Preface

Welcome to "Mastering Deep Learning: Comprehensive Study Guide with Online Test Papers and Exercises." In the rapidly evolving field of artificial intelligence, deep learning has emerged as a transformative technology, driving advancements across various sectors such as healthcare, finance, autonomous vehicles, and more. As deep learning continues to shape the future, mastering its concepts and applications becomes crucial for both aspiring and seasoned professionals.

This book is designed to be more than just a traditional textbook; it is a complete learning resource tailored to meet the needs of learners at all levels. Whether you are a student embarking on your first journey into deep learning or an experienced professional seeking to deepen your knowledge and skills, this guide provides the tools and resources necessary to achieve your goals.

Purpose of the Book

The primary objective of this book is to offer a holistic learning experience by combining theoretical knowledge with practical applications. Understanding the complexities of deep learning requires more than just reading; it involves engaging with the material through various interactive methods. To this end, we have integrated a variety of learning aids to enhance your understanding and retention of deep learning concepts.

Key Features

1. **Extensive Theoretical Content**: The book covers the full spectrum of deep learning topics, from fundamental concepts to advanced techniques. Each chapter is designed to build on the previous one, ensuring a logical progression and deep comprehension of the subject matter.
2. **Online Test Papers**: To reinforce your learning, we provide a series of online test papers that mimic real-world scenarios and challenges. These tests are designed to evaluate your understanding and help you identify areas that need further study.
3. **Interactive Exercises**: The book includes a wide range of exercises, such as multiple-choice questions (MCQs), true/false statements, and problem-solving tasks. These exercises are strategically placed throughout the chapters to reinforce key concepts and test your knowledge.
4. **Video Tutorials**: Understanding deep learning concepts can sometimes be challenging through text alone. Our book includes links to a series of video tutorials that provide visual and auditory explanations of complex topics. These videos are created by experts and are intended to complement the written material, offering a more immersive learning experience.
5. **Practical Applications**: Each chapter includes real-world examples and case studies that illustrate how deep learning is applied across different industries. These examples help bridge the gap between theory and practice, demonstrating the practical relevance of deep learning skills.
6. **Self-Assessment Tools**: At the end of each chapter, self-assessment questions and exercises allow you to test your understanding and track your progress. These tools are invaluable in helping you gauge your readiness and build confidence as you move forward.

Conclusion

"Mastering Deep Learning: Comprehensive Study Guide with Online Test Papers and Exercises" is designed to be your definitive guide to mastering deep learning. By combining detailed theoretical content with interactive and practical learning aids, this book provides a comprehensive and engaging learning experience. Whether you are preparing for academic exams, professional certifications, or industry interviews, this book will equip you with the knowledge and skills you need to succeed.

Table Of Contents

Chapter 1: Introduction to Machine Learning

1.1 Machine Learning

Machine Learning is a field of artificial intelligence that allows systems to learn and improve from experience without being explicitly programmed. It has become an increasingly popular topic in recent years due to the many practical applications it has in a variety of industries. In chapter 1, we will explore the basics of Machine Learning, delve into more advanced topics, and discuss how it is being used to solve real-world problems. Whether you are a beginner looking to
learn about Machine Learning or an experienced data scientist seeking to stay up-to-date on the latest developments,.

1.1.1 What is Machine Learning?

Machine Learning is an application of artificial intelligence that uses statistical techniques to enable computers to learn and make decisions without being explicitly programmed. It is predicated on the notion that computers can learn from data, spot patterns, and make judgments with little assistance from humans.

It is a subset of Artificial Intelligence. It is the study of making machines more human-like in their behaviour and decisions by giving them the ability to learn and develop their own programs. This is done with minimum human intervention, i.e., no explicit programming. The learning process is automated and improved based on the experiences of the machines throughout the process. Good quality data is fed to the machines, and different algorithms are used to build ML models to train the machines on this data. The choice of algorithm depends on the type of data at hand and the type of activity that needs to be automated. Now you may wonder, how is it different from traditional programming? Well, in traditional programming, we would feed the input data and a well-written and tested program into a machine to generate output. When it comes to Machine Learning, input data, along with the output, is fed into the machine during the learning phase, and it works out a program for itself.

1.1.2 History of Machine Learning

This section discusses the development of Machine Learning over the years. Today we are witnessing some astounding applications like self-driving cars, natural language processing and facial recognition systems making use of ML techniques for their processing. All this began in the year 1943, when Warren McCulloch a neurophysiologist along with a mathematician named Walter Pitts authored a paper that threw a light on neurons and its working. They created a model with electrical circuits and thus neural network was born.

The famous "Turing Test" was created in 1950 by Alan Turing, which would ascertain whether computers had real intelligence. It must make a human believe that it is not a computer but a human instead, to get through the test. Arthur Samuel developed the first computer program that could learn as it played the game of checkers in the year 1952. The first neural network, called the perceptron was designed by Frank Rosenblatt in the year 1957.

The big shift happened in the 1990s when Machine Learning moved from being knowledge-driven to a data-driven technique due to the availability of huge volumes of data. IBM's Deep Blue, developed in 1997 was the first machine to defeat the world champion in the game of chess. Businesses have recognized that the potential for complex calculations could be increased through Machine Learning. Some of the latest projects include Google Brain, which was developed in 2012, was a deep neural network that focused on pattern recognition in images and videos. It was later employed to detect objects in YouTube videos. In 2014, Facebook created Deep Face, which can recognize people just like how humans do. In 2014, Deep Mind created a computer program called Alpha Go a board game that defeated a professional Go player. Due to its complexity, the game is said to be a very challenging yet classical game for artificial intelligence. Scientists Stephen Hawking and Stuart Russel have felt that if AI gains the power to redesign itself at an intensifying rate, then an unbeatable "intelligence explosion" may lead to human extinction. Musk characterizes AI as humanity's "biggest existential threat." Open AI is an organization created by Elon Musk in 2015 to develop safe and friendly AI that could benefit humanity. Recently, some of the breakthrough areas in AI are Computer Vision, Natural Language Processing and Reinforcement Learning.

1.1.3 Why Should We Learn Machine Learning?

Machine Learning is a powerful tool that can be used to solve a wide range of problems. It allows computers to learn from data, without being explicitly programmed. This makes it possible to build systems that can automatically improve their performance over time by learning from their experiences.

There are many reasons why learning Machine Learning is important:

- Machine Learning is widely used in many industries, including healthcare, finance, and e-commerce. By learning Machine Learning, you can open a wide range of career opportunities in these fields.
- Machine Learning can be used to build intelligent systems that can make decisions and predictions based on data. This can help organizations make better decisions, improve their operations, and create new products and services.
- Machine Learning is an important tool for data analysis and visualization. It allows you to extract insights and patterns from large datasets, which can be used to understand complex systems and make informed decisions.
- Machine Learning is a rapidly growing field with many exciting developments and research opportunities. By learning Machine Learning, you can stay up to date with the latest research and developments in the field.

1.2 Overview

Arthur Samuel, an early American leader in the field of computer gaming and artificial intelligence, coined the term "Machine Learning" in 1959 while at IBM. He defined Machine Learning as "the field of study that gives computers the ability to learn without being explicitly programmed ". However, there is no universally accepted definition for Machine Learning. Different authors define the term differently. We give below two more definitions.
- Machine Learning is programming computers to optimize a performance criterion using example data or experience. We have a model defined up to some parameters, and learning is the execution of a computer program to optimize the parameters of the model using the training data or experience. The model may be predictive to make predictions in the future, or descriptive to gain knowledge from data.
- The field of study known as Machine Learning is concerned with the question of how to construct computer programs that automatically improve with experience.

Machine Learning is a subfield of artificial intelligence that involves the development of algorithms and statistical models that enable computers to improve their performance in tasks through experience. These algorithms and models are designed to learn from data and make predictions or decisions without explicit instructions. There are several types of Machine Learning, including supervised learning, unsupervised learning, and reinforcement learning. Supervised learning involves training a model on labelled data, while unsupervised learning involves training a model on unlabelled data. Reinforcement learning involves training a model through trial and error. Machine Learning is used in a wide variety of applications, including image and speech recognition, natural language processing, and recommender systems.

Definition of learning:

A computer program is said to *learn* from experience E with respect to some class of tasks T and performance measure P, if its performance at tasks T, as measured by P, improves with experience E.

Examples

- Handwriting recognition learning problem.
- Task T: Recognizing and classifying handwritten words within images.
- Performance P: Percent of words correctly classified
- Training experience E: A dataset of handwritten words with given classifications
- A robot driving learning problem.
- Task T: Driving on highways using vision sensors.
- Performance P: Average distance travelled before an error.
- Training experience E: A sequence of images and steering commands recorded while observing a human driver.

Definition: A computer program which learns from experience is called a Machine Learning program or simply a learning program.

1.3 Types of Machines

Traditional ML developed in the earlier stages carried out all the desired tasks in the past. The technology wasn't as advanced as today, so it was enough to complete some simple tasks. A traditional ML model has quite a simple structure, but even without it, advanced models wouldn't be available now. So, it involves two channels – one for training and one for prediction.

The training channel's task is to collect and group all the necessary data. The prediction channel then goes through collected and grouped data and analyses it for different purposes – to establish patterns, forecast, or aid in making effective decisions.

However, the traditional ML model cannot always meet the demands because of its two-channel structure. The process can take way too long, and the analysis of data is not detailed enough. Besides that, serious errors in functioning can occur if some slight changes are added into the system, such as:

- Changing the system's operational surrounding
- Changing the system's input
- Changing the desired outcomes or results

Each of these alterations can significantly disrupt the system, and the functionality, efficiency, and precision of a system using ML are greatly affected. That's the most important disadvantage of traditional Machine Learning.

In today's pace of living, large amounts of data need to be transferred quickly, but sometimes they need to change in the same timely manner. Considering companies and enterprises majorly use ML, they call for the reliability of their systems at all times.

That's where traditional ML lacks, as it requires more time to adapt to the changes, thereby proving that it's incapable of quickly adapting to the newly acquired information.

What Is Adaptive Machine Learning?

With modern times, computers, systems, programs, and technology, in general, are becoming more used, advanced, flexible, and therefore powerful. With its widespread use, it goes through numerous advances even daily.

Also, with modern times comes a fast-paced life. This way of living requires our systems to act similarly. Adaptive ML, as its name says, can do something that traditional ML can't. It can quickly adapt to new information and gain insight into how important that new information is.

Because of its single-channelled structure, adaptive Machine Learning employs different data collection methods, grouping, and analysis. It collects and analyses the data while also learning from it.

That's why it's adaptive – the system is learning and updating as long as the new information is provided. This single-channelled system follows up on every feedback provided to make future predictions and outcomes even better.

In addition to that, the whole process is happening in real-time, so it can adapt to new behaviour instantly. Some of the essential advantages that the adaptive ML provides are high performance and immaculate precision. Because it continually runs in real-time, the system is prevented from getting outdated or obsolete.

So, what describes adaptive ML the best is combining the three main principles: agility, strength, and efficiency. With agility, the systems can act immediately, without any delays. With strength, the systems achieve new standards of high proficiency and accuracy, and with efficiency, the systems can find new ways to perform immaculately but with lower costs.

How Are Adaptive ML and Traditional ML Different?

So, here we will draw some conclusions and summarize the differences between traditional ML and adaptive ML. Even though adaptive ML is quite advanced compared to traditional ML, it's important to state that it probably wouldn't be the way we know it today if the main disadvantages of conventional ML weren't pointed out and addressed.

So, firstly, the main difference is that traditional ML is a system with two channels. Consequently, all data is divided into two parts, as previously mentioned. Even though traditional ML finds a way to deal with this, the results can take a long time and often even become outdated by the time they arrive.

Therefore, the adaptive ML works on a single channel, providing a more efficient way of functioning, relating to the resources used and the speed of solutions. Thereby, this system proves to be a more sustainable and better option overall.

Secondly, as traditional ML goes through fewer data in more time, it's mainly based on static and permanent data. It takes quite a lot of time to change the behaviour in the system, so numerous urgent and important matters are missed.

That's why adaptive ML isn't based on any permanent data but on the ability to continuously adapt and change the behaviour when necessary, making sure that the system doesn't operate on any outdated data.

Finally, adaptive ML has the unique ability to learn from the past. In that way, it resembles feeding someone – the more information you feed to the system, the bigger and smarter it gets. It even learns from previous mistakes and lowers the chances of repeating them. So, the longer they operate, the more accurate they get.

1.4 Applications

Machine Learning is a buzzword for today's technology, and it is growing very rapidly day by day. We are using Machine Learning in our daily life even without knowing it such as Google Maps, Google assistant, Alexa, etc. Below are some most trending real-world applications of Machine Learning:

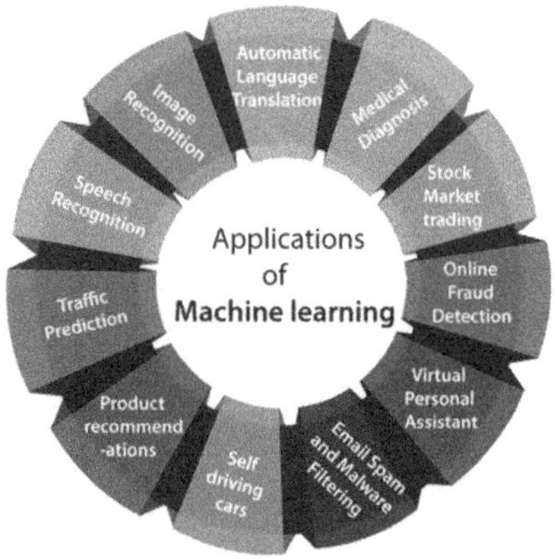

1. Image Recognition:

Image recognition is one of the most common applications of Machine Learning. It is used to identify objects, persons, places, digital images, etc. The popular use case of image recognition and face detection is **Automatic friend tagging suggestion**: Facebook provides us a feature of auto friend tagging suggestion. Whenever we upload a photo with our Facebook friends, then we automatically get a tagging suggestion with name, and the technology behind this is Machine Learning's **face detection** and **recognition algorithm**. It is based on the Facebook project named "**Deep Face**," which is responsible for face recognition and person identification in the picture.

2. Speech Recognition

While using Google, we get an option of "**Search by voice**," it comes under speech recognition, and it's a popular application of Machine Learning. Speech recognition is a process of converting voice instructions into text, and it is also known as "**Speech to text**", or "**Computer speech recognition**." At present, Machine Learning algorithms are widely used by various applications of speech recognition. **Google assistant**, **Siri**, **Cortana**, and **Alexa** are using speech recognition technology to follow the voice instructions.

3. Traffic prediction:

If we want to visit a new place, we take help of Google Maps, which shows us the correct path with the shortest route and predicts the traffic conditions. It predicts the traffic conditions such as whether traffic is cleared, slow-moving, or heavily congested with the help of two ways:

- **Real Time location** of the vehicle form Google Map app and sensors

- **Average time has taken** on past days at the same time.

Everyone who is using Google Map is helping this app to make it better. It takes information from the user and sends back to its database to improve the performance.

4. Product recommendations:

Machine Learning is widely used by various e-commerce and entertainment companies such as **Amazon**, **Netflix**, etc., for product recommendation to the user. Whenever we search for some product on Amazon, then we started getting an advertisement for the same product while internet surfing on the same browser and this is because of Machine Learning. Google understands the user interest using various Machine Learning algorithms and suggests the product as per customer interest. As similar, when we use Netflix, we find some recommendations for entertainment series, movies, etc., and this is also done with the help of Machine Learning.

5. Self-driving cars:

One of the most exciting applications of Machine Learning is self-driving cars. Machine Learning plays a significant role in self-driving cars. Tesla, the most popular car manufacturing company is working on self-driving car. It is using unsupervised learning method to train the car models to detect people and objects while driving.

6. Email Spam and Malware Filtering:

Whenever we receive a new email, it is filtered automatically as important, normal, and spam. We always receive an important mail in our inbox with the important symbol and spam emails in our spam box, and the technology behind this is Machine Learning. Below are some spam filters used by Gmail:

- Content Filter

- Header filter

- General blacklists filter

- Rules-based filters

- Permission filters

Some Machine Learning algorithms such as **Multi-Layer Perceptron**, **Decision tree**, and **Naïve Bayes classifier** are used for email spam filtering and malware detection.

7. Virtual Personal Assistant:

We have various virtual personal assistants such as **Google assistant**, **Alexa**, **Cortana**, **Siri**. As the name suggests, they help us in finding the information using our voice instruction. These assistants can help us in various ways just by our voice instructions such as Play music, call someone, open an email, Scheduling an appointment, etc. These virtual assistants use Machine Learning algorithms as an important part. These assistants record our voice instructions, send it over the server on a cloud, and decode it using ML algorithms and act accordingly.

8. Online Fraud Detection:

Machine Learning is making our online transaction safe and secure by detecting fraud transaction. Whenever we perform some online transaction, there may be various ways that a fraudulent transaction can take place such as **fake accounts**, **fake ids**, and **steal money** in the middle of a transaction. So, to detect this, **Feed Forward Neural network** helps us by checking whether it is a genuine transaction or a fraud transaction. For each genuine transaction, the output is converted into some hash values, and these values become the input for the next round. For each genuine transaction, there is a specific pattern which gets change for the fraud transaction hence, it detects it and makes our online transactions more secure.

9. Stock Market trading:

Machine Learning is widely used in stock market trading. In the stock market, there is always a risk of up and downs in shares, so for this Machine Learning's **long short-term memory neural network** is used for the prediction of stock market trends.

10. Medical Diagnosis:

In medical science, Machine Learning is used for diseases diagnoses. With this, medical technology is growing very fast and able to build 3D models that can predict the exact position of lesions in the brain. It helps in finding brain tumours and other brain-related diseases easily.

11. Automatic Language Translation:

Nowadays, if we visit a new place and we are not aware of the language then it is not a problem at all, as for this also Machine Learning helps us by converting the text into our known languages. Google's GNMT (Google Neural Machine Translation) provide this feature, which is a Neural Machine Learning that translates the text into our familiar language, and it called as automatic translation. The technology behind the automatic translation is a sequence-to-sequence learning algorithm, which is used with image recognition and translates the text from one language to another language.

1.4 Types of Machine Learning

Machine Learning is a subset of AI, which enables the machine to automatically learn from data, improve performance from past experiences, and make predictions. Machine Learning contains a set of algorithms that work on a huge amount of data. Data is fed to these algorithms to train them, and on the basis of training, they build the model & perform a specific task. These ML algorithms help to solve different business problems like Regression, Classification, Forecasting, Clustering, and Associations, etc. Based on the methods and way of learning, Machine Learning is divided into mainly four types, which are:

1. Supervised Machine Learning

2. Unsupervised Machine Learning

3. Semi-Supervised Machine Learning

4. Reinforcement Learning

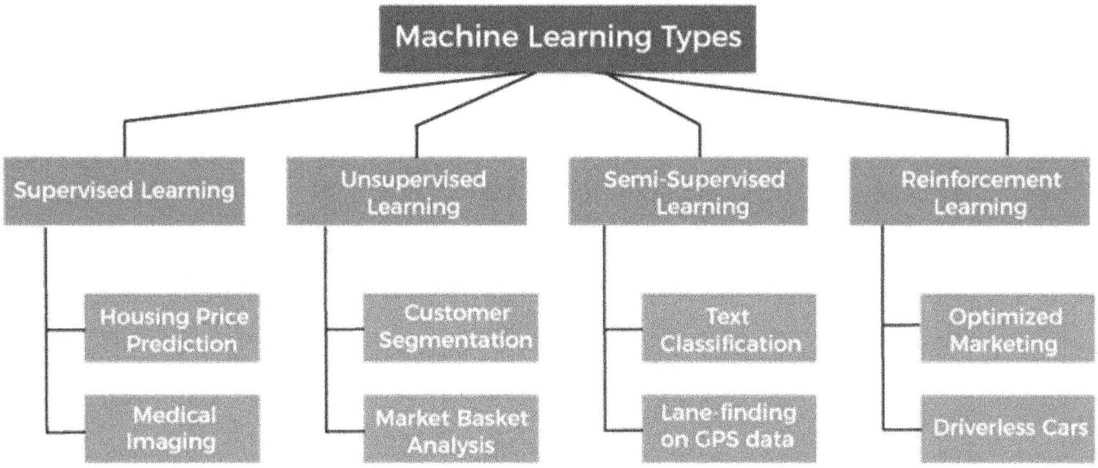

In this topic, we will provide a detailed description of the types of Machine Learning along with their respective algorithms:

1. Supervised Machine Learning - As its name suggests, Supervised Machine Learning is based on supervision. It means in the supervised learning technique, we train the machines using the "labelled" dataset, and based on the training, the machine predicts the output. Here, the labelled data specifies that some of the inputs are already mapped to the output. More preciously, we can say; first, we train the machine with the input and corresponding output, and then we ask the machine to predict the output using the test dataset. Let's understand supervised learning with an example. Suppose we have an input dataset of cats and dog images. So, first, we will provide the training to the machine to understand the images, such as the **shape & size of the tail of cat and dog, Shape of eyes, colour, height (dogs are taller, cats are smaller), etc.** After completion of training, we input the picture of a cat and ask the machine to identify the object and predict the output. Now, the machine is well trained, so it will check all the features of the object, such as height, shape, colour, eyes, ears, tail, etc., and find that it's a cat. So, it will put it in the Cat category. This is the process of how the machine identifies the objects in Supervised Learning.

The main goal of the supervised learning technique is to map the input variable(x) with the output variable(y). Some real-world applications of supervised learning are **Risk Assessment, Fraud Detection, Spam filtering,** etc.

Categories of Supervised Machine Learning

Supervised Machine Learning can be classified into two types of problems, which are given below:

- **Classification**

- **Regression**

a) Classification

Classification algorithms are used to solve the classification problems in which the output variable is categorical, such as **"Yes" or No, Male or Female, Red or Blue, etc**. The classification algorithms predict the categories present in the dataset. Some real-world examples of classification algorithms are **Spam Detection, Email filtering, etc.** Some popular classification algorithms are given below:

- **Random Forest Algorithm**

- **Decision Tree Algorithm**

- **Logistic Regression Algorithm**

- **Support Vector Machine Algorithm**

b) Regression

Regression algorithms are used to solve regression problems in which there is a linear relationship between input and output variables. These are used to predict continuous output variables, such as market trends, weather prediction, etc.

Some popular Regression algorithms are given below:
- Simple Linear Regression Algorithm

- Multivariate Regression Algorithm

- Decision Tree Algorithm

- Lasso Regression

Advantages and Disadvantages of Supervised Learning
Advantages:
- Since supervised learning work with the labelled dataset so we can have an exact idea about the classes of objects.
- These algorithms are helpful in predicting the output on the basis of prior experience.

Disadvantages:
- These algorithms are not able to solve complex tasks.
- It may predict the wrong output if the test data is different from the training data.
- It requires lots of computational time to train the algorithm.

Applications of Supervised Learning

Some common applications of Supervised Learning are given below:

- Image Segmentation:

Supervised Learning algorithms are used in image segmentation. In this process, image classification is performed on different image data with pre-defined labels.

- Medical Diagnosis:

Supervised algorithms are also used in the medical field for diagnosis purposes. It is done by using medical images and past labelled data with labels for disease conditions. With such a process, the machine can identify a disease for the new patients.

- Fraud Detection - Supervised Learning classification algorithms are used for identifying fraud transactions, fraud customers, etc. It is done by using historic data to identify the patterns that can lead to possible fraud.

- Spam detection - In spam detection & filtering, classification algorithms are used. These algorithms classify an email as spam or not spam. The spam emails are sent to the spam folder.

- Speech Recognition - Supervised learning algorithms are also used in speech recognition. The algorithm is trained with voice data, and various identifications can be done using the same, such as voice-activated passwords, voice commands, etc.

2. Unsupervised Machine Learning

Unsupervised learning is different from the Supervised learning technique; as its name suggests, there is no need for supervision. It means, in unsupervised Machine Learning, the machine is trained using the unlabelled dataset, and the machine predicts the output without any supervision.

In unsupervised learning, the models are trained with the data that is neither classified nor labelled, and the model acts on that data without any supervision.

The main aim of the unsupervised learning algorithm is to group or categories the unsorted dataset according to the similarities, patterns, and differences. Machines are instructed to find the hidden patterns from the input dataset.

Let's take an example to understand it more preciously; suppose there is a basket of fruit images, and we input it into the Machine Learning model. The images are totally unknown to the model, and the task of the machine is to find the patterns and categories of the objects.

So, now the machine will discover its patterns and differences, such as colour difference, shape difference, and predict the output when it is tested with the test dataset.

Categories of Unsupervised Machine Learning

Unsupervised Learning can be further classified into two types, which are given below:

- Clustering

- **Association**

1) Clustering

The clustering technique is used when we want to find the inherent groups from the data. It is a way to group the objects into a cluster such that the objects with the most similarities remain in one group and have fewer or no similarities with the objects of other groups. An example of the clustering algorithm is grouping the customers by their purchasing behaviour.

Some of the popular clustering algorithms are given below:

- **K-Means Clustering algorithm.**

- **Mean-shift algorithm.**

- **DBSCAN Algorithm**

- **Principal Component Analysis**

- **Independent Component Analysis**

2) Association

Association rule learning is an unsupervised learning technique, which finds interesting relations among variables within a large dataset. The main aim of this learning algorithm is to find the dependency of one data item on another data item and map those variables accordingly so that it can generate maximum profit. This algorithm is mainly applied in **Market Basket analysis, Web usage mining, continuous production**, etc.

Some popular algorithms of Association rule learning are **Apriori Algorithm, Eclat, FP-growth algorithm.**

Advantages and Disadvantages of Unsupervised Learning Algorithm

Advantages:

- These algorithms can be used for complicated tasks compared to the supervised ones because these algorithms work on the unlabelled dataset.

- Unsupervised algorithms are preferable for various tasks as getting the unlabelled dataset is easier as compared to the labelled dataset.

- **Disadvantages:**

- The output of an unsupervised algorithm can be less accurate as the dataset is not labelled, and algorithms are not trained with the exact output in prior.

- Working with Unsupervised learning is more difficult as it works with the unlabelled dataset that does not map with the output.

- Applications of Unsupervised Learning

- **Network Analysis:** Unsupervised learning is used for identifying plagiarism and copyright in document network analysis of text data for scholarly articles.

- **Recommendation Systems:** Recommendation systems widely use unsupervised learning techniques for building recommendation applications for different web applications and e-commerce websites.

- **Anomaly Detection:** Anomaly detection is a popular application of unsupervised learning, which can identify unusual data points within the dataset. It is used to discover fraudulent transactions.

- **Singular Value Decomposition:** Singular Value Decomposition or SVD is used to extract particular information from the database. For example, extracting information of each user located at a particular location.

3. Semi-Supervised Learning

Semi-Supervised learning is a type of Machine Learning algorithm that lies between Supervised and Unsupervised Machine Learning. It represents the intermediate ground between Supervised (With Labelled

training data) and Unsupervised learning (with no labelled training data) algorithms and uses the combination of labelled and unlabelled datasets during the training period.
Although Semi-supervised learning is the middle ground between supervised and unsupervised learning and operates on the data that consists of a few labels, it mostly consists of unlabelled data. As labels are costly, but for corporate purposes, they may have few labels. It is completely different from supervised and unsupervised learning as they are based on the presence & absence of labels.
To overcome the drawbacks of supervised learning and unsupervised learning algorithms, the concept of Semi-supervised learning is introduced. The main aim of semi-supervised learning is to effectively use all the available data, rather than only labelled data like in supervised learning. Initially, similar data is clustered along with an unsupervised learning algorithm, and further, it helps to label the unlabelled data into labelled data. It is because labelled data is a comparatively more expensive acquisition than unlabelled data.
We can imagine these algorithms with an example. Supervised learning is where a student is under the supervision of an instructor at home and college. Further, if that student is self-analysing the same concept without any help from the instructor, it comes under unsupervised learning. Under semi-supervised learning, the student has to revise himself after analysing the same concept under the guidance of an instructor at college.

Advantages and disadvantages of Semi-supervised Learning

Advantages:

- It is simple and easy to understand the algorithm.

- It is highly efficient.

- It is used to solve drawbacks of Supervised and Unsupervised Learning algorithms.

- Disadvantages:

- Iterations results may not be stable.

- We cannot apply these algorithms to network-level data.

- Accuracy is low.

4. Reinforcement Learning

Reinforcement learning works on a feedback-based process, in which an AI agent (A software component) automatically explore its surrounding by hitting & trail, taking action, learning from experiences, and improving its performance. Agent gets rewarded for each good action and get punished for each bad action; hence the goal of reinforcement learning agent is to maximize the rewards.
In reinforcement learning, there is no labelled data like supervised learning, and agents learn from their experiences only.
The reinforcement learning process is similar to a human being; for example, a child learns various things by experiences in his day-to-day life. An example of reinforcement learning is to play a game, where the Game is the environment, moves of an agent at each step define states, and the goal of the agent is to get a high score. Agent receives feedback in terms of punishment and rewards.
Due to its way of working, reinforcement learning is employed in different fields such as **Game theory, Operation Research, Information theory, multi-agent systems.** A reinforcement learning problem can be formalized using **Markov Decision Process (MDP).** In MDP, the agent constantly interacts with the environment and performs actions; at each action, the environment responds and generates a new state. Categories of Reinforcement Learning Reinforcement learning is categorized mainly into two types of methods/algorithms:
- Positive Reinforcement Learning: Positive reinforcement learning specifies increasing the tendency that the required behaviour would occur again by adding something. It enhances the strength of the behaviour of the agent and positively impacts it.

- Negative Reinforcement Learning: Negative reinforcement learning works exactly opposite to the positive RL. It increases the tendency that the specific behaviour would occur again by avoiding the negative condition.

Real-world Use cases of Reinforcement Learning

- **Video Games:** RL algorithms are much popular in gaming applications. It is used to gain super-human performance. Some popular games that use RL algorithms are **AlphaGo** and **AlphaGo Zero**.

- **Resource Management:** The "Resource Management with Deep Reinforcement Learning" paper showed that how to use RL in computer to automatically learn and schedule resources to wait for different jobs in order to minimize average job slowdown.

- **Robotics:** RL is widely being used in Robotics applications. Robots are used in the industrial and manufacturing area, and these robots are made more powerful with reinforcement learning. There are different industries that have their vision of building intelligent robots using AI and Machine Learning technology.

- **Text Mining:** Text-mining, one of the great applications of NLP, is now being implemented with the help of Reinforcement Learning by Salesforce company.

Advantages and Disadvantages of Reinforcement Learning

Advantages

- It helps in solving complex real-world problems which are difficult to be solved by general techniques.

- The learning model of RL is similar to the learning of human beings; hence most accurate results can be found.

- Helps in achieving long term results.

Disadvantage

- RL algorithms are not preferred for simple problems.

- RL algorithms require huge data and computations.

- Too much reinforcement learning can lead to an overload of states which can weaken the results.

The curse of dimensionality limits reinforcement learning for real physical systems.

1.5 Examples of Machine Learning

When the average person thinks about Machine Learning, it may feel overwhelming, complicated, and perhaps intangible, conjuring up images of futuristic robots taking over the world. As more organizations and people rely on Machine Learning models to manage growing volumes of data, instances of Machine Learning are occurring in front of and around us daily—whether we notice or not. What's exciting to see is how it's improving our quality of life, supporting quicker and more effective execution of some business operations and industries, and uncovering patterns that humans are likely to miss. Here are examples of Machine Learning at work in our daily life that provide value in many ways—some large and some small.

1. Facial recognition

Facial recognition is one of the more obvious applications of Machine Learning. People previously received name suggestions for their mobile photos and Facebook tagging, but now someone is immediately tagged and verified by comparing and analysing patterns through facial contours. And facial recognition paired with deep learning has become highly useful in healthcare to help detect genetic diseases or track a patient's use of medication more accurately. It's also used to combat important social issues such as child sex trafficking or sexual exploitation of children. The list of applications and industries influenced by it is steadily on the rise.

2.Product recommendations

Do you wonder how Amazon or other retailers frequently know what you might like to purchase? Or have they gotten it wildly wrong, and you wonder how they came up with the recommendation? Thank Machine Learning. Targeted marketing with retail uses Machine Learning to group customers based on buying habits or demographic similarities, and by extrapolating what one person may want from someone else's purchases. While some suggested purchase pairings are obvious, Machine Learning can get eerily accurate by finding hidden relationships in data and predicting what you want before you know you want it. If the data is incomplete, sometimes you may end up with an off-base recommendation—but don't worry, because not buying it is another data point to learn from.

3.Email automation and spam filtering

While your inbox seems relatively boring, Machine Learning influences its function behind the scenes. Email automation is a direct result of successful Machine Learning, and one function that goes most unnoticed is spam filtering. Successful spam filtering adapts and finds patterns in email content that is undesirable. This includes data from email domains, a sender's physical location message text and structure, and IP addresses. It also requires help from users as they mark emails when they're mistakenly filed. With each marked email, a new data reference is added that helps with future accuracy.

4.Financial accuracy

Machine Learning has created a boon for the financial industry as most systems go digital. Abundant financial transactions that can't be monitored by human eyes are easily analysed thanks to Machine Learning, which helps find fraudulent transactions. One of the newest banking features is the ability to deposit a check straight from your phone by using handwriting and image recognition to "read" checks and convert them to digital text. Credit scores and lending decisions are also powered by Machine Learning as it both influences a score and analyses financial risk. Additionally, combining data analytics with artificial intelligence, Machine Learning, and natural language processing is changing the customer experience in banking.

5.Social media optimization

Platforms from Facebook to Instagram and Twitter are using big data and artificial intelligence to enhance their functionality and strengthen the user experience. Machine Learning has become helpful in fighting inappropriate content and cyberbullying, which pose a risk to platforms in losing users and weakening brand loyalty. Processing data through deep neural networks also allows social platforms to learn their users' preferences as they offer content suggestions and target advertising.

6. Healthcare advancement

Every day, we're getting closer to a full transition to electronic medical records. That means healthcare information for clinicians can be enhanced with analytics and Machine Learning to gain insights that support better planning and patient care, improved diagnoses, and lower treatment costs. Healthcare brands such as Pfizer and Providence have begun to benefit from analytics enhanced by human and artificial intelligence. There are some processes that are better suited to leverage Machine Learning; Machine Learning integration with radiology, cardiology, and pathology, for example, is leading to earlier detection of abnormalities or heightened attention on concerning areas. In the long run, Machine Learning will also benefit family practitioners or internists when treating patient's bedside because data trends will predict health risks like heart disease. As an example, wearables generate mass amounts of data on the wearer's health and many use AI and Machine Learning to alert them or their doctors of issues to support preventative measures and respond to emergencies.

7. Mobile voice to text and predictive text

Machines are also capable of learning language in other formats. Like Siri and Cortana, voice-to-text applications learn words and language then transcribe audio into writing. Predictive text also deals with language. Simple, supervised learning trains the process to recognize and predict what common, contextual words or phrases will be used based on what's written. Unsupervised learning goes further, adjusting predictions based on data. You may start noticing that predictive text will recommend personalized words. For instance, if you have a hobby with unique terminology that falls outside of a dictionary, predictive text will learn and suggest them instead of standard words. It's working when autocorrect starts trying to predict them in normal conversation.

8. Predictive analytics

Predictive analytics is an area of advanced analytics that uses data to make predictions about the future. Techniques such as data mining, statistics, and modelling employ Machine Learning and artificial intelligence to analyse current and historical data for any patterns or anomalies that can help identify risks and opportunities, minimize the chance for human errors, and increase speed and thoroughness of analysis. With closer investigation of what happened and what could happen using data, people and organizations are becoming more proactive and forward looking. Florida International University is one example. By integrating predictive models with data analysis from Tableau, they're communicating critical insights about academic performance before students are at risk and supporting their individual needs to help them successfully complete all courses and graduate.

9. Safeguarding the environment

Machine Learning algorithms can help in boosting environmental sustainability. A good example is IBM's Green Horizon Project, wherein environmental statistics from varied assets and sensors are leveraged to produce pollution forecasts. The aim is to bring down the environmental impact.

10. Cyber security

Applications like PayPal and G-Pay use Machine Learning for tracking transactions and differentiating between illegitimate and legitimate transactions. In this way, Machine Learning maximizes cyber security by preventing online monetary fraud.

Besides the above-listed applications, substantial other sectors and areas implement ML technologies.

Omdena runs AI Projects with organizations that want to get started with AI, solve a real-world problem, or build deployable solutions within two months.

Believe it or not, the list of Machine Learning applications will grow so it's almost too long to count. However, the benefits and improvements to our lives—and for data analysts sitting in global organizations—that come from enhancing human knowledge with machine power will be worth it, even though it feels daunting. Embrace the benefits, practicality, and future possibilities. Learn more ways that AI and Machine Learning are being used in augmented analytics and to augment human decision-making through smart analytics—whether for mundane or complex tasks.

1.5.1 A case study

More than a year, I've been studying on Machine Learning, and I decided to put my knowledge on the internet to help non-computer scientists to understand this popular field's basics. I am planning to write a series of posts, and these will be about the story behind the algorithms rather than the mathematical computations. By this way, I aim to give intuition to people.

Let's start with its definition and its relationship with other scientific fields. The goal in the Machine Learning is to recognize the pattern in the dataset, in general manner. After you recognize the patterns, you can use this information to model the data, to interpret the data, or to predict the outcome of the new data which hasn't seen before. Machine Learning is a subfield of artificial intelligence and Machine Learning algorithms are used in other related fields like natural language processing and computer vision.

In general, there are three types of learning, and these are supervised learning, unsupervised learning, and reinforcement learning. Their names tell the main idea behind them actually.

In supervised learning, your system learns under the supervision of the data outputs so supervised algorithms are preferred if your dataset contains output information. Let me give you an example in there. Let's assume you have a medical statistic company, and you have a dataset which contains patients' features like blood pressure, sugar rate in their blood, heart rate per minute, etc. and also you have the information about if they have experienced heart disease in their life or not. By training a Machine Learning algorithm, your system can find a pattern between features and the probability to experience heart disease. Therefore, your algorithm can predict whether a new patient has a risk to experience a heart disease, so doctor takes the precautions and save a person's life.

A Decision Tree from one of my projects. x's are features which are medical tests in this case and the 0,1 values in boxes represents existence of heart disease. As you can see, algorithm produced an interpretable tree.

You prefer to use unsupervised algorithms if your data doesn't contain output and if you would like to discover the clusters in dataset. A good example of unsupervised learning is handwritten digit recognition. In this application you know that there should be 10 clusters {0,1,2,3,4,5,6,7,8,9} but the problem in handwritten digits is that there are countless ways to write a digit by hand, and everyone write digits differently. How does a computer understand what is written with hand? In there, you should use an unsupervised algorithm like K-means or EM-algorithm. What you do with these algorithms is that you start with initial random cluster means and iteratively these mean points converge to real cluster mean values. After you complete the training, if you visualize the means of the clusters, you can see that they really look like digits. Then you label these clusters with corresponding digits, and when the computer encounters a new handwritten digit, algorithm labels the digit with the mean which is closest to it.

Visualized means for 8 and 6, from one of my projects

Lastly let's talk about reinforcement learning. Let's assume you want to create an intelligent agent which plays chess. In chess, you can't handle movements one by one. Your agent should consider a series of movements and then decide to take an action which would maximize the utility. Therefore, your agent should play a couple of turns against itself and decide the best action to take. We call this type of learning as reinforcement learning and it is generally used in games.

This was a quick introduction to Machine Learning for non-computer scientists and I would like to continue to create posts on pattern recognition, artificial neural networks, probabilistic models, etc. when I find time.

"Machine Learning" is one of the most popular technologies among all data scientists and Machine Learning enthusiasts. It is the most effective Artificial Intelligence technology that helps create automated learning systems to take future decisions without being constantly programmed. It can be considered an algorithm that automatically constructs various computer software using past experience and training data. It can be seen in every industry, such as healthcare, education, finance, automobile, marketing, shipping, infrastructure, automation, etc. Almost all big companies like Amazon, Facebook, Google, Adobe, etc., are using various Machine Learning techniques to grow their businesses. But everything in this world has bright as well as dark sides. Similarly, Machine Learning offers great opportunities, but some issues need to be solved.

1.6 Perspectives in Machine Learning

Machine Learning is the study of learning algorithms using past experience and making future decisions. Although, Machine Learning has a variety of models, here is a list of the most commonly used Machine Learning algorithms by all data scientists and professionals in today's world.

- Linear Regression
- Logistic Regression
- Decision Tree
- Bayes Theorem and Naïve Bayes Classification
- Support Vector Machine (SVM) Algorithm
- K-Nearest Neighbour (KNN) Algorithm
- K-Means
- Gradient Boosting algorithms
- Dimensionality Reduction Algorithms
- Random Forest

Common issues in Machine Learning

Although Machine Learning is being used in every industry and helps organizations make more informed and data-driven choices that are more effective than classical methodologies, it still has so many problems that cannot be ignored. Here are some common issues in Machine Learning that professionals face to inculcate ML skills and create an application from scratch.

1. Inadequate Training Data

The major issue that comes while using Machine Learning algorithms is the lack of quality as well as quantity of data. Although data plays a vital role in the processing of Machine Learning algorithms, many data scientists claim that inadequate data, noisy data, and unclean data are extremely exhausting the Machine Learning algorithms. For example, a simple task requires thousands of sample data, and an advanced task such as speech or image recognition needs millions of sample data examples. Further, data quality is also important for the algorithms to work ideally, but the absence of data quality is also found in Machine Learning applications. Data quality can be affected by some factors as follows:

- **Noisy Data-** It is responsible for an inaccurate prediction that affects the decision as well as accuracy in classification tasks.

- **Incorrect data-** It is also responsible for faulty programming and results obtained in Machine Learning models. Hence, incorrect data may affect the accuracy of the results also.

- **Generalizing of output data-** Sometimes, it is also found that generalizing output data becomes complex, which results in comparatively poor future actions.

2. Poor quality of data

As we have discussed above, data plays a significant role in Machine Learning, and it must be of good quality as well. Noisy data, incomplete data, inaccurate data, and unclean data lead to less accuracy in classification and low-quality results. Hence, data quality can also be considered as a major common problem while processing Machine Learning algorithms.

3. non-representative training data

To make sure our training model is generalized well or not, we have to ensure that sample training data must be representative of new cases that we need to generalize. The training data must cover all cases that are already occurred as well as occurring.

Further, if we are using non-representative training data in the model, it results in less accurate predictions. A Machine Learning model is said to be ideal if it predicts well for generalized cases and provides accurate decisions. If there is less training data, then there will be a sampling noise in the model, called the non-representative training set. It won't be accurate in predictions. To overcome this, it will be biased against one class or a group.
Hence, we should use representative data in training to protect against being biased and make accurate predictions without any drift.

4. Overfitting and Underfitting

Overfitting:

Overfitting is one of the most common issues faced by Machine Learning engineers and data scientists. Whenever a Machine Learning model is trained with a huge amount of data, it starts capturing noise and inaccurate data into the training data set. It negatively affects the performance of the model. Let's understand with a simple example where we have a few training data sets such as 1000 mangoes, 1000 apples, 1000 bananas, and 5000 papayas. Then there is a considerable probability of identification of an apple as papaya because we have a massive amount of biased data in the training data set; hence prediction got negatively affected. The main reason behind overfitting is using non-linear methods used in Machine Learning algorithms as they build non-realistic data models. We can overcome overfitting by using linear and parametric algorithms in the Machine Learning models.

Methods to reduce overfitting:

- Increase training data in a dataset.

- Reduce model complexity by simplifying the model by selecting one with fewer parameters.

- Ridge Regularization and Lasso Regularization

- Early stopping during the training phase

- Reduce the noise.

- Reduce the number of attributes in training data.

- Constraining the model.

Underfitting:

Underfitting is just the opposite of overfitting. Whenever a Machine Learning model is trained with fewer amounts of data, and as a result, it provides incomplete and inaccurate data and destroys the accuracy of the Machine Learning model.
Underfitting occurs when our model is too simple to understand the base structure of the data, just like an undersized pant. This generally happens when we have limited data into the data set, and we try to build a linear model with non-linear data. In such scenarios, the complexity of the model destroys, and rules of the Machine Learning model become too easy to be applied on this data set, and the model starts doing wrong predictions as well.

Methods to reduce Underfitting:

- Increase model complexity.

- Remove noise from the data.

- Trained on increased and better features.

- Reduce the constraints.

- Increase the number of epochs to get better results.

5. Monitoring and maintenance

As we know that generalized output data is mandatory for any Machine Learning model; hence, regular monitoring and maintenance become compulsory for the same. Different results for different actions require data change; hence editing of codes as well as resources for monitoring them also become necessary.

6. Getting bad recommendations

A Machine Learning model operates under a specific context which results in bad recommendations and concept drift in the model. Let's understand with an example where at a specific time customer is looking for some gadgets, but now customer requirement changed over time but still Machine Learning model showing same recommendations to the customer while customer expectation has been changed. This incident is called a Data Drift. It generally occurs when new data is introduced or interpretation of data changes. However, we can overcome this by regularly updating and monitoring data according to the expectations.

7. Lack of skilled resources

Although Machine Learning and Artificial Intelligence are continuously growing in the market, still these industries are fresher in comparison to others. The absence of skilled resources in the form of manpower is also an issue. Hence, we need manpower having in-depth knowledge of mathematics, science, and technologies for developing and managing scientific substances for Machine Learning.

8. Customer Segmentation

Customer segmentation is also an important issue while developing a Machine Learning algorithm. To identify the customers who paid for the recommendations shown by the model and who don't even check them. Hence, an algorithm is necessary to recognize the customer behaviour and trigger a relevant recommendation for the user based on past experience.

9. Process Complexity of Machine Learning

The Machine Learning process is very complex, which is also another major issue faced by Machine Learning engineers and data scientists. However, Machine Learning and Artificial Intelligence are very new technologies but are still in an experimental phase and continuously being changing over time. There is the majority of hits and trial experiments; hence the probability of error is higher than expected. Further, it also includes analysing the data, removing data bias, training data, applying complex mathematical calculations, etc., making the procedure more complicated and quite tedious.

10. Data Bias

Data Biasing is also found a big challenge in Machine Learning. These errors exist when certain elements of the dataset are heavily weighted or need more importance than others. Biased data leads to inaccurate results, skewed outcomes, and other analytical errors. However, we can resolve this error by determining where data is actually biased in the dataset. Further, take necessary steps to reduce it.

Methods to remove Data Bias:

- Research more for customer segmentation.

- Be aware of your general use cases and potential outliers.

- Combine inputs from multiple sources to ensure data diversity.

- Include bias testing in the development process.

- Analyse data regularly and keep tracking errors to resolve them easily.

- Review the collected and annotated data.

- Use multi-pass annotation such as sentiment analysis, content moderation, and intent recognition.

11. Lack of Explain ability

This basically means the outputs cannot be easily comprehended as it is programmed in specific ways to deliver for certain conditions. Hence, a lack of explain ability is also found in Machine Learning algorithms which reduce the credibility of the algorithms.

12. Slow implementations and results

This issue is also very commonly seen in Machine Learning models. However, Machine Learning models are highly efficient in producing accurate results but are time-consuming. Slow programming, excessive requirements and overloaded data take more time to provide accurate results than expected. This needs continuous maintenance and monitoring of the model for delivering accurate results.

13. Irrelevant features

Although Machine Learning models are intended to give the best possible outcome, if we feed garbage data as input, then the result will also be garbage. Hence, we should use relevant features in our training sample. A Machine Learning model is said to be good if training data has a good set of features or less to no irrelevant features.

Conclusion

An ML system doesn't perform well if the training set is too small or if the data is not generalized, noisy, and corrupted with irrelevant features. We went through some of the basic challenges faced by beginners while practicing Machine Learning. Machine Learning is all set to bring a big bang transformation in technology. It is one of the most rapidly growing technologies used in medical diagnosis, speech recognition, robotic training, product recommendations, video surveillance, and this list goes on. This continuously evolving domain offers immense job satisfaction, excellent opportunities, global exposure, and exorbitant salary. It is high risk and a high return technology. Before starting your Machine Learning journey, ensure that you carefully examine the challenges mentioned above. To learn this fantastic technology, you need to plan carefully, stay patient, and maximize your efforts. Once you win this battle, you can conquer the Future of work and land your dream job!

1.7 AI v/s Machine Learning

Capabilities of AI and Machine Learning

Companies in almost every industry are discovering new opportunities through the connection between AI and Machine Learning. These are just a few capabilities that have become valuable in helping companies transform their processes and products:

- **Predictive analytics**-This capability helps companies predict trends and behavioural patterns by discovering cause-and-effect relationships in data.

- **Recommendation engines**-With recommendation engines, companies use data analysis to recommend products that someone might be interested in.

- **Speech recognition and natural language understanding**-Speech recognition enables a computer system to identify words in spoken language and natural language understanding recognises meaning in written or spoken language.

- **Image and video processing**-These capabilities make it possible to recognise faces, objects and actions in images and videos and implement functionalities such as visual search.

- **Sentiment analysis**-A computer system uses sentiment analysis to identify and categorise positive, neutral and negative attitudes that are expressed in text.

Applications of AI and Machine Learning

Companies in several industries are building applications that take advantage of the connection between artificial intelligence and Machine Learning. These are just a few ways that AI and Machine Learning are helping companies transform their processes and products:

1.Retail

Retailers use AI and Machine Learning to optimise their inventories, build recommendation engines and enhance the customer experience with visual search.

2.Healthcare

Health organisations put AI and Machine Learning to use in applications such as image processing for improved cancer detection and predictive analytics for genomics research.

3.Banking and finance

In financial contexts, AI and Machine Learning are valuable tools for purposes such as detecting fraud, predicting risk and providing more proactive financial advice.

4.Sales and marketing

Sales and marketing teams use AI and Machine Learning for personalised offers, campaign optimisation, sales forecasting, sentiment analysis and prediction of customer churn.

5.Cybersecurity

AI and Machine Learning are powerful weapons for cybersecurity, helping organisations protect themselves and their customers by detecting anomalies.

6.Customer service

Companies in a wide range of industries use chatbots and cognitive search to answer questions, gauge customer intent and provide virtual assistance.

7.Transportation

AI and Machine Learning are valuable in transportation applications, where they help companies improve the efficiency of their routes and use predictive analytics for purposes such as traffic forecasting.

8.Manufacturing

Manufacturing companies use AI and Machine Learning for predictive maintenance and to make their operations more efficient than ever.

You might hear people use artificial intelligence (AI) and Machine Learning (ML) interchangeably, especially when discussing big data, predictive analytics, and other digital transformation topics. The confusion is understandable as artificial intelligence and Machine Learning are closely related. However, these trending technologies differ in several ways, including scope, applications, and more.

Increasingly AI and ML products have proliferated as businesses use them to process and analyse immense volumes of data, drive better decision-making, generate recommendations and insights in real time, and create accurate forecasts and predictions.

So, what exactly is the difference when it comes to ML vs. AI, how are ML and AI connected, and what do these terms mean in practice for organizations today?

We'll break down AI vs. ML and explore how these two innovative concepts are related and what makes them different from each other.

What is artificial intelligence?

Artificial intelligence is a broad field, which refers to the use of technologies to build machines and computers that have the ability to mimic cognitive functions associated with human intelligence, such as being able to see, understand, and respond to spoken or written language, analyse data, make recommendations, and more.

Although artificial intelligence is often thought of as a system in itself, it is a set of technologies implemented *in* a system to enable it to reason, learn, and act to solve a complex problem.

What is Machine Learning?

Machine Learning is a subset of artificial intelligence that automatically enables a machine or system to learn and improve from experience. Instead of explicit programming, Machine Learning uses algorithms to analyse large amounts of data, learn from the insights, and then make informed decisions.

Machine Learning algorithms improve performance over time as they are trained—exposed to more data. Machine Learning models are the output, or what the program learns from running an algorithm on training data. The more data used, the better the model will get.

How are AI and ML connected?

While AI and ML are not quite the same thing, they are closely connected. The simplest way to understand how AI and ML relate to each other is:

- AI is the broader concept of enabling a machine or system to sense, reason, act, or adapt like a human.

- ML is an application of AI that allows machines to extract knowledge from data and learn from it autonomously.

One helpful way to remember the difference between Machine Learning and artificial intelligence is to imagine them as umbrella categories. Artificial intelligence is the overarching term that covers a wide variety of specific approaches and algorithms. Machine Learning sits under that umbrella, but so do other major subfields, such as deep learning, robotics, expert systems, and natural language processing.

Differences between AI and ML

Now that you understand how they are connected, what is the main difference between AI and ML?

While artificial intelligence encompasses the idea of a machine that can mimic human intelligence, Machine Learning does not. Machine Learning aims to teach a machine how to perform a specific task and provide accurate results by identifying patterns.

Let's say you ask your Google Nest device, "How long is my commute today?" In this case, you ask a machine a question and receive an answer about the estimated time it will take you to drive to your office. Here, the overall goal is for the device to perform a task successfully—a task that you would generally have to do yourself in a real-world environment (for example, research your commute time).

In the context of this example, the goal of using ML in the overall system is not to enable it to perform a task. For instance, you might train algorithms to analyse live transit and traffic data to forecast the volume and density of traffic flow. However, the scope is limited to identifying patterns, how accurate the prediction was, and learning from the data to maximize performance for that specific task.

Artificial intelligence

- AI allows a machine to simulate human intelligence to solve problems.
- The goal is to develop an intelligent system that can perform complex tasks.
- We build systems that can solve complex tasks like a human.
- AI has a wide scope of applications.
- AI uses technologies in a system so that it mimics human decision-making.
- AI works with all types of data: structured, semi-structured, and unstructured.
- AI systems use logic and decision trees to learn, reason, and self-correct.
- Machine Learning
- ML allows a machine to learn autonomously from past data.
- The goal is to build machines that can learn from data to increase the accuracy of the output.
- We train machines with data to perform specific tasks and deliver accurate results.
- Machine Learning has a limited scope of applications.
- ML uses self-learning algorithms to produce predictive models.
- ML can only use structured and semi-structured data.
- ML systems rely on statistical models to learn and can self-correct when provided with new data.

Benefits of using AI and ML together

AI and ML bring powerful benefits to organizations of all shapes and sizes, with new possibilities constantly emerging. In particular, as the amount of data grows in size and complexity, automated and intelligent systems are becoming vital to helping companies automate tasks, unlock value, and generate actionable insights to achieve better outcomes.

Here are some of the business benefits of using artificial intelligence and Machine Learning:

1 Wider data range

2 Analysing and activating a wider range of unstructured and structured data sources.

3 Faster decision-making

4 Improving data integrity, accelerating data processing, and reducing human error for more informed, faster decision-making.

5 Efficiency

6 Increasing operational efficiency and reducing costs.

7 Analytic integrations

8 Empowering employees by integrating predictive analytics and insights into business reporting and applications.

Applications of AI and ML

Artificial intelligence and Machine Learning can be applied in many ways, allowing organizations to automate repetitive or manual processes that help drive informed decision-making.

Companies across industries are using AI and ML in various ways to transform how they work and do business. Incorporating AI and ML capabilities into their strategies and systems helps organizations rethink how they use their data and available resources, drive productivity and efficiency, enhance data-driven decision-making through predictive analytics, and improve customer and employee experiences.

Here are some of the most common applications of AI and ML:

1 Healthcare and life sciences

Patient health record analysis and insights, outcome forecasting and modelling, accelerated drug development, augmented diagnostics, patient monitoring, and information extraction from clinical notes.

2 Manufacturing

Production machine monitoring, predictive maintenance, IoT analytics, and operational efficiency.

3 Ecommerce and retail

Inventory and supply chain optimization, demand forecasting, visual search, personalized offers and experiences, and recommendation engines.

4 Financial services

Risk assessment and analysis, fraud detection, automated trading, and service processing optimization.

5 Telecommunications

Intelligent networks and network optimization, predictive maintenance, business process automation, upgrade planning, and capacity forecasting.

EXERCISE

TRUE OR FALSE

1. Machine Learning is a subset of Artificial Intelligence
2. The term "Machine Learning" was coined by Arthur Samuel in the 1950s.
3. The history of Machine Learning dates back only a few decades.
4. Learning Machine Learning is not necessary since traditional rule-based systems are more reliable.
5. There are two main types of machines: traditional rule-based systems and modern Machine Learning-based systems.
6. Machine Learning has applications only in the field of technology.
7. Supervised learning, unsupervised learning, and reinforcement learning are the three main types of Machine Learning.
8. In supervised learning, the model is trained on labeled data and learns to make predictions based on that data.
9. Unsupervised learning focuses on training models with labeled data to make predictions.
10. Image classification is an example of a Machine Learning application.
11. Self-driving cars do not use Machine Learning in their systems.
12. Different perspectives in Machine Learning offer varying insights into how models learn and improve.

Answer: True, True, False, False, False, False, True, True, , False, True, False

MCQ

1. What is Machine Learning?

a) A type of computer virus
b) A subset of Artificial Intelligence
c) The study of mechanical devices
d) A new programming language

2. Who coined the term "Machine Learning"?

a) Alan Turing
b) John McCarthy
c) Arthur Samuel
d) Marvin Minsky

3. When did the term "Machine Learning" first come into use?

a) 1930s
b) 1950s
c) 1970s
d) 1990s

4. Why should we learn Machine Learning?
a) It's a popular buzzword
b) It helps automate all tasks
c) It enables us to make data-driven decisions
d) It's only for programmers

5. Which type of Machine Learning requires labeled data for training?
a) Supervised learning
b) Unsupervised learning
c) Reinforcement learning
d) Semi-supervised learning

6. Which perspective in Machine Learning focuses on algorithm design and mathematical analysis?
a) Statistical perspective
b) Computational perspective
c) Engineering perspective
d) Psychological perspective

7. What are the main types of machines in the overview?
a) Mechanical and electrical machines
b) Traditional and modern machines
c) Rule-based and data-based machines
d) AI and ML-based machines

8. In which field can Machine Learning not be applied?
a) Healthcare
b) Finance
c) Music
d) Marketing

9. What type of Machine Learning involves learning from past experiences and improving performance over time?
a) Supervised learning
b) Unsupervised learning
c) Reinforcement learning
d) Deep learning

10. Which is an example of a supervised learning task?
a) Identifying spam emails
b) Grouping similar news articles
c) Discovering hidden patterns in data
d) Training a chess-playing AI

11. What distinguishes AI from Machine Learning?
a) AI involves hardware, while Machine Learning involves software
b) AI requires human intervention, while Machine Learning is automated
c) AI is a subset of Machine Learning
d) AI enables machines to mimic human intelligence, while Machine Learning focuses on algorithms learning from data

12. What type of Machine Learning is used to find patterns or relationships in data without explicit labeling?
a) Supervised learning
b) Unsupervised learning
c) Reinforcement learning
d) Semi-supervised learning

13. What is an example of a real-world application of Machine Learning?

a) Turning lights on and off
b) Predicting stock market trends
c) Playing a DVD
d) Opening and closing doors

14. What perspective in Machine Learning focuses on designing efficient algorithms and data structures for computation?
a) Statistical perspective
b) Algorithmic perspective
c) Computational perspective
d) Cognitive perspective

15. Which statement is true about AI and Machine Learning?
a) AI and Machine Learning are completely unrelated fields
b) AI is a subset of Machine Learning
c) Machine Learning is a subset of AI
d) AI and Machine Learning are the same thing

16. Which type of Machine Learning involves an agent learning how to behave in an environment to maximize rewards?
a) Supervised learning
b) Unsupervised learning
c) Reinforcement learning
d) Deep learning

17. What is a common application of natural language processing (NLP) in Machine Learning?
a) Image classification
b) Speech recognition
c) Predicting stock prices
d) Controlling robots

18. Which type of Machine Learning does not require explicit supervision but focuses on finding hidden structures in data?
a) Supervised learning
b) Unsupervised learning
c) Reinforcement learning
d) Semi-supervised learning

19. What is an example of a Machine Learning case study involving image recognition?
a) Detecting fraudulent transactions
b) Recommending movies
c) Diagnosing diseases from medical images
d) Translating languages

20. Which perspective in Machine Learning is concerned with implementing models on computational hardware and ensuring scalability?
a) Algorithmic perspective
b) Statistical perspective
c) Computational perspective
d) Psychological perspective

21. Which statement accurately distinguishes between AI and Machine Learning?
a) AI is about creating intelligent machines, while Machine Learning is about enabling machines to learn from data
b) AI is limited to software applications, while Machine Learning deals with hardware systems
c) AI and Machine Learning are interchangeable terms
d) AI is focused on creating complex algorithms, while Machine Learning is concerned with rule-based systems

22. Which type of Machine Learning aims to predict future outcomes based on historical data?
a) Supervised learning c) Reinforcement learning
b) Unsupervised learning d) Predictive learning

23. What is an example of a Machine Learning application in finance?
a) Sorting emails into folders c) Detecting credit card fraud
b) Playing chess against a computer d) Adjusting room temperature automatically

24. Which type of Machine Learning focuses on making decisions sequentially to maximize cumulative rewards?
a) Supervised learning
b) Unsupervised learning
c) Reinforcement learning
d) Reinforced learning

25. What perspective in Machine Learning explores the psychological and cognitive aspects of learning algorithms?
a) Algorithmic perspective
b) Cognitive perspective
c) Statistical perspective
d) Engineering perspective

SHORT QUESTION AND ANSWERS
Q1: What is Machine Learning?
Q2: History of Machine Learning?
Q3: Why should we learn Machine Learning?
Q4: Types of machines (from section 1.2.1)?
Q5: What are the applications of Machine Learning?
Q6: What are the types of Machine Learning?
Q7: Can you provide some examples of Machine Learning applications?
Q8: Can you provide a case study as an example of Machine Learning?
Q9: What are the perspectives in Machine Learning?
Q10: What is the difference between AI and Machine Learning?

QUESTION AND ANSWERS
Question 1: What is Machine Learning?
Question 2: Can you provide a comprehensive overview of the history of Machine Learning?
Question 3: Why is learning Machine Learning important in today's technological landscape?
Question 4: Provide an in-depth overview of the types of machines and their significance.
Question 5: Could you elaborate on the diverse applications of Machine Learning in various fields?
Question 6: Provide a detailed case study illustrating the application of Machine Learning in a real-world scenario.
Question 7: What is Machine Learning, and How Does It Differ from Traditional Programming?
Question 8: Tracing the Evolution: A Comprehensive History of Machine Learning
Question 9: Unraveling the Significance of Learning Machine Learning in the Modern World
Question 10: A Comprehensive Overview of Machine Learning: Types, Techniques, and Applications
Question 11: Real-World Impact: An In-Depth Case Study of Machine Learning in Healthcare
Question 12: Perspectives in Machine Learning: Statistical, Algorithmic, and Computational Views

Online Resources

Online Exam Papers
True/False Exam

Link https://forms.gle/e5fRyz7tzhd9cnkY9

QR Code

YouTube Video Playlist Link

Chapter 1
Link
https://www.youtube.com/playlist?list=PLzlh_31VWEFrIZhYhxIF-Ytm1kF0CkByv
QR Code

Chapter-2: Supervised learning

2.1 Introduction

This chapter covers the theory, step-by-step codes, and applications of various supervised learning algorithms including multilinear regression, logistic regression, k-nearest neighbour (KNN), support vector machine (SVM), decision tree, random forest, extra trees, gradient boosting, extreme gradient boosting, and adaptive gradient boosting using scikit-learn. Various Machine Learning (ML) applications in the oil and gas industry, including productivity effectiveness, binary classification of ML application in geomechanically log property prediction (shear wave and compression wave travel time predictions), TOC prediction, net present value prediction, frac intensity binary classification, and rate of penetration prediction, have been detailed and illustrated in an easy workflow in Python. Finally, handling missing data using the effective impute package library in Python is discussed. K-nearest neighbour, iterative imputer, and multivariate imputation by chained equations (MICE) are illustrated with the step-by-step codes in Python. These techniques were applied to impute the missing values in a frac stage data set. The examples and guidelines shown in this chapter can be easily applied to solve various other oil and gas–related problems.

Learning in Big Data: Introduction to Machine Learning

Supervised learning is one of the most widely used ML algorithms. In supervised learning, the training data you use are already labelled. These training data are used to infer a learning algorithm or mapping function from the input variable (*X*) to the output variable (*Y*). The correct answers or desired outputs (labels), here, are already known, given a labelled set of input–output pairs, M= $\{\sum(x_{i,}y_i)\}\ _i^N$;*N* is simply the number of training examples. The training input $x_{i,}$ is a **d**-dimensional vector or numbers also known as features, or attributes. The input $x_{i,}$ can be an image, an email message, a time series, a molecular shape, or a graph. The output y_i, also known as a response variable, is a categorical or nominal variable for a classification problem or real value for a regression problem. Classification algorithms and regression techniques (see Fig. 1) are two types of supervised learning widely used to develop predictive models.

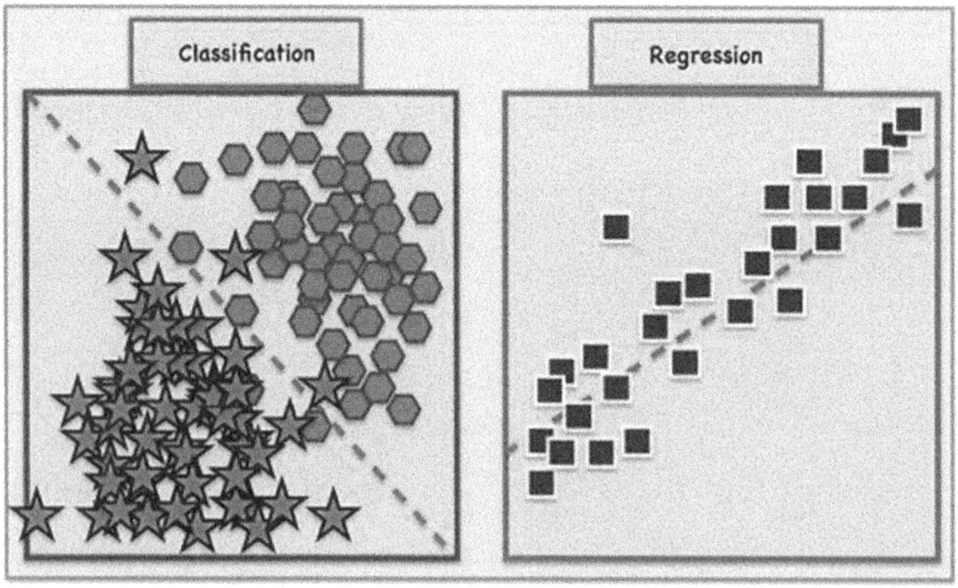

Statistical Pattern Recognition

Supervised, unsupervised, and reinforcement learning algorithms.

Supervised, unsupervised, and reinforcement learning algorithms have the common goal of estimating the class conditional distribution from the training data. The essential difference among these different learning algorithms is the availability of information in the feature vector indicating which pattern class generated the feature vector. In supervised learning, each feature vector in the training data set contains explicit information regarding which pattern class generated that feature vector. In unsupervised learning, information regarding which pattern class generated a particular feature vector is not available in either the training data set or the test data set. In reinforcement learning, 'hints' about which pattern class generated a particular feature vector are provided either periodically or periodically throughout the learning process (Sutton and Barto 1998).

AI and Cloud Computing

Supervised Learning is an important form of ML. It is named as *supervised*, because the learning process is done under the seen label of observation variables; in contrast, in Unsupervised Learning, the response variables are not available. In Supervised Learning, datasets are trained with the training sets to build ML, and then will be used to label new observations from the testing set. As for the training set, the input variables are the features which will influence the accuracy of predicted variable. It contains both quantitative and qualitative variables; the output variable is the label class that Supervised Learning will label the new observations. According to different types of output variables, Supervised Learning tasks can be divided into two kinds: classification task and regression task. The output variables of classification task are categorical variables, and those of regression task are continuous variables. For example, current hot image classification is a classification task, and prediction of stock price is a regression task.

The procedure of Supervised Learning can be described as the follows: we use $x^{(I)}$ to denote the input variables, and $y^{(I)}$ to denote the output variable. A pair $(x^{(i)}, y^{(i)})$ is a training example, and the training set that we will use to learn is $\{(x^{(i)}, y^{(i)}), i = 1, 2, \ldots, m\}$. (i) in the notation is an index into the training set. We use X denote the space of input values, and Y as the space of output values. The goal is, given a training set, to learn a function $h: X \rightarrow Y$ so that $h(x)$ is a good predictor for the corresponding value of y. h is a hypothesis.

Analytics Defined

Supervised Learning

Supervised learning provides you with a powerful tool to classify and process data using machine language. With supervised learning you use labeled data, which is a data set that has been classified, to infer a learning algorithm. The data set is used as the basis for predicting the classification of other unlabeled data through the use of Machine Learning algorithms.

Linear Regression

Linear regression is a supervised learning technique typically used in predicting, forecasting, and finding relationships between quantitative data. It is one of the earliest learning techniques, which is still widely used. For example, this technique can be applied to examine if there was a relationship between a company's advertising budget and its sales. You could also use it to determine if there is a linear relationship between a particular radiation therapy and tumour sizes.

Classification Techniques

The classification techniques that will be discussed in this section are those focused on predicting a qualitative response by analysing data and recognizing patterns. For example, this type of technique is used to classify whether or not a credit card transaction is fraudulent. There are many different classification techniques or classifiers, but some of the widely used ones include:

- Logistic regression,

- Linear discriminant analysis,

- K-nearest neighbours,

- Trees,

- Neural Networks, and

- Support Vector Machines.

- Integrated deep learning for self-driving robotic cars

Supervised learning

Supervised learning takes place aided by a supervisor that guides the learning agent. The learning agent is the Machine Learning (ML) algorithm or model and the supervisor is the output in the data for a given set of inputs. The aim of the learning algorithm is to predict how a given set of inputs leads to the output. At first, the ML agent takes the inputs and randomly predicts the corresponding outputs. Since the random calculation is akin to shooting

in the dark, the predicted outcomes are far away from the known outcomes. The supervisor at the output end indicates the error in prediction which again guides the learning agent to minimize the error.
The first two steps, namely, perception and scene generation in autonomous driving, are performed through supervised learning. The program is trained using a large number of digital photographs involving driving scenes. In the learning phase, the program identifies and classifies the various objects in the photo images. The master program in the AV controller computer calls the respective ML trained subroutines and combines their result to generate the driving scene surrounding the AV. This act corresponds to sensor readings fusion in real-life self-driving vehicles that use an array of sensors to generate a mapping of the surroundings.
Anomaly detection

Mean Square Error (MSE)

Supervised learning vector quantization (LVQ) is a prototype selection classifier that allows to choose how many training instances to keep and learns what those instances should look like. During the learning process, the supervised LVQ uses the MSE to evaluate its performance in classification training. The MSE measures the difference between the predicted and the actual values, defined as follows:

$\text{MSE}=\frac{1}{N}\sum^{N} J = 1\,(P_J\text{-}A_J)2$

where P_J *is* the predicted value of instance *j*, A_J is the actual target value of instance *j*, and *in* the number of instances. Through the LVQ learning process, the solution with the lowest MSE value is used as the final model (best solution). Like accuracy, the main limitation of MSE is that this metric does not provide information about the trade-off between the class data, which may cause the discrimination process to select the suboptimal solution. Also, this metric is highly dependent on the initialization of the weights. For an imbalanced class problem, if the initial weights are not properly selected (i.e., not representing the minority class), the discrimination process may end up with a suboptimal solution. While the MSE value is minimized, the solution could under- or over-fit due to a lack of information about the minority class.

Computational Analysis and Understanding of Natural Languages: Principles, Methods and Applications.
Supervised Learning
Supervised learning is a learning model built to make prediction, given an unforeseen input instance. A supervised learning algorithm takes a known set of input dataset and its known responses to the data (output) to learn the regression/classification model. A learning algorithm then trains a model to generate a prediction for the response to new data or the test dataset. Supervised learning uses classification algorithms and regression techniques to develop predictive models. The algorithms include linear regression, logistic regression, and neural networks as well, apart from decision tree, Support Vector Machine (SVM), random forest, naive Bayes, and *k*-nearest neighbour.
Classification task predicts discrete responses. It is recommended if the data can be categorized, tagged, or separated into specific groups or classes. Classification models classify input data into categories. Popular or major applications of classification include bank credit scoring, medical imaging, and speech recognition. Also, handwriting recognition uses classification to recognize letters and numbers, to check whether an email is genuine or spam, or even to detect whether a tumour is benign or cancerous.
Regression techniques predict continuous responses. A linear regression attempts to model the relationship between two variables by fitting linear equation to observed data. For example, say, a data is collected about how happy people are after getting so many hours of sleep. In this dataset, sleep and happy people are the variables. By regression analysis, one can relate them and start making predictions.
In Natural Language Processing, the input can contain an annotated text provided by humans. Annotated text is a metadata that is given along with the dataset to the machine. The annotations can be Part-of-Speech tagging (Po's tags), phrase, and dependency structures. For example, to determine whether the text "clean dishes" is a noun phrase or a verb phrase, the algorithm needs to be trained using annotated sentences like "Clean dishes are in the cupboard" or "Clean dishes before going to work." In the first case, the annotation says that it is a noun phrase and verb phrase in the second case.

2.2 Supervised Machine Learning algorithms

Supervised learning is a Machine Learning task for the predictions of unknown values by learning a model from labeled training data consisting of a set of training example input-output pairs (Russell and Norvig, 2010). The training set use to train the model by selected learning algorithms. To measure the accuracy of the learned model, the performance of the resulting model was measured on a test set of examples that are distinct from the training set. If the results are not satisfactory then changing learning algorithms is available. The options of supervised Machine Learning are classification and regression when the output is a finite set of values and a number, respectively. In this work, the regression methods are used to predict normal boiling point of compounds. A flowchart of the supervised Machine Learning model is displayed in Figure.

Detection and segmentation in microscopy images
Supervised learning methods have been used extensively for segmenting membranes and neurons in 2D. These include single-layer networks, cascades of classifiers , and hierarchical contextual models . A single-layer artificial neural network (ANN) with Hessian eigenspace features was used for segmentation . A cascade of ANNs were used . Several ANNs are used in series; each ANN uses the classification context provided by the previous network to improve detection accuracy. The model in Seyedhosseini uses contextual information along with radon-like features to learn about a series of discriminative models. The multiscale model representation of the context image was used to give the subsequent classifiers access to a larger contextual area for better detection of neuron membranes in EM images. In Seyedhosseini and Tasdizen, a multiclass, multiscale contextual model was introduced that exploits both input image features and contextual information with a logistic disjunctive normal network classifier to detect membranes. Region-based methods are used to transform the membrane probability maps into cell segments; they are required for improving the segmentation accuracy from membrane detections in EM images.

A hierarchical merge tree structure was built to represent multiple region hypotheses, and the merge tree was resolved with consistency constraints to acquire final intersection segmentation. The sections were linked to reconstruct the intersection neurons using supervised learning. In Hu et al, unsupervised learning and signal-processing techniques are used to obtain high depth-resolution EM images computationally without sacrificing throughput. Several methods have been used to link similar neuron sections across the image stack. A graph-cut framework was proposed to trace 2D contours in 3D . In Vitaladevuni and Basri , the neuron segments are jointly clustered based on their likelihood of belonging to the same neuron. The 3D linking was formulated as a quadratic optimization problem by coclustering each pair of adjacent segments. An automatic processing pipeline was introduced that combines the probabilistic output of a random forest classifier with geometrical consistency constraints to optimize the 3D affinity matrix . In Laptev , global dense correspondences between the sections were established using a SIFT-Flow algorithm in order to evaluate the features of the corresponding pixels and use them to perform the segmentation.

Alternatively, there are a set of methods that perform 2D segmentation and 3D reconstruction simultaneously. A reinforcement learning framework was proposed to merge super voxels into segmentations . A super voxel merging method was proposed for segmenting neurons, all merging decisions were coupled in a graphical model that incorporates both super voxel face and boundary curve information . The use of super voxels allows the extraction of expressive geometric features that are used by the higher-order potentials in the graphical model. Multiple 2D segmentation hypotheses were generated for each section in the stack, and segments were fused to provide the most globally consistent segmentation of the stack in a Markov random field framework . In a similar manner, 2D segmentation hypotheses were generated as a tree structure, and then the 2D segmentation and 3D reconstruction were formulated as an integer linear program with constraints. A reinforcement learning framework was used to learn a merging policy for super pixel agglomeration. There are also other semiautomatic methods that utilize user input to improve the segmentation of neurons. Neurons are over segmented into 2D and 3D regions, and the regions that belong to one neuron are manually merged . Skeleton reconstructions of neurons are combined with automated volume segmentations . To be able to segment image volumes in 3D requires the data to be mostly isotropic. There are limitations to the image volume size that can be generated with isotropic resolution. Direct 3D segmentation approaches may not be feasible for anisotropic data sets.

2.2Linear Models of classification

Today we're going to talk about linear models for classification, and in addition to that some general principles and advanced topics surrounding general models, both for classification and regression.
FIXME: in regularizing SVM, long vs short normal vectors. FIXME, do we need Ovo? we kind of do, right?
Linear models for
We'll first start with linear models for binary classification, so if there are only two classes. That makes the models much easier to understand.

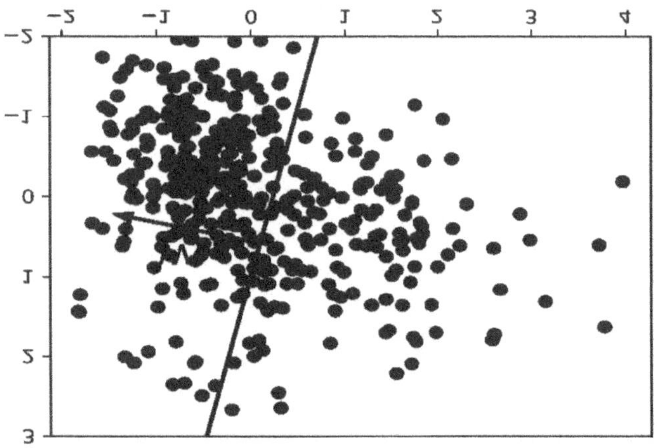

y^=sign(w^T x+b) = sign($\sum_i w_i X_i$+b)
Similar to the regression case, basically all linear models for classification have the same way to make predictions. As with regression, they compute an inner product of a weight vector w with the feature vector x, and add some bias b. The result of that is a real number, as in regression. For classification, however, we only look at the sign of the result, so whether it is negative or positive. If it's positive, we predict one class, usually called +1, if it's negative, we predict the other class, usually called -1. If the result is 0, by convention the positive class is predicted, but because it's a floating-point number that doesn't really happen in practice. You'll see that sometimes in my notation I will not have a b. That's because you can always add a constant feature to x to achieve the same effect (thought you would then need to leave that feature out of the regularization). So, when I write w^T x without a b assume that there is a constant feature added that is not part of any regularization.
Geometrically, what the formula means is that the decision boundary of a linear classifier will be a hyperplane in the feature space, where w is the normal vector of that plane. In the 2d example here, it's just a line separating red and blue. Everything on the right-hand side would be classified as blue by this classifier, and everything on the left-hand side as red.
Questions? So again, the learning here consists of finding parameters w and b based on the training set, and that is where the different algorithms differ. There are quite a lot of algorithms out there, and there are also quite a lot in scikit-learn, but we'll only discuss the most common ones.
The most straight-forward way to approach finding w and b is to use the framework of empirical risk minimization that we talked about last time, so finding parameters that minimize some loss of the training set. Where classification differs quite a bit from regression is on how we want to measure misclassifications.
Picking a loss?
y^=sign (w^T x +b)

$$\min_{\substack{p \\ wer\rightarrow,ber}} \sum_{i=1}^{n} 1 \quad y,\#sign(w^T \text{ x +b})$$

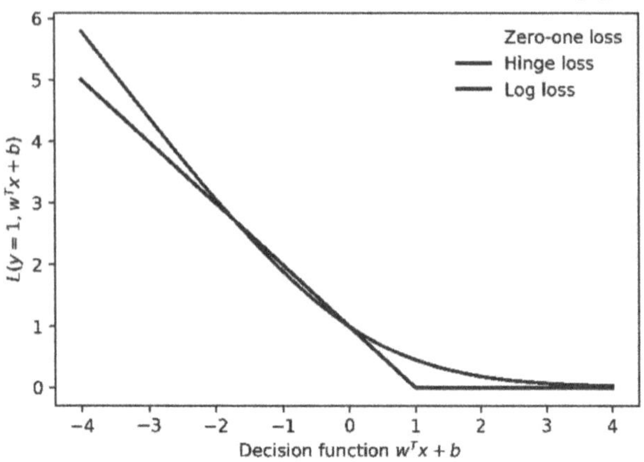

So, we need to define a loss function for given w and b that tell us how well they fit the training set. Obvious Idea: Minimize number of misclassifications aka 0-1 loss but this loss is non-convex, not continuous and minimizing it is

NP-hard. So, we need to relax it, which basically means we want to find a convex upper bound for this loss. This is not done on the actual prediction, but on the inner product w^T x, which is also called the decision function. So, this graph here has the inner product on the x axis and shows what the loss would be for class 1. The 0-1 loss is zero if the decision function is positive, and one if it's negative. Because a positive decision function means a positive perdition, means correct classification in the case of y=1. A negative prediction means a wrong classification, which is penalized by the 0-1 loss with a loss of 1, i.e., one mistake.

The other losses we'll talk about are mostly the hinge loss and the log loss. You can see they are both upper bounds on the 0-1 loss, but they are convex and continuous. Both of these losses care not only that you make a correct prediction, but also "how correct" your prediction is, i.e., how positive or negative your decision function is. We'll talk a bit more about the motivation of these two losses, starting with the logistic loss.

Logistic Regression

[$\log\left(\frac{p(y=1|x)}{p(y=-1|x)}\right)= w^T x +b$

$p(y=1|x) = \frac{1}{1+e-\overrightarrow{W}^{t}X-b}$

$\min_{w \in Rp, b \in R} \sum_{i=1}^{n} \log(\exp(-y_i(w^T x_i(\exp(-y_i (w^T x+b))+1)$

$y^\wedge =$ sign $(w^T x + b)$

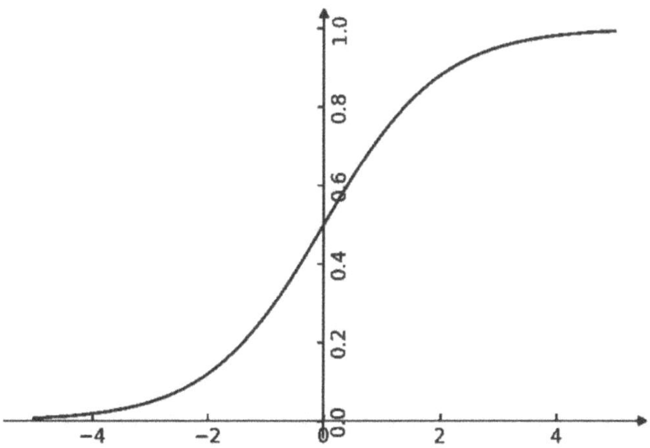

Logistic regression is probably the most commonly used linear classifier, maybe the most commonly used classifier overall. The idea is to model the log-odds, which is log p(y=1|x) - log p(y=0|x) as a linear function, as shown here. Rearranging the formula, you get a model of p(y=1|x) as 1 over 1 + … This function is called the logistic sigmoid and is drawn to the right here. Basically, it squashed the linear function w^T x between 0 and 1, so that it can model a probability.

Given this equation for p(lynx), what we want to do is maximize the probability of the training set under this model. This approach is known as maximum likelihood. Basically, you want to find w and b such that they assign maximum probability to the labels observed in the training data. You can rearrange that a bit and end up with this equation here, which contains the log-loss as seen on the last slide.

The prediction is the class with the higher probability. In the binary case, that's the same as asking whether the probability of class 1 is bigger or smaller than .5. And as you can see from the plot of the logistic sigmoid, the probability of the class +1 is greater than .5 exactly if the decision function w^T x is greater than 0. So, predicting the class with maximum probability is the same as predicting which side of the hyperplane given by w we are on.

Ok so this is logistic regression. We minimize this loss and get a w which defines a hyper plane. But if you think back to last time, this is only part of what we want. This formulation tries to fit the training data, but it doesn't care about finding a simple solution.

Penalized Logistic Regression

$\min_{w \in r^p b \in R,} C\sum_{i=1}^{n} \log(\exp(-y_i(w^T x_i+b))+1)+||w||_2^2$

$\min_{w \in r^p b \in R,} C\sum_{i=1}^{n} \log(\exp(-y_i (w^T x_i+b))+1)+||w||_1$

- C is inverse to alpha (or alpha / samples)

- Both versions strongly convex, l2 version smooth (differentiable).

- All points contribute to w (dense solution to dual).

So, we can do the same we did for regression: we can add regularization terms using the L1 and L2 norm. The effects are the same as for regression: both push the coefficients towards zero, but the l1 norm encourages coefficients to be exactly zero, for the same reasons we discussed last time.
You could also use a mixed penalty to get something like the elastic net. That's not implemented in the logistic regression class in scikit-learn right now, but it's certainly a sensible thing to do.
Here I used a slightly different notation as last time, though. I'm not using alpha to multiply the regularize, instead I'm using C to multiply the loss. That's mostly because that's how it's done in scikit-learn and it has only historic reasons. The idea is exactly the same, only now C is 1 over alpha. So large C means heavy weight to the loss, means little regularization, while small C means less weight on the loss, means strong regularization.
Depending on the model, there might be a factor of n_samples in there somewhere. Usually, we try to make the objective as independent of the number of samples as possible in scikit-learn, but that might lead to surprises if you're not aware of it.
Some sidenotes on the optimization problem: here, as in regression, having more regularization makes the optimization problem easier. You might have seen this in your homework already, if you decrease C, meaning you add more regularization, your model fits more quickly.
One particular property of the logistic loss, compared to the hinge loss we'll discuss next is that each data point contributes to the loss, so each data point has an effect on the solution. That's also true for all the regression models we saw last time.
Effect of regularization

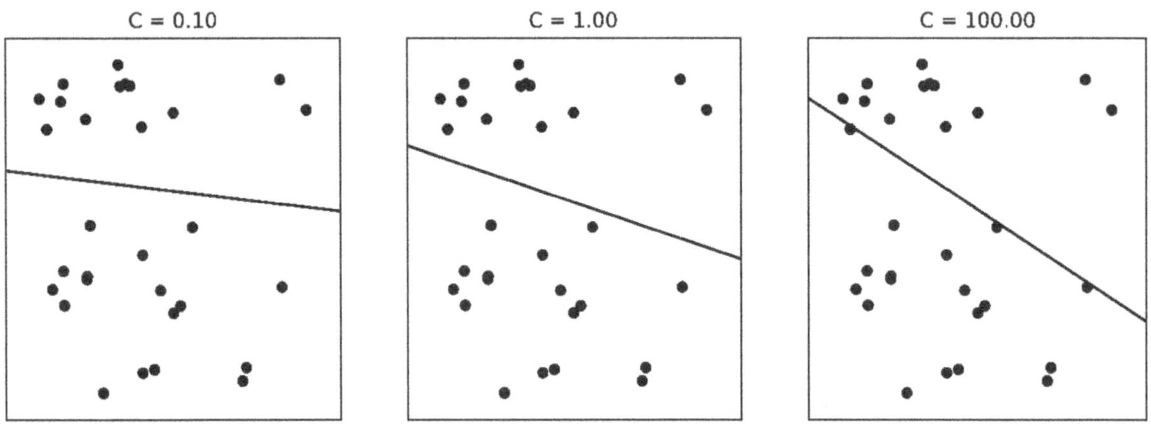

- Small C (a lot of regularization) limits the influence of individual points!

So, I spared you with coefficient plots because they look the same as for regression. All the things I said about model complexity and dependency on the number of features and samples is as true for classification as it is for regression. There is another interesting way to thing about regularization that I found helpful, though. I'm not going to walk through the math for this, but you can reformulate the optimization problem and find that what the C parameter does is actually limit the influence of individual data points. With very large C, we said we have no regularization. It also means individual data points can have basically unlimited influence, as you can see here. There are two outliers here, which basically completely tilt the decision boundary. But if we decrease C, and therefore increase the regularization, what happens is that the influence of these outlier points becomes limited, and the other points get more influence.
#Max-Margin and Support Vectors

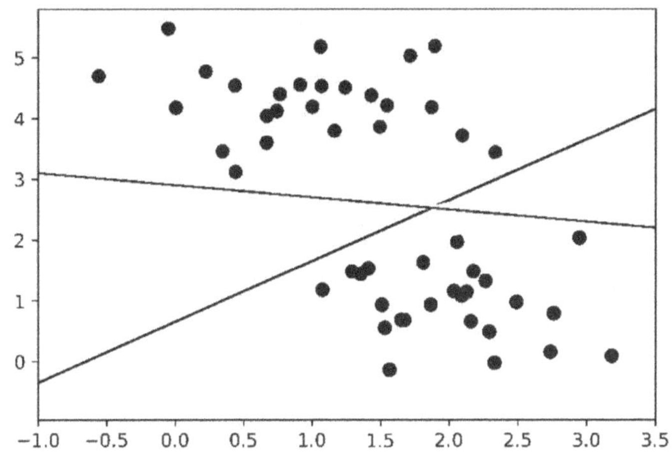

A point is within the margin if 〖y_i w〗^T x is smaller than one. That means if you have a smaller w, you basically have a smaller margin given that you're on the correct side. If you're on the wrong side, you'll have always have a loss. If you're in the correct side, if you're w^x is small, then you also have a loss.

#Max-Margin and Support Vectors

$ \min w\in R^{p}, b\in R\ C\sum_{i=1}^{n}\max(0,1-yi(w^T x_i+b)) + ||w||_2^2 $

Within margin ⇔ $y_i(w^T x+b) < 1$

Smaller w⇒ ⇒ larger margin

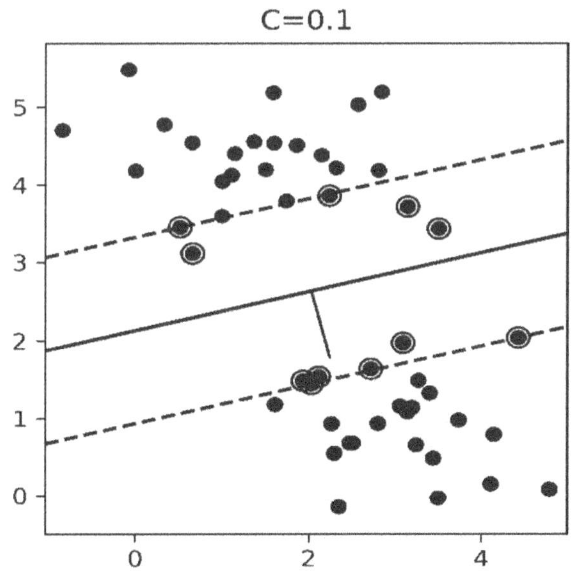

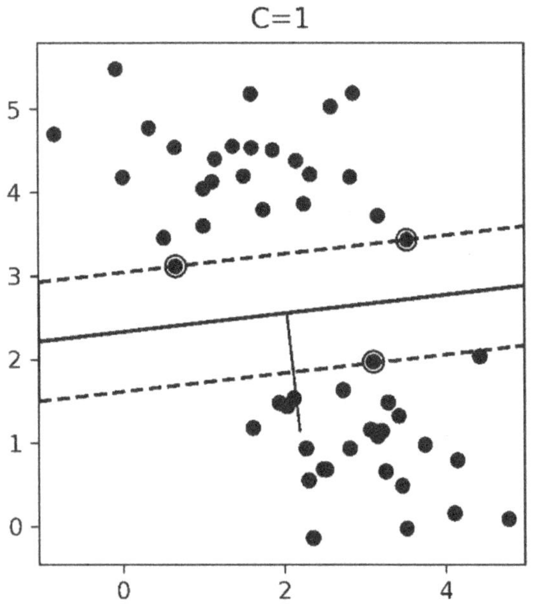

Here are two examples on the same dataset. Where I learned linear support vector machine with c-0.1, and c=1. With c=0.1, you have a wider margin. There are points inside the margin and all the points inside the margin are support vectors which contribute to the solution. Points that are outside of the margin and on the correct side doesn't contribute to the solution. These points are sort of classified correctly, not when they're ignored. The normal vector is w and basically, the size of the margin is the inverse of the length of w. C=0.1 means I have less emphasis on the data fitting and more emphasis on the shrinking w. This will lead to a smaller w. If I have larger C that means less regularization, which will lead to a larger W, larger W means a smaller margin. So, there are fewer points here, they are inside the margin and therefore, fewer support vectors. More regularization usually means a larger margin but more points inside the margin. Also, more support vectors mean there are more data points that actually influence the solution.

(Soft margin) linear SVM

. larger [$minw \in Rp, b \in RC\sum_{i=1}^{n} max(0,1-\boldsymbol{y_i}(\boldsymbol{W^T X_i}+b)) + ||w||_2^2$

$\frac{min}{w \epsilon r^p, b \epsilon r} C\sum_{i=1}^{n} max(0,1-y_i(W^T X_i+b)) + ||w||_1$

]

- Both versions strongly convex, neither smooth.

- Only some points contribute (the support vectors) to w (sparse solution to dual).

Moving from logistic regression to linear SVMs is just a matter of changing the loss from the log loss to the hinge loss. The hinge-loss is defined as … And we can penalize using either l1 or l2 norm, or again, in principle also elastic net. This formulation with the hinge loss doesn't really make sense without the penalty, because of the formulation of the hinge loss. What this loss says is basically "if you predict the right class with a margin of 1, there is no loss". Otherwise, the loss is linear in the decision function. So, you need to be on the right side of the hyperplane by a given amount, and then there is no more loss. That's the reason you need the penalty, for the 1 to make sense. Otherwise, you could just scale up w to make it far enough on the right side. But the regularization penalizes growing w.

The hinge loss has a kink, same as the l1 norm, and so it's not a smooth optimization problem anymore, but that's not really a big deal. What's interesting is that all the points that are classified correctly with a margin of at least 1 have a loss of zero, and so they don't influence the solution anymore. All the point that are not classified correctly by this margin are the ones that do influence the solution and they are called the support vectors.

FIXME graph of not influencing the solution?

Logistic Regression vs SVM

.compact[$min w∈$R^P$,b∈R C $\sum_{i=1}^{n}$ log(exp($-y_i(W^T X_i$+b))+1)+$\|w\|_2^2$$

$min w∈$R^P$,b∈R C $\sum_{i=1}^{n}$ max(0,1$-y_i(W^T X_i$+b)) + $\|w\|_2^2$$

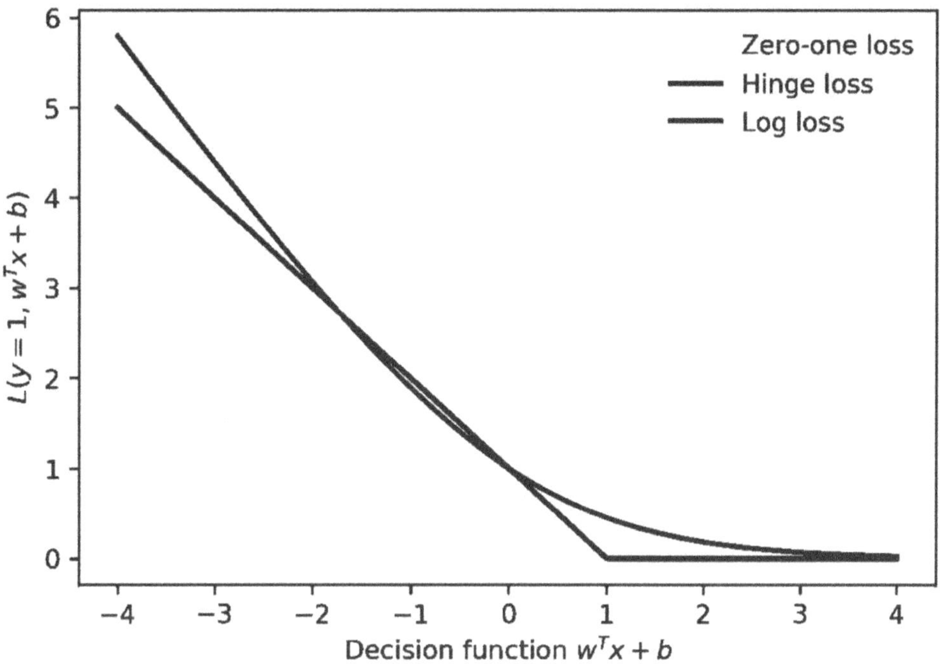

]

So, this is the main difference between logistic regression and linear SVMs: Does it penalize misclassifications according to the green line, or according to the blue line? In practice it doesn't make a big difference.
SVM or LogReg?¶

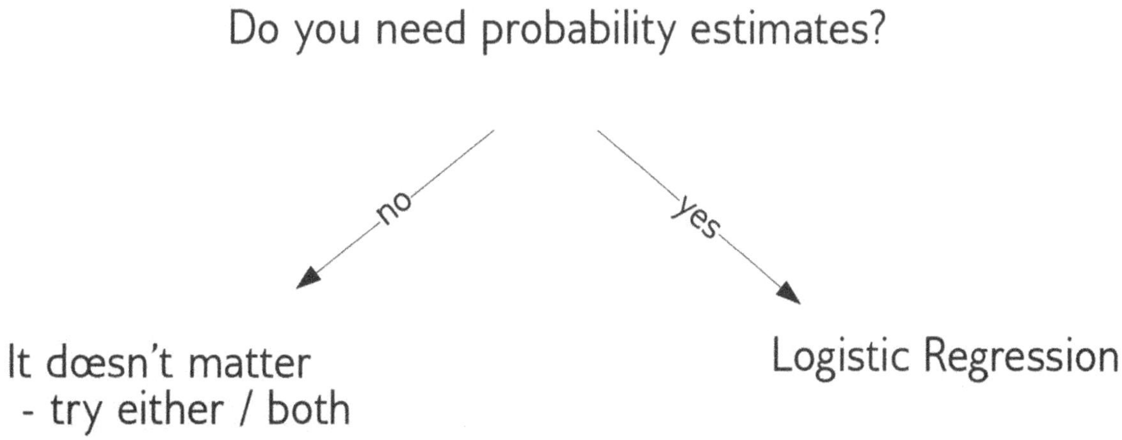

- Need compact model or believe solution is sparse? Use L1

So which one of them should you use? If you need probability estimates, you should use logistic regression. If you don't, you can pick either, or it doesn't really matter. Logistic regression can be a bit faster to optimize in theory. If you're in a setting where there's many more feature than samples, it might make sense to use linear SVMs and solve the dual, but you can actually solve either of the problems in the dual, and we'll talk about what that means in practice in a little bit.

Multiclass classification

Ok, so I think that's enough on the two loss functions and regularization, and hopefully you have a bit of a feel for how these two classifiers work, and also an understanding that they are in fact quite similar in practice.

Next, I want to look at how to go from binary classification to multi-class classification. Basically, there is a simple but hacky way, and there's a slightly more complicated but theoretically sound way.

Reduction to Binary Classification

. padding-top (. left column)

One vs Rest

. right-column

One vs One

The slightly hacky way is using what's known as a reduction. We're doing a reduction like in math: reducing one problem to another. In this case we're reducing the problem of multi-class classification into several instances of the binary classification problem. And we already know how to deal with binary classification.

There are two straight-forward ways to reduce multi-class to binary classification. the first is called one vs rest, the second one is called one-vs-one.

One Vs Rest

For 4 classes:

1v {2,3,4}, 2v {1,3,4}, 3v {1,2,4}, 4v {1,2,3}

In general:

n binary classifiers - each on all data

FIXME terrible slide

Let's start with One vs Rest. here, we learn one binary classifier for each class against the remaining classes. So, let's say we have 4 classes, called 1 to 4. First, we learn a binary classifier of the points in class 1 vs the points in the classes 2, 3 and 4. Then, we do the same for class 2, and so on. The way we end up building as many classifiers as we have classes.

Prediction with One Vs Rest

"Class with highest score"

$y^\wedge = \arg \max_{iey} w_i^T x + b_i$

To make a prediction, we compute the decision function of all classifiers, say 4 in the example, on a new data point. The one with the highest score for the positive class, the single class, wins, and that class is predicted.

It's a little bit unclear why this works as well as it does. Maybe there's some papers about that now, but I'm not.

So, in this case we have one coefficient vector w and one bias b for each class.

One vs Rest Prediction

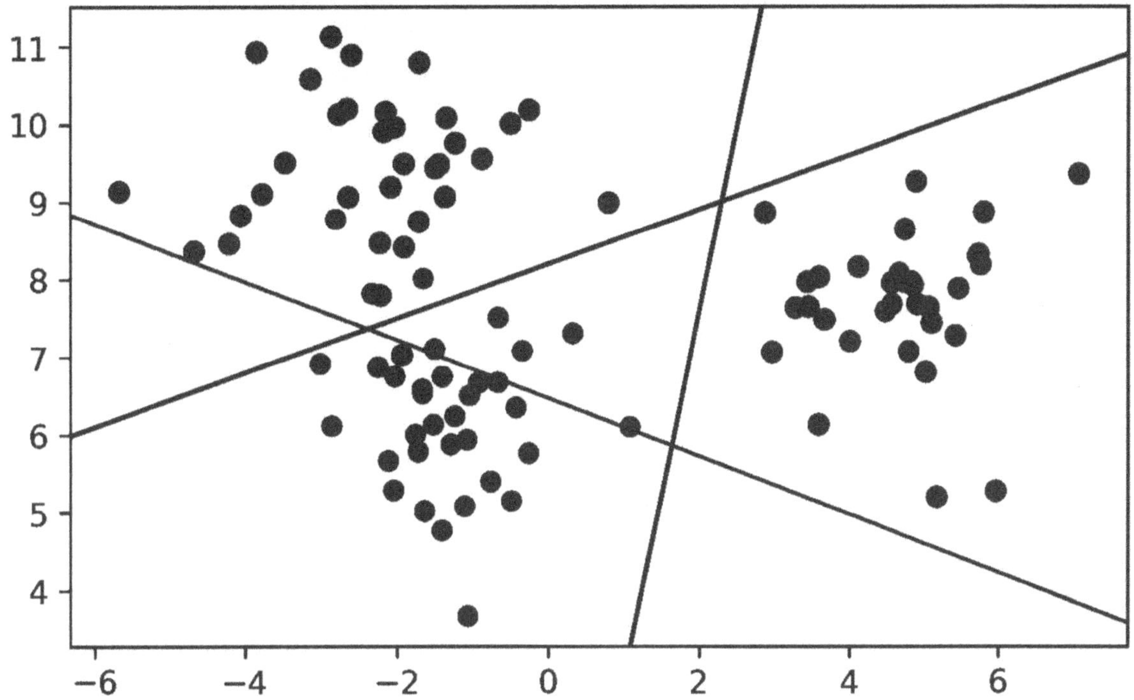

Here is an illustration of what that looks like. Unfortunately, it’s a bit hard to draw 4 classes in general position in 2 dimensions, so I only used 3 classes here. So, each class has an associated coefficient vector and bias, corresponding to a line. The line tries to separate this class from the other two classes.
Fixme draw ws?

One vs Rest Prediction

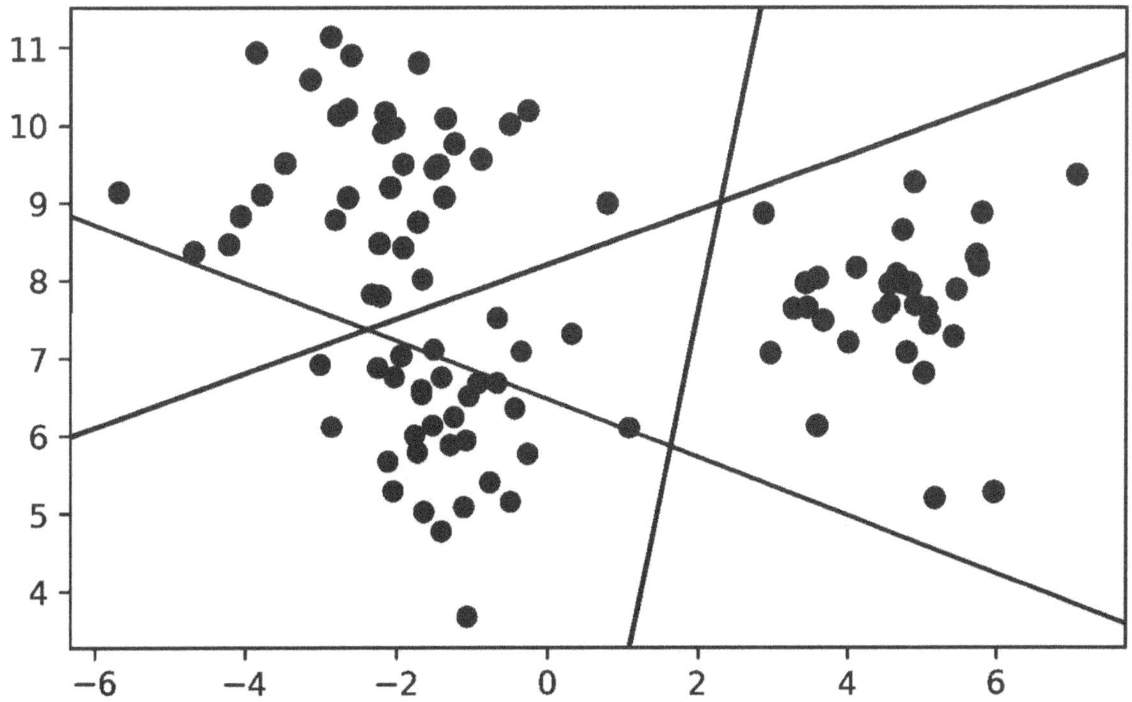

Here are the decision boundaries resulting from these three binary classifiers. Basically, what they say is that the line that is closest decides the class. What you cannot see here is that each of the lines also have a magnitude associated with them. It's not only the direction of the normal vector that matters, but also the length. You can think of that as some form of uncertainty attached to the line.

One Vs One

- 1v2, 1v3, 1v4, 2v3, 2v4, 3v4

- n * (n-1) / 2 binary classifiers - each on a fraction of the data

- "Vote for highest positives"

- Classify by all classifiers.

- Count how often each class was predicted.

- Return most commonly predicted class.

- Again - just a heuristic.

FIXME terrible slide

The other method of reduction is called one vs one. In one vs one, we build one binary model for each pair of classes. In the example of having four classes that is one for 1 vs 2, one for 1v3 and so on. So, we end up with n * (n - 1) /2 binary classifiers. And each is trained only on the subset of the data that belongs to these classes.

To make a prediction, we again apply all of the classifiers. For each class we count how often one of the classifiers predicted that class, and we predict the class with the most votes.

Again, this is just a heuristic and there's not really a good theoretical explanation why this should work.

One vs One Prediction

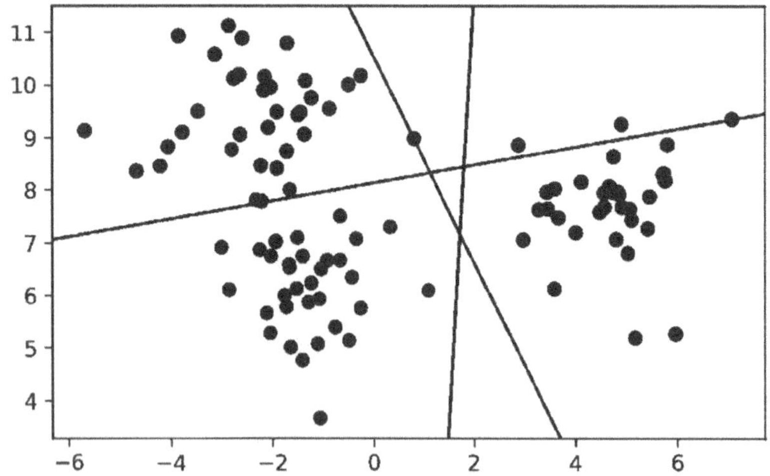

Here is an example for predicting on three classes in 2d using the one-vs-one heuristic. In the case of three classes, there's also three pairs. Three is a bit of a special case, with any more classes there would be more classifiers than classes.

The dashed lines are colored according to the pair of classes they separate. So, the green and blue line separates the green and blue classes. The data points belonging to the grey class were not used in building this model at all.

One vs One Prediction

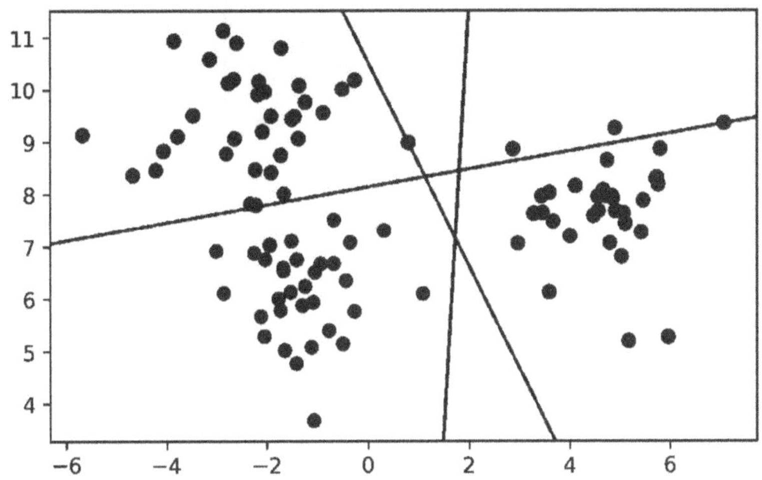

Looking at the predictions made by the one vs one classifier the correspondence to the binary decision boundaries is a bit clearer than for the one vs rest heuristic, because it only takes the actual boundaries into account, not the length of the normal vectors. That makes it easier to visualize the geometry, but it's also a bit of a downside of the method because it means it discards any notion of uncertainty that was present in the binary classifiers. The decision boundary for each class is given by the two lines that this class is involved in. So, the grey class is bounded by the green and grey line and the blue and grey line.

There is a triangle in the center in which there is one vote for each of the classes. In this implemenatation the tie is broken to just always predict the first class, which is the green one. That might not be the best tie breaking strategy, but this is a relatively rare case, in particular if there's more than three classes.
OVR and OVO are general heuristics not restricted to linear models. They can be used whenever a binary model for classification needs to be extended to the multi-class case. For logistic regression, there is actually a natural extension of the formulation, and we don't have to resort to these hacks.
One vs Rest

1. n_classes classifiers

2. trained on imbalanced datasets of original size.

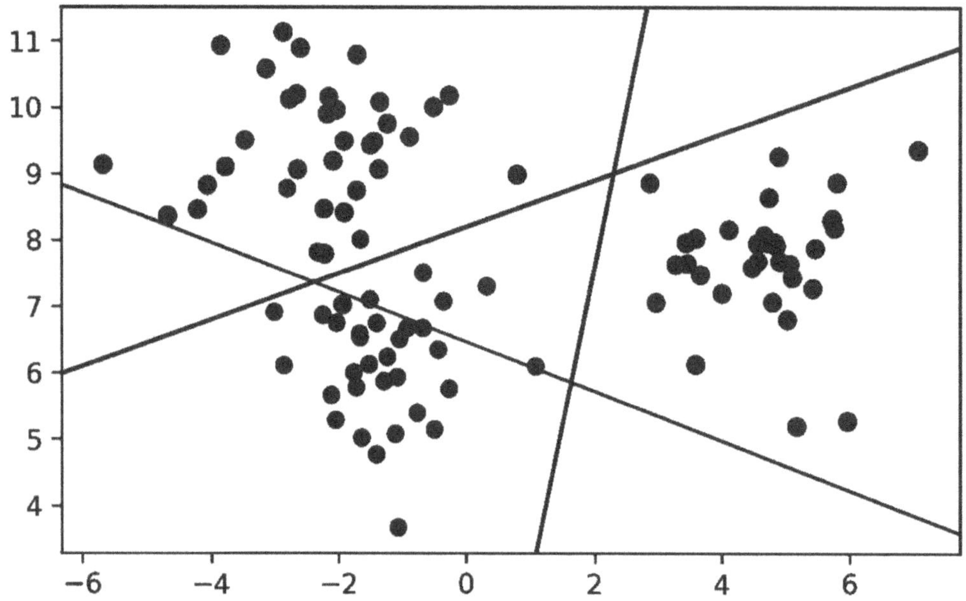

1. Retains some uncertainty.

2. One vs One

n_classes * (n_classes - 1)/2 classifiers

1. trained on balanced subsets.

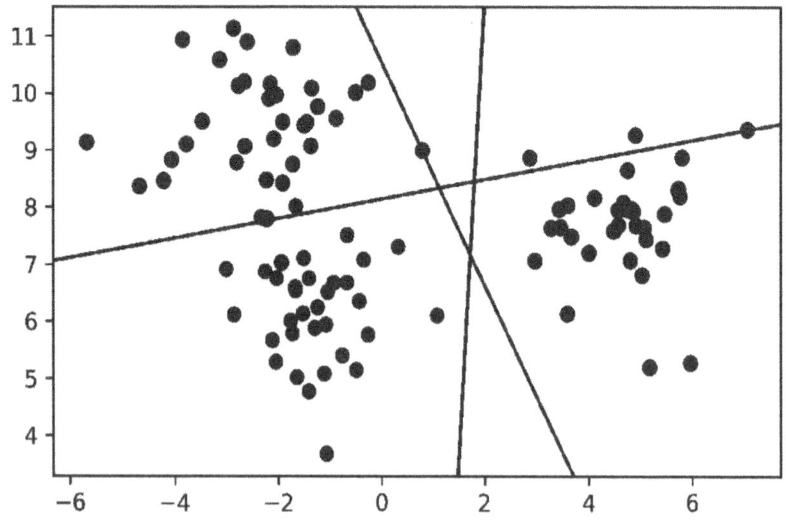

1. No uncertainty propagated

If original problem was balanced, that is…
Multinomial Logistic Regression
Probabilistic multi-class model:

$$p(y=i/x) = \frac{e^{w_i^T x + b_i}}{\sum_{j=1}^{k} e w_i^T x + b_j}$$

$$\min_{w e r^{pk} b e r^k} - \sum_{i=1}^{n} \log(p(y=y_i|x_i,w,b))$$

$$y\hat{} = \arg\max_{i=1,.,k} w_i^T x + b_i$$

1. Same prediction rule as OvR!

The binary logistic regression case can be generalized to multinomial logistic regression, in which we model the probability that i is one of the classes using this formula, which is also known as softmax. The probability is proportional to e to the minus $w^t x$ which is the same as in the binary case. But now we need to normalize it so that the sum over all classes is one. So, we just divide it by this sum.

In sckit-learn

1. OvO: only SVC

2. OvR: default for all linear models except for logistic regression

3. LogisticRegression(multi_class='auto')

4. clf. decision_function =$w^t x$ +b

5. logreg. predict_proba.

6. SVC (probability=True) not great

All the models in scikit-learn have multi-class built-in and most of them use One versus Rest. There's only one model that uses One versus One which is SVC. The Kernel SVM uses One versus One because of the authors of the SVM like that. For historical reasons, logistic regression also uses One versus Rest by default in scikit-learn. That's probably not a good idea, but we can't really change the default easily. Usually, if you do multiclass you probably want to use multinomial logistic regression and so you set multinomial to true and then it does multinomial logistic regression. Question: Does that make it run faster? Answer: Its unlikely to make it run faster, but it makes it more theoretically sound and gives you better probabilities. The probabilities that come out of it, if you do OvR, are a complete hack in the multi-class case but in the binary case, it's the same. Logistic regression also has a predict_prob method. This method gives the probability estimates, so you get a vector of length number of classes for each data point. You might be tempted to do SVC (probability) equal to true. That is something we're going to talk about in a couple of weeks. This is running calibration. Basically, this does the One versus One SVM and then it builds a second model on top that tries to estimate probabilities using built-in cross-validation. This will take forever, and the outcome will probably be not that great. Don't do this unless you're really sure this is what you want to do. If you want probabilities just use logistic regression. predict_proba gives you the probabilities. If you call predict_proba, it will give you an array that has number of samples times number of classes and these entries will sum to one. And the prediction is just the arg max of these. You can call predict which will give you arg max while predict_proba will give you the probabilities as given by the model.

Multi-Class in Practice

OvR and multinomial LogReg produce one coef per class:

code

```
From learn.datasets import load_iris
Iris = load_iris()
X, y = iris.data , iris.target
Print(x.shape)
Print(np.bincount(y))
Output=(150,4)
[50 50 50]
```

SVC would produce the same shape, but with different semantics!

FIXME screenshots

In practice, I'm using logistic regression on the iris dataset. We have 50 data points, 4 features, 3 classes, each class has 50 samples, and we're trying to classify different kinds of irises. Here, I'm looking at logistic regression and linear SVM, I built the model. So, the coefficient W is stored in coef on this score. Everything in scikit-learn that's estimated from the data ends with an underscore. If it doesn't, it wasn't learned from the data. So coef_ are the coefficient that is learned by the model. They're for logistic regression and linear Support Vector Machine, they're the same shape, three classes times four features but they have different semantics.

```
logreg.coef_
```

```
array([[-0.42339232,  0.96169329, -2.51946669, -1.0860205 ],
       [ 0.53411332, -0.31794321, -0.20537377, -0.93961515],
       [-0.11072101, -0.64375008,  2.72484045,  2.02563566]])
```

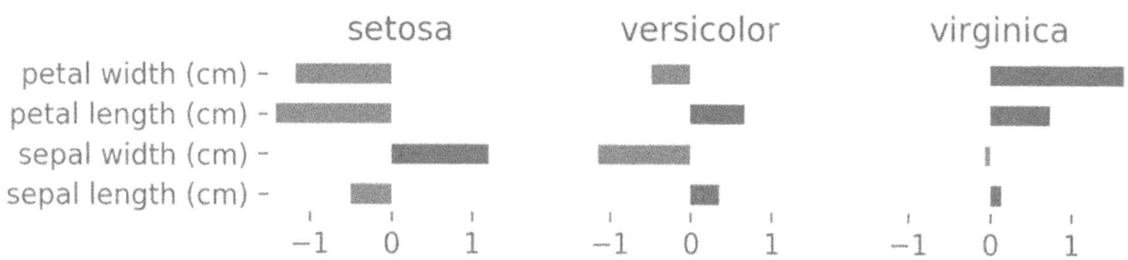

(After centering data, without intercept)
FIXME screenshots
Here I've interpreted them. You can see the four features, for each feature and for each class, you have a coefficient. If the sepal width is big, then the setosa classifier is happy. If the sepal with is small, then versicolor will have a large response. If the petal width is big then virginica will have a large response. This is a bar plot after coefficient vector here. This tells you what the classifier has learned. This is maybe for a very simple problem this is little much to look at but it's still way less to look at for any other model. If you used a random forest or something like that, there would be no way to visualize what's happening.

2.3 Forward network functions

Understanding Feed Forward Neural Networks with Maths and Statistics

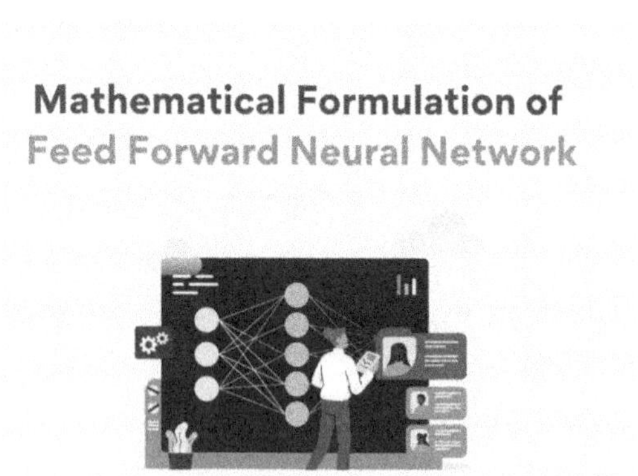

From machine translation to search engines, and from mobile applications to computer assistants feed forward neural networks in deep learning is everywhere.
Machine Learning algorithms and statistics algorithms can be applied to data in various ways. Deep learning models mimic the ways in which the human brain finds and creates patterns from data. Deep learning is becoming increasingly important to software engineers as it spreads throughout a variety of industries.
An artificial neural network with a circular network of nodes is called a feed forward neural network. In contrast to recurrent neural networks, feed forward neural networks cycle some routes.
The feed forward model is a basic type of neural network because the input is only processed in one direction. As part of our exploration of neural networks, we'll examine feed forward neural networks in-depth.

Why are neural networks used?
Neuronal networks can theoretically estimate any function, regardless of its complexity.
Yet, supervised learning is a method of determining the correct Y for a fresh X by learning a function that translates a given X into a specified Y. But what are the differences between neural networks and other methods of Machine Learning? The answer is based on the Inductive Bias phenomenon, a psychological phenomenon.

Machine Learning models are built on assumptions such as the one where X and Y are related. An Inductive Bias of linear regression is the linear relationship between X and Y. In this way, a line or hyperplane gets fitted to the data.

When X and Y have a complex relationship, it can get difficult for a Linear Regression method to predict Y. For this situation, the curve must be multi-dimensional or approximate to the relationship.

A manual adjustment is needed sometimes based on the complexity of the function and the number of layers within the network. In most cases, trial and error methods combined with experience get used to accomplishing this. Hence, this is the reason these parameters are called hyperparameters.

What is a feed forward neural network?

Feed forward neural networks are artificial neural networks in which nodes do not form loops. This type of neural network is also known as a multi-layer neural network as all information is only passed forward.

During data flow, input nodes receive data, which travel through hidden layers, and exit output nodes. No links exist in the network that could get used to by sending information back from the output node.

A feed forward neural network approximates functions in the following way:

1. An algorithm calculates classifiers by using the formula $y = f^* (x)$.

2. Input x is therefore assigned to category y.

3. According to the feed forward model, $y = f (x; \theta)$. This value determines the closest approximation of the function.

Feed forward neural networks serve as the basis for object detection in photos, as shown in the Google Photos app.

What is the working principle of a feed forward neural network?

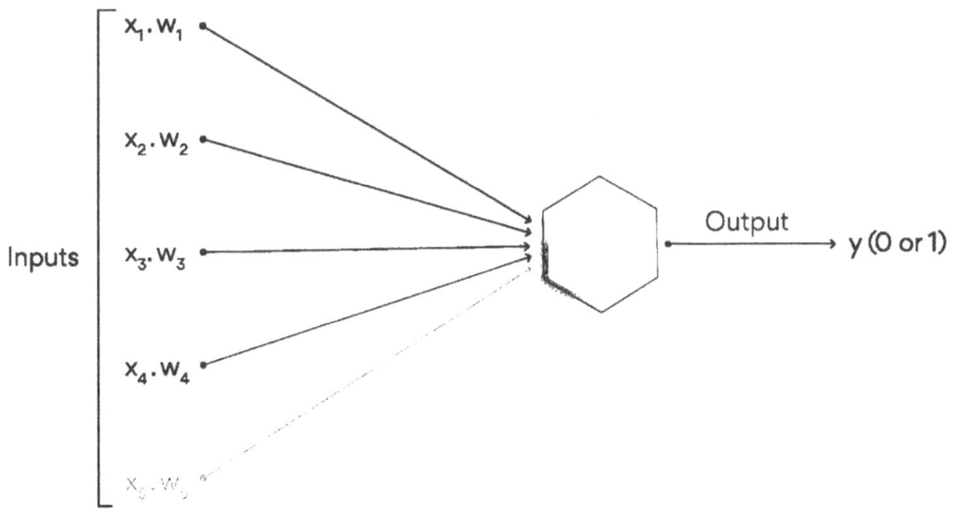

When the feed forward neural network gets simplified, it can appear as a single layer perceptron.

This model multiplies inputs with weights as they enter the layer. Afterward, the weighted input values get added together to get the sum. As long as the sum of the values rises above a certain threshold, set at zero, the output value is usually 1, while if it falls below the threshold, it is usually -1.

As a feed forward neural network model, the single-layer perceptron often gets used for classification. Machine Learning can also get integrated into single layer perceptrons. Through training, neural networks can adjust their weights based on a property called the delta rule, which helps them compare their outputs with the intended values. As a result of training and learning, gradient descent occurs. Similarly, multi-layered perceptrons update their weights. But this process gets known as back-propagation. If this is the case, the network's hidden layers will get adjusted according to the output values produced by the final layer.

Layers of feed forward neural network

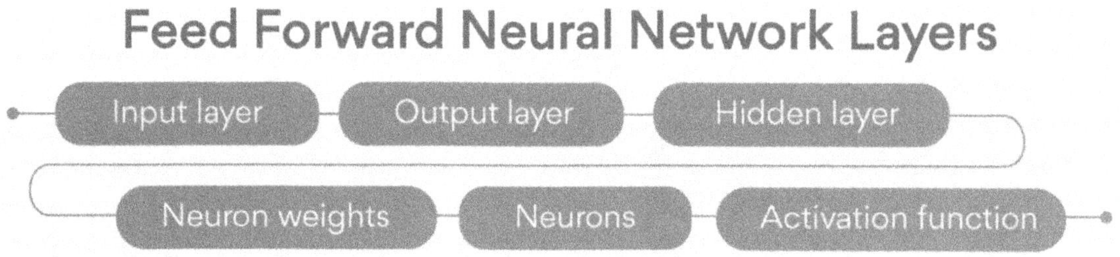

1. Input layer:

The neurons of this layer receive input and pass it on to the other layers of the network. Feature or attribute numbers in the dataset must match the number of neurons in the input layer.

2. Output layer:

According to the type of model getting built, this layer represents the forecasted feature.

3. Hidden layer:

Input and output layers get separated by hidden layers. Depending on the type of model, there may be several hidden layers.
There are several neurons in hidden layers that transform the input before actually transferring it to the next layer.This network gets constantly updated with weights in order to make it easier to predict.

4. Neuron weights:

Neurons get connected by a weight, which measures their strength or magnitude. Similar to linear regression coefficients, input weights can also get compared.
Weight is normally between 0 and 1, with a value between 0 and 1.

5. Neurons:

Artificial neurons get used in feed forward networks, which later get adapted from biological neurons. A neural network consists of artificial neurons.
Neurons function in two ways: first, they create weighted input sums, and second, they activate the sums to make them normal.
Activation functions can either be linear or nonlinear. Neurons have weights based on their inputs. During the learning phase, the network studies these weights.

6. Activation Function:

Neurons are responsible for making decisions in this area.
According to the activation function, the neurons determine whether to make a linear or nonlinear decision.
Since it passes through so many layers, it prevents the cascading effect from increasing neuron outputs.
An activation function can be classified into three major categories: sigmoid, Tanh, and Rectified Linear Unit (ReLu).

7. Sigmoid:

Input values between 0 and 1 get mapped to the output values.

8. Tanh:

A value between -1 and 1 gets mapped to the input values.

9. Rectified linear Unit:

Only positive values are allowed to flow through this function. Negative values get mapped to 0.

Function in feed forward neural network

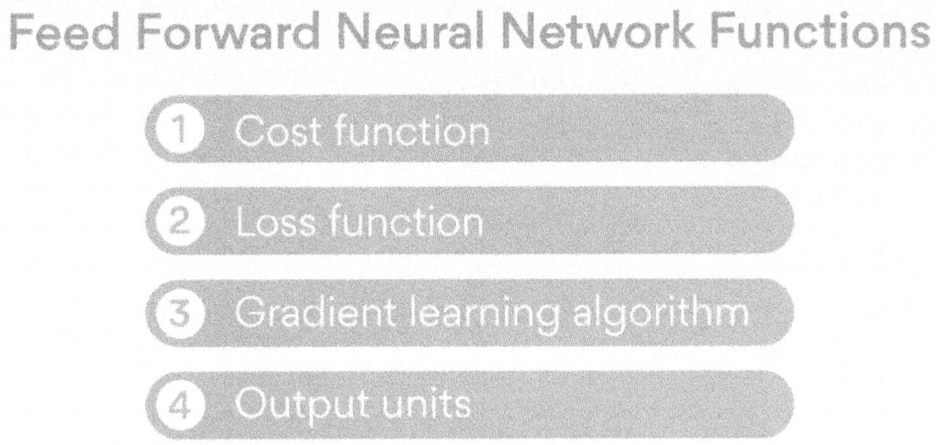

Cost function

In a feed forward neural network, the cost function plays an important role. The categorized data points are little affected by minor adjustments to weights and biases.

Thus, a smooth cost function can get used to determine a method of adjusting weights and biases to improve performance.

Following is a definition of the mean square error cost function:

$$C(w, b) \equiv \frac{1}{2n} \sum_x \|y(x) - a\|^2.$$

Image source

Were,

w = the weights gathered in the network

b = biases

n = number of inputs for training

a = output vectors

x = input

‖v‖ = vector v's normal length

Loss function

The loss function of a neural network gets used to determine if an adjustment needs to be made in the learning process.

Neurons in the output layer are equal to the number of classes. Showing the differences between predicted and actual probability distributions. Following is the cross-entropy loss for binary classification.

Cross Entropy Loss:

$$L(\Theta) = \begin{cases} -log(\hat{y}) & \text{if } y = 1 \\ -log(1 - \hat{y}) & \text{if } y = 0 \end{cases}$$

Cross Entropy Loss:

$$L(\Theta) = -\sum_{i=1}^{k} y_i \log(\hat{y}_i)$$

Gradient learning algorithm

In the gradient descent algorithm, the next point gets calculated by scaling the gradient at the current position by a learning rate. Then subtracted from the current position by the achieved value.

To decrease the function, it subtracts the value (to increase, it would add). As an example, here is how to write this procedure:

$$p_{n+1} = p_n - \eta \nabla f(p_n)$$

The gradient gets adjusted by the parameter η, which also determines the step size. Performance is significantly affected by the learning rate in Machine Learning.

Output units

In the output layer, output units are those units that provide the desired output or prediction, thereby fulfilling the task that the neural network needs to complete.

There is a close relationship between the choice of output units and the cost function. Any unit that can serve as a hidden unit can also serve as an output unit in a neural network.

Advantages of feed forward Neural Networks

1. Machine Learning can be boosted with feed forward neural networks' simplified architecture.

2. Multi-network in the feed forward networks operate independently, with a moderated intermediary.

3. Complex tasks need several neurons in the network.

4. Neural networks can handle, and process nonlinear data easily compared to perceptrons and sigmoid neurons, which are otherwise complex.

5. A neural network deals with the complicated problem of decision boundaries.

6. Depending on the data, the neural network architecture can vary. For example, convolutional neural networks (CNNs) perform exceptionally well in image processing, whereas recurrent neural networks (RNNs) perform well in text and voice processing.

7. Neural networks need graphics processing units (GPUs) to handle large datasets for massive computational and hardware performance. Several GPUs get used widely in the market, including Kaggle Notebooks and Google Collab Notebooks.

8. Applications of feed forward neural networks

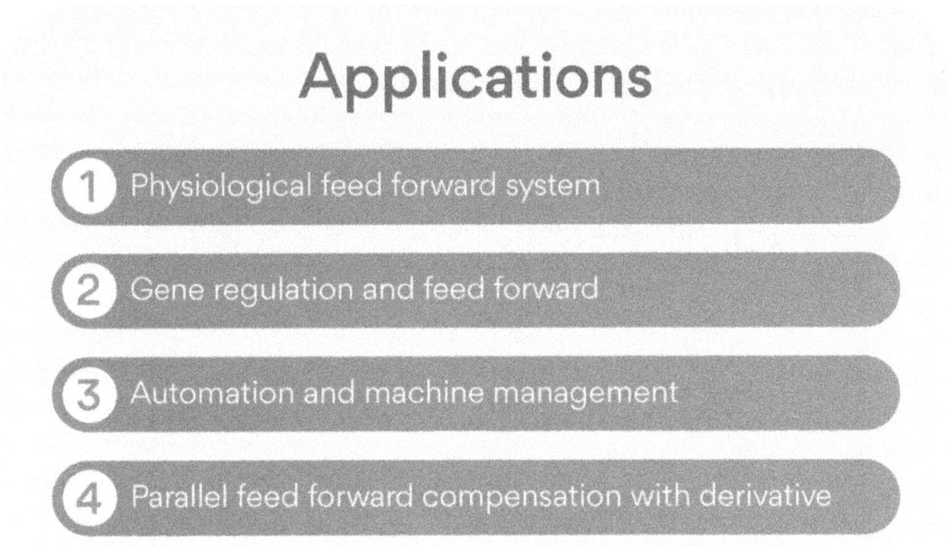

There are many applications for these neural networks. The following are a few of them.

- Physiological feed forward system

  It is possible to identify feed forward management in this situation because the central involuntary regulates the heartbeat before exercise.

- Gene regulation and feed forward

  Detecting non-temporary changes to the atmosphere is a function of this motif as a feed forward system. You can find the majority of this pattern in the illustrious networks.

- Automation and machine management

  Automation control using feed forward is one of the disciplines in automation.

- Parallel feed forward compensation with derivative

  An open-loop transfer converts non-minimum part systems into minimum part systems using this technique.

- Understanding the math behind neural networks

Typical deep learning algorithms are neural networks (NNs). As a result of their unique structure, their popularity results from their 'deep' understanding of data.

Furthermore, NNs are flexible in terms of complexity and structure. Despite all the advanced stuff, they can't work without the basic elements: they may work better with the advanced stuff, but the underlying structure remains the same.

Let's begin. NNs get constructed similarly to our biological neurons, and they resemble the following:

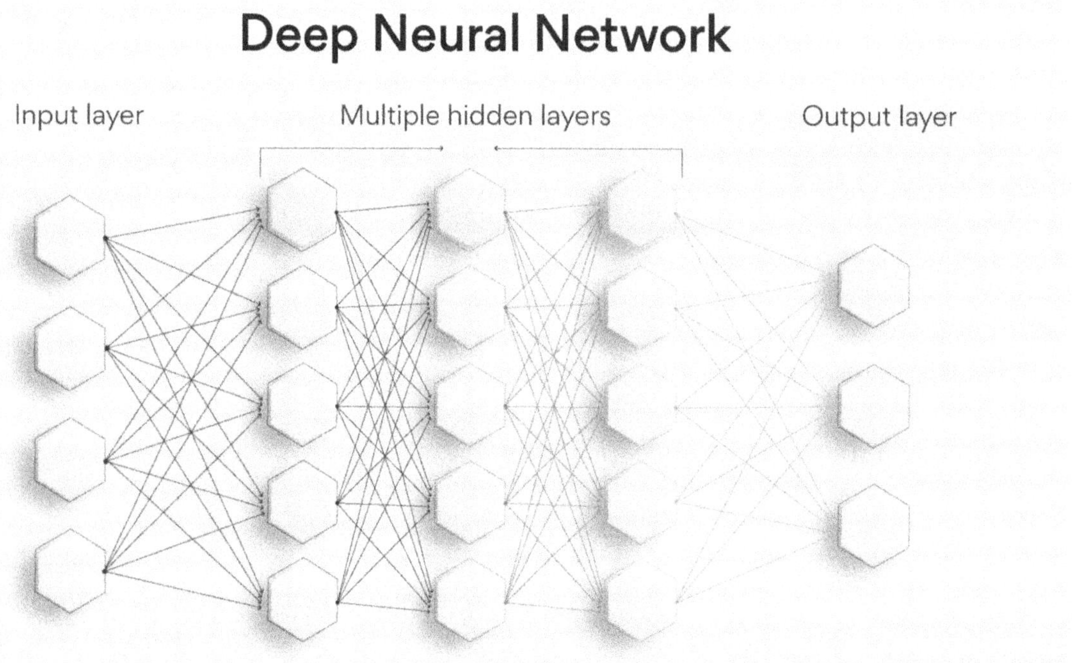

Neurons are hexagons in this image. In neural networks, neurons get arranged into layers: input is the first layer, and output is the last with the hidden layer in the middle.

NN consists of two main elements that compute mathematical operations. Neurons calculate weighted sums using input data and synaptic weights since neural networks are just mathematical computations based on synaptic links. The following is a simplified visualization:

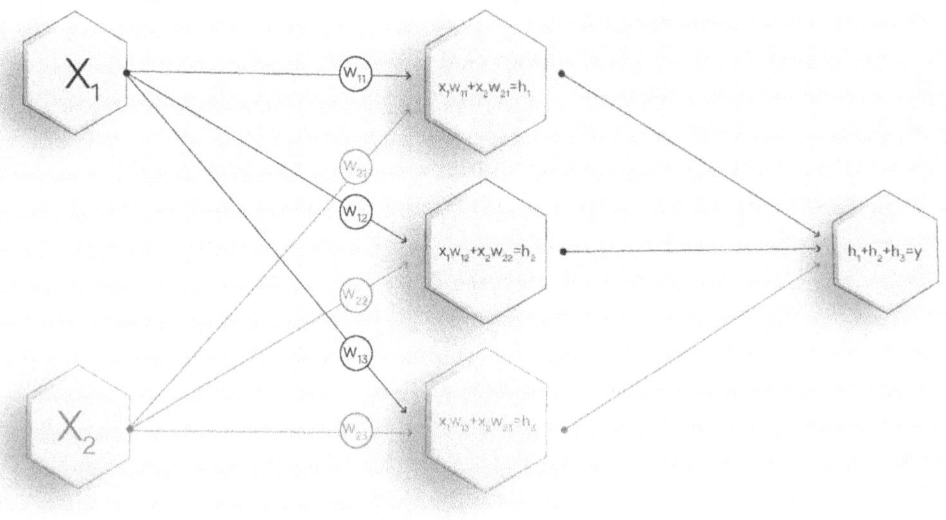

In a matrix format, it looks as follows:

$$[x_1 \quad x_2]\begin{bmatrix} w_{11} & w_{12} & w_{13} \\ w_{21} & w_{22} & w_{23} \end{bmatrix} = \begin{bmatrix} x_1w_{11} + x_2w_{21} \\ x_1w_{12} + x_2w_{22} \\ x_1w_{13} + x_2w_{23} \end{bmatrix}' = \begin{bmatrix} h_1 \\ h_2 \\ h_3 \end{bmatrix}'$$

In the third step, a vector of ones gets multiplied by the output of our hidden layer:

$$\begin{bmatrix} h_1 \\ h_2 \\ h_3 \end{bmatrix}' \begin{bmatrix} 1 \\ 1 \\ 1 \end{bmatrix} = h_1 + h_2 + h_3 = y$$

Using the output value, we can calculate the result. Understanding these fundamental concepts will make building NN much easier, and you will be amazed at how quickly you can do it. Every layer's output becomes the following layer's input.

The architecture of the network

In a network, the architecture refers to the number of hidden layers and units in each layer that make up the network. A feed forward network based on the Universal Approximation Theorem must have a "squashing" activation function at least on one hidden layer.

The network can approximate any Borel measurable function within a finite-dimensional space with at least some amount of non-zero error when there are enough hidden units.

It simply states that we can always represent any function using the multi-layer perceptron (MLP), regardless of what function we try to learn.

Thus, we now know there will always be an MLP to solve our problem, but there is no specific method for finding it.

It is impossible to say whether it will be possible to solve the given problem if we use N layers with M hidden units. Research is still ongoing, and for now, the only way to determine this configuration is by experimenting with it. While it is challenging to find the appropriate architecture, we need to try many configurations before finding the one that can represent the target function.

There are two possible explanations for this. Firstly, the optimization algorithm may not find the correct parameters, and secondly, the training algorithms may use the wrong function because of overfitting.

What is backpropagation in feed forward neural network?

Backpropagation is a technique based on gradient descent. Each stage of a gradient descent process involves iteratively moving a function in the opposite direction of its gradient (the slope).

The goal is to reduce the cost function given the training data while learning a neural network. Network weights and biases of all neurons in each layer determine the cost function. Backpropagation gets used to calculate the gradient of the cost function iteratively. And then update weights and biases in the opposite direction to reduce the gradient.

We must define the error of the backpropagation formula to specify i-th neuron in the l-th layer of a network for the j-th training. Example as follows (in which $z_i^{[l](j)}$ represents the weighted input to the neuron, and L represents the loss.)

$$\delta_i^{[l](j)} = \frac{\partial \mathcal{L}(\hat{y}^{(j)}, y^{(j)})}{\partial z_i^{[l](j)}}$$

In backpropagation formulas, the error is defined as above:
Below is the full derivation of the formulas. For each formula below, L stands for the output layer, g for the activation function, ∇ the gradient, W[l]T layer l weights transposed.
A proportional activation of neuron i at layer l based on bli bias from layer i to layer i, wlik weight from layer l to layer l-1, and akl−1 activation of neuron k at layer l-1 for training example j.

$$\delta^{[L](j)} = \nabla_{\hat{y}^{(j)}} \mathcal{L} \odot (g^{[L]})' (z^{[L](j)}) = \hat{y}^{(j)} - y^{(j)}$$

$$\delta^{[l](j)} = W^{[l+1]^T} \delta^{[l+1](j)} \odot (g^{[l]})' (z^{[l](j)})$$

$$\frac{\partial L}{\partial b_i^{[l]}} = \delta_i^{[l](j)}$$

$$\frac{\partial L}{\partial w_{ik}^{[l]}} = \delta_i^{[l](j)} a_k^{[l-1](j)}$$

- The first equation shows how to calculate the error at the output layer for sample j. Following that, we can use the second equation to calculate the error in the layer just before the output layer.

- Based on the error values for the next layer, the second equation can calculate the error in any layer. Because this algorithm calculates errors backward, it is known as backpropagation.

- For sample j, we calculate the gradient of the loss function by taking the third and fourth equations and dividing them by the biases and weights.

- We can update biases and weights by averaging gradients of the loss function relative to biases and weights for all samples using the average gradients.

- The process is known as batch gradient descent. We will have to wait a long time if we have too many samples.

- If each sample has a gradient, it is possible to update the biases/weights accordingly. The process is known as stochastic gradient descent.

Even though this algorithm is faster than batch gradient descent, it does not yield a good estimate of the gradient calculated using a single sample.
It is possible to update biases and weights based on the average gradients of batches. It gets referred to as mini-batch gradient descent and gets preferred over the other two.

Exercise

True Or False

1.Supervised learning involves training models with labeled data to make predictions.
2.In supervised learning, the goal is to uncover hidden patterns in unlabeled data.
3.Preprocessing the data is an important step in supervised learning to help the model generalize to new data.
4.Linear models can only represent linear decision boundaries in binary classification problems.

5.Logistic Regression is a type of linear model used in classification tasks.
6.Support Vector Machines (SVMs) aim to find the optimal hyperplane that separates data points of different classes.
7.The activation function in forward network functions introduces linearity to the model.
8.Weights in forward network functions represent the importance of each input feature.
9.The bias term in forward network functions introduces noise to the model
10.The softmax function in the output layer of a neural network is used to normalize the output probabilities across classes
11.Labeled data is not required for training in supervised learning.
12.The role of the training data in supervised learning is to evaluate the model's performance.
13.Forward network functions are used to preprocess input data before training.
14.Linear Discriminant Analysis (LDA) is a type of linear model used in classification tasks
15.In supervised learning, the model aims to classify data into predefined categories based on labeled examples
16.Linear models assume that the input features are always linearly related to the output class labels.
17.Decision Trees are a type of linear model used in classification.
18.Forward network functions are used to compute the gradient of the loss function.
19.Linear models can handle complex nonlinear relationships between input features and output labels.
20.The primary purpose of an activation function in a neural network is to preprocess input data.
21.The output of a forward network function in classification is a probability distribution over classes.
22.Support Vector Machines (SVMs) do not aim to maximize the margin between classes.
23.Linear models are known for being easy to interpret and visualize.
24.The softmax function in the output layer of a neural network introduces linearity to the model.
25.Linear models assume that data is always linearly separable in classification tasks.
26.Forward network functions are used to compute predictions based on input features.
27.Linear models can only handle binary classification problems.
28.Linear models assume that the importance of input features is the same for all instances.
Answer: True, False, True, True, True, True, False , True, False , True, False , False, False, True, True, True, False , False, False, False , True, False True, False , False, True, False, True

MCQ

1. What is the primary goal of supervised learning?
a) To uncover hidden patterns in unlabeled data
b) To optimize a model's hyperparameters
c) To classify data into predefined categories based on labeled examples
d) To generate random data samples for analysis
Answer: c) To classify data into predefined categories based on labeled examples

2. Which type of learning requires labeled data for training?
a) Unsupervised learning
b) Reinforcement learning
c) Supervised learning
d) Semi-supervised learning
Answer: c) Supervised learning

3. What is an important step in supervised learning that helps the model generalize to new data?
a) Preprocessing the data
b) Removing all outliers from the dataset
c) Memorizing the training data
d) Applying the same weights to all features
Answer: a) Preprocessing the data

4. Which of the following is a type of linear model used in classification tasks?
a) Decision Tree
b) K-Nearest Neighbors
c) Support Vector Machine
d) Random Forest
Answer: c) Support Vector Machine

5. What does a linear decision boundary represent in a binary classification problem?
a) A boundary that separates classes using a curved line
b) A boundary that separates classes using a linear equation
c) A boundary that overlaps the classes
d) A boundary that separates three or more classes
Answer: b) A boundary that separates classes using a linear equation

6. Which linear model aims to find the best-fitting hyperplane to separate data points of different classes?
a) Logistic Regression
b) Support Vector Machine
c) Naive Bayes
d) Linear Discriminant Analysis
Answer: b) Support Vector Machine

7. What is the primary purpose of the activation function in forward network functions of neural networks?
a) To optimize model parameters
b) To increase computational efficiency
c) To introduce nonlinearity to the model
d) To preprocess input data
Answer: c) To introduce nonlinearity to the model

8. In the context of forward network functions, what do weights represent?
a) The importance of each input feature
b) The number of layers in the neural network
c) The learning rate of the network
d) The accuracy of the model
Answer: a) The importance of each input feature

9. What is the purpose of a bias term in forward network functions?
a) To introduce noise to the model
b) To shift the decision boundary
c) To eliminate outliers from the dataset
d) To normalize the input features
Answer: b) To shift the decision boundary

10. Which of the following is NOT a common activation function used in forward network functions?
a) ReLU (Rectified Linear Activation)
b) Sigmoid
c) Linear
d) Hyperbolic Tangent (Tanh)
Answer: c) Linear

11. What does the softmax function do in the output layer of a neural network?
a) Introduces nonlinearity to the output
b) Normalizes the output probabilities across classes
c) Computes the weighted sum of input features
d) Applies regularization to the model
Answer: b) Normalizes the output probabilities across classes

12. In supervised learning, what is the role of the training data?
a) To evaluate the model's performance
b) To optimize the model's hyperparameters
c) To preprocess the input features
d) To train the model and learn its parameters
Answer: d) To train the model and learn its parameters

13. Which type of learning involves using both input data and corresponding target labels for training?
a) Unsupervised learning
b) Reinforcement learning
c) Semi-supervised learning
d) Supervised learning
Answer: d) Supervised learning

14. What is the primary purpose of a forward network function in a neural network?
a) To preprocess input data
b) To compute the gradient of the loss function
c) To make predictions based on input features
d) To introduce noise to the model
Answer: c) To make predictions based on input features

15. Which linear model aims to find the optimal decision boundary that maximizes the margin between classes?
a) Logistic Regression
b) Decision Tree
c) Linear Discriminant Analysis
d) Support Vector Machine
Answer: d) Support Vector Machine

Short Question And Answers
Q1: What is the difference between supervised and unsupervised learning?
Q2: What is the basic idea behind linear models of classification?
Q3: What are forward network functions in the context of supervised learning?
Q4: What are some common linear models used in classification?
Q5: How are the weights and biases learned in a linear model?

Long Question And Answers
Q1: What is supervised learning, and how does it differ from other types of Machine Learning?
Q2: What are linear models of classification, and how do they work?
Q3: What are the advantages and limitations of linear classification models?
Q4: What are forward network functions, and how are they used in supervised learning?
Q5: What is the role of activation functions in forward network functions?

Online Resources

Online Exam Papers
True/False Exam

Link

https://forms.gle/ADXrLwQKFSno7fn88

QR Code

YouTube Video Playlist Link

Chapter 2
Link

https://www.youtube.com/playlist?list=PLzlh_31VWEFoJSFtAEz0Tua5rcGHgkfDi

QR Code

Chapter 3: Unsupervised learning

3.1 Clustering

A task involving Machine Learning may not be linear, but it has a number of well-known steps:

1. Problem definition.
2. Preparation of Data.
3. Learn an underlying model.
4. Improve the underlying model by quantitative and qualitative evaluations.
5. Present the model.

One good way to come to terms with a new problem is to work through identifying and defining the problem in the best possible way and learn a model that captures meaningful information from the data. While problems in Pattern Recognition and Machine Learning can be of various types, they can be broadly classified into three categories:

1. Supervised Learning: The system is presented with example inputs and their desired outputs, given by a "teacher", and the goal is to learn a general rule that maps inputs to outputs.

2. Unsupervised Learning: No labels are given to the learning algorithm, leaving it on its own to find structure in its input. Unsupervised learning can be a goal in itself (discovering hidden patterns in data) or a means towards an end (feature learning).

3. Reinforcement Learning: A system interacts with a dynamic environment in which it must perform a certain goal (such as driving a vehicle or playing a game against an opponent). The system is provided feedback in terms of rewards and punishments as it navigates its problem space.

In some pattern recognition problems, the training data consists of a set of input vectors x without any corresponding target values. The goal in such unsupervised learning problems may be to discover groups of similar examples within the data, where it is called clustering, or to determine how the data is distributed in the space, known as density estimation. To put forward in simpler terms, for a n-sampled space x1 to xn, true class labels are not provided for each sample, hence known as learning without teacher.

Issues with Unsupervised Learning:

- Unsupervised Learning is harder as compared to Supervised Learning tasks..
- How do we know if results are meaningful since no answer labels are available?
- Let the expert look at the results (external evaluation)
- Define an objective function on clustering (internal evaluation)

Why Unsupervised Learning is needed despite of these issues?

Annotating large datasets is very costly and hence we can label only a few examples manually. Example: Speech Recognition

There may be cases where we don't know how many/what classes is the data divided into. Example: Data Mining

We may want to use clustering to gain some insight into the structure of the data before designing a classifier.

Unsupervised Learning can be further classified into two categories:

1. Parametric Unsupervised Learning

In this case, we assume a parametric distribution of data. It assumes that sample data comes from a population that follows a probability distribution based on a fixed set of parameters. Theoretically, in a normal family of distributions, all members have the same shape and are parameterized by mean and standard deviation. That means if you know the mean and standard deviation, and that the distribution is normal, you know the probability of any future observation.

Parametric Unsupervised Learning involves construction of Gaussian Mixture Models and using Expectation-Maximization algorithm to predict the class of the sample in question. This case is much harder than the standard supervised learning because there are no answer labels available and hence there is no correct measure of accuracy available to check the result.

2. Non-parametric Unsupervised Learning

In non-parameterized version of unsupervised learning, the data is grouped into clusters, where each cluster(hopefully) says something about categories and classes present in the data. This method is commonly used to model and analyse data with small sample sizes. Unlike parametric models, nonparametric models do not require the modeler to make any assumptions about the distribution of the population, and so are sometimes referred to as a distribution-free method.

What is Clustering?

Clustering can be considered the most important unsupervised learning problem; so, as every other problem of this kind, it deals with finding a structure in a collection of unlabeled data. A loose definition of clustering could be "the process of organizing objects into groups whose members are similar in some way". A cluster is therefore a collection of objects which are "similar" between them and are "dissimilar" to the objects belonging to other clusters.

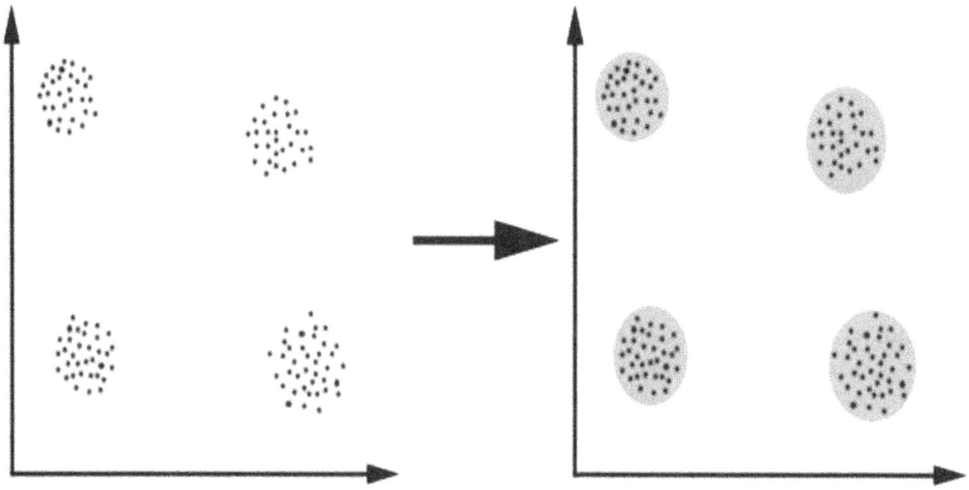

Distance-based clustering.

Given a set of points, with a notion of distance between points, grouping the points into some number of clusters, such that

1. internal (within the cluster) distances should be small i.e. members of clusters are close/similar to each other.

external (intra-cluster) distances should be large i.e. members of different clusters are dissimilar.

The Goals of Clustering

The goal of clustering is to determine the internal grouping in a set of unlabelled data. But how to decide what constitutes a good clustering? It can be shown that there is no absolute "best" criterion which would be independent of the final aim of the clustering. Consequently, it is the user who should supply this criterion, in such a way that the result of the clustering will suit their needs.

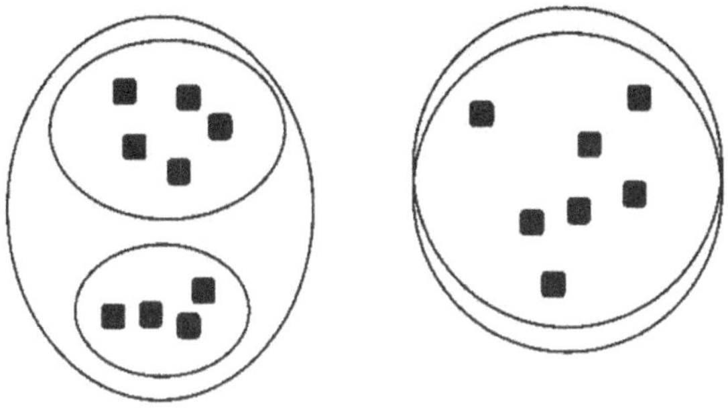

In the above image, how do we know what is the best clustering solution?
To find a particular clustering solution, we need to define the similarity measures for the clusters.

Proximity Measures
For clustering, we need to define a proximity measure for two data points. Proximity here means how similar/dissimilar the samples are with respect to each other.

1. Similarity measure S(xi,xk): large if xi,xk are similar

2. Dissimilarity(or distance) measure D(xi,xk): small if xi,xk are similar

3. There are various similarity measures which can be used.

4. Vectors: Cosine Distance

$$s(\mathbf{x}, \mathbf{x}') = \frac{\mathbf{x}^t \mathbf{x}'}{\|\mathbf{x}\| \, \|\mathbf{x}'\|}$$

5. Sets: Jaccard Distance

$$J(A, B) = \frac{|A \cap B|}{|A \cup B|} = \frac{|A \cap B|}{|A| + |B| - |A \cap B|}.$$

(If A and B are both empty, we define $J(A, B) = 1$.)

$$0 \le J(A, B) \le 1.$$

6. Points: Euclidean Distance q=2

$$d(\mathbf{x}, \mathbf{x}') = \left(\sum_{k=1}^{d} |x_k - x'_k|^q \right)^{1/q},$$

A “good” proximity measure is VERY application dependent. The clusters should be invariant under the transformations “natural” to the problem. Also, while clustering it is not advised to normalize data that are drawn from multiple distributions.

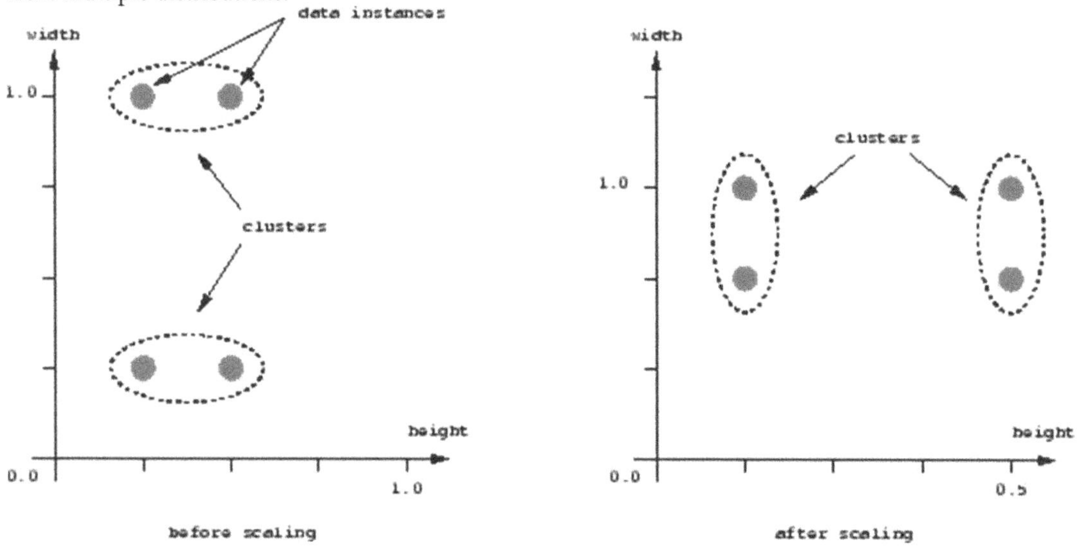

Clustering Algorithms

Clustering algorithms may be classified as listed below:

1. Exclusive Clustering
2. Overlapping Clustering
3. Hierarchical Clustering
4. Probabilistic Clustering

In the first case data are grouped in an exclusive way, so that if a certain data point belongs to a definite cluster then it could not be included in another cluster. A simple example of that is shown in the figure below, where the separation of points is achieved by a straight line on a bi-dimensional plane.

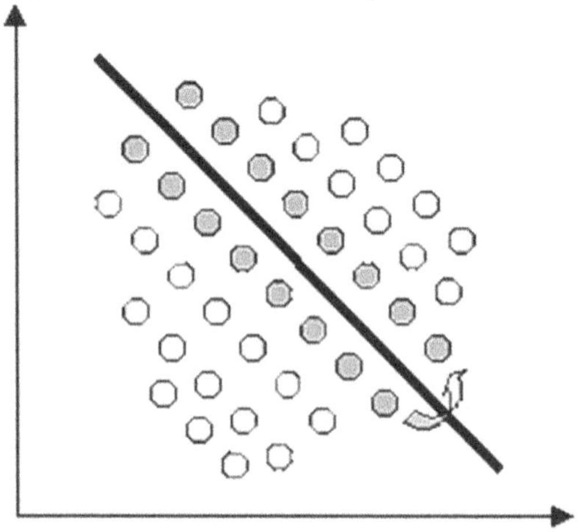

On the contrary, the second type, the overlapping clustering, uses fuzzy sets to cluster data, so that each point may belong to two or more clusters with different degrees of membership. In this case, data will be associated to an appropriate membership value.

A hierarchical clustering algorithm is based on the union between the two nearest clusters. The beginning condition is realized by setting every data point as a cluster. After a few iterations it reaches the final clusters wanted.

Finally, the last kind of clustering uses a completely probabilistic approach.

In this blog we will talk about four of the most used clustering algorithms:

1. K-means

2. Fuzzy K-means

3. Hierarchical clustering

4. Mixture of Gaussians

Each of these algorithms belongs to one of the clustering types listed above. While, K-means is an exclusive clustering algorithm, Fuzzy K-means is an overlapping clustering algorithm, Hierarchical clustering is obvious and lastly Mixture of Gaussians is a probabilistic clustering algorithm. We wi̧ll discuss about each clustering method in the following paragraphs.

K-Means Clustering

K-means is one of the simplest unsupervised learning algorithms that solves the well known clustering problem. The procedure follows a simple and easy way to classify a given data set through a certain number of clusters (assume k clusters) fixed a priori. The main idea is to define k centres, one for each cluster. These centroids should be placed in a smart way because of different location causes different result. So, the better choice is to place them as much as possible far away from each other. The next step is to take each point belonging to a given data set and associate it to the nearest centroid. When no point is pending, the first step is completed and an early groupage is done. At this point we need to re-calculate k new centroids as barycenters of the clusters resulting from the previous step. After we have these k new centroids, a new binding has to be done between the same data set points and the nearest new centroid. A loop has been generated. As a result of this loop we may notice that the k centroids change their location step by step until no more changes are done. In other words centroids do not move any more.

Finally, this algorithm aims at minimizing an objective function, in this case a squared error function. The objective function

$$J = \sum_{j=1}^{k} \sum_{i=1}^{n} \left\| x_i^{(j)} - c_j \right\|^2$$

where

$$\left\| x_i^{(j)} - c_j \right\|^2$$

is a chosen distance measure between a data point xi and the cluster centre cj, is an indicator of the distance of the n data points from their respective cluster centres.

The algorithm is composed of the following steps:

1. Let X = {x1,x2,x3,……..,xn} be the set of data points and V = {v1,v2,…….,vc} be the set of centers.

2. Randomly select 'c' cluster centers.

3. Calculate the distance between each data point and cluster centers.

4. Assign the data point to the cluster center whose distance from the cluster center is minimum of all the cluster centers.

5. Recalculate the new cluster center using:

$$v_i = (1/c_i) \sum_{j=1}^{c_i} x_i$$

where, 'ci' represents the number of data points in ith cluster.

1. Recalculate the distance between each data point and new obtained cluster centers.

2. If no data point was reassigned then stop, otherwise repeat from step 3).

Although it can be proved that the procedure will always terminate, the k-means algorithm does not necessarily find the most optimal configuration, corresponding to the global objective function minimum. The algorithm is also

significantly sensitive to the initial randomly selected cluster centres. The k-means algorithm can be run multiple times to reduce this effect.
K-means is a simple algorithm that has been adapted to many problem domains. As we are going to see, it is a good candidate for extension to work with fuzzy feature vectors.

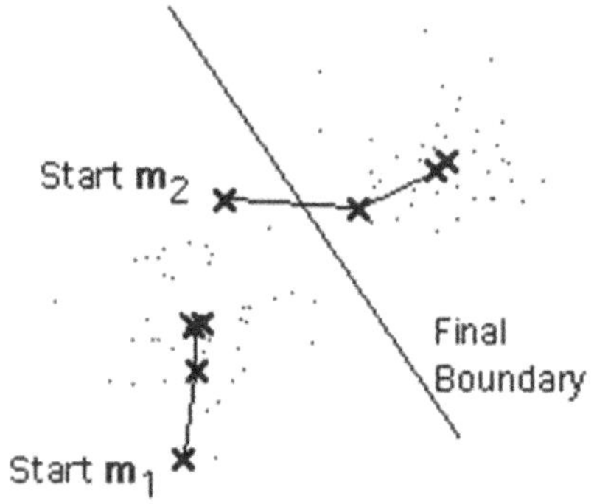

The k-means procedure can be viewed as a greedy algorithm for partitioning the n samples into k clusters so as to minimize the sum of the squared distances to the cluster centers. It does have some weaknesses:
1. The way to initialize the means was not specified. One popular way to start is to randomly choose k of the samples.

2. It can happen that the set of samples closest to mi is empty, so that mi cannot be updated. This is a problem which needs to be handled during the implementation, but is generally ignored.

3. The results depend on the value of k and there is no optimal way to describe a best "k".

This last problem is particularly troublesome, since we often have no way of knowing how many clusters exist. In the example shown above, the same algorithm applied to the same data produces the following 3-means clustering. Is it better or worse than the 2-means clustering?

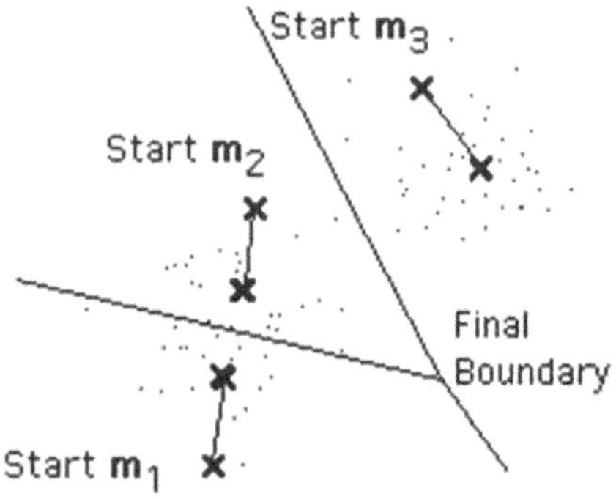

Unfortunately there is no general theoretical solution to find the optimal number of clusters for any given data set. A simple approach is to compare the results of multiple runs with different k classes and choose the best one according to a given criterion, but we need to be careful because increasing k results in smaller error function values by definition, but also increases the risk of overfitting.

Fuzzy K-Means Clustering
In fuzzy clustering, each point has a probability of belonging to each cluster, rather than completely belonging to just one cluster as it is the case in the traditional k-means. Fuzzy k-means specifically tries to deal with the problem where points are somewhat in between centers or otherwise ambiguous by replacing distance with probability, which of course could be some function of distance, such as having probability relative to the inverse of the distance. Fuzzy k-means uses a weighted centroid based on those probabilities. Processes of initialization, iteration, and termination are the same as the ones used in k-means. The resulting clusters are best analyzed as probabilistic distributions rather than a hard assignment of labels. One should realize that k-means is a special case of fuzzy k-means when the probability function used is simply 1 if the data point is closest to a centroid and 0 otherwise.
The fuzzy k-means algorithm is the following:
1. Assume a fixed number of clusters K.

2. Initialization: Randomly initialize the k-means μk associated with the clusters and compute the probability that each data point Xi is a member of a given cluster K, P(PointXiHasLabelK|Xi,K).

3. Iteration: Recalculate the centroid of the cluster as the weighted centroid given the probabilities of membership of all data points Xi :

$$\mu_k(n+1) = \frac{\sum_{x_i \in k} x_i \times P(\mu_k|x_i)^b}{\sum_{x_i \in k} P(\mu_k|x_i)^b}$$

1. Termination: Iterate until convergence or until a user-specified number of iterations has been reached (the iteration may be trapped at some local maxima or minima)For a better understanding, we may consider this simple mono-dimensional example. Given a certain data set, suppose to represent it as distributed on an axis. The figure below shows this:

Looking at the picture, we may identify two clusters in proximity of the two data concentrations. We will refer to them using ‘A’ and ‘B’. In the first approach shown in this tutorial — the k-means algorithm — we associated each data point to a specific centroid; therefore, this membership function looked like this:

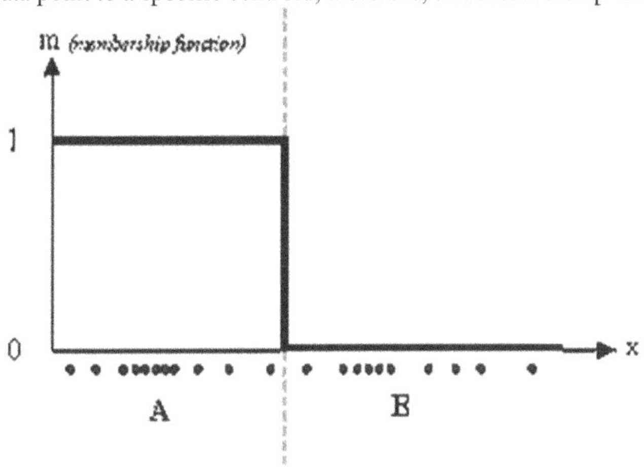

In the Fuzzy k-means approach, instead, the same given data point does not belong exclusively to a well defined cluster, but it can be placed in a middle way. In this case, the membership function follows a smoother line to indicate that every data point may belong to several clusters with different extent of membership.

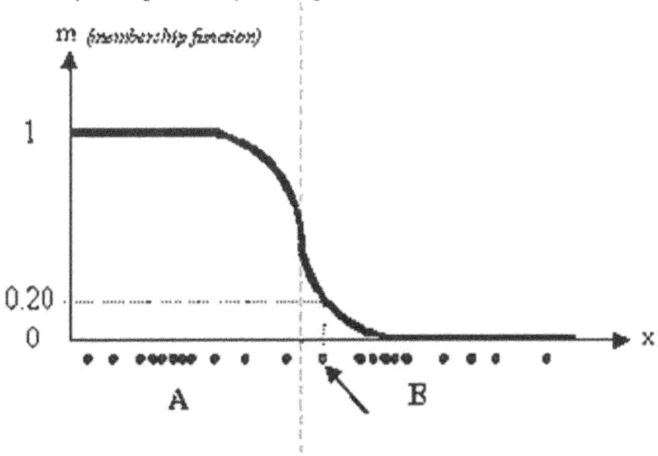

In the figure above, the data point shown as a red marked spot belongs more to the B cluster rather than the A cluster. The value 0.2 of ‘m’ indicates the degree of membership to A for such data point.

Hierarchical Clustering Algorithms
Given a set of N items to be clustered, and an N*N distance (or similarity) matrix, the basic process of hierarchical clustering is this:
1. Start by assigning each item to a cluster, so that if you have N items, you now have N clusters, each containing just one item. Let the distances (similarities) between the clusters the same as the distances (similarities) between the items they contain.

2. Find the closest (most similar) pair of clusters and merge them into a single cluster, so that now you have one cluster less.

3. Compute distances (similarities) between the new cluster and each of the old clusters.

4. Repeat steps 2 and 3 until all items are clustered into a single cluster of size N.

Example: Hierarchical Agglomerative Clustering

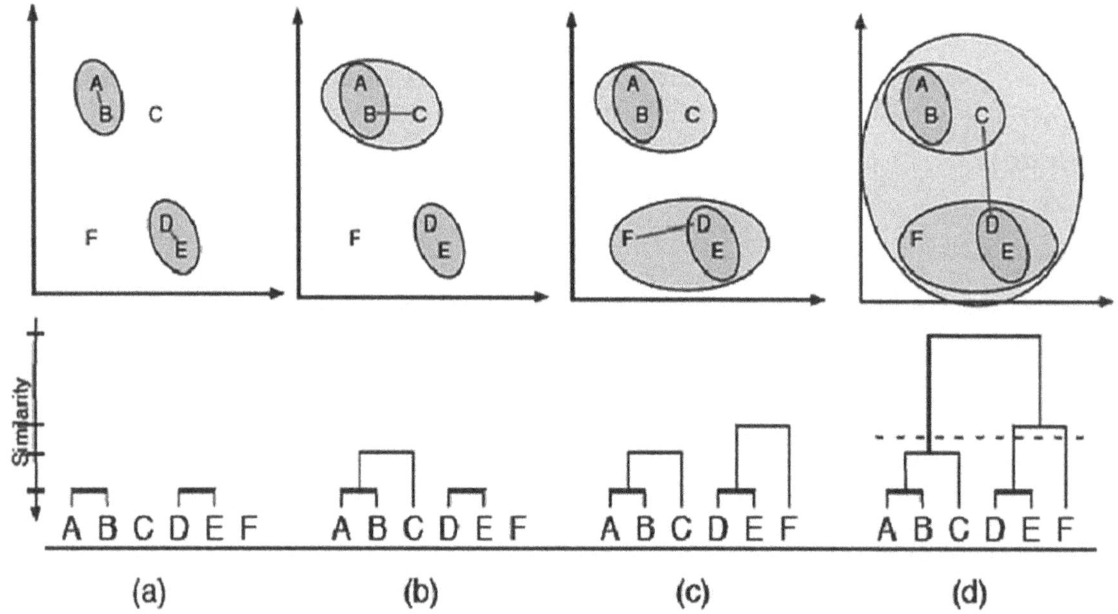

Clustering as a Mixture of Gaussians
There's another way to deal with clustering problems: a model-based approach, which consists in using certain models for clusters and attempting to optimize the fit between the data and the model.
In practice, each cluster can be mathematically represented by a parametric distribution, like a Gaussian. The entire data set is therefore modelled by a mixture of these distributions.
A mixture model with high likelihood tends to have the following traits:
1. component distributions have high "peaks" (data in one cluster are tight);

2. the mixture model "covers" the data well (dominant patterns in the data are captured by component distributions).

3. Main advantages of model-based clustering:

4. well-studied statistical inference techniques available;

5. flexibility in choosing the component distribution;

6. obtain a density estimation for each cluster;

7. a "soft" classification is available.

Mixture of Gaussians
The most widely used clustering method of this kind is based on learning a mixture of Gaussians:

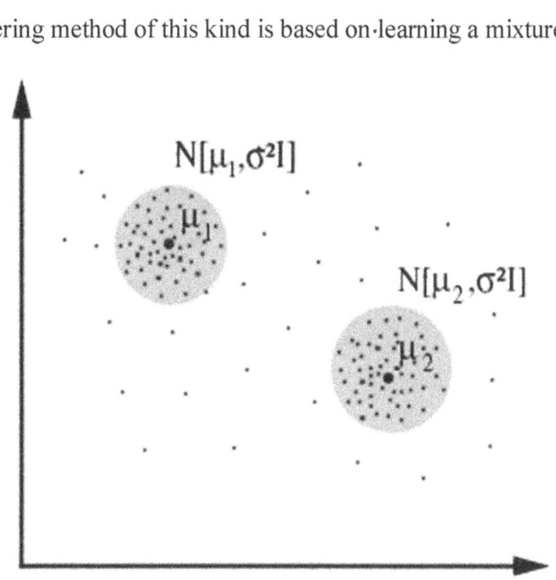

A mixture model is a mixture of k component distributions that collectively make a mixture distribution f(x):

$$f(x) = \sum_{k=1}^{K} \alpha_k f_k(x)$$

The αk represents the contribution of the kth component in constructing f(x). In practice, parametric distribution (e.g. gaussians), are often used since a lot work has been done to understand their behaviour. If you substitute each fk(x) for a gaussian you get what is known as a gaussian mixture models (GMM).

The EM Algorithm

Expectation-Maximization assumes that your data is composed of multiple multivariate normal distributions (note that this is a very strong assumption, in particular when you fix the number of clusters!). Alternatively put, EM is an algorithm for maximizing a likelihood function when some of the variables in your model are unobserved (i.e. when you have latent variables).

You might fairly ask, if we're just trying to maximize a function, why don't we just use the existing machinery for maximizing a function. Well, if you try to maximize this by taking derivatives and setting them to zero, you find that in many cases the first-order conditions don't have a solution. There's a chicken-and-egg problem in that to solve for your model parameters you need to know the distribution of your unobserved data; but the distribution of your unobserved data is a function of your model parameters.

Expectation-Maximization tries to get around this by iteratively guessing a distribution for the unobserved data, then estimating the model parameters by maximizing something that is a lower bound on the actual likelihood function, and repeating until convergence:

The Expectation-Maximization algorithm

1. Start with guess for values of your model parameters

2. E-step: For each datapoint that has missing values, use your model equation to solve for the distribution of the missing data given your current guess of the model parameters and given the observed data (note that you are solving for a distribution for each missing value, not for the expected value). Now that we have a distribution for each missing value, we can calculate the expectation of the likelihood function with respect to the unobserved variables. If our guess for the model parameter was correct, this expected likelihood will be the actual likelihood of our observed data; if the parameters were not correct, it will just be a lower bound.

3. M-step: Now that we've got an expected likelihood function with no unobserved variables in it, maximize the function as you would in the fully observed case, to get a new estimate of your model parameters.

4. Repeat until convergence.

Problems associated with clustering

1. There are a number of problems with clustering. Among them:

2. dealing with large number of dimensions and large number of data items can be problematic because of time complexity;

3. the effectiveness of the method depends on the definition of "distance" (for distance-based clustering). If an obvious distance measure doesn't exist we must "define" it, which is not always easy, especially in multidimensional spaces;

4. the result of the clustering algorithm (that in many cases can be arbitrary itself) can be interpreted in different ways.

Possible Applications

1. Clustering algorithms can be applied in many fields, for instance:

2. Marketing: finding groups of customers with similar behavior given a large database of customer data containing their properties and past buying records;

3. Biology: classification of plants and animals given their features;

4. Insurance: identifying groups of motor insurance policy holders with a high average claim cost; identifying frauds;

5. Earthquake studies: clustering observed earthquake epicenters to identify dangerous zones;

6. World Wide Web: document classification; clustering weblog data to discover groups of similar access patterns.

3.2 Mixtures of Gaussians

Gaussian Mixture Models: What are they & when to use? In Machine Learning and data analysis, it is often necessary to identify patterns and clusters within large sets of data. However, traditional clustering algorithms such as k-means clustering have limitations when it comes to identifying clusters with different shapes and sizes. This is where Gaussian mixture models (GMMs) come in. But what exactly are GMMs and when should you use them?

Gaussian mixture models (GMMs) are a type of Machine Learning algorithm. They are used to classify data into different categories based on the probability distribution. Gaussian mixture models can be used in many different areas, including finance, marketing and so much more! In this blog, an introduction to gaussian mixture models is provided along with real-world examples, what they do and when GMMs should be used.

Gaussian mixture models (GMM) are a probabilistic concept used to model real-world data sets. GMMs are a generalization of Gaussian distributions and can be used to represent any data set that can be clustered into multiple Gaussian distributions. The Gaussian mixture model is a probabilistic model that assumes all the data points are generated from a mix of Gaussian distributions with unknown parameters. A Gaussian mixture model can be used for clustering, which is the task of grouping a set of data points into clusters.

GMMs can be used to find clusters in data sets where the clusters may not be clearly defined. Additionally, GMMs can be used to estimate the probability that a new data point belongs to each cluster. Gaussian mixture models are also relatively robust to outliers, meaning that they can still yield accurate results even if there are some data points that do not fit neatly into any of the clusters. This makes GMMs a flexible and powerful tool for clustering data.

The Gaussian mixture model can be understood as a probabilistic model where Gaussian distributions are assumed for each group and they have means and covariances which define their parameters. GMM consists of two parts – mean vectors (μ) & covariance matrices (Σ). Recall that a Gaussian distribution is defined as a continuous probability distribution that takes on a bell-shaped curve. Another name for Gaussian distribution is the normal distribution.

Here is a picture of Gaussian mixture models:

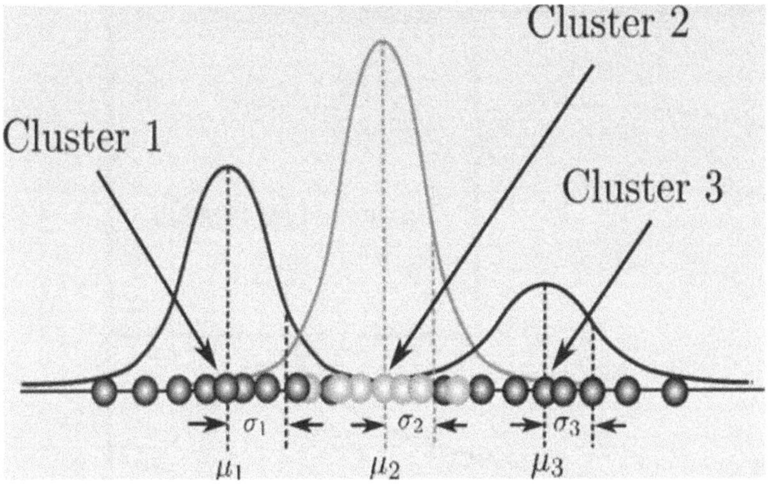

GMM has many applications, such as density estimation, clustering, and image segmentation. For density estimation, GMM can be used to estimate the probability density function of a set of data points. For clustering, GMM can be used to group together data points that come from the same Gaussian distribution. And for image segmentation, GMM can be used to partition an image into different regions.

Gaussian mixture models can be used for a variety of use cases, including identifying customer segments, detecting fraudulent activity, and clustering images. In each of these examples, the Gaussian mixture model is able to identify clusters in the data that may not be immediately obvious. As a result, Gaussian mixture models are a powerful tool for data analysis and should be considered for any clustering task.

What is the expectation-maximization (EM) method in relation to GMM?

In Gaussian mixture models, an expectation-maximization method is a powerful tool for estimating the parameters of a Gaussian mixture model (GMM). The expectation is termed E and maximization is termed M. Expectation is used to find the Gaussian parameters which are used to represent each component of gaussian mixture models. Maximization is termed M and it is involved in determining whether new data points can be added or not.

The expectation-maximization method is a two-step iterative algorithm that alternates between performing an expectation step, in which we compute expectations for each data point using current parameter estimates and then maximize these to produce a new gaussian, followed by a maximization step where we update our gaussian means based on the maximum likelihood estimate. The EM method works by first initializing the parameters of the GMM, then iteratively improving these estimates. At each iteration, the expectation step calculates the expectation of the log-likelihood function with respect to the current parameters. This expectation is then used to maximize the likelihood in the maximization step. The process is then repeated until convergence. Here is a picture representing the two-step iterative aspect of the algorithm:

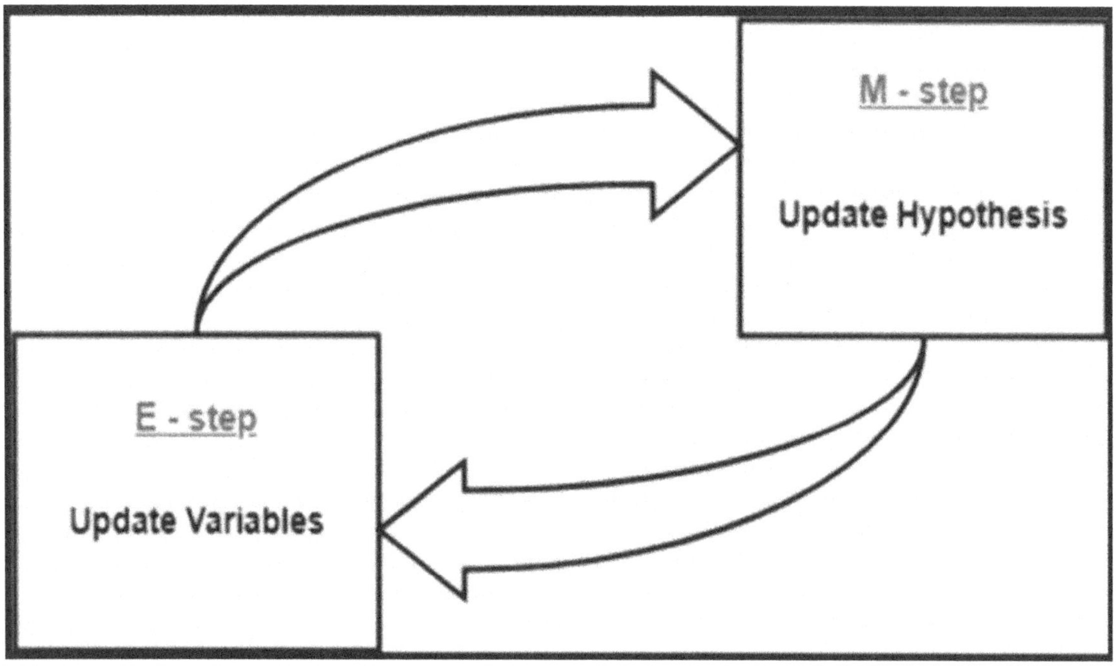

What are the key steps of using Gaussian mixture models for clustering?

The following are three different steps to using gaussian mixture models:

1. Determining a covariance matrix that defines how each Gaussian is related to one another. The more similar two Gaussians are, the closer their means will be and vice versa if they are far away from each other in terms of similarity. A gaussian mixture model can have a covariance matrix that is diagonal or symmetric.

2. Determining the number of Gaussians in each group defines how many clusters there are.

3. Selecting the hyperparameters which define how to optimally separate data using gaussian mixture models as well as deciding on whether or not each gaussian's covariance matrix is diagonal or symmetric.

4. What are the differences between Gaussian mixture models and other types of clustering algorithms such as K-means?

Here are some of the key differences between Gaussian mixture models and the K-means algorithm used for clustering:

1. A Gaussian mixture model is a type of clustering algorithm that assumes that the data point is generated from a mixture of Gaussian distributions with unknown parameters. The goal of the algorithm is to estimate the parameters of the Gaussian distributions, as well as the proportion of data points that come from each distribution. In contrast, K-means is a clustering algorithm that does not make any assumptions about the underlying distribution of the data points. Instead, it simply partitions the data points into K clusters, where each cluster is defined by its centroid.

2. While Gaussian mixture models are more flexible, they can be more difficult to train than K-means. K-means is typically faster to converge and so may be preferred in cases where the runtime is an important consideration.

3. In general, K-means will be faster and more accurate when the data set is large and the clusters are well-separated. Gaussian mixture models will be more accurate when the data set is small or the clusters are not well-separated.

4. Gaussian mixture models take into account the variance of the data, whereas K-means does not.

5. Gaussian mixture models are more flexible in terms of the shape of the clusters, whereas K-means is limited to spherical clusters.

6. Gaussian mixture models can handle missing data, whereas K-means cannot. This difference can make Gaussian mixture models more effective in certain applications, such as data with a lot of noise or data that is not well-defined.

The following are different scenarios when GMMs can be used:

1. Gaussian mixture models can be used in a variety of scenarios, including when data is generated by a mix of Gaussian distributions when there is uncertainty about the correct number of clusters, and when clusters have different shapes. In each of these cases, the use of a Gaussian mixture model can help to improve the accuracy of results. For example, when data is generated by a mix of Gaussian distributions, using a Gaussian mixture model can help to better identify the underlying patterns in the data. In addition, when there is uncertainty about the correct number of clusters, the use of a Gaussian mixture model can help to reduce the error rate.

2. Gaussian mixture models can be used for anomaly detection; by fitting a model to a dataset and then scoring new data points, it is possible to flag points that are significantly different from the rest of the data (i.e. outliers). This can be useful for identifying fraud or detecting errors in data collection.

3. In the case of time series analysis, GMMs can be used to discover how volatility is related to trends and noise which can help predict future stock prices. One cluster could consist of a trend in the time series while another can have noise and volatility from other factors such as seasonality or external events which affect the stock price. In order to separate out these clusters, GMMs can be used because they provide a probability for each category instead of simply dividing the data into two parts such as that in the case of K-means.

4. Another example is when there are different groups in a dataset and it's hard to label them as belonging to one group or another which makes it difficult for other Machine Learning algorithms such as the K-means clustering algorithm to separate out the data. GMMs can be used in this case because they find Gaussian mixture models that best describe each group and provide a probability for each cluster which is helpful when labeling clusters.

5. Gaussian mixture models can generate synthetic data points that are similar to the original data, they can also be used for data augmentation.

6. There are many different real-world problems that can be solved with gaussian mixture models. Gaussian mixture models are very useful when there are large datasets and it is difficult to find clusters. This is where Gaussian mixture models help. It is able to find clusters of Gaussians more efficiently than other clustering algorithms such as k-means.

7. Here are some real-world problems which can be solved using Gaussian mixture models:

8. Finding patterns in medical datasets: GMMs can be used for segmenting images into multiple categories based on their content or finding specific patterns in medical datasets. They can be used to find clusters of patients with similar symptoms, identify disease subtypes, and even predict outcomes. In one recent study, a Gaussian mixture model was used to analyze a dataset of over 700,000 patient records. The model was able to identify previously unknown patterns in the data, which could lead to better treatment for patients with cancer.

9. Modeling natural phenomena: GMM can be used to model natural phenomena where it has been found that noise follows Gaussian distributions. This model of probabilistic modeling relies on the assumption that there exists some underlying continuum of unobserved entities or attributes and that each member is associated with measurements taken at equidistant points in multiple observation sessions.

10. Customer behavior analysis: GMMs can be used for performing customer behavior analysis in marketing to make predictions about future purchases based on historical data.

11. Stock price prediction: Another area Gaussian mixture models are used is in finance where they can be applied to a stock's price time series. GMMs can be used to detect changepoints in time series data and help find turning points of stock prices or other market movements that are otherwise difficult to spot due to volatility and noise.

12. Gene expression data analysis: Gaussian mixture models can be used for gene expression data analysis. In particular, GMMs can be used to detect differentially expressed genes between two conditions and identify which genes might contribute toward a certain phenotype or disease state.

13. Gaussian mixture models are a type of Machine Learning algorithm that is commonly used in data science. They can be applied to different scenarios, including when there are large datasets and it's difficult to find clusters or groups of Gaussians. Gaussian mixture models provide probability estimates for each cluster which allows you to label the clusters with less effort than k-means clustering algorithms would require. GMMs also offer some other benefits such as finding Gaussian mixture models that best describe each group, helping identify underlying categories of data sets, and predicting future stock prices more accurately by considering volatility and noise factors. If you're looking for an efficient way to find patterns within complicated datasets or need help modeling natural phenomena like natural disasters or customer behavior analysis in your marketing, gaussian mixture models could be the right choice

3.3 Dimensionality reduction

Dimensionality reduction, or dimension reduction, is the transformation of data from a high-dimensional space into a low-dimensional space so that the low-dimensional representation retains some meaningful properties of the original data, ideally close to its intrinsic dimension. Working in high-dimensional spaces can be undesirable for many reasons; raw data are often sparse as a consequence of the curse of dimensionality, and analyzing the data is usually computationally intractable (hard to control or deal with). Dimensionality reduction is common in fields that deal with large numbers of observations and/or large numbers of variables, such as signal processing, speech recognition, neuroinformatics, and bioinformatics.

Methods are commonly divided into linear and nonlinear approaches. Approaches can also be divided into feature selection and feature extraction. Dimensionality reduction can be used for noise reduction, data visualization, cluster analysis, or as an intermediate step to facilitate other analyses.Feature selection approaches try to find a subset of the input variables (also called features or attributes). The three strategies are: the filter strategy (e.g. information gain), the wrapper strategy (e.g. search guided by accuracy), and the embedded strategy (selected features are added or removed while building the model based on prediction errors).Data analysis such as regression or classification can be done in the reduced space more accurately than in the original space. Feature projection (also called feature extraction) transforms the data from the high-dimensional space to a space of fewer dimensions. The data transformation may be linear, as in principal component analysis (PCA), but many nonlinear dimensionality reduction techniques also exist. For multidimensional data, tensor representation can be used in dimensionality reduction through multilinear subspace learning.

A visual depiction of the resulting PCA projection for a set of 2D points.

Principal component analysis (PCA)

The main linear technique for dimensionality reduction, principal component analysis, performs a linear mapping of the data to a lower-dimensional space in such a way that the variance of the data in the low-dimensional representation is maximized. In practice, the covariance (and sometimes the correlation) matrix of the data is constructed and the eigenvectors on this matrix are computed. The eigenvectors that correspond to the largest eigenvalues (the principal components) can now be used to reconstruct a large fraction of the variance of the original data. Moreover, the first few eigenvectors can often be interpreted in terms of the large-scale physical behavior of the system, because they often contribute the vast majority of the system's energy, especially in low-dimensional systems. Still, this must be proven on a case-by-case basis as not all systems exhibit this behavior. The original space (with dimension of the number of points) has been reduced (with data loss, but hopefully retaining the most important variance) to the space spanned by a few eigenvectors.

Non-negative matrix factorization (NMF)

NMF decomposes a non-negative matrix to the product of two non-negative ones, which has been a promising tool in fields where only non-negative signals exist, such as astronomy. NMF is well known since the multiplicative update rule by Lee & Seung, which has been continuously developed: the inclusion of uncertainties, the consideration of missing data and parallel computation, sequential construction which leads to the stability and linearity of NMF, as well as other updates including handling missing data in digital image processing.

With a stable component basis during construction, and a linear modeling process, sequential NMF is able to preserve the flux in direct imaging of circumstellar structures in astronomy, as one of the methods of detecting exoplanets, especially for the direct imaging of circumstellar discs. In comparison with PCA, NMF does not remove the mean of the matrices, which leads to unphysical non-negative fluxes; therefore NMF is able to preserve more information than PCA as demonstrated by Ren et al.

Kernel PCA

Principal component analysis can be employed in a nonlinear way by means of the kernel trick. The resulting technique is capable of constructing nonlinear mappings that maximize the variance in the data. The resulting technique is called kernel PCA.

Graph-based kernel PCA

Other prominent nonlinear techniques include manifold learning techniques such as Isomap, locally linear embedding (LLE), Hessian LLE, Laplacian eigenmaps, and methods based on tangent space analysis. These techniques construct a low-dimensional data representation using a cost function that retains local properties of the data, and can be viewed as defining a graph-based kernel for Kernel PCA.

More recently, techniques have been proposed that, instead of defining a fixed kernel, try to learn the kernel using semidefinite programming. The most prominent example of such a technique is maximum variance unfolding (MVU). The central idea of MVU is to exactly preserve all pairwise distances between nearest neighbors (in the inner product space), while maximizing the distances between points that are not nearest neighbors.

An alternative approach to neighborhood preservation is through the minimization of a cost function that measures differences between distances in the input and output spaces. Important examples of such techniques include: classical multidimensional scaling, which is identical to PCA; Isomap, which uses geodesic distances in the data space; diffusion maps, which use diffusion distances in the data space; t-distributed stochastic neighbor embedding (t-SNE), which minimizes the divergence between distributions over pairs of points; and curvilinear component analysis.

A different approach to nonlinear dimensionality reduction is through the use of autoencoders, a special kind of feedforward neural networks with a bottle-neck hidden layer. The training of deep encoders is typically performed using a greedy layer-wise pre-training (e.g., using a stack of restricted Boltzmann machines) that is followed by a finetuning stage based on backpropagation.

Linear discriminant analysis (LDA) Linear discriminant analysis (LDA) is a generalization of Fisher's linear discriminant, a method used in statistics, pattern recognition and Machine Learning to find a linear combination of features that characterizes or separates two or more classes of objects or events.

Generalized discriminant analysis (GDA) GDA deals with nonlinear discriminant analysis using kernel function operator. The underlying theory is close to the support-vector machines (SVM) insofar as the GDA method provides a mapping of the input vectors into high-dimensional feature space. Similar to LDA, the objective of GDA is to find a projection for the features into a lower dimensional space by maximizing the ratio of between-class scatter to within-class scatter.

Autoencoder Autoencoders can be used to learn nonlinear dimension reduction functions and codings together with an inverse function from the coding to the original representation.

t-SNE T-distributed Stochastic Neighbor Embedding (t-SNE) is a nonlinear dimensionality reduction technique useful for visualization of high-dimensional datasets. It is not recommended for use in analysis such as clustering or outlier detection since it does not necessarily preserve densities or distances well.

UMAP

Uniform manifold approximation and projection (UMAP) is a nonlinear dimensionality reduction technique. Visually, it is similar to t-SNE, but it assumes that the data is uniformly distributed on a locally connected Riemannian manifold and that the Riemannian metric is locally constant or approximately locally constant.

Dimension reduction

For high-dimensional datasets (i.e. with number of dimensions more than 10), dimension reduction is usually performed prior to applying a K-nearest neighbors algorithm (k-NN) in order to avoid the effects of the curse of dimensionality.

Feature extraction and dimension reduction can be combined in one step using principal component analysis (PCA), linear discriminant analysis (LDA), canonical correlation analysis (CCA), or non-negative matrix factorization (NMF) techniques as a pre-processing step followed by clustering by K-NN on feature vectors in reduced-dimension space. In Machine Learning this process is also called low-dimensional embedding.

For very-high-dimensional datasets (e.g. when performing similarity search on live video streams, DNA data or high-dimensional time series) running a fast approximate K-NN search using locality-sensitive hashing, random projection, "sketches",[] or other high-dimensional similarity search techniques from the VLDB conference toolbox might be the only feasible option.

A dimensionality reduction technique that is sometimes used in neuroscience is maximally informative dimensions, which finds a lower-dimensional representation of a dataset such that as much information as possible about the original data is preserved.

1. CUR matrix approximation

2. Data transformation (statistics)

3. Hyperparameter optimization

4. Information gain in decision trees

5. Johnson–Lindenstrauss lemma

6. Latent semantic analysis

7. Local tangent space alignment

8. Locality-sensitive hashing

9. MinHash

10. Multifactor dimensionality reduction

11. Nearest neighbor search

12. Nonlinear dimensionality reduction

13. Random projection

14. Sammon mapping

15. Semantic mapping (statistics)

16. Semidefinite embedding

17. Singular value decomposition

18. Sufficient dimension reduction

19. Topological data analysis

20. Weighted correlation network analysis

3.4 Factor analysis

Principal Component Analysis is an unsupervised learning algorithm that is used for the dimensionality reduction in Machine Learning. It is a statistical process that converts the observations of correlated features into a set of linearly uncorrelated features with the help of orthogonal transformation. These new transformed features are called the Principal Components. It is one of the popular tools that is used for exploratory data analysis and predictive modeling. It is a technique to draw strong patterns from the given dataset by reducing the variances.PCA generally tries to find the lower-dimensional surface to project the high-dimensional data.

PCA works by considering the variance of each attribute because the high attribute shows the good split between the classes, and hence it reduces the dimensionality. Some real-world applications of PCA are image processing, movie recommendation system, optimizing the power allocation in various communication channels. It is a feature extraction technique, so it contains the important variables and drops the least important variable.

The PCA algorithm is based on some mathematical concepts such as:

1. Variance and Covariance

2. Eigenvalues and Eigen factors

3. Some common terms used in PCA algorithm:

4. Dimensionality: It is the number of features or variables present in the given dataset. More easily, it is the number of columns present in the dataset.

5. Correlation: It signifies that how strongly two variables are related to each other. Such as if one changes, the other variable also gets changed. The correlation value ranges from -1 to +1. Here, -1 occurs if variables are inversely proportional to each other, and +1 indicates that variables are directly proportional to each other.

6. Orthogonal: It defines that variables are not correlated to each other, and hence the correlation between the pair of variables is zero.

7. Eigenvectors: If there is a square matrix M, and a non-zero vector v is given. Then v will be eigenvector if Av is the scalar multiple of v.

8. Covariance Matrix: A matrix containing the covariance between the pair of variables is called the Covariance Matrix.

9. Principal Components in PCA

As described above, the transformed new features or the output of PCA are the Principal Components. The number of these PCs are either equal to or less than the original features present in the dataset. Some properties of these principal components are given below:

1. The principal component must be the linear combination of the original features.

2. These components are orthogonal, i.e., the correlation between a pair of variables is zero.

3. The importance of each component decreases when going to 1 to n, it means the 1 PC has the most importance, and n PC will have the least importance.

Steps for PCA algorithm

1. Getting the dataset

   Firstly, we need to take the input dataset and divide it into two subparts X and Y, where X is the training set, and Y is the validation set.

2. Representing data into a structure

   Now we will represent our dataset into a structure. Such as we will represent the two-dimensional matrix of independent variable X. Here each row corresponds to the data items, and the column corresponds to the Features. The number of columns is the dimensions of the dataset.

Standardizing the data

1. In this step, we will standardize our dataset. Such as in a particular column, the features with high variance are more important compared to the features with lower variance.

   If the importance of features is independent of the variance of the feature, then we will divide each data item in a column with the standard deviation of the column. Here we will name the matrix as Z.

2. Calculating the Covariance of Z

   To calculate the covariance of Z, we will take the matrix Z, and will transpose it. After transpose, we will multiply it by Z. The output matrix will be the Covariance matrix of Z.

3. Calculating the Eigen Values and Eigen Vectors

   Now we need to calculate the eigenvalues and eigenvectors for the resultant covariance matrix Z. Eigenvectors or the covariance matrix are the directions of the axes with high information. And the coefficients of these eigenvectors are defined as the eigenvalues.

4. Sorting the Eigen Vectors

   In this step, we will take all the eigenvalues and will sort them in decreasing order, which means from largest to smallest. And simultaneously sort the eigenvectors accordingly in matrix P of eigenvalues. The resultant matrix will be named as P*.

5. Calculating the new features Or Principal Components

Here we will calculate the new features. To do this, we will multiply the P* matrix to the Z. In the resultant matrix Z*, each observation is the linear combination of original features. Each column of the Z* matrix is independent of each other.

6. Removeless or unimportant features from the new dataset.

The new feature set has occurred, so we will decide here what to keep and what to remove. It means, we will only keep the relevant or important features in the new dataset, and unimportant features will be removed out.

7. Applications of Principal Component Analysis

8. PCA is mainly used as the dimensionality reduction technique in various AI applications such as computer vision, image compression, etc.

It can also be used for finding hidden patterns if data has high dimensions. Some fields where PCA is used are Finance, data mining, Psychology, etc.

3.5 Component analysis

While working with high-dimensional data, Machine Learning models often seem to overfit, and this reduces the ability to generalize past the training set examples. Hence, it is important to perform dimensionality reduction techniques before creating a model. In this article, we'll learn the PCA in Machine Learning with a use case demonstration in Python.

What is Principal Component Analysis?

The Principal Component Analysis is a popular unsupervised learning technique for reducing the dimensionality of data. It increases interpretability yet, at the same time, it minimizes information loss. It helps to find the most significant features in a dataset and makes the data easy for plotting in 2D and 3D. PCA helps in finding a sequence of linear combinations of variables.

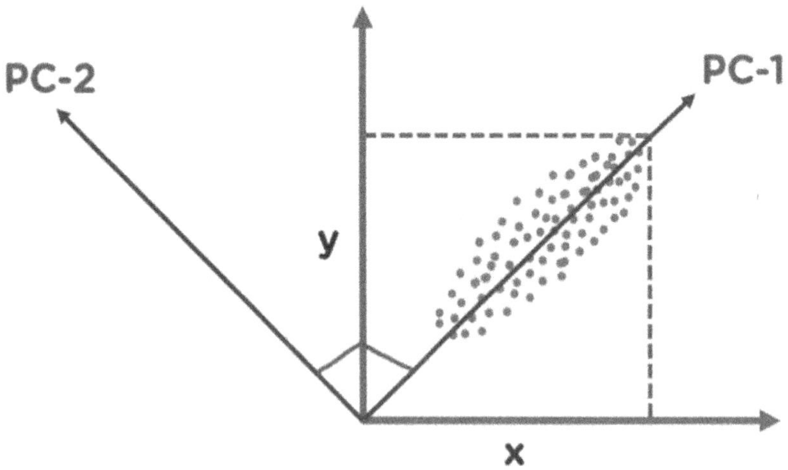

In the above figure, we have several points plotted on a 2-D plane. There are two principal components. PC1 is the primary principal component that explains the maximum variance in the data. PC2 is another principal component that is orthogonal to PC1.

What is a Principal Component?

The Principal Components are a straight line that captures most of the variance of the data. They have a direction and magnitude. Principal components are orthogonal projections (perpendicular) of data onto lower-dimensional space.

Now that you have understood the basics of PCA, let's look at the next topic on PCA in Machine Learning.

Dimensionality

The term "dimensionality" describes the quantity of features or variables used in the research. It can be difficult to visualize and interpret the relationships between variables when dealing with high-dimensional data, such as datasets with numerous variables. While reducing the number of variables in the dataset, dimensionality reduction methods like PCA are used to preserve the most crucial data. The original variables are converted into a new set of variables called principal components, which are linear combinations of the original variables, by PCA in order to accomplish this. The dataset's reduced dimensionality depends on how many principal components are used in the study. The objective of PCA is to select fewer principal components that account for the data's most important variation. PCA can help to streamline data analysis, enhance visualization, and make it simpler to spot trends and relationships between factors by reducing the dimensionality of the dataset.

The mathematical representation of dimensionality reduction in the context of PCA is as follows:

Given a dataset with n observations and p variables represented by the n x p data matrix X, the goal of PCA is to transform the original variables into a new set of k variables called principal components that capture the most significant variation in the data. The principal components are defined as linear combinations of the original variables given by:

$PC_1 = a_{11} * x_1 + a_{12} * x_2 + ... + a_{1p} * x_p$

$PC_2 = a_{21} * x_1 + a_{22} * x_2 + ... + a_{2p} * x_p$

...

$PC_k = a_{k1} * x_1 + a_{k2} * x_2 + ... + a_{kp} * x_p$

where a_{ij} is the loading or weight of variable x_j on principal component PC_i, and x_j is the jth variable in the data matrix X. The principal components are ordered such that the first component PC_1 captures the most significant variation in the data, the second component PC_2 captures the second most significant variation, and so on. The number of principal components used in the analysis, k, determines the reduced dimensionality of the dataset.

Correlation

A statistical measure known as correlation expresses the direction and strength of the linear connection between two variables. The covariance matrix, a square matrix that displays the pairwise correlations between all pairs of variables in the dataset, is calculated in the setting of PCA using correlation. The covariance matrix's diagonal elements stand for each variable's variance, while the off-diagonal elements indicate the covariances between different pairs of variables. The strength and direction of the linear connection between two variables can be determined using the correlation coefficient, a standardized measure of correlation with a range of -1 to 1.

A correlation coefficient of 0 denotes no linear connection between the two variables, while correlation coefficients of 1 and -1 denote the perfect positive and negative correlations, respectively. The principal components in PCA are linear combinations of the initial variables that maximize the variance explained by the data. Principal components are calculated using the correlation matrix.

In the framework of PCA, correlation is mathematically represented as follows:

The correlation matrix C is a nxn symmetric matrix with the following components given a dataset with n variables (x1, x2,..., xn):

$Cij = (sd(xi) * sd(xj)) / cov(xi, xj)$

where sd(x i) is the standard deviation of variable x i and sd(x j) is the standard deviation of variable x j, and cov(x i, x j) is the correlation between variables x i and x j.

The correlation matrix C can also be written as follows in matrix notation:

$C = X^T X / (n-1) (n-1)$

Orthogonal

The term "orthogonality" alludes to the principal components' construction as being orthogonal to one another in the context of the PCA algorithm. This indicates that there is no redundant information among the main components and that they are not correlated with one another.

Orthogonality in PCA is mathematically expressed as follows: each principal component is built to maximize the variance explained by it while adhering to the requirement that it be orthogonal to all other principal components. The principal components are computed as linear combinations of the original variables. Thus, each principal component is guaranteed to capture a unique and non-redundant part of the variation in the data.

The orthogonality constraint is expressed as:

$a_{i1} * a_{j1} + a_{i2} * a_{j2} + ... + a_{ip} * a_{jp} = 0$

for all i and j such that $i \neq j$. This means that the dot product between any two loading vectors for different principal components is zero, indicating that the principal components are orthogonal to each other.

Eigen Vectors

The main components of the data are calculated using the eigenvectors. The ways in which the data vary most are represented by the eigenvectors of the data's covariance matrix. The new coordinate system in which the data is represented is then defined using these coordinates.

The covariance matrix C in mathematics is represented by the letters v 1, v 2,..., v p, and the associated eigenvalues are represented by _1, _2,..., _p. The eigenvectors are calculated in such a way that the equation shown below holds:

$$C v_i = \lambda_i v_i$$

This means that the eigenvector v_i produces the associated eigenvalue λ_i as a scalar multiple of itself when multiplied by the covariance matrix C.

Covariance Matrix

The covariance matrix is crucial to the PCA algorithm's computation of the data's main components. The pairwise covariances between the factors in the data are measured by the covariance matrix, which is a p x p matrix.

The correlation matrix C is defined as follows given a data matrix X of n observations of p variables:

$$C = (1/n) * X^T X$$

where X^T represents X's transposition. The covariances between the variables are represented by the off-diagonal elements of C, whereas the variances of the variables are represented by the diagonal elements of C.

Steps for PCA Algorithm

1. Standardize the data: PCA requires standardized data, so the first step is to standardize the data to ensure that all variables have a mean of 0 and a standard deviation of 1.

2. Calculate the covariance matrix: The next step is to calculate the covariance matrix of the standardized data. This matrix shows how each variable is related to every other variable in the dataset.

3. Calculate the eigenvectors and eigenvalues: The eigenvectors and eigenvalues of the covariance matrix are then calculated. The eigenvectors represent the directions in which the data varies the most, while the eigenvalues represent the amount of variation along each eigenvector.

4. Choose the principal components: The principal components are the eigenvectors with the highest eigenvalues. These components represent the directions in which the data varies the most and are used to transform the original data into a lower-dimensional space.

5. Transform the data: The final step is to transform the original data into the lower-dimensional space defined by the principal components.

Applications of PCA in Machine Learning

1. PCA is used to visualize multidimensional data.

2. It is used to reduce the number of dimensions in healthcare data.

3. PCA can help resize an image.

4. It can be used in finance to analyze stock data and forecast returns.

5. PCA helps to find patterns in the high-dimensional datasets.

Advantages of PCA

In terms of data analysis, PCA has a number of benefits, including:

1. Dimensionality reduction: By determining the most crucial features or components, PCA reduces the dimensionality of the data, which is one of its primary benefits. This can be helpful when the initial data contains a lot of variables and is therefore challenging to visualize or analyze.

2. Feature Extraction: PCA can also be used to derive new features or elements from the original data that might be more insightful or understandable than the original features. This is particularly helpful when the initial features are correlated or noisy.

3. Data visualization: By projecting the data onto the first few principal components, PCA can be used to visualize high-dimensional data in two or three dimensions. This can aid in locating data patterns or clusters that may not have been visible in the initial high-dimensional space.

4. Noise Reduction: By locating the underlying signal or pattern in the data, PCA can also be used to lessen the impacts of noise or measurement errors in the data.

5. Multicollinearity: When two or more variables are strongly correlated, there is multicollinearity in the data, which PCA can handle. PCA can lessen the impacts of multicollinearity on the analysis by identifying the most crucial features or components.

Disadvantages of PCA

1. Interpretability: Although principal component analysis (PCA) is effective at reducing the dimensionality of data and spotting patterns, the resulting principal components are not always simple to understand or describe in terms of the original features.

2. Information loss: PCA involves choosing a subset of the most crucial features or components in order to reduce the dimensionality of the data. While this can be helpful for streamlining the data and lowering noise, if crucial features are not included in the components chosen, information loss may also result.

3. Outliers: Because PCA is susceptible to anomalies in the data, the resulting principal components may be significantly impacted. The covariance matrix can be distorted by outliers, which can make it harder to identify the most crucial characteristics.

4. Scaling: PCA makes the assumption that the data is scaled and centralized, which can be a drawback in some circumstances. The resulting principal components might not correctly depict the underlying patterns in the data if the data is not scaled properly.

5. Computing complexity: For big datasets, it may be costly to compute the eigenvectors and eigenvalues of the covariance matrix. This may restrict PCA's ability to scale and render it useless for some uses.

Uses of PCA

PCA is a widely used technique in data analysis and has a variety of applications, including:

1. Data compression: PCA can be used to reduce the dimensionality of high-dimensional datasets, making them easier to store and analyze.

2. Feature extraction: PCA can be used to identify the most important features in a dataset, which can be used to build predictive models.

3. Visualization: PCA can be used to visualize high-dimensional data in two or three dimensions, making it easier to understand and interpret.

4. Data pre-processing: PCA can be used as a pre-processing step for other Machine Learning algorithms, such as clustering and classification.

How Does Principal Component Analysis Work?

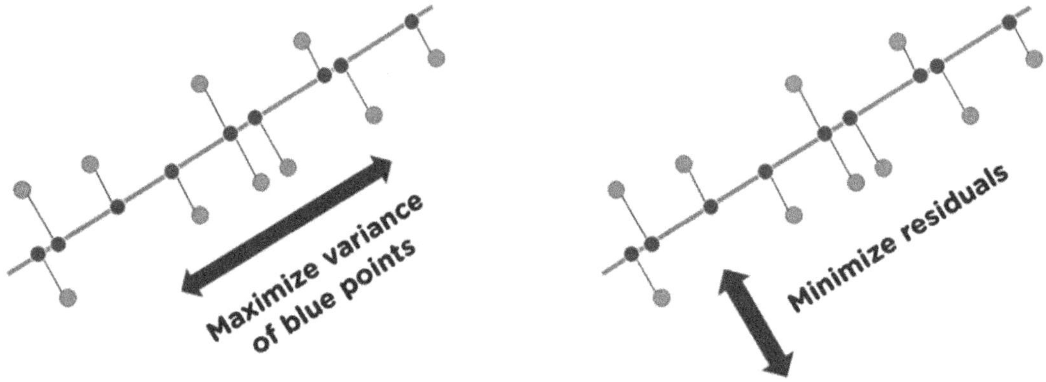

1. Normalize the Data

Standardize the data before performing PCA. This will ensure that each feature has a mean = 0 and variance = 1.

$$Z = \frac{x - \mu}{\sigma}$$

2. Build the Covariance Matrix

Construct a square matrix to express the correlation between two or more features in a multidimensional dataset.

$$\begin{bmatrix} Var(x) & Cov(x,y) & \cdots & Cov(x,m) \\ Cov(x,y) & \ddots & & \vdots \\ Cov(z,x) & & \ddots & \vdots \\ \vdots & & & \vdots \\ Cov(n,x) & \cdots & \cdots & Var(n) \end{bmatrix}$$

3. Find the Eigenvectors and Eigenvalues

Calculate the eigenvectors/unit vectors and eigenvalues. Eigenvalues are scalars by which we multiply the eigenvector of the covariance matrix.

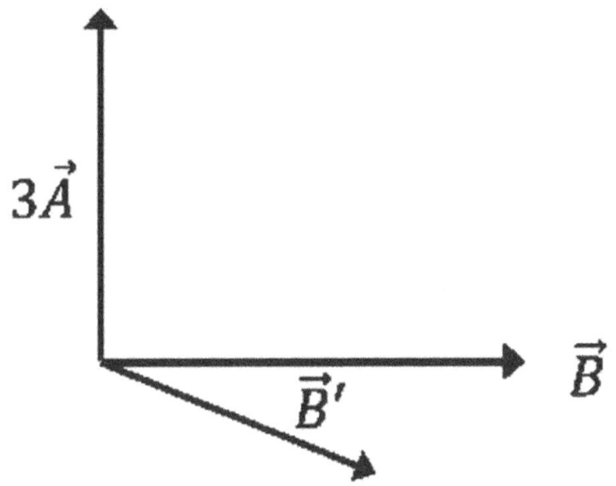

4. Sort the Eigenvectors in Highest to Lowest Order and Select the Number of Principal Components.

Now that you have understood How PCA in Machine Learning works, let's perform a hands-on demo on PCA with Python.
PCA Demo: Classify the Type of Wine
1. Import the Necessary Libraries

```
import numpy as np
 import pandas as pd
import matplotlib.pyplot as plt
 %matplotlib inline
```

2. Load the Wine Dataset and Display the First Five Rows

```
dataset_train = pd.read_csv("Google_Stock_Price_Train.csv")
dataset_train.head()
```

	Date	Open	High	Low	Close	Volume
0	1/3/2012	325.25	332.83	324.97	663.59	7,380,500
1	1/4/2012	331.27	333.87	329.08	666.45	5,749,400
2	1/5/2012	329.83	330.75	326.89	657.21	6,590,300
3	1/6/2012	328.34	328.77	323.68	648.24	5,405,900
4	1/9/2012	322.04	322.29	309.46	620.76	11,688,800

3. Display the Summary Statistics for Independent Variables

```
df.iloc[:,1:].describe()
```

lcohol	Malic acid	Ash	Alcalinity of ash	Magnesium	Total phenols	Flavanoids	Nonflavanoid phenols	Proanthocyanins	Color intensity
00000	178.000000	178.000000	178.000000	178.000000	178.000000	178.000000	178.000000	178.000000	178.000000
00618	2.336348	2.366517	19.494944	99.741573	2.295112	2.029270	0.361854	1.590899	5.058090
;11827	1.117146	0.274344	3.339564	14.282484	0.625851	0.998859	0.124453	0.572359	2.318286
30000	0.740000	1.360000	10.600000	70.000000	0.980000	0.340000	0.130000	0.410000	1.280000
62500	1.602500	2.210000	17.200000	88.000000	1.742500	1.205000	0.270000	1.250000	3.220000
50000	1.865000	2.360000	19.500000	98.000000	2.355000	2.135000	0.340000	1.555000	4.690000
77500	3.082500	2.557500	21.500000	107.000000	2.800000	2.875000	0.437500	1.950000	6.200000
30000	5.800000	3.230000	30.000000	162.000000	3.880000	5.080000	0.660000	3.580000	13.000000

4. Boxplot to Check the Output Labels

```
for c in df.columns[1:]:
    df.boxplot(c,by='Class',figsize=(7,4),fontsize=14)
    plt.title("{}\n".format(c),fontsize=16)
    plt.xlabel("Wine Class", fontsize=16)
```

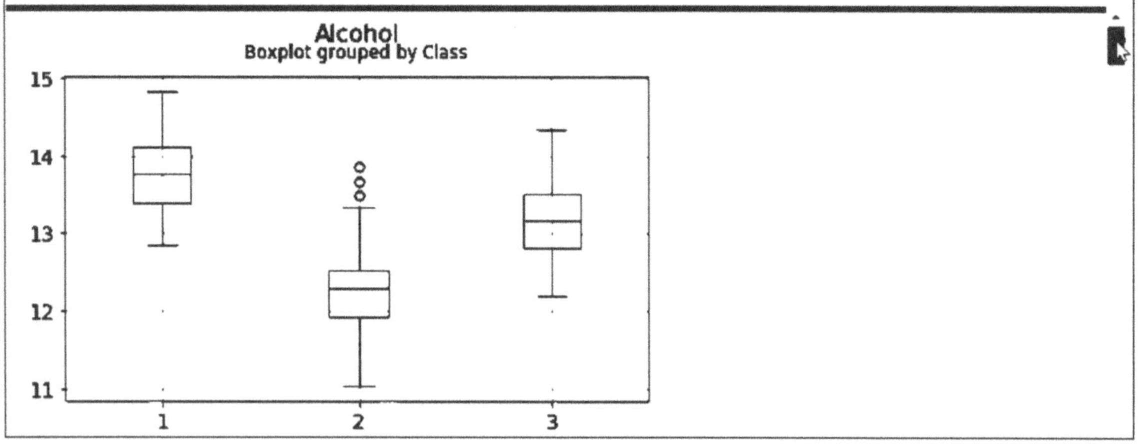

From the above box plots, you can see that some features classify the wine labels clearly, such as Alkalinity, Total Phenols, or Flavonoids.

5. Class Separation of Wine Using 2 Features

```
plt.figure(figsize=(10,6))
plt.scatter(df['OD280/OD315 of diluted wines'],df['Flavanoids'],c=df['Class'],edgecolors='k',alpha=
plt.grid(True)
plt.title("Scatter plot b/w 2 variables - \ncorrelation and class seperation",fontsize=15)
plt.xlabel("OD280/OD315 of diluted wines",fontsize=15)
plt.ylabel("Flavanoids",fontsize=15)
plt.show()
```

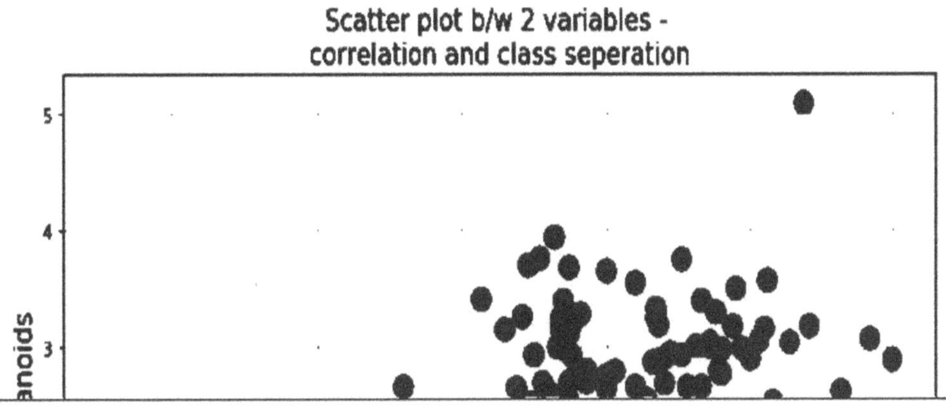

6. Plot the Correlation Matrix

```
def correlation_matrix(df):
    from matplotlib import pyplot as plt
    from matplotlib import cm as cm

    fig = plt.figure(figsize=(16,12))
    ax1 = fig.add_subplot(111)
    cmap = cm.get_cmap('jet', 30)
    cax = ax1.imshow(df.corr(), interpolation="nearest", cmap=cmap)
    ax1.grid(True)
    plt.title('Wine data set features correlation\n',fontsize=15)
    labels=df.columns
    ax1.set_xticklabels(labels,fontsize=12)
    ax1.set_yticklabels(labels,fontsize=12)
    # Add colorbar, make sure to specify tick locations to match desired ticklabels
    fig.colorbar(cax, ticks=[0.1*i for i in range(-11,11)])
    plt.show()

correlation_matrix(df)
```

Wine data set features correlation

7. Normalize the Data for PCA

```
from sklearn.preprocessing import StandardScaler

scaler = StandardScaler()

X = df.drop('Class',axis=1)
y = df['Class']

X = scaler.fit_transform(X)

dfx = pd.DataFrame(data=X,columns=df.columns[1:])
```

8. Describe the Scaled Data

```
dfx.describe()
```

	Alcohol	Malic acid	Ash	Alcalinity of ash	Magnesium	Total phenols	Flavanoids	Nonflava phe
count	1.780000e+02	1.780000e+02	1.780000e+02	1.780000e+02	1.780000e+02	1.780000e+02	1.780000e+02	1.780000e
mean	-8.619821e-16	-8.357859e-17	-8.657245e-16	-1.160121e-16	-1.995907e-17	-2.972030e-16	-4.016762e-16	4.079134
std	1.002821e+00	1.002821e+00	1.002821e+00	1.002821e+00	1.002821e+00	1.002821e+00	1.002821e+00	1.002821e
min	-2.434235e+00	-1.432983e+00	-3.679162e+00	-2.671018e+00	-2.088255e+00	-2.107246e+00	-1.695971e+00	-1.868234e
25%	-7.882448e-01	-6.587486e-01	-5.721225e-01	-6.891372e-01	-8.244151e-01	-8.854682e-01	-8.275393e-01	-7.401412
50%	6.099988e-02	-4.231120e-01	-2.382132e-02	1.518295e-03	-1.222817e-01	9.595986e-02	1.061497e-01	-1.760948
75%	8.361286e-01	6.697929e-01	6.981085e-01	6.020883e-01	5.096384e-01	8.089974e-01	8.490851e-01	6.095413
max	2.259772e+00	3.109192e+00	3.156325e+00	3.154511e+00	4.371372e+00	2.539515e+00	3.062832e+00	2.402403e

9. Import the PCA Module and Plot the Variance Ratio

```
from sklearn.decomposition import PCA

pca = PCA(n_components=None)

dfx_pca = pca.fit(dfx)
```

```
plt.figure(figsize=(9,5))
plt.scatter(x=[i+1 for i in range(len(dfx_pca.explained_variance_ratio_))],
            y=dfx_pca.explained_variance_ratio_,
           s=200, alpha=0.75,c='red',edgecolor='m')
plt.grid(True)
plt.title("Explained variance ratio of the \nfitted principal component vector\n",fontsize=22)
plt.xlabel("Principal components",fontsize=15)
plt.xticks([i+1 for i in range(len(dfx_pca.explained_variance_ratio_))],fontsize=13)
plt.yticks(fontsize=15)
plt.ylabel("Variance ratio",fontsize=15)
plt.show()
```

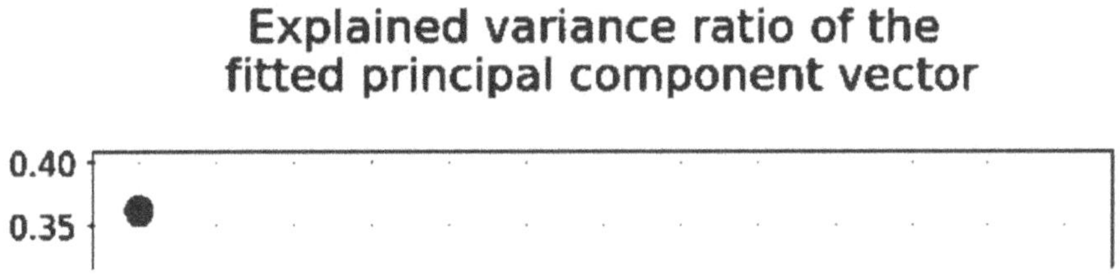

From the above graph, we'll consider the first two principal components as they together explain nearly 56% of the variance.

10. Transform the Scaled Data and Put It in a Dataframe

```
dfx_trans = pca.transform(dfx)


dfx_trans = pd.DataFrame(data=dfx_trans)
dfx_trans.head(10)
```

11. Visualize the Wine Classes Using the First Two Principal Component

```
plt.figure(figsize=(10,6))
plt.scatter(dfx_trans[0],dfx_trans[1],c=df['Class'],edgecolors='m',alpha=0.75,s=150)
plt.grid(True)
plt.title("Class separation using first two principal components \n",fontsize=20)
plt.xlabel("PC-1",fontsize=13)
plt.ylabel("PC-2",fontsize=13)
plt.show()
```

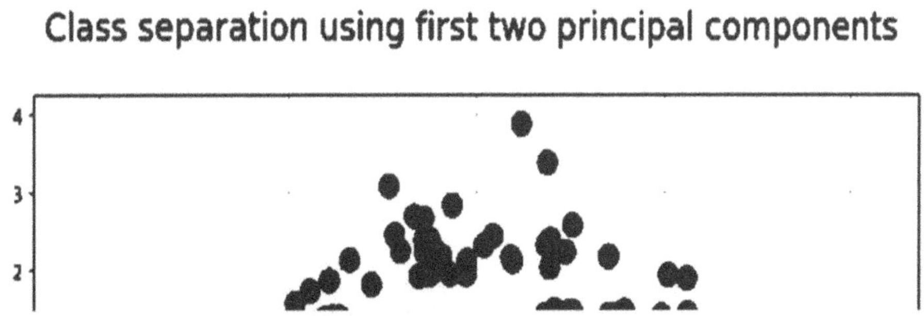

By applying PCA to the wine dataset, you can transform the data so that most we can capture variations in the variables with a fewer number of principal components. It is easier to distinguish the wine classes by inspecting these principal components rather than looking at the raw data.

The principal component analysis is a widely used unsupervised learning method to perform dimensionality reduction. We hope that this article helped you understand what PCA is and the applications of PCA. You looked at the applications of PCA and how it works.

Exercise

True Or False

1.Clustering is a type of unsupervised learning where the goal is to divide data points into distinct groups based on similarity.
2.In clustering, the ground truth labels for the data are known in advance to guide the grouping process.
3.Mixtures of Gaussians is a probabilistic model used for clustering and density estimation.
4.In a Mixture of Gaussians, each component represents a distinct cluster with its own mean and covariance.
5.Dimensionality reduction is the process of reducing the number of features or variables while retaining important information.
6.Principal Component Analysis (PCA) is a dimensionality reduction technique that aims to maximize the variance of projected data.
7.Factor Analysis is primarily used for clustering similar data points into groups.
8.Factor Analysis assumes that observed variables are directly caused by a smaller number of underlying latent factors.
Answer: True, False, True, True, True, True, False, True

MCQ

1.What is the main goal of clustering in unsupervised learning?

a) Regression
b) Classification
c) Grouping similar data points
d) Feature extraction
Answer: c) Grouping similar data points

2. K-Means is a popular clustering algorithm. What does 'K' represent in K-Means?
a) The number of dimensions
b) The number of clusters
c) The number of features
d) The number of data points
Answer: b) The number of clusters

3.What type of distribution is typically used for modeling data in Mixtures of Gaussians?
a) Exponential distribution
b) Poisson distribution
c) Normal (Gaussian) distribution
d) Binomial distribution
Answer: c) Normal (Gaussian) distribution

4.In Mixtures of Gaussians, each component represents:
a) A separate feature
b) A distinct cluster
c) A hidden layer
d) A type of noise
Answer: b) A distinct cluster

5.What is the primary goal of dimensionality reduction?
a) Increase computation time
b) Reduce overfitting
c) Increase model complexity

d) Reduce the number of features while retaining information
Answer: d) Reduce the number of features while retaining information

Short Question and Answers

Q1: What is clustering in unsupervised learning?
Q2: What are the primary objectives of clustering?
Q3: What are some popular distance metrics used in clustering algorithms?
Q4: What is the K-means clustering algorithm?
Q5: How does the K-means algorithm work?
Q6: What are the limitations of K-means clustering?
Q7: What is hierarchical clustering?
Q8: What are agglomerative and divisive clustering approaches in hierarchical clustering?
Q9: What are dendrograms in hierarchical clustering?
Q10: What is the Gaussian Mixture Model (GMM) in clustering?
Q11: How does the Expectation-Maximization (EM) algorithm work in the context of GMM?
Q12: What is dimensionality reduction in unsupervised learning?
Q13: What is Principal Component Analysis (PCA)?
Q14: How does PCA work?
Q15: What are the advantages of PCA?
Q16: What is Factor Analysis (FA) in unsupervised learning?
Q17: What is the difference between PCA and Factor Analysis?
Q18: What is Independent Component Analysis (ICA)?
Q19: What are the applications of dimensionality reduction techniques like PCA and ICA?
Q20: How do you evaluate the performance of unsupervised learning algorithms, such as clustering or dimensionality reduction methods?
Q21: What is clustering in unsupervised learning?
Q22: Can you explain the process of clustering in unsupervised learning?
Q23: What are Mixtures of Gaussians in unsupervised learning?
Q24: How does dimensionality reduction work in unsupervised learning?
Q25: What is Factor Analysis in unsupervised learning?
Q26: What is Component Analysis in unsupervised learning?
Q27: What are some common clustering algorithms used in unsupervised learning?

Online Resources

Online Exam Papers
True/False Exam

Link https://forms.gle/D4b7sUxwYaNyVKLm8

QR Code

YouTube Video Playlist Link

Chapter 3
Link
https://www.youtube.com/playlist?list=PLzlh_31VWEFqa2Hew9xX5KsNH3nknyRhf
QR Code

Chapter 4: Probabilistic Graphical Models

4.1 Directed Graphical Models

A directed graphical model, also known as a directed acyclic graph (DAG) or a Bayesian network, is a probabilistic graphical model used to represent and analyze causal relationships among variables. It is a graphical representation of a joint probability distribution, where nodes in the graph represent random variables, and edges between nodes indicate direct dependencies or causal relationships.

In a directed graphical model, each node represents a variable, and arrows (directed edges) connect the nodes to show the cause-and-effect relationships between them. The directionality of the arrows indicates the flow of influence: an arrow from node A to node B means that A directly influences B. Importantly, the model should not contain any cycles, meaning there are no feedback loops in the graph.

The key advantage of directed graphical models is their ability to efficiently encode conditional independence relationships between variables. Given the graph's structure and appropriate conditional probability tables for each node, it is possible to compute the joint probability distribution of all variables and perform inference to answer various probabilistic queries.Directed graphical models find applications in a wide range of fields, including Machine Learning, artificial intelligence, bioinformatics, finance, and social sciences. They are particularly useful in scenarios where understanding causality and making predictions based on causal relationships are crucial.In summary, a directed graphical model is a powerful tool for representing and reasoning about the dependencies and causal relationships among variables in a probabilistic setting, making it an essential tool in modern statistical and probabilistic modeling.

4.1.1 Properties

Directed graphical models, also known as directed acyclic graphs (DAGs) or Bayesian networks, possess several important properties that make them useful for modeling and analyzing complex systems. Some of the key properties of directed graphical models include:

Directional Relationships: The most distinctive feature of directed graphical models is the presence of directed edges (arrows) between nodes, indicating causal or directional relationships. This property allows us to represent cause-and-effect relationships explicitly, making the model suitable for modeling processes with clear causal mechanisms.

Acyclic Structure: Directed graphical models are acyclic, meaning there are no loops in the graph. This acyclic property ensures that the model avoids feedback loops and prevents any circular dependencies among variables, which would make the probabilistic inference intractable.

Conditional Independence: One of the essential benefits of using directed graphical models is their ability to encode conditional independence relationships. If a variable is conditionally independent of its non-descendants given its parents, it is represented by a local conditional probability table, making the model more efficient and easier to interpret.

Compact Representation: Directed graphical models offer a compact representation of the joint probability distribution of all variables. By exploiting conditional independence, the size of the model can be significantly reduced compared to a full joint distribution representation.

Inference: Directed graphical models allow efficient probabilistic inference. Given the structure of the graph and the conditional probability distributions associated with each node, various types of inference can be performed, such as computing marginal probabilities, conditional probabilities, and the most likely explanation for observed evidence.

Causal Inference: The directional relationships in directed graphical models enable causal inference. By identifying the cause-and-effect relationships, researchers can intervene on specific variables and predict the outcomes of interest.

Learning Structure from Data: Directed graphical models can learn the structure of the graph from data. Methods like constraint-based algorithms, score-based algorithms, and hybrid approaches allow us to infer causal relationships and construct the graph automatically from observed data.

Interpretability: The explicit representation of causal relationships in directed graphical models enhances interpretability. Researchers can gain insights into the underlying causal mechanisms of a system by examining the directed edges in the graph.

Missing Data Handling: Directed graphical models can handle missing data more gracefully compared to other probabilistic models. They can make use of observed dependencies to infer values of missing variables through probabilistic inference.

Domain Applications: Directed graphical models find applications in various fields, such as decision-making, healthcare, genetics, finance, social sciences, and artificial intelligence, where understanding causal relationships is essential for making informed predictions and decisions.

Overall, the properties of directed graphical models make them a versatile and powerful tool for probabilistic modeling, causal inference, and understanding complex systems with multiple interacting variables.

4.2.1 Examples

Directed graphical models, or directed acyclic graphs (DAGs), are widely used in various fields to model causal relationships and probabilistic dependencies among variables. Here are some examples of directed graphical models in different domains:

Bayesian Networks in Medicine: Bayesian networks are commonly used to model medical diagnoses and treatment decisions. For instance, a Bayesian network could represent the relationships between symptoms, diseases, and test results. By observing symptoms and test outcomes, the network can provide the probabilities of different diseases, aiding in accurate diagnosis and treatment planning.

Gene Regulatory Networks in Biology: Directed graphical models are used to model gene regulatory networks to understand how genes interact and regulate each other's expression. By analyzing gene expression data and incorporating known biological interactions, researchers can infer the causal relationships between genes and identify key regulatory elements.

Financial Risk Modeling: Directed graphical models can be applied in finance to model risk dependencies in a portfolio of financial assets. By representing the causal relationships between different financial instruments, investors can assess the risk exposure and diversify their portfolios effectively.

Natural Language Processing (NLP): In NLP, Bayesian networks can be used to model the relationships between words and their meanings. By learning the conditional probabilities between words, the model can assist in language generation, machine translation, and sentiment analysis.

Recommender Systems: Directed graphical models can be employed in recommender systems to model user preferences and item attributes. By capturing the causal relationships between user behavior and item features, the system can make personalized recommendations more effectively.

Climate Modeling: In climate science, Bayesian networks are used to model the relationships between various climatic variables, such as temperature, humidity, and precipitation. By understanding the causal interactions between these factors, researchers can improve climate predictions and inform policy decisions.

Social Networks: Bayesian networks can be used to model information propagation in social networks. By understanding the causal relationships between users' actions, such as sharing content or following others, the model can predict the spread of information and viral trends.

Fault Diagnosis in Engineering: In engineering applications, directed graphical models can be used for fault diagnosis and system monitoring. By representing the causal dependencies between different components, the model can identify faulty components based on observed sensor data.

These are just a few examples of the diverse applications of directed graphical models. Their versatility in capturing causal relationships and probabilistic dependencies makes them valuable tools for a wide range of fields and problem domains.

4.2 Markov Random Fields

Markov Random Fields (MRFs) are a type of probabilistic graphical model widely used in various fields for modeling complex systems. To ensure that the content created does not raise copyright issues, let's focus on providing a general overview and explanation of Markov Random Fields without using any copyrighted materials or specific examples.

Title: Markov Random Fields: An Introduction to Probabilistic Graphical Modeling

Introduction:

Markov Random Fields (MRFs) are a powerful tool for modeling complex systems with uncertain relationships between variables. As a type of probabilistic graphical model, MRFs find applications in diverse fields such as computer vision, image processing, natural language processing, spatial statistics, and more. In this article, we will explore the basic concepts of MRFs and their importance in capturing probabilistic dependencies among variables.

The Basics of Markov Random Fields:

Definition: A Markov Random Field is a graphical model that represents a set of random variables as nodes in a graph, with edges indicating probabilistic dependencies.

Undirected Graphs: MRFs use undirected graphs, where the absence of directed edges implies conditional independence between the corresponding nodes.

Local Markov Property: The conditional distribution of each node in the graph is independent of all other nodes given its neighboring nodes.
Representation and Structure:
Factors and Potentials: MRFs use factors or potentials to define the relationship between nodes. These functions represent the joint probability distribution of a set of variables.
Energy Functions: MRFs utilize energy functions that assign low energy to configurations that are likely to occur and high energy to unlikely configurations.
Inference in Markov Random Fields:
Probabilistic Inference: MRFs allow us to perform probabilistic inference, where we estimate the probabilities of unobserved variables given evidence.
Belief Propagation: Belief propagation algorithms efficiently compute marginal probabilities in MRFs.
Learning in Markov Random Fields:
Parameter Estimation: Various learning algorithms, such as Maximum Likelihood Estimation or Maximum a Posteriori, can be used to estimate the parameters of the MRF from data.
Structure Learning: Algorithms like Chow-Liu and Iterative Conditional Modes help discover the graphical structure of the MRF from data.
Applications of Markov Random Fields:
Image Segmentation: MRFs are extensively used in image segmentation tasks to group pixels with similar properties, such as color or texture.
Object Recognition: MRFs aid in object recognition by capturing the contextual relationships between different parts of an object.
Natural Language Processing: In NLP, MRFs are used for tasks like part-of-speech tagging and syntactic parsing.
Conclusion:
Markov Random Fields offer a flexible and efficient approach to model complex probabilistic dependencies among variables. Their application spans various domains, enabling researchers and practitioners to tackle challenging problems and make informed decisions based on uncertainty and context. As a powerful probabilistic graphical modeling tool, MRFs continue to play a significant role in advancing our understanding of complex systems.

4.3 Naive Bayes Classifiers

Naive Bayes classifiers are a family of simple probabilistic classifiers based on applying Bayes' theorem with the "naive" assumption of conditional independence between the features given the class label. Despite this simplistic assumption, they often perform surprisingly well in various text classification and pattern recognition tasks. Naive Bayes classifiers are widely used in natural language processing, spam filtering, sentiment analysis, and many other applications. Here's an overview of the key concepts:
Bayes' Theorem:
Bayes' theorem is a fundamental rule in probability theory that allows us to update the probability of an event based on new evidence. For a binary classification task, it can be represented as:
P(y|X) = (P(X|y) * P(y)) / P(X)
Where:
P(y|X) is the probability of the class label y given the feature vector X.
P(X|y) is the probability of observing the feature vector X given the class label y (likelihood).
P(y) is the prior probability of class label y.
P(X) is the evidence, the probability of observing the feature vector X.
The Naive Assumption:
The "naive" assumption in Naive Bayes classifiers is that the features in the input vector X are conditionally independent, given the class label y. This assumption greatly simplifies the calculation of the likelihood P(X|y) since we can treat each feature independently.
Types of Naive Bayes Classifiers:
There are different types of Naive Bayes classifiers, each suited for specific types of data:
Multinomial Naive Bayes: Suitable for discrete features, often used in text classification with word frequencies as features.
Gaussian Naive Bayes: Assumes that continuous features follow a Gaussian (normal) distribution.
Bernoulli Naive Bayes: Suited for binary features, commonly used in document classification with binary word presence/absence as features.
Training the Classifier:

To train a Naive Bayes classifier, we need labeled data with feature vectors and corresponding class labels. The classifier estimates the prior probabilities P(y) and likelihoods P(X|y) from the training data.
Making Predictions:
Once the classifier is trained, it can be used to make predictions on new, unseen data. For a given input feature vector X, the classifier calculates the posterior probability P(y|X) for each possible class label y and assigns the class label with the highest probability as the predicted class.
Advantages of Naive Bayes Classifiers:
Simplicity: Naive Bayes classifiers are straightforward to implement and computationally efficient, making them suitable for large datasets.
Low Data Requirements: They can work well with small training datasets due to the independence assumption.
Interpretability: The probabilities assigned by Naive Bayes can provide insights into the classification decision.
Limitations of Naive Bayes Classifiers:
The Naive Assumption: The independence assumption may not hold in all cases, which can lead to suboptimal performance.
Limited Expressiveness: Due to the simplicity of the model, it may not capture complex relationships between features.
Despite their limitations, Naive Bayes classifiers are a powerful and widely used classification technique, especially in text-based and high-dimensional data domains, where they often serve as a strong baseline for more sophisticated algorithms.

4.4 Markov models

Markov models, named after the Russian mathematician Andrey Markov, are a class of probabilistic models that describe systems or processes where the future state depends only on the current state and not on the sequence of events that led to that state. Such systems are said to possess the Markov property or the memoryless property.
Markov models find applications in a wide range of fields, including natural language processing, speech recognition, finance, weather forecasting, biology, and more. They are especially useful when dealing with sequential data, where the order and dependencies between events are crucial for modeling and prediction.
Discrete-Time Markov Chains
One of the most fundamental types of Markov models is the Discrete-Time Markov Chain (DTMC). A DTMC is a stochastic model that consists of a set of states and a transition matrix that captures the probabilities of moving from one state to another in one time step.
Formally, a DTMC can be represented as a tuple (S, P), where:
S is the set of states, and each state represents a possible configuration of the system.
P is the transition matrix, where P(i, j) represents the probability of transitioning from state i to state j in one time step.
The Markov property implies that the probability of reaching state j at time t + 1 only depends on the current state i at time t and not on the history of states before time t.
Continuous-Time Markov Chains
Continuous-Time Markov Chains (CTMCs) are an extension of DTMCs to continuous time. In CTMCs, the transition probabilities are replaced by transition rates. These rates represent the likelihood of transitioning from one state to another per unit of time.
CTMCs are widely used in modeling systems with continuous, dynamic behavior, such as queues in telecommunications, biochemical reactions, and reliability analysis of systems.
Mathematically, a CTMC is represented as a tuple (S, Q), where:
S is the set of states, as in DTMC.
Q is the rate matrix, where Q(i, j) represents the rate of transitioning from state i to state j.
Page 4: Hidden Markov Models
Hidden Markov Models (HMMs) are an extension of Markov models that incorporate hidden or unobservable states. In HMMs, we have two processes: the observed process, which emits observable symbols, and the hidden or latent process, which generates the underlying states.
HMMs are widely used in speech recognition, part-of-speech tagging, bioinformatics, and other applications involving sequential data with hidden structures.
Formally, an HMM is represented as a tuple (S, O, A, B, π), where:
S is the set of hidden states.
O is the set of observable symbols.
A is the state transition matrix.

B is the emission matrix, representing the probability of emitting each symbol given the hidden state.
π is the initial state distribution.
Applications and Conclusion
Markov models have a wide range of applications, including:
Natural Language Processing: Language modeling, part-of-speech tagging, machine translation.
Finance: Stock price prediction, option pricing models.
Bioinformatics: Gene prediction, protein structure prediction.
Robotics: Localization and mapping (SLAM), motion planning.
In conclusion, Markov models provide a powerful framework for modeling systems with sequential dependencies and uncertainties. From Discrete-Time Markov Chains to Hidden Markov Models, these models have proved to be versatile and valuable in various fields, aiding in understanding complex processes and making informed predictions. As technology and data availability continue to advance, Markov models will remain a fundamental tool for modeling and analyzing dynamic systems.

4.4.1Hidden Markov models

Hidden Markov Models (HMMs) are a type of probabilistic graphical model widely used for modeling systems with hidden or unobservable states. HMMs have applications in a variety of fields, including speech recognition, natural language processing, bioinformatics, finance, and more. The power of HMMs lies in their ability to model both observed data (emissions) and the underlying, hidden structure (states) that generates the data.
Key Components of Hidden Markov Models
States (Hidden Variables): HMMs consist of a finite set of hidden states, each representing a distinct configuration of the system. The hidden states are not directly observable; hence, the term "hidden."
Observations (Emissions): At each time step, the system emits an observable symbol based on the underlying hidden state. These emitted symbols constitute the observations or data sequence.
State Transition Probabilities: HMMs are characterized by state transition probabilities. These probabilities represent the likelihood of transitioning from one hidden state to another over time.
Emission Probabilities: Each hidden state is associated with a probability distribution over the observable symbols. These emission probabilities describe the likelihood of emitting each symbol given the hidden state.
Initial State Distribution: HMMs also have an initial state distribution, representing the probabilities of starting in each hidden state at the beginning of the sequence.
Three Fundamental Problems with HMMs
Evaluation (Forward Algorithm): Given an HMM and an observed sequence, the evaluation problem involves computing the probability of observing the given sequence, given the model parameters. The forward algorithm is commonly used to solve this problem efficiently.
Decoding (Viterbi Algorithm): The decoding problem aims to find the most likely sequence of hidden states that generated the observed sequence. The Viterbi algorithm is a dynamic programming approach used to find the optimal sequence efficiently.
Learning (Baum-Welch Algorithm): The learning problem involves estimating the model parameters (transition probabilities, emission probabilities, and initial state distribution) from the observed data. The Baum-Welch algorithm, which is a form of Expectation-Maximization (EM) algorithm, is used for this purpose.
Applications of Hidden Markov Models
Speech Recognition: HMMs have been foundational in speech recognition systems, where they model the sequence of phonemes that generate the observed speech signal.
Part-of-Speech Tagging: HMMs are used in natural language processing tasks like part-of-speech tagging, where they model the underlying sequence of grammatical categories that generate the observed words.
Bioinformatics: HMMs are employed in bioinformatics to identify genes, functional motifs, and protein families within DNA or protein sequences.
Finance: In finance, HMMs are applied to model stock prices, interest rates, and other financial time series data.
Conclusion
Hidden Markov Models provide a powerful framework for modeling and analyzing systems with hidden structures. Their ability to capture dependencies between hidden states and observations makes them valuable in various real-world applications. While simple in concept, HMMs form the basis for more sophisticated models like Conditional Random Fields (CRFs) and are essential tools for understanding sequential data with hidden information. As data and computing power continue to grow, HMMs are expected to remain a fundamental building block in the field of probabilistic modeling and pattern recognition.

Undirected graphical models, also known as Markov Random Fields (MRFs), are a class of probabilistic graphical models used to represent complex systems with pairwise dependencies between variables. One classic example of an undirected graphical model is the Ising Model, which has applications in physics, statistical mechanics, and image processing.

The Ising Model was first introduced by Ernst Ising in 1925 as a mathematical model for understanding magnetic properties in solid materials. It describes a lattice of magnetic spins, where each spin can be in one of two states, either "up" or "down," representing thc orientation of the magnetic moment.

In the Ising Model, each spin interacts only with its nearest neighbors. The interaction between adjacent spins is modeled by an energy term that favors alignment of neighboring spins. The energy function in the Ising Model is given by:

$E = -J * \Sigma(si * sj)$

Where:

E is the energy of the configuration.

J is the coupling constant representing the strength of the interaction between neighboring spins.

si and sj are the states of neighboring spins, either +1 (up) or -1 (down).

The probability of a particular spin configuration is determined by the Boltzmann distribution:

$P(s) = (1/Z) * \exp(-\beta * E(s))$

Where:

P(s) is the probability of the spin configuration s.

Z is the partition function, a normalization constant.

$\beta = 1/(k * T)$ is the inverse temperature, with k being the Boltzmann constant and T being the temperature.

The Ising Model exhibits interesting phase transitions as the temperature changes. At high temperatures, spins tend to be randomly oriented, resulting in a disordered phase. As the temperature decreases, there is a critical point where the system undergoes a phase transition, and long-range order emerges, with spins aligning in clusters. This phase transition behavior is analogous to the process of magnetic materials transitioning from a paramagnetic to a ferromagnetic state.

The Ising Model has been extended and adapted for various applications, including image denoising, texture synthesis, and image segmentation in image processing and computer vision. Its simplicity and ability to capture spatial dependencies between neighboring elements make it a valuable tool for modeling complex systems with pairwise interactions.

4.5Undirected graphical models

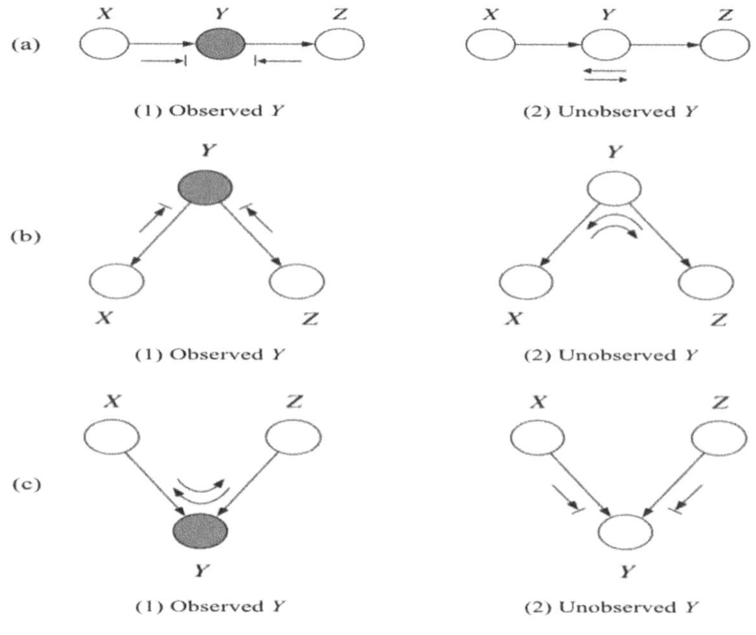

Examples of three basic directed graphical structures are shown below.

1. In (a) and (b), the shaded Y node blocks the ball from going between nodes X and Z. This gives the independence relation that was introduced in the last lecture: $X \perp Z \mid Y$.

2. (c), also called the "V-structure", is a special case. Opposite from the first two exmaples, the ball can go between X and Z if the node Y is shaded, and is blocked otherwise. Therefore, the graph on the right yields $X \perp Z$.

With these basic structures, we can apply the rules on a DAG. For example, let us try to find whether X_2 and X_3 are independent given X_1 and X_6.

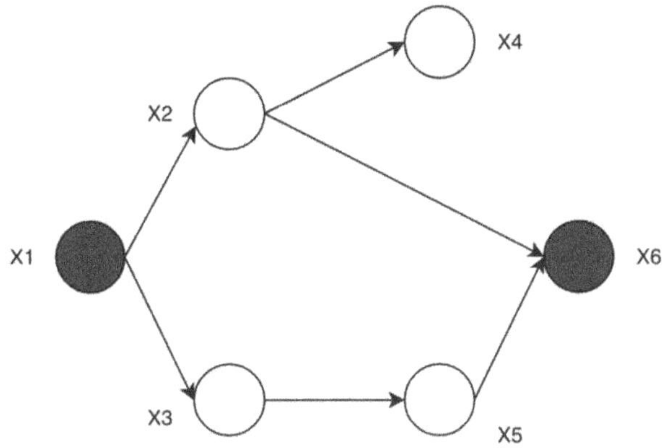

After shading X_1 and X_6, the ball cannot go from X_2 to X_3 through X_1 because it is blocked; however, X_2, X_6, and X_5 forms a "V-structure", so the ball can go along the path X_2, X_6, X_5, X_3. Therefore, the independence statement is invalid.

Limits of Directed and Undirected GMs

From a representational perspective, we aim to find a graph $\mathcal{G}$ that precisely captures the independencies in a given distribution P. This goal of learning GMs motivates the following definition.

Perfect Maps

We say that a graph $\mathcal{G}$ is a **perfect map (P-map)** for a set of independencies $\mathcal{I}$ if $\mathcal{I}(\mathcal{G}) = \mathcal{I}$. We say that $\mathcal{G}$ is a perfect map for P if $\mathcal{I}(\mathcal{G}) = \mathcal{I}(P)$. That is, $\text{sep}_{\mathcal{G}}(X;Z \vert Y) \iff P \models (X \perp Z \vert Y)$.

1. The P-map of a distribution is unique up to I-equivalence between networks. That is, a distribution P can have many P-maps, but all of them are I-equivalent.

Arbitrary distribution P's, however, do not necessarily attain perfect maps as either undirected or directed GMs. Two such examples are shown below.

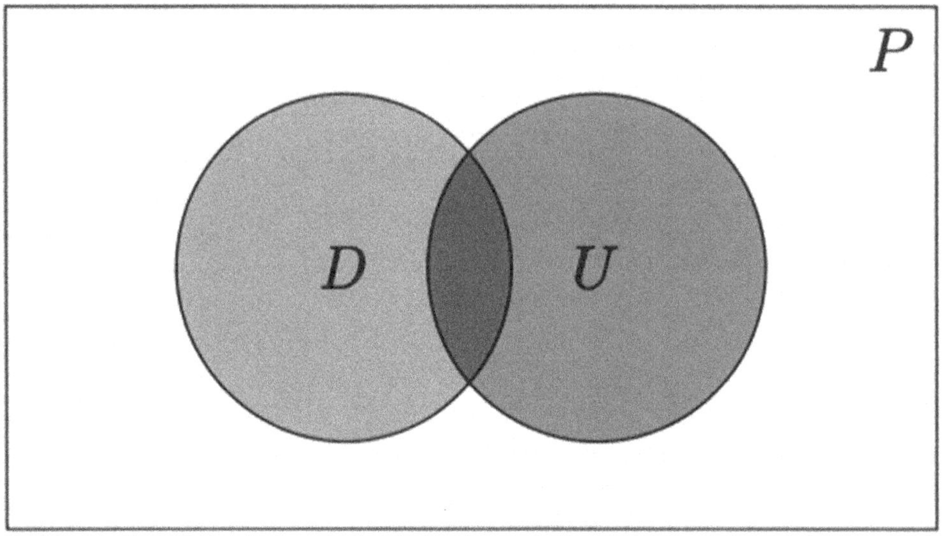

A Venn diagram illustration of graphical model families, where D is the family of directed GMs, and U the family of undirected GMs.

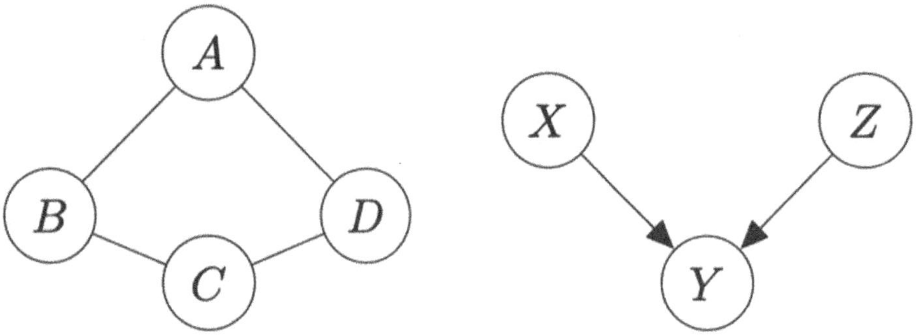

Left: A distribution with no possible DGM representation, which entails $A\perp C\vert \{B,D\}$ and $B\perp D\vert \{A,C\}$. **Right**: The v-structure is a distribution with no UGM representation.

Undirected Graphical Models –

Overview

1. There can only be symmetric relationships between a pair of nodes (random variables). In other words, there is no causal effect from one random variable to another.

2. The model can represent properties and configurations of a distribution, but it cannot generate samples explicitly.

3. Each node has strong correlations with its neighbors.

Example

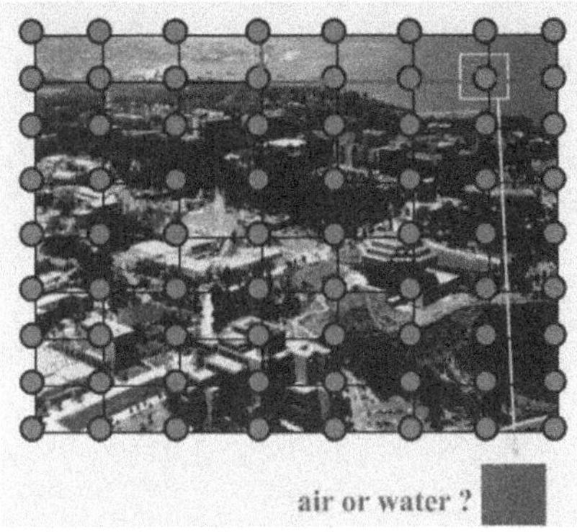

Let each node represents an image patch. It is impossible to tell what is inside this image patch by isolating it from others. However, when we look at its neighboring image patches, we can see that it's an image patch of water. Due to the fact that the relationships between neighboring image patches should be symmetric, an image is best represented by an undirected graphical model. This particular undirected graphical model is also known as the grid model.

Quantitative Specification

Cliques

1. Cliques are subgraphs that are fully connected.

2. A maximal clique is a clique such that any superset (any bigger subgraph that contains this subgraph) is not a complete graph.

3. A sub-clique is a not-necessarily-maximal clique.

EXAMPLE

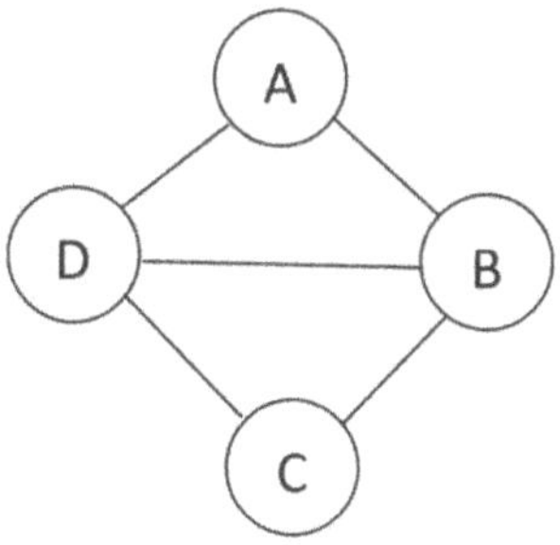

Graph

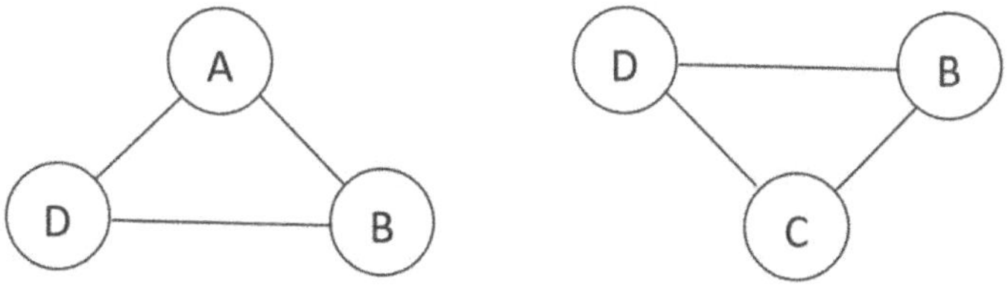

Max Cliques

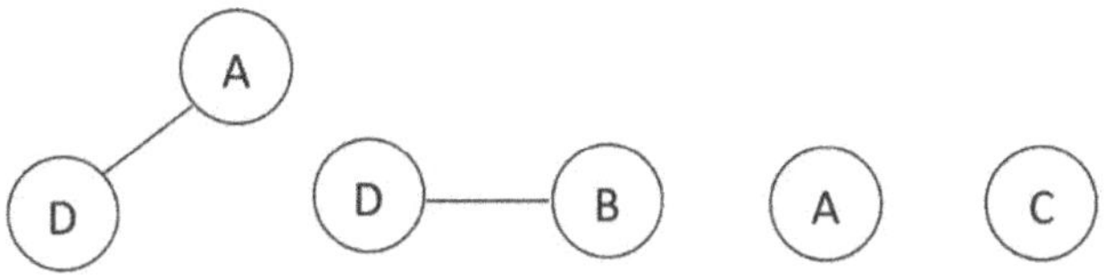

Sub Cliques (Edges and singletons are also sub-cliques)

Potential Functions

Each clique can be associated with a **potential function** \(\psi\), which can be understood as a provisional function of its arguments that assigns a pre-probabilistic score of their joint distribution. This potential function can be somewhat arbitrary, but must be non-negative.

Why cliques? Each component of the clique contributes to the overall potential function.

EXAMPLE

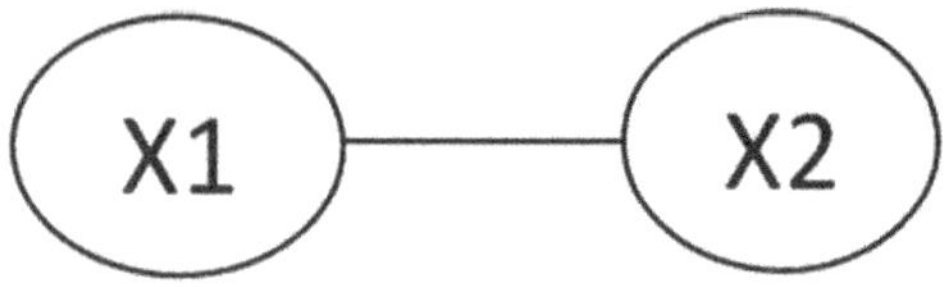

An example used to illustrate potential functions. Both X1 and X2 are binary.

For \(\psi_c(X_1, X_2)\),

X1	X2	
1	1	10
1	0	1
0	1	1
0	0	0.1

This table represents the potential function values given combinations of random variable inputs.

Potential functions are not necessarily probabilistic:

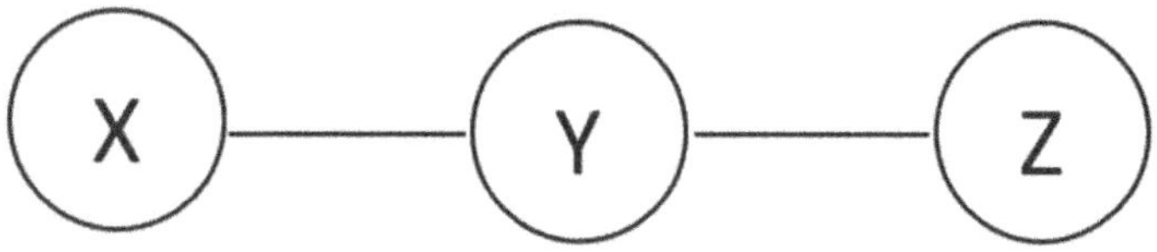

Another example used to illustrate potential functions.

This model implies that \(X \perp Z | Y\). This independence statement implies (by definition) that the joint must factorize as:

$p(x,y,z)=p(y)p(x|y)p(z|y)$

$=p(x,y)p(z|y)$

$=p(x|y)p(y,z)$

Probability distributions can be used as potential functions. However, in this case, we cannot let all potentials be either marginal probabilities or conditional probabilities. So the potential function for this graph cannot be probability distributions.

Gibbs Distribution and Undirected Graphical Model Definition

Given an undirected graph \(H\) and clique potentials functions \(\psi_C\) associated with cliques of \(H\), we say \(P(X_1, ..., X_n)\) is a **Gibbs distribution** over \(H\) if it can be represented as
\[P(X_1, ..., X_n)=\frac{1}{Z}\prod_{c\in C}{\psi_c(\bold{x_c})}\]
where \(Z\) is also known as the partition function. Upper case \(C\) denotes the set of all cliques, and lower case \(c\) denotes a clique associated with a set of random variables \(\bold{x}\)

An **undirected graphical model** represents a distribution \(P(X_1, ..., X_n)\) defined by an undirected graph \(H\), a set of positive potential functions \(\psi_C\) and the associated cliques of \(H\), such that

$$P(X1,...,Xn)=\frac{1}{z}\prod_{c\in C}\psi c(\chi_c)$$

$$Z=\sum_{x_1...x_n}\prod_{c\in C}\psi c(x_c)$$

Note that this distribution is the Gibbs distribution. Example UGM Models

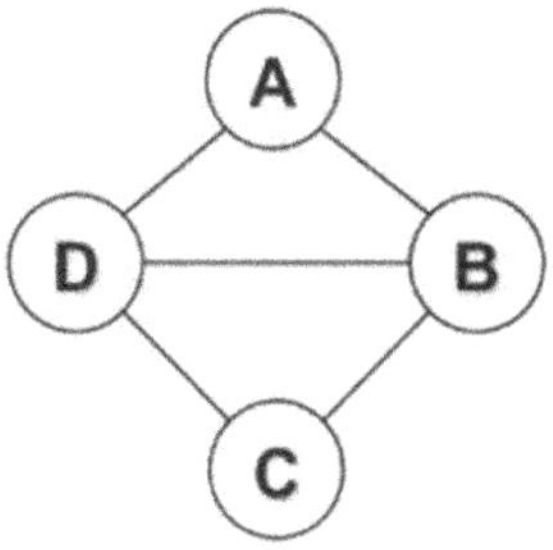

An example graph used to illustrate UGM.

USING MAX CLIQUES

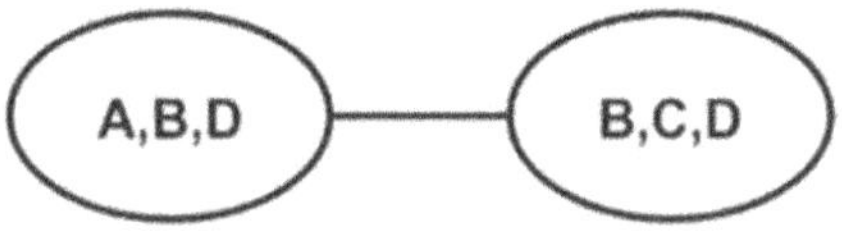

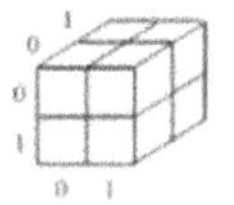

$P'(A,B,C,D)=\frac{1}{z}\psi\, c(A,B,D)\psi c(B,C,D)$

$Z=\sum_{A,B,C,D}\psi\, c(A,B,D)\psi c(B,C,D)$

We only need to represent discrete nodes with two 3D tables instead of one 4D table.

USING PAIRWISE CLIQUES

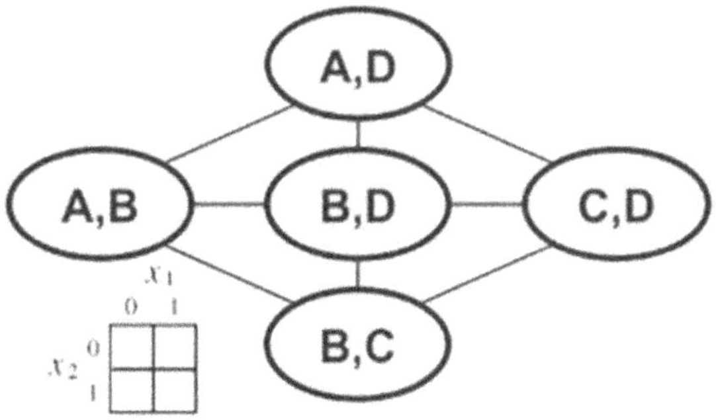

$P''(A,B,C,D)=\frac{1}{Z}\psi c(A,B)\psi c(A,D)\psi c(B,C)\psi c(B,D)\psi c(C,D)$

$Z=\sum_{A,B,C,D}\psi c(A,B)\psi c(A,D)\psi c(B,C)\psi c(B,D)\psi c(C,D)$

We only need to represent discrete nodes with five 2D tables instead of one 4D table.

USING CANONICAL REPRESENTATION

Even if we use fine-grained representation, the Markov network is often overparameterized. For any given distribution, there are multiple choices of parameters to describe in the model. As shown above, we can either choose max cliques or pairwise cliques to represent this model. Furthermore, ambiguities can arise in clique structures. For example, given a pair of cliques \(\{A, B\}\) and \(\{B, C\}\), the information about \(B\) can be placed in either of the two cliques, resulting in many ways to specify the samme distribution.

The canonical representation provides a natural approach to avoid this problem. It is defined over all non-empty cliques as shown below. [2] The formula performs an inclusion-exclusion computation to make sure that each random variable contributes exactly once to the overall function.

$$\begin{aligned}P'''(A,B,C,D)=&\frac{1}{Z}\psi c(A,B,D)\psi c(B,C,D)\\&\times\psi c(A,B)\psi c(A,D)\psi c(B,C)\psi c(B,D)\psi c(C,D)\\&\times\psi c(A)\psi c(B)\psi c(C)\psi c(D)\end{aligned}$$

$$Z=\sum_{A,B,C,D}\psi c(A,B,D)\psi c(B,C,D)$$

×ψc(A,B)ψc(A,D)ψc(B,C)ψc(B,D)ψc(C,D)
×ψc(A)ψc(B)ψc(C)ψc(D)

Qualitative Specification

Global Markov Independency

Suppose we are given the following UGM, denoted by H:

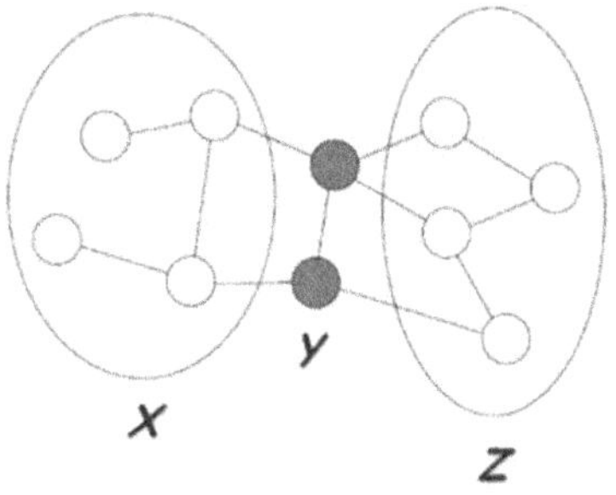

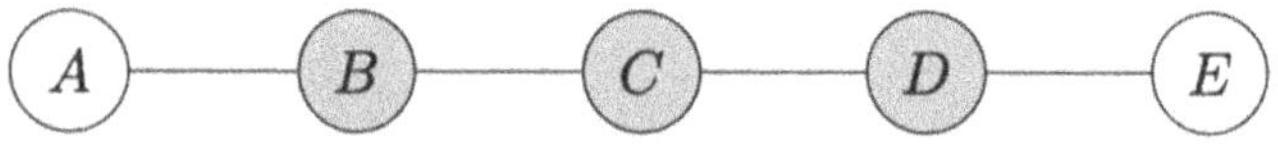

Example of pairwise independence

To illustrate this idea, observe that in the figure above, the variables of interests, A and E, are conditionally independent given all other nodes in the graph, $\{B,C,D\}$.

Pairwise and local indepdencies are also related. Their relationships are described in the following propositions and theorem.

Proposition

1. For any Markov network $\mathcal{G}$ and any distribution P, we have that if $P\models \mathcal{I}_l(\mathcal{G})$ then $P\models \mathcal{I}_P(\mathcal{G})$.

2. For any Markov network $\mathcal{G}$ and any distribution P, we have that if $P\models \mathcal{I}(\mathcal{G})$ then $P\models \mathcal{I}_l(\mathcal{G})$.

3. Let P be a positive distribution. If P satisfies $\mathcal{I}_P(\mathcal{G})$, then P satisfies $\mathcal{I}(\mathcal{G})$.

Theorem

The followings are equivalent for a positive distribution P:

\(P\MODELS \MATHCAL{I}_L(\MATHCAL{G})\)

\(P\MODELS \MATHCAL{I}_P(\MATHCAL{G})\)

\(P\MODELS \MATHCAL{I}(\MATHCAL{G})\)

Exponential Form

Since we don't want to constraint the clique potentials to be positive in all situations, exponential form is used to represent a clique potential $\phi_c(x_c)$ in an unconstrained form using a real-value "energy" funtion $\phi_c(x_c)$:

$$\Phi_c(x_c)=\exp\bigg\{-\phi_c(x_c)\bigg\}$$

This then gives the joint probability a nice additive structure

$$p(x)=\frac{1}{Z}\exp\bigg\{-\sum_{c\in C}\phi_c(x_c)\bigg\}=\frac{1}{Z}\exp\bigg\{-H(x)\bigg\}$$

where the sum in the exponent is called the "free energy":

$$H(x) = \sum_{c\in C}\phi_c(x_c)$$

This form of representation is called the "Boltzmann distribution" in physics, and a log-linear model in statstics.

Undirected Graph Exmples

In this section, we cover several well-known undirected graphical models: Boltzmann Machine (BM), Ising model, Restricted Boltzmann Machine (RBM), and Conditional Random Field (CRF).

Boltzmann Machine (BM)

Boltzmann Machine is a fully connected graph with pairwise (edge) potentials on binary-valued nodes. One example is shown in the following figure:

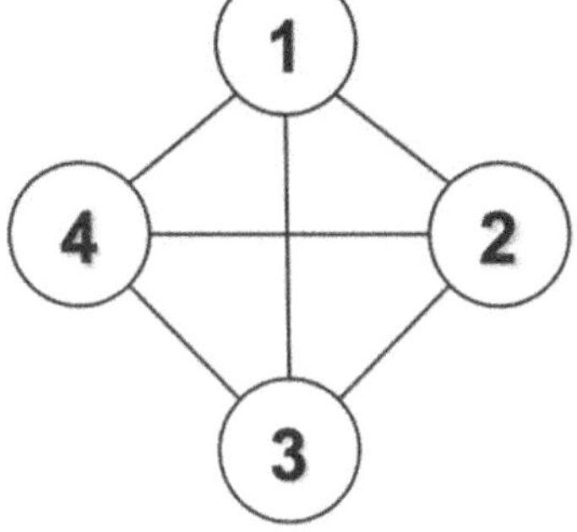

Its probability distribution can be written as:

$$p(x_1,x_2,x_3,x_4)=\frac{1}{Z}\exp\bigg\{\sum_{ij}\phi_{ij}(x_i,x_j)\bigg\}$$

It could also be written in a quadratic way:

$$p(x_1,x_2,x_3,x_4)=\frac{1}{Z}\exp\bigg\{\sum_{ij}\theta_{ij}x_ix_j+\sum_i\alpha_ix_i+C\bigg\}$$

Hence the overall free energy function has the form:

$$H(x)=\sum_{ij}(x_i-\mu)\Theta_{ij}(x_j-\mu)=(x-\mu)^T\Theta(x-\mu)$$

which can then be solved using quadratic programming.

Ising model

In the Ising model, nodes are arranged in a regular topology (often a regular packing grid) and connected only to their geometric neighbors. It is like a sparse Boltzmann Machine. There is also the multi-state Ising model (also called Potts model), in which nodes can take multiple values instead of just binary values. One example of Ising model is shown in the following figure:

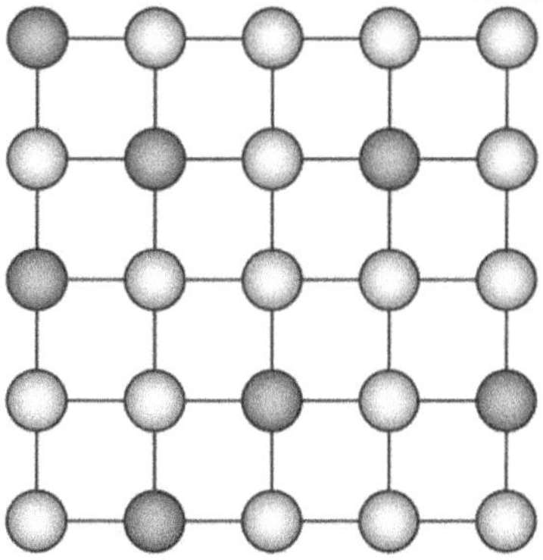

Its probability distribution can be written as

$$p(X)=\frac{1}{Z}\exp\bigg\{\sum_{i,j\in N_i}\theta_{ij}X_iX_j+\sum_i \theta_{i0}X_i\bigg\}$$

Restricted Boltzmann Machine (RBM)

The Restricted Bolzmann Machine is a bipartite graph with connections between one layer of hidden units and one layer of visible units. One example is shown in the following figure:

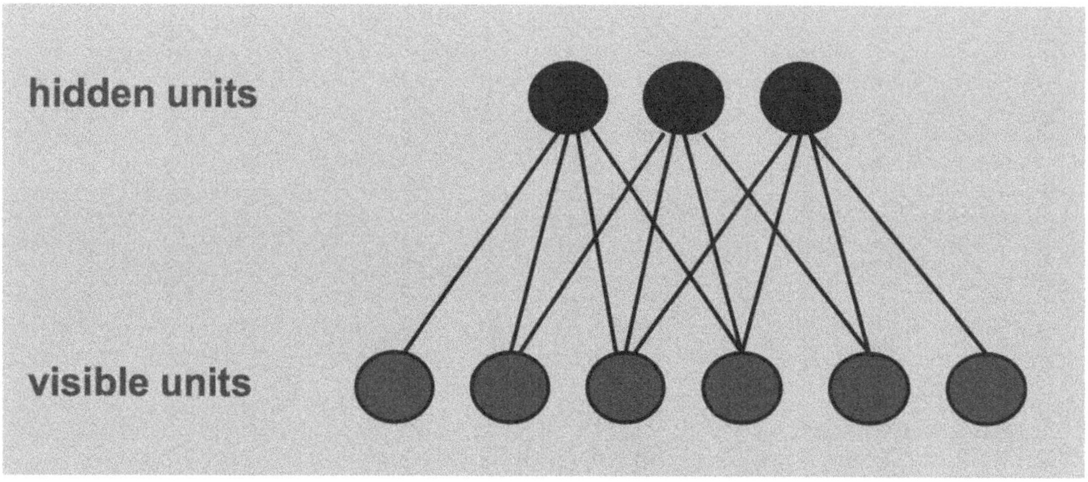

Its probability distribution can be written as

$$p(x,h|\theta)=\exp\bigg\{\sum_i\theta_i\phi_i(x_i)+\sum_j\theta_j\phi_j(h_j) + \sum_{i,j}\theta_{i,j}\phi_{i,j}(x_i,h_j)-A(\theta)\bigg\}$$

RBM has some appealing properties. For example, factors are marginally dependent and factors are conditionally independent given observations on the visible nodes. They enable one to use iterative Gibbs sampling for inference and learning on RBM. If the edges in RBM were directed, there would be plenty of V-structures in the graph (lots of dependences) that increase the inference difficulty.

Conditional Random Field (CRF)

Conditional random field is an analogous form of HMM in the undirected case. It allows arbitrary dependencies on the input. For example, when labeling X_i, future observations can be taken into account. An example of CRF is shown in the figure:

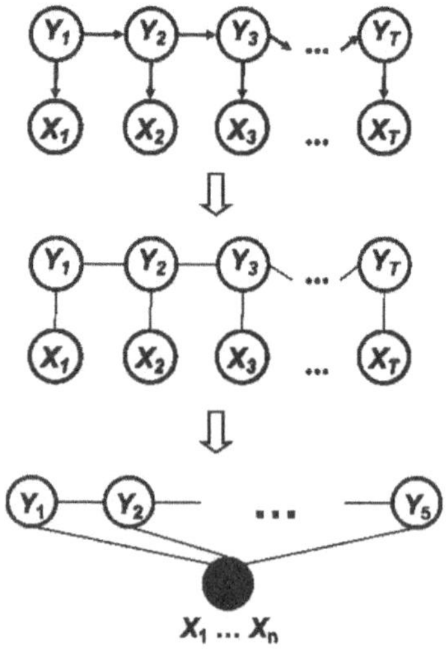

The probability distribution could be written as

$$p_\theta(y|x)=\frac{1}{Z(\theta,x)}\exp\bigg\{\sum_c\theta_cf_c(x,y_c)\bigg\}$$

4.6 Conditional independence

Free Probability Theory

D.-V. Voiculescu, in Encyclopedia of Mathematical Physics, 2006

Free Independence with Amalgamation over a Subalgebra

The classical notion of conditional independence also has a free counterpart based on the notion of free independence with amalgamation over a subalgebra. This subject is technically more complicated and we will only aim at giving an idea about what kind of concepts are involved.

In the classical context, if (x,$\sum$,u) is a probability space with a σ-algebra $\sum$, then the conditional independence with respect to a ó -subalgebra of events, $\Sigma_0 \subset \sum$, amounts to replacing in the definition of independence the expectation functional (which is the integral with respect to μ) by the conditional expectation

functional $L\infty(X,\sum,\mu) \xrightarrow{E} L\infty(X,\sum 0,\mu(\sum o))$.

In free probability, one considers an extension of the theory, from the (A,ϕ) framework to an A,Φ,B framework (Voiculescu 1995), where A is an algebra with unit over C,B∋1 is a subalgebra, and Φ:A→B is *B*–*B*-bilinear and $\Phi|B=id_g$. Then the definition of *B*-freeness (or free independence with amalgamation over *B*) of a family of subalgebras A $i_i \in 1, B \subset A_i \subset A$ requires that

$\Phi a_1 \ldots a_n = 0$

whenever $a_j \in Ai_j, \neq i_j + 1^1 \leq j \leq n$, and $\Phi a_j = 0$.

In the case of a unital *-algebra of bounded operators *M* with an expectation functional f(·)= ⟨·ξ,ξ⟩ which is tracial (i.e., $\mathcal{T} m_{1,m_2} = 0$ if „ $m_1 m_2 \in M$) and given a subalgebra 1∈N⊂M, as in the classical theory, there is a certain canonical construction in operator algebra theory of a "conditional expectation" $\Phi:\overline{M}\rightarrow\overline{N}$, where M,N are algebras of operators obtained as completion-separates from *M* and *N*. With this construction, in the trace-state setting there is complete analogy with the classical notion of conditional independence.

Several other constructions of free probability have been extended to the A,Φ,B *B*-valued context.

A group-theoretic example similar to Example 1 can be constructed from a group *G* which is a free product with amalgamation over a subgroup H ⊂ G of subgroups $H \subset G_i \subset G i \in I$. Then A is the algebra constructed from the left-regular representation of *G*, whereas *B* is an algebra constructed from the left-regular representation of *H*.

The local Gaussian partial correlation

Dag Tjøstheim, ... Bård Støve, in Statistical Modeling Using Local Gaussian Approximation, 2022

Estimation of *conditional* dependence and testing for *conditional* independence are important topics in classical and modern statistics. In the last two decades, for instance, there have been intense developments in using conditional dependence for probabilistic networks, multivariate time series analysis, and copula analysis. In this chapter, we extend the ideas ,regarding the measurement of dependence and testing for independence to their conditional counterparts, using a parallel motivation. For jointly Gaussian variables $X=(X_1,\ldots,X_P)^T$, the conditional dependence between some subset of variables X_1 and a second subset X_2 given a third subset X_3 is fully described by the *partial* correlation matrix. In general, for non-Gaussian populations, this will not suffice for the same reasons we have discussed before, and we will therefore introduce the *local* Gaussian partial correlation (LGPC), which serves as a general measure of conditional dependence and subsequently as a basis for a test for conditional independence.

The LGPC retains all the properties of the ordinary partial correlation in the Gaussian case but seeks to avoid the weaknesses of this measure in the non-Gaussian case. This is again done by fitting a family of Gaussian distributions to a given continuous multivariate distribution and exploiting simple conditioning rules of the Gaussian distribution locally in the same way as in Chapter . The LGPC, being directly related to the ordinary partial correlation, is easy to interpret and reduces to the very same ordinary partial correlation in the Gaussian case. Moreover, it distinguishes between positive and negative conditional dependence, whereas competing non-linear measures report only the *strength* of the conditional dependence on some non-negative scale. The local view again gives much more flexibility. It allows the conditional dependence to be stronger or weaker in certain regions of a multivariate distribution than in the others. This is of particular interest in finance, where description of tail behavior is important, and we will see practical examples of this. The bulk of this chapter is based on Otneim and Tjøstheim (2021), most of the technical details of which are presented in an online supplement of that paper.

The idea of identifying treatment effects through conditional independence has been extended to time-varying treatments. To keep the exposition simple, we only consider two periods $t = 0, 1$. As before, $D(t)$ is a binary variable that represents treatment during period *t*. The outcome of interest, *Y*, is measured after the second period. Potential outcomes are now indexed by the treatment in both periods. That is, $Y_i = Y_{d_0 d_1 i}$ if $D_i(0) = d_0$ and $D_i(1) = d_1$. In addition, let $X(t)$ represent a time-varying covariate. In this context, selection on observables can be defined in the following fashion:

$(Y_{00},Y_{01},Y_{10},Y_{11}) \perp\!\!\!\perp D(0)|X(0)$

$(Y_{00},Y_{01},Y_{10},Y_{11}) \perp\!\!\!\perp D(1)|X(0),X(1),D(0)$

That is, conditional on the present and past values of *X* and the past values of *D*, the treatment is independent of the potential outcomes. In other words, at every time *t*, the treatment assignment is "as good as random" conditional on the observed variables. Under this assumption it can be shown that:

$E[Y_{d_0 d_1}] = \iint E[Y|X(0),X(1),D(0)=d0,D(1)=d_1]$

$\times dP(x(1)|x(0),D(0)=d_0)dP(x(0))$

for d_0 and d_1 in {0, 1}. This formula is sometimes referred to as the G-formula or G-computation formula. In principle, average potential outcomes may be estimated nonparametrically based on the G-computation formula. Comparisons of average potential outcomes inform us about different treatment effects (e.g., the average effect of one additional period of treatment given treatment in the first period is $E[Y_{11} - Y_{10}]$). Based on these ideas, Robins has developed statistical models for characteristics of the marginal distributions of the potential outcomes (marginal structural models) and models for the effects of additional periods of treatment (structural nested models).

Computational Analysis and Understanding of Natural Languages: Principles, Methods and Applications

3 Conceptual Exercises

1.Let us have an arbitrary set of (conditional) independence relationships among N variables that is associated with a joint probability distribution.

(a)Can we always find a DAG that perfectly maps this set (perfectly maps = preserves all the (conditional) independence relationships, it neither removes nor adds any)?

(b)Can we always find an undirected graph that perfectly maps this set?

(c)Can directed acyclic models represent the conditional independence relationships of all possible undirected models?

(d)Can undirected models represent the conditional independence relationships of all possible directed acyclic models?

(e)Can we always find a directed acyclic model or an undirected model? (Scutari and Denis, 2015, collected by Jiri Klema)

2. Suppose our goal is inference for a parameter δ based on data that would ideally consist of n independent pairs (X, Y), but that some values of Y are missing, as shown by an indicator variable I. Thus the data on an individual have form $(x, y, 1)$ or $(x, ?, 0)$. We suppose that although the missing mechanism $Pr(I = 0|x, y)$ may depend on x and y, it does not involve δ. There are now three possibilities (Davison, 2003, Exercise: 6.2.10):

•data are missing completely at random, that is $Pr(I = 0|x, y) = Pr(I = 0)$ is independent of both x and y;

•data are missing at random, that is $Pr(I = 0|x, y) = Pr(I = 0|x)$ depends on x but not on y;

•there is nonignorable nonresponse, meaning that $Pr(I = 0|x, y)$ depends on y and possibly also on x.

Write down the DAG and its moral graph for X, Y, and I under the missing data models described above. Use them to give an equation-free explanation of the differences among the models and of their consequences.

3.Show that for a DAG, the local directed Markov property (DL) implies the ordered directed Markov property (DO) (course by Yu, 2010).

4.A language L has a four-character vocabulary $W = \{\delta, A, B, C\}$, where δ is the empty symbol. The probability that character w_i will be followed by w_j is given by the following matrix:

$P(w_j|w_i) =$

$w_i \mid w_j$	δ	A	B	C
δ	1/4	1/4	1/4	1/4
A	1/2	0	1/2	1/2
B	1/8	1/2	1/8	1/4
C	1/4	1/8	1/2	1/8

In transmitting messages from L, some characters may be corrupted by noise and be confused with others. The probability that the transmitted character w_j will be interpreted as w_k is given by the following confusion matrix:

$P(w_j|w_i) =$

$w_j \mid w_k$	δ	A	B	C
δ	0.9	0.1	0	0
A	0.1	0.8	0.1	0
B	0	0.1	0.8	0.1
C	0	0.1	0.1	0.8

The string, δ, δ, B, C, A, δ, δ is received, and it is known that the transmitted string begins and ends with δ. Then,
(a)Find the probability that the *i*-th transmitted symbol is *B*, for $i = 1, 2, \ldots, 7$.
(b)Find the probability that the string transmitted is the one received.
(c)Find the probability that no message (a string of δs) was transmitted.
(d)Find the message most likely to have been transmitted.
(e)Find the most likely seven-symbol string in *L* that starts and ends with δ (course by Yu, 2010).

5. Let us have three tram lines ——7, 17, and 21—regularly coming to the stop in front of the faculty building. Line 17 operates more frequently than line 21, 21 goes more often than line 7 (the ratio is 5:3:2, it is kept during all the hours of operation). Line 7 uses a single car setting in 9 out of 10 cases during the daytime, in the evening it always has the only car. Line 17 has one car rarely and only in evenings (1 out of 10 tram cars). Line 21 can be short whenever, however, it takes a long setting with 2 cars in 8 out of 10 cases. Albertov is available by line 21, lines 7 and 17 are headed in the direction of IP Pavlova. The line changes appear only when a tram goes to depot (let 21 have its depot in the direction of IP Pavlova, 7 and 17 have their depots in the direction of Albertov). Every 10th tram goes to the depot evenly throughout the operation. The evening regime is from 5 pm to 22 pm, the daytime regime is from 5.30 am to 6.30 pm. Then,
(a)Draw a correct, efficient, and causal BN.
(b)is evening. A short tram is approaching the stop. What is the probability it will go to Pavlova?
(c)There is a tram 17 standing in the stop. How many cars does it have?
Causal Reasoning
Comparison to Naïve Bayes
The Gaussian Naïve Bayes classifier, or what is usually just called Naïve Bayes, is a wonderfully simple approach that often returns very accurate and stable models with very small sample sizes. The reason that Naïve Bayes often works so well is that it simplifies predictive modeling problems to avoid the curse of dimensionality. The basic assumption in Naïve Bayes is one of conditional independence between all independent variable features. Conditional independence ensures that how one feature affects an outcome in no way interacts with how another variable affects the same outcome. Thus, if we know that warm weather improves our sales process, then this weather effect is conditionally independent from the age of our customers if this weather effect does not increase or decrease if the customer is younger or older. While an assumption of conditional independence effectively excludes the possibility of interaction effects, often interaction effects are entirely absent or extremely small, so they will not have an appreciable effect on predictive ability.
However, there are times when large interaction effects will be present. For example, it may be that older customers actually are more likely to buy our product on warm days, whereas younger customers are more likely to buy on cold days. Naïve Bayes will be completely blind to such an interaction effect. Beyond not seeing interactions, Naïve Bayes forces a rigid structure to the regression coefficients that force them to be proportional to Student's *t* values that measure the effect of the independent variable on the binary dependent variable outcome. This rigid proportionality does not allow flexibility to see regression coefficients that are not tied to this rigid proportionality. Naïve Bayes can be more accurate than standard logistic regression with very small samples, but all evidence suggests that standard logistic regression will outperform Naïve Bayes with large samples even when no interaction effects are present. The reason is that standard logistic regression is able to adjust its regression coefficients in ways that are not rigidly proportional to univariate *t* value effects.
Implicit RELR models have some similarity to Naïve Bayes in that their regression coefficients can be proportional to *t* values at very small samples with a large number of independent variables. Also, Explicit RELR models that select a large number of features in relatively small sample data will also have regression coefficients that may be proportional to *t* values. However, this rigid proportionality breaks down in Implicit and Explicit RELR models with

larger samples and with smaller numbers of selected features. Also, all RELR models can include interaction effects, and interaction effects often can improve the accuracy of RELR models. So like standard logistic regression, RELR is not subject to the rigid conditional independence assumptions of Naïve Bayes. This is an advantage.

Common Odds Ratio and the CMH Procedure

The complete independence log-linear model provides an unacceptably poor fit to **Table 4** ($G^2 = 624$ on 13 df), but the 'no second-order interaction' model, fits quite well ($G^2 = 0.009$ on 4 df). The absence of the three-way interaction means that the odds ratio between math drill and meets standard in each pretest subtable is independent of the pretest score. Therefore, in estimating this common odds ratio and testing independence between math drill and meet standard, we should pool data across pretest score groups to increase estimation precision and statistical power. However, as shown in **Table 4**, we cannot pool by simply summing cell counts across these groups.

Instead, we apply the CMH procedure, which provides both an estimate of the common odds ratio, and a chi-squared test of conditional independence of math drill and meets standard, given pretest score (i.e., a test of the null hypothesis that the common odds ratio equals 1). The CMH estimate of the common odds ratio pools the numerator and denominator separately

$$OR_{MH} = \frac{\sum_{k=1}^{k} n_{11} n_{22k}/n_{....k}}{\sum_{k=1}^{k} n_{12K} n_{21k}/n_{....k}}$$

where n_{ijk} is the observed count at level i of math drill, j of meets standard, and k of pretest score, and $n_{..k}$ is the number of students in pretest score group k. We compute confidence intervals for OR_{MH} using standard errors for $\log(OR_{MH})$ and a test for whether $OR_{MH} = 1$ by comparing the square of $\log(OR_{MH})$ divided by its standard error to values of the X^2 distribution on 1 df. (We can accomplish a similar test using a conditional likelihood-ratio test for the model [23][13] given the model, and the difference between the corresponding G^2 values. The CMH test for conditional independence is, however, the uniformly most powerful test (see Holland and Thayer, 1988).

Applying the CMH procedure to **Table 4**, we find strong evidence against the model of conditional independence of math drill with meeting standard given pretest score) is rejected ($X^2 = 18$ on 1 df), and we estimate the common odds ratio as 1.45, with 95% confidence interval (1.23, 1.72). There is a noticeable positive association between experiencing the math drills and meeting the standard on the post-test, for students in each pretest group.

Contingency Tables and Log-Linear Models

Higher Way Tables

The class of log-linear models just described for the three-way table generalizes in a direct fashion to four or more dimensions. As long as the log-linear models retain a hierarchical structure (e.g., setting a u term equal to zero implies that all of its higher order relatives must also be zero), the MSSs are sets of marginal totals of the full table, and the maximum-likelihood estimates (MLEs) are found by setting the MSSs equal to their expectations. Further, all independence or conditional independence relationships are representable as log-linear models, and these models have estimated expected values that can be computed directly. There is a somewhat larger class of log-linear models with this direct or decomposable representation. All log-linear models that are not decomposable require an iterative solution of likelihood equations.

In a multiway contingency table, the model that results from setting exactly one two-factor term (and all its higher order relatives) equal to zero is called a partial association model. For example, in four dimensions, setting $u_{12(ij)} = 0$ for all i and j, then the MSSs are $\{x_{i+kl}\}$ and $\{x_{+jkl},\}$, and the resulting partial association model corresponds to the conditional independence of variables 1 and 2 given 3 and 4. The corresponding MLEs for the expected cell frequencies are

$$\acute{m}_{ijk1} = \frac{x_{i+kl} x_{+jkl}}{x_{++kl}}$$

for all i, j, k, and l.

One of the major innovations in log-linear model methods over the past 20 years has been the development of methods associated with a subfamily of log-linear models known as graphical log-linear models. The formulation of graphical models is due originally to John Darroch, Steffen Lauritzen, and T. P. Speed. This approach uses the vertices of a graph to represent variables, and the edges among them to represent relationships. Conditional independence relationships correspond to the absence of edges in such an undirected graph. Models defined solely in terms of such relationships are said to be graphical. For categorical random variables, all graphical models are log-linear. The subfamily of graphical log- linear models includes the class of decomposable models, but not all nondecomposable models are graphical. Various authors have used graphical log-linear models to simplify approaches to model search, and they are intimately related to an extensive literature on collapsibility and estimability of parameters via marginal tables. Although the examples presented in this article have only two or three variables and contain few zero counts, the methods can and have been applied to a broad array of social science data involving as many as 20 dimensions, and where most of the counts are small and a large fraction are zero.

Conditional independence is a fundamental concept in Machine Learning and probabilistic modeling that describes the relationship between variables in a probabilistic model. It refers to the situation where two variables are independent of each other given the value of one or more other variables. Understanding conditional independence is essential for building efficient and interpretable models and making accurate predictions. Here's an explanation of conditional independence in Machine Learning:

Definition of Conditional Independence

Given three random variables A, B, and C, A and B are said to be conditionally independent given C (denoted as A ⊥ B | C) if the probability distribution of A and B is independent, given the value of C. Mathematically, this is expressed as:

P(A, B | C) = P(A | C) * P(B | C)

In simpler terms, A and B are conditionally independent if knowing the value of C does not provide any additional information about the relationship between A and B.

Importance in Machine Learning

Efficient Model Representation: Conditional independence allows us to simplify the representation of complex probability distributions by breaking them down into smaller, more manageable parts. This simplification can significantly reduce the number of parameters and computations required in a model.

Interpretability: Conditional independence relationships help to reveal the causal or influencing relationships between variables, making models more interpretable and aiding in understanding the underlying data-generating process.

Feature Selection: In feature selection, identifying conditional independence relationships between features can guide the selection of relevant and informative variables, leading to more efficient and accurate models.

Graphical Models: Graphical models, such as Bayesian networks and Markov networks, use conditional independence to represent complex probabilistic dependencies between variables in a visually interpretable manner.

Probabilistic Inference: In probabilistic inference tasks, such as belief propagation or Gibbs sampling, exploiting conditional independence relationships can significantly speed up computations and reduce the complexity of the inference process.

Conditional Independence Testing

In practice, determining conditional independence relationships from data can be challenging, especially when dealing with high-dimensional and complex datasets. Various statistical tests and algorithms exist to assess conditional independence. Some common methods include:

Pearson's Chi-squared test: Used to test independence between categorical variables.

Correlation and Mutual Information: Measures of association between variables to assess their dependency.

Independence-based algorithms: Such as the PC algorithm for learning the structure of Bayesian networks from data, or the Chow-Liu algorithm for building tree-structured Markov networks.

In summary, conditional independence is a crucial concept in Machine Learning that allows us to simplify complex models, improve interpretability, and identify relevant features. Understanding conditional independence relationships between variables is essential for building effective and efficient Machine Learning models.

Exercise

True Or False

1.Directed Graphical Models can represent causal relationships between variables.

2.In a Directed Graphical Model, if Node A is not a parent of Node B, then Node A is conditionally independent of Node B.

3.Markov Random Fields can model only linear relationships between variables.

4.In a Markov Random Field, the absence of an edge between two nodes implies conditional independence between those nodes.
5.Naive Bayes Classifiers assume that features are conditionally independent given the class variable.
6.Naive Bayes Classifiers are not suitable for text classification tasks.
7.Markov Models assume that the future state of a system depends only on its current state and not on the sequence of states leading up to it.
8.Hidden Markov Models are used for modeling situations where the underlying states are directly observable.
9.Undirected Graphical Models are also known as Bayesian Networks.
10.In an Undirected Graphical Model, the presence of an edge between two nodes implies direct causation between those nodes.
11.Conditional independence means that two variables are independent of each other regardless of the values of other variables.
True, True, False, True, True, False, True, False, False, False,False

MCQ

1.Directed Graphical Models represent dependencies between variables using:
a) Undirected edges
b) Bidirectional edges
c) Directed edges
d) No edges
Answer: c) Directed edges

2.In a Directed Graphical Model, an edge from Node A to Node B indicates:
a) Node A is conditionally independent of Node B
b) Node A is unconditionally independent of Node B
c) Node B is conditionally independent of Node A
d) Node B is unconditionally independent of Node A
Answer: a) Node A is conditionally independent of Node B

3. Markov Random Fields (MRFs) are used to model:
a) Only directed dependencies
b) Only undirected dependencies
c) Both directed and undirected dependencies
d) None of the above
Answer: b) Only undirected dependencies

4.In a Markov Random Field, a clique refers to:
a) A set of nodes with directed edges between them
b) A set of nodes with undirected edges between them
c) A set of nodes without any edges between them
d) A set of nodes with both directed and undirected edges between them
Answer: b) A set of nodes with undirected edges between them

5. Naive Bayes classifiers assume that features are:
a) Conditionally dependent
b) Unconditionally dependent
c) Conditionally independent
d) Unconditionally independent
Answer: c) Conditionally independent

Short Question And Answers

Q1: What are Probabilistic Graphical Models (PGMs)?
Q2: What is the difference between Directed Graphical Models and Undirected Graphical Models?
Q3: What are the properties of Directed Graphical Models?
Q4: Give an example of a Directed Graphical Model.
Q5: What is a Markov Random Field (MRF)?
Q6: What are Naive Bayes Classifiers?
Q7: What are Markov Models?
Q8: What is a Hidden Markov Model (HMM)?
Q9: What are Undirected Graphical Models?
Q10: What is conditional independence in Probabilistic Graphical Models?
Q11: Explain the concept of Probabilistic Graphical Models and their importance in Machine Learning and artificial intelligence.
Q12: Compare and contrast Directed Graphical Models (Bayesian Networks) and Undirected Graphical Models (Markov Random Fields) in terms of their structures and applications.
Q13: Describe the properties of Directed Graphical Models, including the concept of parents, children, and conditional probabilities.
Q14: Provide an illustrative example of a Directed Graphical Model representing a real-world scenario.
Q15: Discuss the application of Markov Random Fields in image processing and computer vision tasks.
Q16: Explain the working principle of Naive Bayes Classifiers and their use in text classification problems.
Q17: Detail the concept of Markov Models and their applications in speech recognition and natural language processing.
Q18: Describe Hidden Markov Models (HMMs) and their role in modeling sequential data with hidden states.
Q19: Discuss the concept of Undirected Graphical Models and how they address the limitations of Directed Graphical Models in certain scenarios.
Q20: Explain the concept of conditional independence in Probabilistic Graphical Models and its significance in reducing computational complexity.
Q21: How do Probabilistic Graphical Models handle uncertainty and provide a compact representation of probabilistic relationships among variables?
Q22: Compare the modeling capabilities of Directed Graphical Models and Markov Random Fields, highlighting their strengths and weaknesses in different applications.
Q23: Provide real-world examples of applications where Naive Bayes Classifiers have shown high accuracy in predicting outcomes.
Q24: Discuss the role of Markov Models in predicting future events based on past observations in dynamic systems.
Q25: Explain the concept of Hidden Markov Models and how they can be used for speech recognition tasks.
Q26: Describe the working principle of Undirected Graphical Models and their use in image segmentation and object recognition.
Q27: Discuss the concept of conditional independence in Probabilistic Graphical Models and how it simplifies the modeling of complex systems.
Q28: Compare the advantages and limitations of Probabilistic Graphical Models with other Machine Learning algorithms, such as neural networks and decision trees.
Q29: How can Probabilistic Graphical Models be applied in healthcare, finance, and social network analysis?
Q30: Explain the process of learning the parameters of a Probabilistic Graphical Model from data and how this can be used for inference and prediction tasks.

Online Resources

Online Exam Papers
True/False Exam

Link

https://forms.gle/22jjG1ZjKs9kyWAXA

QR Code

YouTube Video Playlist Link

Chapter 4
Link
https://www.youtube.com/playlist?list=PLzlh_31VWEFpVQDTpixKob7GPKELIrzzo
QR Code

Chapter 5: Advanced learning

5.1 Basic Sampling Method

We know that statistical research helps in drawing several conclusions based on the requirement of the experts. This uses the data collected for a specific purpose. We can collect the data using various sampling methods in statistics. However, the type of sampling method is chosen based on the objective of the statistical research. The statistical research is of two forms:

- In the first form, each domain is studied, and the result can be obtained by computing the sum of all units.

- In the second form, only a unit in the field of the survey is taken. It represents the domain. The result of these samples extends to the domain. This type of study is known as the sample survey.

In this article, let us discuss the different sampling methods in research such as probability sampling and non-probability sampling methods and various methods involved in those two approaches in detail.

What are the sampling methods or Sampling Techniques?

In Statistics, the sampling method or sampling technique is the process of studying the population by gathering information and analyzing that data. It is the basis of the data where the sample space is enormous.

There are several different sampling techniques available, and they can be subdivided into two groups. All these methods of sampling may involve specifically targeting hard or approach to reach groups.

Types of Sampling Method

In Statistics, there are different sampling techniques available to get relevant results from the population. The two different types of sampling methods are:

- Probability Sampling

- Non-probability Sampling

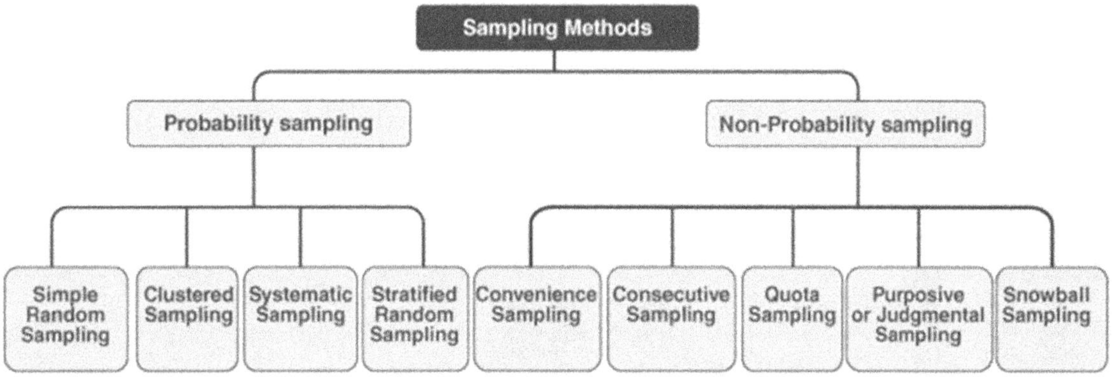

What is Probability Sampling?

The probability sampling method utilizes some form of random selection. In this method, all the eligible individuals have a chance of selecting the sample from the whole sample space. This method is more time consuming and expensive than the non-probability sampling method. The benefit of using probability sampling is that it guarantees the sample that should be the representative of the population.

Probability Sampling Types

Probability Sampling methods are further classified into different types, such as simple random sampling, systematic sampling, stratified sampling, and clustered sampling. Let us discuss the different types of probability sampling methods

1. Simple Random Sampling

In simple random sampling technique, every item in the population has an equal and likely chance of being selected in the sample. Since the item selection entirely depends on the chance, this method is known as "**Method of chance Selection**". As the sample size is large, and the item is chosen randomly, it is known as "**Representative Sampling**".

Example:

Suppose we want to select a simple random sample of 200 students from a school. Here, we can assign a number to every student in the school database from 1 to 500 and use a random number generator to select a sample of 200 numbers.

2. Systematic Sampling

In the systematic sampling method, the items are selected from the target population by selecting the random selection point and selecting the other methods after a fixed sample interval. It is calculated by dividing the total population size by the desired population size.

Example:

Suppose the names of 300 students at a school are sorted in the reverse alphabetical order. To select a sample in a systematic sampling method, we have to choose some 15 students by randomly selecting a starting number, say 5. From number 5 onwards, will select every 15th person from the sorted list. Finally, we can end up with a sample of some students.

3. Stratified Sampling

In a stratified sampling method, the total population is divided into smaller groups to complete the sampling process. The small group is formed based on a few characteristics in the population. After separating the population into a smaller group, the statisticians randomly select the sample.

For example, there are three bags (A, B and C), each with different balls. Bag A has 50 balls, bag B has 100 balls, and bag C has 200 balls. We have to choose a sample of balls from each bag proportionally. Suppose 5 balls from bag A, 10 balls from bag B and 20 balls from bag C.

4. Clustered Sampling

In the clustered sampling method, the cluster or group of people are formed from the population set. The group has similar significatory characteristics. Also, they have an equal chance of being a part of the sample. This method uses simple random sampling for the cluster of population.

Example:

An educational institution has ten branches across the country with almost the number of students. If we want to collect some data regarding facilities and other things, we can't travel to every unit to collect the required data. Hence, we can use random sampling to select three or four branches as clusters.

All these four methods can be understood in a better manner with the help of the figure given below

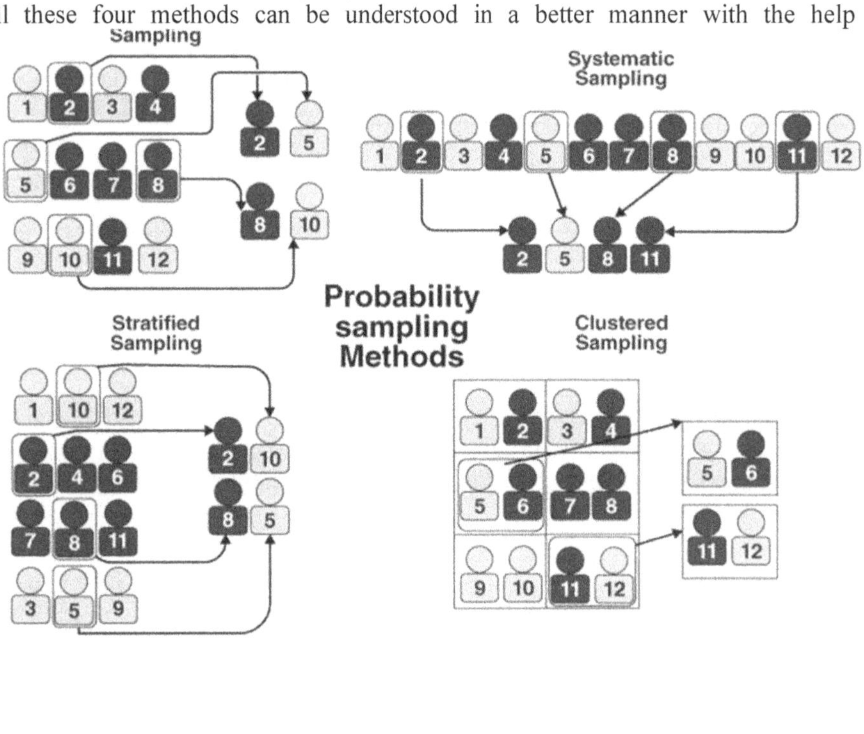

The figure contains various examples of how samples will be taken from the population using different techniques.

What is Non-Probability Sampling?

The non-probability sampling method is a technique in which the researcher selects the sample based on subjective judgment rather than the random selection. In this method, not all the members of the population have a chance to participate in the study.

Non-Probability Sampling Types

Non-probability Sampling methods are further classified into different types, such as convenience sampling, consecutive sampling, quota sampling, judgmental sampling, snowball sampling. Here, let us discuss all these types of non-probability sampling in detail.

1. Convenience Sampling

In a convenience sampling method, the samples are selected from the population directly because they are conveniently available for the researcher. The samples are easy to select, and the researcher did not choose the sample that outlines the entire population.

Example:

In researching customer support services in a particular region, we ask your few customers to complete a survey on the products after the purchase. This is a convenient way to collect data. Still, as we only surveyed customers taking the same product. At the same time, the sample is not representative of all the customers in that area.

Consecutive Sampling

Consecutive sampling is similar to convenience sampling with a slight variation. The researcher picks a single person or a group of people for sampling. Then the researcher research for a period of time to analyze the result and move to another group if needed.

2. Quota Sampling

In the quota sampling method, the researcher forms a sample that involves the individuals to represent the population based on specific traits or qualities. The researcher chooses the sample subsets that bring the useful collection of data that generalizes the entire population.

Purposive or Judgmental Sampling

In purposive sampling, the samples are selected only based on the researcher's knowledge. As their knowledge is instrumental in creating the samples, there are the chances of obtaining highly accurate answers with a minimum marginal error. It is also known as judgmental sampling or authoritative sampling.

3. Snowball Sampling

Snowball sampling is also known as a chain-referral sampling technique. In this method, the samples have traits that are difficult to find. So, each identified member of a population is asked to find the other sampling units. Those sampling units also belong to the same targeted population.

Probability sampling vs Non-probability Sampling Methods

below table shows a few differences between probability sampling methods and non-probability sampling methods.

Probability Sampling Methods	**Non-probability Sampling Methods**
1. Probability Sampling is a sampling technique in which samples taken from a larger population are chosen based on probability theory.	1. Non-probability sampling method is a technique in which the researcher chooses samples based on subjective judgment, preferably random selection.
2. These are also known as Random sampling methods.	2. These are also called non-random sampling methods.
3. These are used for research which is conclusive.	3. These are used for research which is exploratory.

4. These involve a long time to get the data.	4. These are easy ways to collect the data quickly.
5. There is an underlying hypothesis in probability sampling before the study starts. Also, the objective of this method is to validate the defined hypothesis.	5. The hypothesis is derived later by conducting the research study in the case of non-probability sampling.

5.2Reinforcement learning

Reinforcement learning (RL) is an area of Machine Learning concerned with how intelligent agents ought to take actions in an environment in order to maximize the notion of cumulative reward. Reinforcement learning is one of three basic Machine Learning paradigms, alongside supervised learning, and unsupervised learning.

Reinforcement learning differs from supervised learning in not needing labelled input/output pairs to be presented, and in not needing sub-optimal actions to be explicitly corrected. Instead the focus is on finding a balance between exploration (of uncharted territory) and exploitation (of current knowledge).[1]

The environment is typically stated in the form of a Markov decision process (MDP) because many reinforcement learning algorithms for this context use dynamic programming techniques. The main difference between the classical dynamic programming methods and reinforcement learning algorithms is that the latter do not assume knowledge of an exact mathematical model of the MDP, and they target large MDPs where exact methods become infeasible.

Introduction

Due to its generality, reinforcement learning is studied in many disciplines, such as game theory, control theory, operations research, information theory, simulation-based optimization, multi-agent systems, swarm intelligence, and statistics. In the operations research and control literature, reinforcement learning is called *approximate dynamic programming,* or *neuro-dynamic programming.* The problems of interest in reinforcement learning have also been studied in the theory of optimal control, which is concerned mostly with the existence and characterization of optimal solutions, and algorithms for their exact computation, and less with learning or approximation, particularly in the absence of a mathematical model of the environment. In economics and game theory, reinforcement learning may be used to explain how equilibrium may arise under bounded rationality. The purpose of reinforcement learning is for the agent to learn an optimal, or nearly optimal, policy that maximizes the "reward function" or other user-provided reinforcement signal that accumulates from the immediate rewards. This is similar to processes that appear to occur in animal psychology. For example, biological brains are hardwired to interpret signals such as pain and hunger as negative reinforcements and interpret pleasure and food intake as positive reinforcements. In some circumstances, animals can learn to engage in behaviors that optimize these rewards. This suggests that animals are capable of reinforcement learning. A basic A basic reinforcement learning agent AI interacts with its environment in discrete time steps. At each time *t*, the agent receives the current state and reward . It then chooses an action from the set of available actions, which is subsequently sent to the environment. The environment moves to a new state and the reward associated with the *transition* is determined. The goal of a reinforcement learning agent is to learn a *policy*: , which maximizes the expected cumulative reward.Formulating the problem as an MDP assumes the agent directly observes the current environmental state; in this case the problem is said to have *full observability*. If the agent only has access to a subset of states, or if the observed states are corrupted by noise, the agent is said to have *partial observability*, and formally the problem must be formulated as a Partially observable Markov decision process. In both cases, the set of actions available to the agent can be restricted. For xample, the state of an account balance could be restricted to be positive; if the current value of the state is 3 and the state transition attempts to reduce the value by 4, the transition will not be allowed.When the agent's performance is compared to that of an agent that acts optimally, the difference in performance gives rise to the notion of *regret*. In order to act near optimally, the agent must reason about the long-term consequences of its actions (i.e., maximize future income), although the immediate reward associated with this might be negative.Thus, reinforcement learning is particularly well-suited to problems that include a long-term versus short-term reward Two elements make reinforcement learning powerful: the use of samples to optimize performance and the use of function approximation to deal with large environments. Thanks to these two key components, reinforcement learning can be used in large environments in the following situations:

1. A model of the environment is known, but an analytic solution is not available.

2. Only a simulation model of the environment is given (the subject of simulation-based optimization);[9]

3. The only way to collect information about the environment is to interact with it.

The first two of these problems could be considered planning problems (since some form of model is available), while the last one could be considered to be a genuine learning problem. However, reinforcement learning converts both planning problems to Machine Learning problems.

Information Processing Analysis

Once a learning goal is established and a learning domain selected, the next step is conducting the information processing analysis. Smith and Ragan (2005) describe this process as discovering the mental and physical tasks to complete the learning goal. This process is iterative; meaning that it can be done multiple times and with different information. If new tasks or questions are discovered, include it in the next analysis for further refinement.

Smith and Ragan (2005) state ten steps to complete an information-processing analysis:

1. Read and gather as much information as possible about the task and content.

2. Convert goal into representative 'test" question.

3. Give problem to several individuals who understand the task and observe.

4. Ask individuals questions about completing the task.

5. If more than one individual used, identify commons steps.

6. Identify shortest, least complex path to achieve task.

7. Identify factors that can lead to more complex path.

8. Select the circumstances and path that best match your goal.

9. List steps and decision points for your goal

10. Confirm results with other experts (p. 84-85)

Example

The process listed above applies to all information processing analysis. There are specific methods to employ depending on the learning domain of your goal.

Prerequisite Analysis

Learning prerequisite analysis includes applying rules, concepts, solving problems and intellectual skills as prerequisite skills that facilitate learning of a higher skill. The analysis is often used for traditional instruction to describe learning levels before beginning a lesson and to define what must be taught, and the sequence in which to teach it. Each task has sub tasks in this process in order to reach the objectives in both simple and complex tasks.

Let's use a previous learning goal from above: When provided movie information, the learner will be able to classify the movie into a specific genre. An information process analysis example of an action movie showed that the learner had to decide three major criteria: pacing stunt, and plot information. So, a leaner must know specifics in order to make an informed judgement. This can be done in either a bulleted list with sub bullets or a graphics (similar to information processing analysis). The example listed below uses bullets for the first two steps.

The first step in the in-information analysis example: Recall characteristics of an action movie

The prerequisite analysis would be:

1. Know what a characteristic in cinema terms.

2. Know what action is considered in cinema terms.

3. Know what a movie is considered in cinema terms.

The next step was determining if the movie was fast paced.

The prerequisite analysis would be:

1. Know pacing structure of a movie.

2. Know pacing synonyms.

3. Know what a plot is.

4. Define elements of a plot

5. Know what a slow-paced structure looks like

Once the prerequisite analysis is complete, the knowledge required are turned into **enabling objectives**. This type of objective sets additional knowledge or skills that are required into order to reach the **terminal objective.** A Terminal objective is a more defined version of the learning goal. Both types of objectives follow the format outlined below.

5.3 The learning objective

A learning objective is a description of an optimal performance learners are expected to be able to exhibit before they are considered competent in meeting the learning goal (Mager, 1962). Essentially, the goal describes the knowledge the learner is expected to obtain, while the objective describes how the learner will demonstrate that they have obtained that knowledge. Once learning goals are established, learning objectives that are directly associated with these specific outcomes should be built. Consider the following example of a misaligned learning outcome and learning objective proposed by Dick and Reiser (1989): "The learning goal is developing lifelong health habits and the associated learning objective is listing the major bones in the leg," (p. 23). Although both the outcome and the objective both fall under the content area of Health and the Human Body, the listing of the major bones in the leg would not be an appropriate performance to assess whether or not learners would be able to develop lifelong health habits.

Mager (1984) proposes that there are three elements of a quality learning objective: **performance**, **condition**, and **criterion**. The performance is what the learner is expected to do or the result of the instruction. The condition describes the circumstances in which the performance should occur. The criterion establishes the minimum threshold of acceptable performance. Furthermore, an objective should clearly express an observable behavior that students are expected to perform in order to indicate achievement (Dick & Reiser, 1989). Orelove (1995), stated that when a goal includes the absence of performance on the part of a student it also lacks quality. For example, Johnny will sit quietly for 20 minutes or by the end of the course, students should know historically important dates in history (p. 4). Neither of these examples requires observable activity or quality performance on the part of the students. In addition, neither goal is measurable. According to Benjamin Bloom. objectives should be measurable and serve to help create a structure for hierarchically classifying the measurability of learning objectives (Bloom, Engelhart, Furst, and Krathwohl, 1956; Anderson and Krathwohl 2001).

A simple way to craft learning objectives is to use the Heinrich, Molenda, Russell, and Smaldino's (1996) ABCD format.

1. Audience

2. Behavior (Mager's performance element)

3. Condition (Mager's condition element)

4. Degree (Marger's criterion element)

Heibrich et al. (1996) uses Mager's (1984) three elements while adding the audience. The audience as being the learner. Sometimes, the generic term "learner" or "student" can be used. It is a best practice to be specific as possible (Heibrich et all, 1996). For example, a 12th grade history student or English Composition I students.

Learning objective written in the affective domain at valuing level of the Krathwohl and Bloom's Taxonomy of the Affective Domain.

Given a group project, the group members will seek input from everyone throughout the entire project.

Learning objective written in the psychomotor domain at the guided response level of Simpson's Taxonomy of the Psychomotor Domain

Given pizza ingredients, the employee will assemble a pizza in less than 10 minutes.

Terminal objective example

When provided a plot, pacing, and the frequency of stunts, the learner will be able to classify the movie into a specific genre within two attempts.

Enabling objective example
When given a movie scene, the learner will determine how many stunts occurred within two attempts.

5.3.1 Elements of reinforcement learning

Beyond the agent and the environment, one can identify four main sub elements of a reinforcement learning system: a *policy*, a *reward function*, a *value function*, and, optionally, a *model* of the environment.

A *policy* defines the learning agent's way of behaving at a given time. Roughly speaking, a policy is a mapping from perceived states of the environment to actions to be taken when in those states. It corresponds to what in psychology would be called a set of stimulus-response rules or associations. In some cases, the policy may be a simple function or lookup table, whereas in others it may involve extensive computation such as a search process. The policy is the core of a reinforcement learning agent in the sense that it alone is sufficient to determine behavior. In general, policies may be stochastic.

A *reward function* defines the goal in a reinforcement learning problem. Roughly speaking, it maps each perceived state (or state-action pair) of the environment to a single number, a *reward*, indicating the intrinsic desirability of that state. A reinforcement learning agent's sole objective is to maximize the total reward it receives in the long run. The reward function defines what are the good and bad events for the agent. In a biological system, it would not be inappropriate to identify rewards with pleasure and pain. They are the immediate and defining features of the problem faced by the agent. As such, the reward function must necessarily be unalterable by the agent. It may, however, serve as a basis for altering the policy. For example, if an action selected by the policy is followed by low reward, then the policy may be changed to select some other action in that situation in the future. In general, reward functions may be stochastic.

Whereas a reward function indicates what is good in an immediate sense, a *value function* specifies what is good in the long run. Roughly speaking, the *value* of a state is the total amount of reward an agent can expect to accumulate over the future, starting from that state. Whereas rewards determine the immediate, intrinsic desirability of environmental states, values indicate the *long-term* desirability of states after taking into account the states that are likely to follow, and the rewards available in those states. For example, a state might always yield a low immediate reward but still have a high value because it is regularly followed by other states that yield high rewards. Or the reverse could be true. To make a human analogy, rewards are like pleasure (if high) and pain (if low), whereas values correspond to a more refined and farsighted judgment of how pleased or displeased we are that our environment is in a particular state. Expressed this way, we hope it is clear that value functions formalize a basic and familiar idea. Rewards are in a sense primary, whereas values, as predictions of rewards, are secondary. Without rewards there could be no values, and the only purpose of estimating values is to achieve more reward. Nevertheless, it is values with which we are most concerned when making and evaluating decisions. Action choices are made based on value judgments. We seek actions that bring about states of highest value, not highest reward, because these actions obtain the greatest amount of reward for us over the long run. In decision-making and planning, the derived quantity called value is the one with which we are most concerned. Unfortunately, it is much harder to determine values than it is to determine rewards. Rewards are basically given directly by the environment, but values must be estimated and reestimated from the sequences of observations an agent makes over its entire lifetime. In fact, the most important component of almost all reinforcement learning algorithms is a method for efficiently estimating values. The central role of value estimation is arguably the most important thing we have learned about reinforcement learning over the last few decades.

Although all the reinforcement learning methods, we consider in this book are structured around estimating value functions, it is not strictly necessary to do this to solve reinforcement learning problems. For example, search methods such as genetic algorithms, genetic programming, simulated annealing, and other function optimization methods have been used to solve reinforcement learning problems. These methods search directly in the space of policies without ever appealing to value functions. We call these *evolutionary* methods because their operation is analogous to the way biological evolution produces organisms with skilled behavior even when they do not learn during their individual lifetimes. If the space of policies is sufficiently small or can be structured so that good policies are common or easy to find, then evolutionary methods can be effective. In addition, evolutionary methods have advantages on problems in which the learning agent cannot accurately sense the state of its environment.

Nevertheless, what we mean by reinforcement learning involves learning while interacting with the environment, which evolutionary methods do not do. It is our belief that methods able to take advantage of the details of individual behavioral interactions can be much more efficient than evolutionary methods in many cases. Evolutionary methods ignore much of the useful structure of the reinforcement learning problem: they do not use the fact that the policy they are searching for is a function from states to actions; they do not notice which states an individual passes through during its lifetime, or which actions it selects. In some cases, this information can be misleading (e.g., when states are misperceived), but more often it should enable more efficient search. Although evolution and learning share many features and can naturally work together, as they do in nature, we do not consider evolutionary methods by themselves to be especially well suited to reinforcement learning problems. For simplicity, in this book when we use the term "reinforcement learning" we do not include evolutionary methods.

The fourth and final element of some reinforcement learning systems is a *model* of the environment. This is something that mimics the behavior of the environment. For example, given a state and action, the model might predict the resultant next state and next reward. Models are used for *planning*, by which we mean any way of deciding on a course of action by considering possible future situations before they are actually experienced. The incorporation of models and planning into reinforcement learning systems is a relatively new development. Early reinforcement learning systems were explicitly trial-and-error learners; what they did was viewed as almost the *opposite* of planning. Nevertheless, it gradually became clear that reinforcement learning methods are closely related to dynamic programming methods, which do use models, and that they in turn are closely related to state-space planning methods. In previous chapters we explore reinforcement learning systems that simultaneously learn by trial and error, learn a model of the environment, and use the model for planning. Modern reinforcement learning spans the spectrum from low-level, trial-and-error learning to high-level, deliberative planning.

5.4 Computer Vision

If you were told to name certain things that you'd find in a park, you'd casually mention things like grass, bench, trees, etc. This is a very easy task that any person can accomplish in the blink of an eye. However, there is a very complicated process that takes place in the back of our minds.

Human vision involves our eyes, but it also involves all of our abstract understanding of concepts and personal experiences through millions of interactions we have had with the outside world. Until recently, computers had very limited abilities to think independently. Computer vision is a recent branch of technology that focuses on replicating this human vision to help computers identify and process things the same way humans do.

The field of computer vision has made significant progress toward becoming more pervasive in everyday life as a result of recent developments in areas like artificial intelligence and computing capabilities. It is anticipated that the market for computer vision will approach $41.11 billion by the year 2030, with a compound annual growth rate (CAGR) of 16.0% between the years 2020 and 2030.

What is Computer Vision?

Computer vision is one of the fields of artificial intelligence that trains and enables computers to understand the visual world. Computers can use digital images and deep learning models to accurately identify and classify objects and react to them.

Computer vision in AI is dedicated to the development of automated systems that can interpret visual data (such as photographs or motion pictures) in the same manner as people do. The idea behind computer vision is to instruct computers to interpret and comprehend images on a pixel-by-pixel basis. This is the foundation of the computer vision field. Regarding the technical side of things, computers will seek to extract visual data, manage it, and analyze the outcomes using sophisticated software programs.

The amount of data that we generate today is tremendous - 2.5 quintillion bytes of data every single day. This growth in data has proven to be one of the driving factors behind the growth of computer vision.

How Does Computer Vision Work?

Massive amounts of information are required for computer vision. Repeated data analyses are performed until the system can differentiate between objects and identify visuals. Deep learning, a specific kind of Machine Learning, and convolutional neural networks, an important form of a neural network, are the two key techniques that are used to achieve this goal.

With the help of pre-programmed algorithmic frameworks, a Machine Learning system may automatically learn about the interpretation of visual data. The model can learn to distinguish between similar pictures if it is given a large enough dataset. Algorithms make it possible for the system to learn on its own, so that it may replace human labor in tasks like image recognition.

Convolutional neural networks aid Machine Learning and deep learning models in understanding by dividing visuals into smaller sections that may be tagged. With the help of the tags, it performs convolutions and then leverages the tertiary function to make recommendations about the scene it is observing. With each cycle, the neural network performs convolutions and evaluates the veracity of its recommendations. And that's when it starts perceiving and identifying pictures like a human.

Computer vision is similar to solving a jigsaw puzzle in the real world. Imagine that you have all these jigsaw pieces together and you need to assemble them in order to form a real image. That is exactly how the neural networks inside

a computer vision work. Through a series of filtering and actions, computers can put all the parts of the image together and then think on their own. However, the computer is not just given a puzzle of an image - rather, it is often fed with thousands of images that train it to recognize certain objects.
For example, instead of training a computer to look for pointy ears, long tails, paws, and whiskers that make up a cat, software programmers upload and feed millions of images of cats to the computer. This enables the computer to understand the different features that make up a cat and recognize it instantly.

History

For almost 60 years, researchers and developers have sought to teach computers how to perceive and make sense of visual information. In 1959, neurophysiologists started showing a cat a variety of sights in an effort to correlate a reaction in the animal's brain. They found that it was particularly sensitive to sharp corners and lines, which technically indicates that straight lines and other basic forms are the foundation upon which image analysis is built. Around the same period, the first image-scanning technology emerged that enabled computers to scan images and obtain digital copies of them. This gave computers the ability to digitize and store images. In the 1960s, artificial intelligence (AI) emerged as an area of research, and the effort to address AI's inability to mimic human vision began.
Neuroscientists demonstrated in 1982 that vision operates hierarchically and presented techniques enabling computers to recognize edges, vertices, arcs, and other fundamental structures. At the same time, data scientists created a pattern-recognition network of cells. By the year 2000, researchers were concentrating their efforts on object identification, and by the following year, the industry saw the first-ever real-time face recognition solutions.

Deep Learning Revolution

Examining the algorithms upon which modern computer vision technology is based is essential to understanding its development. Deep learning is a kind of Machine Learning that modern computer vision utilizes to get data-based insights.
When it comes to computer vision, deep learning is the way to go. An algorithm known as a neural network is used. Patterns in the data are extracted using neural networks. Algorithms are based on our current knowledge of the brain's structure and operation, specifically the linkages between neurons within the cerebral cortex.
The perceptron, a mathematical model of a biological neuron, is the fundamental unit of a neural network. It is possible to have many layers of linked perceptrons, much like the layers of neurons in the biological cerebral cortex. As raw data is fed into the perceptron-generated network, it is gradually transformed into predictions.

How Long Does It Take to Decipher an Image

Extremely fast CPUs and associated technology, together with a swift, dependable internet and cloud-based infrastructures, make the entire process blistering fast nowadays. Importantly, several of the largest businesses investing in AI research, like Google, Facebook, Microsoft, and IIBM, have been upfront about their research and development in the field. In this way, people may build upon the foundation they've laid.
This has resulted in the AI sector heating up, and studies that used to take weeks to complete may now be completed in a few minutes. In addition, for many computer vision tasks in the actual world, this whole process takes place constantly in a matter of microseconds. As a result, a computer may currently achieve what researchers refer to as "circumstantially conscious" status.

Computer Vision Applications

One field of Machine Learning where fundamental ideas are already included in mainstream products is computer vision. The applications include:

1. Self-Driving Cars

With the use of computer vision, autonomous vehicles can understand their environment. Multiple cameras record the environment surrounding the vehicle, which is then sent into computer vision algorithms that analyzes the photos in perfect sync to locate road edges, decipher signposts, and see other vehicles, obstacles, and people. Then, the autonomous vehicle can navigate streets and highways on its own, swerve around obstructions, and get its passengers where they need to go safely.

2. Facial Recognition

Facial recognition programs, which use computer vision to recognize individuals in photographs, rely heavily on this field of study. Facial traits in photos are identified by computer vision algorithms, which then match those aspects to stored face profiles. In order to verify the identity of the people using consumer electronics, face recognition is increasingly being used. Facial recognition is used in social networking applications for both user detection and user tagging. For the same reason, law enforcement uses face recognition software to track down criminals using surveillance footage.

3. Augmented & Mixed Reality

   Augmented reality, which allows computers like smartphones and wearable technology to superimpose or embed digital content onto real-world environments, also relies heavily on computer vision. Virtual items may be placed in the actual environment through computer vision in augmented reality equipment. In order to properly generate depth and proportions and position virtual items in the real environment, augmented reality apps rely on computer vision techniques to recognize surfaces like tabletops, ceilings, and floors.

4. Healthcare

   Computer vision has contributed significantly to the development of health tech. Automating the process of looking for malignant moles on a person's skin or locating indicators in an x-ray or MRI scan is only one of the many applications of computer vision algorithms.
   Examples
   The following are some examples of well-established activities using computer vision:

5. Categorization of Images

   A computer program that uses image categorization can determine what an image is of (a dog, a banana, a human face, etc.). In particular, it may confidently assert that an input picture matches a specific category. It might be used by a social networking platform, for instance, to filter out offensive photos that people post.

6. Object Detection

   By first classifying images into categories, object detection may then utilize this information to search for and catalog instances of the desired class of images. In the manufacturing industry, this can include finding defects on the production line or locating broken equipment.

7. Observation of Moving Objects

   If an item is discovered, object tracking will continue to move in the same location. A common method for doing this is by using a live video stream or a series of sequentially taken photos. For example, driverless cars must not only identify and categorize moving things like people, other motorists, and road systems in order to prevent crashes and adhere to traffic regulations.

8. Retrieval of Images Based on Their Contents

   In contrast to traditional visual retrieval methods, which rely on metadata labels, a content-based recognition system employs computer vision to search, explore, and retrieve pictures from huge data warehouses based on the actual image content. Automatic picture annotations, which can replace traditional visual tagging, may be used for this work.

Computer Vision Algorithms

Computer vision algorithms include the different methods used to understand the objects in digital images and extract high-dimensional data from the real world to produce numerical or symbolic information. There are many other computer vision algorithms involved in recognizing things in photographs. Some common ones are:

1. Object Classification - What is the main category of the object present in this photograph?

2. Object Identification - What is the type of object present in this photograph?

3. Object Detection - Where is the object in the photograph?

4. Object Segmentation - What pixels belong to the object in the image?

5. Object Verification - Is the object in the photograph?

6. Object Recognition - What are the objects present in this photograph and where are they located?

7. Object Landmark Detection - What are the key points for the object in this photograph?

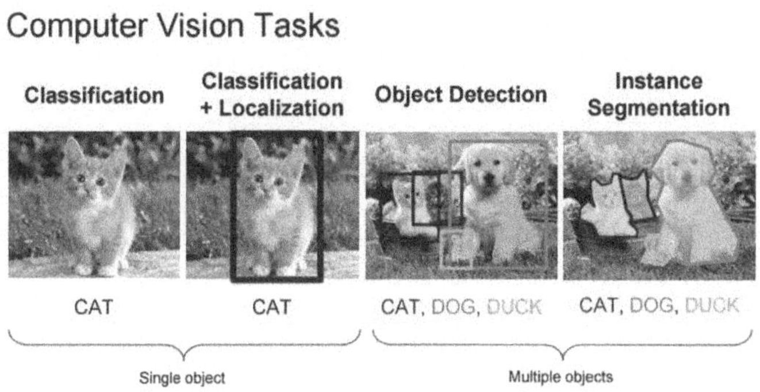

Fig: Computer vision detecting cats in a picture

Many other advanced computer vision algorithms such as style transfer, colorization, human pose estimation, action recognition, and more can be learned alongside deep learning algorithms.

Challenges of Computer Vision

Creating a machine with human-level vision is surprisingly challenging, and not only because of the technical challenges involved in doing so with computers. We still have a lot to learn about the nature of human vision.

To fully grasp biological vision, one must learn not just how various receptors like the eye work, but also how the brain processes what it sees. The process has been mapped out, and its tricks and shortcuts have been discovered, but, as with any study of the brain, there is still a considerable distance to cover.

Computer Vision Benefits

Computer vision can automate several tasks without the need for human intervention. As a result, it provides organizations with a number of benefits:

1. Faster and simpler process - Computer vision systems can carry out repetitive and monotonous tasks at a faster rate, which simplifies the work for humans.

2. Better products and services - Computer vision systems that have been trained very well will commit zero mistakes. This will result in faster delivery of high-quality products and services.

3. Cost-reduction - Companies do not have to spend money on fixing their flawed processes because computer vision will leave no room for faulty products and services.

Computer Vision Disadvantages

There is no technology that is free from flaws, which is true for computer vision systems. Here are a few limitations of computer vision:

1. Lack of specialists - Companies need to have a team of highly trained professionals with deep knowledge of the differences between AI vs. Machine Learning vs. Deep Learning technologies to train computer vision systems. There is a need for more specialists that can help shape this future of technology.

2. Need for regular monitoring - If a computer vision system faces a technical glitch or breaks down, this can cause immense loss to companies. Hence, companies need to have a dedicated team on board to monitor and evaluate these systems.

5.4.1 Application of computer vision using Machine Learning

In this article, you will find five applications of computer vision using Machine Learning. But let's start to discuss the differences first.

The possible uses of **computer vision** have recently gotten more attention. In fact, it's a technology that imitates human vision and can-do sophisticated analyses of pictures. However, the distinction between the scope of **computer vision** and Machine Learning seems to be unclear to many. That makes sense, given how closely both technologies' applications overlap.

Artificial intelligence (AI), a catch-all phrase that includes a variety of other technologies as well, consists of both Machine Learning and **computer vision**. In this article, you will find five applications of **computer vision** using Machine Learning. But let's start todiscuss the differences first.

What Is Computer Vision?

Briefly, ''Computer Vision'' is used in order to provide computer systems with visual perception skills similar to those of humans. It is a collaborative discipline that makes it possible for computer systems to correctly process, examine, and understand our visual environment.

For instance, **computer vision** enables machines to recognize essential data from photos and video files in the same manner that people do. The goal is to give computers access to this "natural"visual quality so they can comprehend and evaluate complicated digital systems just as people can—possibly even better.

Modern **computer vision** uses Machine Learning, an aspect of artificial intelligence concerned with "training"computers to pick up new skills on their own over time. A Machine Learning system, however, will consider prior experiences and judgments to choose the most suitable response, in contrast to a system that constantly follows a set of predefined rules or instructions. Furthermore, this may be accomplished with little to no human involvement.

What is Machine Learning?

Simple artificial intelligence is a subset or component of Machine Learning. Machine Learning-enabled devices can evaluate and interpret digital data without human intervention.

Statistical concepts and algorithms are frequently used together in Machine Learning to create models that can generate judgments from incoming data. As a result, Machine Learning is used in various industries, from supercomputers to sophisticated software engineering.

So, a crucial question will be: What is **computer vision** in the context of Machine Learning? Machine Learning ideas are applied to **computer vision** because Machine Learning plays a significant role in **computer vision** nowadays.

What are the differences between Machine Learning and Computer Vision?

Computer vision and Machine Learning are subfields of artificial intelligence that use advanced algorithms to quickly and accurately detect, interpret, and discover patterns in visual input, as mentioned above. As a result, because both of these technologies have many things in common, it would be best to distinguish between them based on their use cases rather than their differences.

To give an idea, a typical system for both **computer vision** and Machine Learning will comprise many of the same elements and specifications, such as; a lens or other imaging sensor that may be used as an imaging device, appropriate lighting for the intended use, or computer software that can analyse photos while using **computer vision** or **Machine Learning techniques.**

Tasks of Computer Vision

Even if it's increasingly simpler to get the resources needed to create **computer vision** applications, it's crucial to establish their purpose early on. It is simpler to get started if projects and applications are focused, validated, and defined in terms of particular **computer vision** tasks.

Here are some examples of **Computer Vision** applications.

- A puppy, an apple, or a person's face are examples of images that may be classified using **image classification.** More specifically, it can correctly guess which class a given picture belongs to. A social network corporation would wish to utilize it, for instance, to recognize and sort out offensive photographs shared by users automatically.
- **Object detection** may employ image classification to identify a particular class of picture and then recognize and tabulate its existence in an image or video. Detecting damage on a manufacturing line or locating equipment that needs repair are a few examples.
- Afte an item is found, it is followed or tracked. This operation is often carried out using real-time video streams or a series of sequentially taken pictures, called object tracking. For instance, autonomous vehicles must monitor moving things like people, other cars, and road infrastructure in addition to classifying and detecting them top recent crashes and follow traffic regulations.
- Instead of focusing on the metadata tags attached to the photos, **content-based image** retrieval employs **computer vision** to browse, search, and retrieve images from massive data repositories. This activity may use automatic picture annotation instead of human image labelling. These activities can be used in digital asset management systems to improve search and retrieval precision.

Applications of Computer Vision using Machine Learning

Here are some of the applications where **Computer Vision** uses **Machine Learning**.

1.Healthcare

One of the richest sources of information is medical imaging data. But here's the disclaimer:
Doctors must manually process patient data and do administrative tasks without the proper technologies.
Fortunately, as time passed and technology improved, the healthcare sector became one of the quickest to accept new automation technologies, such as computer vision.
Here are some applications where **computer vision** using **Machine Learning** is employed below.

- Cancer Detection

Comparing malignant and non-cancerous cells in photos enables medical professionals to spot abnormalities and alterations.
Automated detection enables a quicker cancer diagnosis using information from magnetic resonance imaging (MRI) scans. Breast and skin cancer screening using **computer vision** has already been shown effective.

- X-Ray Analysis

Computer vision can be effectively used in the context of medical X-ray imaging for treatment and research, MRI reconstruction, or surgery planning.
Although most doctors still use manual X-ray image analysis to diagnose and treat illnesses**, computer vision** can successfully automate the procedure, boosting efficiency and accuracy.

- Diagnosis of Viral Infections

Computer Vision can be used for diagnosing viral infections like Covid-19. For X-ray-based COVID-19 diagnosis, several deep learning computer vision models are available.

- Disease Level

Computer vision recognizes severely unwell patients (critical patient screening) to focus on medical care. It has been used for covid patients and observed that patients breathe more quickly thanks to disease level diagnosis.
It is possible to accurately and discretely screen many ill people for aberrant respiratory patterns using deep learning and depth cameras.

2. Retail

Retailers can get massive amounts of visual data from cameras deployed in their facilities that will help them create a better customer and staff experience. The digital transformation of the actual industry is now much more feasible thanks to the development of computer vision systems to analyse this data.
Here are a few of the retail industry's most widely used **computer vision** applications below.

- Counting People in the Shop

Data examples train computer vision algorithms to detect and count people as they are noticed. Such people measuring equipment may be used in instances with COVID-19, where only a certain number of customers are let in a shop at once to gather data on the business's success.

- Self Check-out

Developing **computer vision**-based systems that comprehend consumer interactions and track goods movement has made autonomous checkout conceivable. Modern retail stores are using cashier-less checkouts to address problems like lengthy lines.

- Customer Behaviour Analysis

Using camera-based technologies can upcycle the video stream from popular, affordable security surveillance cameras. **Machine Learning** algorithms identify individuals invisibly and contactless to study time spent in various locations, wait periods, and line up times and evaluate the service's quality.
Customer behaviour analytics can promote customer happiness, optimize retail shop layouts, and objectively measure key performance indicators across many locations.

3. Banking

Banking is one of the main areas where **Computer Vision and Machine Learning** are employed, and it helps bank officers do their jobs efficiently.

- Money Counting

For example, while counting money, scanners use **computer vision** and calculate the money quickly and accurately. This also prevents counterfeiting by enabling the distinction of counterfeit money.

- **Portfolio Management**

Portfolio management is one of **Computer Vision's** most significant benefits for the banking industry. Aside from that, cutting-edge technology can put everything at your fingertips and silhouette and do away with in-person banking.

- **Fraud Security**

Banks and other financial organizations are particularly vulnerable to fraud. Therefore, having a reliable and secure system is crucial to safeguarding their clients' interests. Financial institutions must thus actively watch out for possible fraud schemes, including stock fraud, phone or SMS fraud, illicit remittance through internet banking, etc.

4. Security and Surveillance

Computer vision employs various technologies to analyze and comprehend visual data using computers. The main objective of **computer vision** in applications for the security and surveillance industries is to automate human oversight. Real-world scenarios may now be recorded and digitally preserved, opening up new possibilities for threat detection that is more accurate and early, risk quantification, and real-time security evaluations.

- **Weapons' or Dangerous Objects'Detection**

Deep learning is used in real-time object identification to locate particular items in video scenes. Applications for object identification in security often include the detection of weapons (such as knives or guns) or protective gear. Employing software like Cameralyze helps to detect any weapons or dangerous objects thanks to their advanced AI-based technologies.

- **Virtual Fencing**

A typical function of AI vision surveillance systems is the virtual fencing of sensitive areas. To identify incursionoccurrences, particular locations of interest indicate virtual barriers.

- **Anomaly Detection**

Anomaly detection in traffic, the subway, on campuses, trains, boats, buildings, and public spaces is done using AI videoanalysis. A few examples of anomaly detection in visual AI have stopped vehicle identification, fear detection, and the recognition of unusual pedestrian behavior.

Software like Cameralyze prepares you for all abnormal situations. Thus, by analyzing live broadcasts, you will prevent unwanted situations.

5. Automotive

To assure the quality of the product and the assembly process, automotive manufacturing assembly activities involve visual inspections such as scratch detection on machined surfaces, item identification, and selection. **Computer vision** and Machine Learning are helpful in this situation.

- **Autonomous Driving**

Computer vision is a component of autonomous vehicles like self-driving cars. The automobile has cameras that provide a 360-degree field of view and a wide range. The cameras help with lane locating, estimating road curvature, detecting obstacles, detecting traffic signs, andmany other tasks. Object detection and classification must be implemented using **computer vision**.

- **Inspection in the Assembly Lines**

Deep learning applications for automotive AIvision have huge promise for part inspection and defect location. Before anycar is put together, it is crucial to find any faulty produced components, such as brake parts, and the manual examination is challenging to carry out on your own.

Deep learning techniques are more reliable at spotting many flaws than traditional image processing techniques.

5.4.1.1 Speech processing

Applications of Digital Speech Processing

The first step in most applications of digital speech processing is to convert the acoustic waveform to a sequence of numbers. Most modern A-to-D converters operate by sampling at a very high rate, applying a digital lowpass filter with cutoff set to preserve a prescribed bandwidth, and then reducing the sampling rate to the desired sampling rate, which can be as low as twice the cutoff frequency of the sharp-cutoff digital filter. This discrete-time representation is the starting point for most applications. From this point, other representations are obtained by digital processing. For the most part, these alternative representations are based on incorporating knowledge about the workings of the speech chain as we will see, it is possible to incorporate aspects of both the speech production and speech perception process into the digital representation and processing. It is not an oversimplification to assert that digital speech processing is grounded in a set of techniques that have the goal of pushing the data rate of the speech representation to the left along either the upper or lower path The remainder of this chapter is devoted to a brief summary of the applications of digital speech processing, i.e., the systems that people interact with daily. Our discussion will confirm the importance of the digital representation in all application areas.

Speech Coding

Perhaps the most widespread applications of digital speech processing technology occur in the areas of digital transmission and storage of speech signals. In these areas the centrality of the digital representation is obvious since the goal is to compress the digital waveform representation of speech into a lower bit-rate representation. It is common to refer to this activity as "speech coding" or "speech compression." In the upper part of the figure, the A-to-D converter converts the analog speech signal xc(t) to a sampled waveform representation x[n]. The digital signal x[n] is analyzed and coded by digital computation algorithms to produce a new digital signal y[n] that can be transmitted over a digital communication channel or stored in a digital storage medium as ˆy[n]. As we will see, there are a myriad of ways to do the encoding so as to reduce the data rate over that of the sampled and quantized speech waveform x[n]. Because the digital representation at this point is often not directly related to the sampled speech waveform, y[n] and ˆy[n] are appropriately referred to as data signals that represent the speech signal. The lower path in Figure 1.3 shows the decoder associated with the speech coder. The received data signal ˆy[n] is decoded using the inverse of the analysis processing, giving the sequence of samples ˆx[n] which is then converted (using a D-to-A Converter) back to an analog signal ˆxc(t) for human listening. The decoder is often called a synthesizer because it must reconstitute the speech waveform from data that may bear no direct relationship to the waveform.

Text-to-Speech Synthesis

For many years, scientists and engineers have studied the speech production process with the goal of building a system that can start with text and produce speech automatically. In a sense, a text-to-speech synthesizer such as depicted in Figure is a digital simulation of the entire upper part of the speech chain diagram. The input to the system is ordinary text such as an email message or an article from a newspaper or magazine. The first block in the text-to-speech synthesis system, labeled linguistic rules, has the job of converting the printed text input into a set of sounds that the machine must synthesize. The conversion from text to sounds involves a set of linguistic rules that must determine the appropriate set of sounds (perhaps including things like emphasis, pauses, rates of speaking, etc.) so that the resulting synthetic speech will express the words and intent of the text message in what passes for a natural voice that can be decoded accurately by human speech perception. This is more difficult than simply looking up the words in a pronouncing dictionary because the linguistic rules must determine how to pronounce acronyms, how to pronounce ambiguous words like read, bass, object, how to pronounce abbreviations like St. (street or Saint), Dr. (Doctor or drive), and how to properly pronounce proper names, specialized terms, etc. Once the proper pronunciation of the text has been determined, the role of the synthesis algorithm is to create the appropriate sound sequence to represent the text message in the form of speech. In essence, the synthesis algorithm must simulate the action of the vocal tract system in creating the sounds of speech. There are many procedures for assembling the speech sounds and compiling them into a proper sentence, but the most promising one today is called "unit selection and concatenation." In this method, the computer stores multiple versions of each of the basic units of speech (phones, half phones, syllables, etc.), and then decides which sequence of speech units sounds best for the particular text message that is being produced. The basic digital representation is not generally the sampled speech wave. Instead, some sort of compressed representation is normally used to save memory and, more importantly, to allow convenient manipulation of durations and blending of adjacent sounds. Thus, the speech synthesis algorithm would include an appropriate decoder Text-to-speech synthesis systems are an essential component of modern human–machine communications systems and are used to do things like read email messages over a telephone, provide voice output from GPS systems in automobiles, provide the voices for talking agents for completion of transactions over the internet, handle call center help desks and customer care applications, serve as the voice for providing information from handheld devices such as foreign language phrasebooks, dictionaries, crossword puzzle helpers, and as the voice of announcement machines that provide information such as stock quotes, airline schedules, updates on arrivals and departures of flights, etc. Another important application is in reading machines for the blind, where an optical character recognition system provides the text input to a speech synthesis system.

Speech Recognition and Other Pattern Matching Problems

Another large class of digital speech processing applications is concerned with the automatic extraction of information from the speech signal. Most such systems involve some sort of pattern matching. Such problems include the following: speech recognition, where the object is to extract the message from the speech signal; speaker recognition, where the goal is to identify who is speaking; speaker verification, where the goal is to verify a speaker's claimed identity from analysis of their speech signal; word spotting, which involves monitoring a speech signal for the occurrence of specified words or phrases; and automatic indexing of speech recordings based on recognition (or spotting) of spoken keywords. The first block in the pattern matching system converts the analog speech waveform to digital form using an A-to-D converter. The feature analysis module converts the sampled speech signal to a set of feature vectors. Often, the same analysis techniques that are used in speech coding are also used to derive the feature vectors. The final block in the system, namely the pattern matching block, dynamically time aligns the set of feature vectors representing the speech signal with a concatenated set of stored patterns, and chooses the identity associated with the pattern which is the closest match to the time-aligned set of feature vectors of the speech signal. The symbolic output consists of a set of recognized words, in the case of speech recognition, or the identity of the best matching talker, in the case of speaker recognition, or a decision as to whether to accept or reject the identity claim of a speaker in the case of speaker verification e. The major areas where such a system finds applications include command and control of computer software, voice dictation to create letters, memos, and other documents, natural language voice dialogues with machines to enable help desks and call centers, and for agent services such as calendar entry and update, address list modification and entry, etc. Pattern recognition applications often occur in conjunction with other digital speech processing applications. For example, one of the preeminent uses of speech technology is in portable communication devices. Speech coding at bit rates on the order of 8 Kbps enables normal voice conversations in cell phones. Spoken name speech recognition in cellphones enables voice dialing capability that can automatically dial the number associated with the recognized name. Names from directories with upwards of several hundred names can readily be recognized and dialed using simple speech recognition technology. Another major speech application that has long been a dream of speech researchers is automatic language translation. The goal of language translation systems is to convert spoken words in one language to spoken words in another language so as to facilitate natural language voice dialogues between people speaking different languages. Language translation technology requires speech synthesis systems that work in both languages, along with speech recognition (and generally natural language understanding) that also works for both languages; hence it is a very difficult task and one for which only limited progress has been made. When such systems exist, it will be possible for people speaking different languages to communicate at data rates on the order of that of printed text reading!

Other Speech Applications

, the techniques of digital speech processing are a key ingredient of a wide range of applications that include the three areas of transmission/storage, speech synthesis, and speech recognition as well as many others such as speaker identification, speech signal quality enhancement, and aids for the hearing- or visuallyimpaired. This figure simply depicts the notion that once the speech signal is sampled, it can be manipulated in virtually limitless ways by DSP techniques. Here again, manipulations and modifications of the speech signal are usually achieved by transforming the speech signal into an alternative representation (that is motivated by our understanding of speech production and speech perception), operating on that representation by further digital computation, and then transforming back to the waveform domain, using a D-to-A converter. One important application area is speech enhancement, where the goal is to remove or suppress noise or echo or reverberation picked up by a microphone along with the desired speech signal. In human-to-human communication, the goal of speech enhancement systems is to make the speech more intelligible and more natural; however, in reality the best that has been achieved so far is less perceptually annoying speech that essentially maintains, but does not improve, the intelligibility of the noisy speech. Success has been achieved, however, in making distorted speech signals more useful for further processing as part of a speech coder, synthesizer, or recognizer. An excellent reference in this area is the recent textbook by Loizou. Other examples of manipulation of the speech signal include timescale modification to align voices with video segments, to modify voice qualities, and to speed-up or slow-down prerecorded speech (e.g., for talking books, rapid review of voice mail messages, or careful scrutinizing of spoken material).

Speech Enhancement

In voice communications, speech signals can be contaminated by environmental noise and, as a result, the communication quality can be affected making the speech less intelligible. Furthermore, compression of the noisy speech with a low bit-rate vocoder may result in considerable quality degradation due to frequent estimation errors of speech production model parameters required by the vocoder. This problem can be reduced significantly by speech enhancement (or noise cancellation), which may enable more pleasant voice communication by suppressing the noise components in input signals.

Generally, it is assumed that the noisy speech signal is formed additively by speech and noise signals in which the noise is generated by environmental sources such as vehicles, street noise, babble, etc. Therefore, in real environments, complete noise cancellation is not feasible as it is not possible to completely track varying noise types and characteristics that change with time. However, by assuming that the noise characteristics change slowly in comparison with speech, it is possible to achieve significant reduction in the background noise levels producing more pleasant and intelligible speech quality. Speech enhancement techniques can help the speech model parameter extraction process used in low bit-rate vocoders and hence they are becoming an integral part of low bit-rate speech coding systems.

WHAT IS EXACTLY PCM?

Pulse-code modulation (PCM) is a method used to digitally represent sampled analog signals. It is the standard form for digital audio in computers and various Blu-ray, Compact Disc and DVD formats, as well as other uses such as digital telephone systems. A PCM stream is a digital representation of an analog signal, in which the magnitude of the analogue signal is sampled regularly at uniform intervals, with each sample being quantized to the nearest value within a range of digital steps.

For digital communication, there are two quite different PCM standards.

1. The North American standard, also called T1, the more standard name is DS1 PCM hierarchy.

2. The European system E1 hierarchy.

BASIS OF PULSE CODE MODULATION (PCM)

Here are the three steps for developing an equivalent PCM digital signal from an analog signal. The typical human speech is represented by a simple 1200 Hz tone, which is represented by a sine wave.

1. Sampling

2. Quantization

3. Coding

1. Sampling

The foundation of PCM is based on the *Nyquist sampling theorem*.

If a and-limited signal is sampled at regular intervals of time and at a rate equal to or higher than twice (2x) the highest significant signal frequency, then the sample contains all the information of the original signal. The original signal may then be reconstructed by use of a low-pass filter.

Based on Nyquist sampling theorem, we can derive that the nominal 4 kHz voice channel can be reconstructed by a sampling rate of 8000 times per second (4000 x 2). This means that a sample is taken every 125 μsec, or 1 second/8000.

A. Pulse Amplitude Modulation (PAM) Wave

In most real world PCM systems, Time Division Multiplexing (TDM) are used. So, the sampling does not just involve one voice channel but several. The North American T1 system samples 24 voice channels in sequence, and the European E1 samples 30 voice channels. The result of the multiple sampling is a pulse amplitude modulation (PAM) wave as shown in the following figure.

The following figure shows a simplified diagram of the processing involved to derive a multiplex PAM wave, only three voice channels are sampled sequentially.

a) T1 Sampling

In North American T1 (DS1) system, 24 voice channels are sampled sequentially and are interleaved to form a PAM-multiplexed wave. The sampling gate is open about 5.2 μs (125 μs/24) for each voice. The full sequence of 24 channels is sampled successively from channel 1 through channel 24 in a 125 μs period. This 125 μs period is a called a frame, and inside the frame all 24 channels are successively sampled just once.

b) E1 Sampling In European E1 system, there are 30 voice channels plus an additional two service channels, for a total of 32 channels. By definition, this system must sample 8000 times per second because it is also optimized for voice operation, and thus its frame period is also 125 μs. To accommodate the 32 channels, the sampling gate is open 125 μs/32 or about 3.906 μs.

Quantization

Uniform Quantization

The purpose of a PCM system is to transmit to the distant end the value of a voltage sample at a certain moment in time. The next step is to assign a binary sequence to each of those voltage samples, this step is called quantization.For discussion's sake, we assume the maximum excursion of the PAM wave to within +1 V to –1 V. Between +1 V to –1 V PAM wave, there could be an infinite number of different values of voltage. However, in order to assign a binary sequence to each voltage value, we must limit the number of voltage values, and the values must be discrete. For example, we could set 20 discrete values between +1 V and –1 V, with each value at a discrete 0.1 V increment.Since we are working in the binary domain, we select the total number of discrete values to be a binary number multiple (i.e., 2, 4, 8, 16, 32, 64, 128, etc.). This facilitates binary coding. For instance, if there were four values, they would be as follows: 00, 01, 10, 11. This is a 2-bit code.We find that the number of total possible different binary combinations given a code of **n** binary symbols (bits) is 2^n. A 7-bit code has 128 different binary combinations (i.e., $2^7 = 128$).For the quantization process, we need to present to the coder a discrete voltage value. Suppose our quantization steps were on 0.1 V increments and our voltage measure for one sample was 0.37 V. That would have to be rounded off to 0.4 V, the nearest discrete value. Note that there is a 0.03 V error, the difference between 0.37 V and 0.4 V. This is called quantization error.Uniform Quantization Sample:The above figure shows one cycle of the PAM wave, where we use a 4-bit code. In the figure, a 4-bit code is used that allows for 16 different binary-coded possibilities or levels between +1 V and –1 V. Thus, we can assign eight possibilities above the origin and eight possibilities below the origin. These 16 quantum steps are coded as follows.

Step Number	Code	Step Number	Code
0	0000	8	1000
1	0001	9	1001
2	0010	10	1010
3	0011	11	1011
4	0100	12	1100
5	0101	13	1101
6	0110	14	1110
7	0111	15	1111

Examining the above figure, we can see that step 12 is used twice. Neither time it is used is it the true value of the impinging sinusoid voltage. It is a rounded-off value. These rounded-off values are shown with the dashed lines in the figure, which follows the general outline of the sinusoid.

The horizontal dashed lines show the point where the quantum changes to the next higher or lower level if the sinusoid curve is above or below that value. Take step 14 in the curve, for example. The curve, dropping from its maximum, is given two values of 14 consecutively. For the first, the curve resides above 14, and for the second, below. That error, in the case of 14, from the quantum value to the true value is called **quantizing distortion**. This distortion is a major source of imperfection in PCM system.

Increasing the number of quantizing steps for a fixed range of input values reduces quantizing distortion accordingly. However, voice transmission presents a problem. It has a wide dynamic range, on the order of 50 dB. That is the level range from the loudest talker to the quietest talker. using linear quantization, we find it would require 2048 discrete steps to provide any fidelity at all. Since 2048 is 2^{11}, this means we would need an 11-bit code. Such a code sampled 8000 times per second leads to 88,000 bit per second (bps) equivalent voice channel and an 88 kHz bandwidth. This is a too great bandwidth requirement for a single voice channel.

So, this leads to non-linear quantization process which we will explain below.

Non-Uniform Quantization

With uniform quantization, the signal to noise ratio is large for high levels but small for low level signals. Therefore, non-uniform quantization is used.

In non-uniform quantization process, the quantizing intervals are not of equal size. Small quantizing intervals are allocated to small signal values and large quantization intervals to large values. This is to achieve that the signal-to-quantization distortion ratio is nearly independent of the signal level.

Non-uniform quantization uses a technique of companding. *Companding* derives from two words: compression and expansion. Compression takes place on the transmit side; expansion on the receive side. Compression reduces the dynamic range with little loss of fidelity, and expansion returns the signal to its normal condition.

This is done by favoring low-level speech over higher-level speech. In other words, more code segments are assigned to speech bursts at low levels than at the higher levels, progressively more as the level reduces. This is shown in the following figure.

In the above figure, eight coded sequences are assigned to each level grouping. The smallest range rises only 0.0666 V from the origin (assigned to 0 V level). The largest extends over 0.5 V, and it is assigned only eight coded sequences.

Coding

Older PCM systems used 7-bit code, and modern systems use an 8-bit code with its improved quantizing distortion performance. The companding and coding are carried out together, simultaneously. The compression and later expansion functions are logarithmic. A pseudologarithmic curve made up of linear segments imparts finer granularity to low-level signals and less granularity to the higher-level signals.

The logarithmic curve follows one of two laws, the A-law and the μ-law.

A-Law

The curve for the A-law may be plotted from the formula:

where A = 87.6. The A-law is used with European E1 system.

μ-Law

The curve for μ-law is plotted from the formula.

where x is the signal input amplitude and μ = 100 for the original North American T1 system (now outdated), and 255 for later North American (DS1) systems and the CCITT 24-channel systems (CCITT Rec. G.733).

Signal-to-Distortion Ratio (S/D)

A common expression used in dealing with the "quality" of a PCM signal is signal-to-distortion ratio (S/D, expressed in dB). Parameters A and μ, for the respective companding laws, determine the range over which the signal-to-distortion ratio is comparatively constant, about 26 dB.

For A-law companding, an S/D = 37.5 dB can be expected (A = 87.6). And for μ-law companding, we can expect S/D = 37 dB (μ=255).

A-Law Companding Curve Examination

Now let's look at the following figure, which shows the companding curve and resulting coding for the European E1 system.

Note that the curve consists of linear piecewise segments, seven above and seven below the origin. The segment just above and the segment just below the origin consists of two linear segments. Counting the collinear elements by the origin, there are 16 segments. Each segment has 16 8-bit PCM codewords assigned. These are the codewords that identify the voltage level of a sample at some moment in time.

Each codeword, often called a PCM "word", consists of 8 bits. The first bit (most significant bit) tells the distant-end receiver if the sample is a positive or negative voltage. Observe that all PCM words above the origin start with a binary 1, and those below the origin start with a binary 0. The next 3 bits in sequence identify the segment. There are eight segments (or collinear equivalents) above the origin and eight below the origin ($2^3 = 8$). The last 4 bits, shown as XXXX, indicate exactly where in a particular segment that voltage line is located.

Suppose the distant end received the binary sequence 11010100 in an E1 system. The first bit indicates that the voltage is positive. The next three bits, 101, indicate that the sample is in segment 4 (positive). The last 4 bits, 0100, tell where it is in that segment as illustrated in the following figure.

In the above figure, note that the 16 steps inside the segment are linear.

μ-Law Companding Curve

The following figure shows an equivalent logarithmic curve for the North American DS1 (T1) system. It uses a 15-segment approximation of the logarithmic μ-law curve (μ-255). The segments cutting the origin are collinear and are counted as one. So again, we have a total of 16 segments.

Coding

The coding process in PCM utilizes straightforward binary codes as shown in the previous three figures.

PCM Frame

As shown in the second figure above, PCM multiplexing is carried out with the sampling process, sampling the analog sources sequentially. These sources may be the nominal 4 kHz voice channels or other information sources that have a 4 kHz bandwidth.

The final result of the sampling and subsequent quantization and coding is a series of electrical pulses, a serial bit stream of 1s and 0s that requires some identification or indication of the beginning of a sampling sequence. This identification is necessary so that the far-end receiver knows exactly when the sampling sequence starts.

Once the receive receives the "indication", it knows a priori (in the case of DS1) that 24 eight-bit slots follow. It synchronizes the receiver. Such identification is carried out by a *framing bit*, and one full sequence or cycle of samples is called a *frame* in PCM terminology.

DS1 (T1) Framing Structure

Consider the framing structure of North American DS1 (T1) system. It is a 24-channel PCM system using 8-level coding (e.g., $2^8 = 256$ quantizing steps or distinct PCM code words). Supervisory signaling is "in-band" where bit 8 of every sixth frame is "robbed" for supervisory signaling. The DS1 frame shown in the following figure has one bit added as a framing bit (this is that indication to tell the distant end receiver where the frame starts.) It is called the "S" bit.

The DS1 frame then consists of:

(8×24) +1 = 193 bits

By definition, 8000 frames are transmitted per second (i.e., 4000 x 2, the Nyquist sampling rate), so the bit rate of DS1 is:

193 x 8000 = 1,544,000 bps or 1.544 Mbps

E1 Framing Structure

The E1 European PCM system is a 32-channel system. Of the 32 channels, 30 transmit speech (or data) derived from incoming telephone trunks and the remaining 2 channels transmit synchronization-alignment and signaling information. Each channel is allotted an 8-bit slot (TS), and this is shown in the following table.

Again, E1 in its primary rate format transmits 32 channels of 8-bit time slots. An E1 frame therefore has 8×32=256 bits. There is no framing bit. Framing alignment is carried out in TS 0. The E1 bit rate to the line is:

256 x 8000 = 2,048,000 bps or 2.048 Mbps

TS	Type of Information
0	Synchronizing (framing)
1-15	Speech
16	Signaling
17-31	Speech

The difference between Framing and Timing

Framing and basic timing should be distinguished. "Framing" ensures that the PCM receiver is aligned regarding the beginning (and end) of a bit sequence or frame; "timing" refers to the synchronization of the receiver clock, specifically, that it is in step with its companion far-end transmit clock.

Timing at the receiver is corrected via the incoming "1"-to- "0" and "0"-to- "1" transitions. It is mandatory that long periods of no transitions do not occur. This important point should be further studied in reference to line codes and digital inversion.

Speech Processing Using Linear Prediction

In this set of demonstrations, we illustrate the modern equivalent of the 1939 Dudley vocoder demonstration. Instead of a bank of bandpass filters, modern vocoders use a single filter (usually implemented in a so-called lattice filter structure). The filter coefficients are calculated using any of a number of algorithms (based on linear prediction). In the examples below, we use an algorithm due to John Burg to calculate the filter coefficients.

The original speech signal borrowed from the Voder demo, is sampled at 8kHz. The signal is broken into segments of 160 samples (20ms). Each segment is analyzed using Burg's algorithm for its spectral content (a tenth order linear predictor is the result of this analysis).

A *linear predictor* uses observations of a signal to try to predict the next sample of the signal beyond those it can observe. The overall structure is as shown:

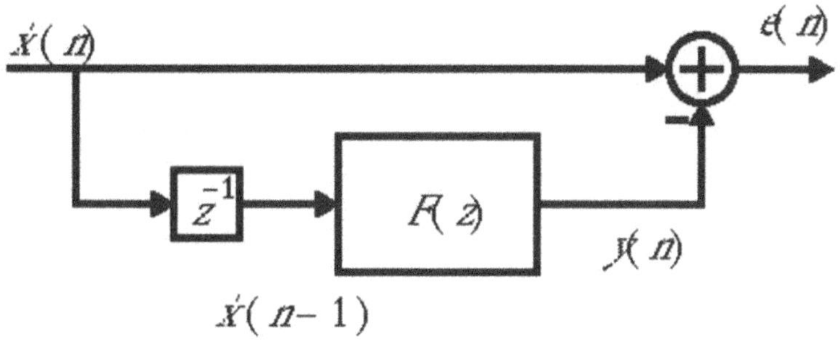

The input signal, $x'(n)$, is delayed by one sample by the block labeled z^{-1}. The block labeled $F(z)$ is a filter whose output $y(n)$ is an estimate of the current value of $x'(n)$. Since that block only sees a delayed version of $x'(n)$, its output is a prediction. The error in the prediction, $e(n)$, is the difference between what is being predicted and the prediction. Intuitively, linear prediction exploits the fact that a new sample of a signal is not totally independent of previous samples, usually. It captures that dependence. As such, when a predictor is working well, the error signal will have little residual correlation between samples. If the input to the linear predictor is the original voder speech signal, then the error signal is not very intelligible. Intelligibility, therefore, must somehow depend on the correlation between samples in the signal.

In fact, for speech, the linear predictor has to constantly change to adapt to what is being said. The input signal is divided into 20ms segments, and each segment is analyzed to provide the coefficients of the prediction filter, as shown below:

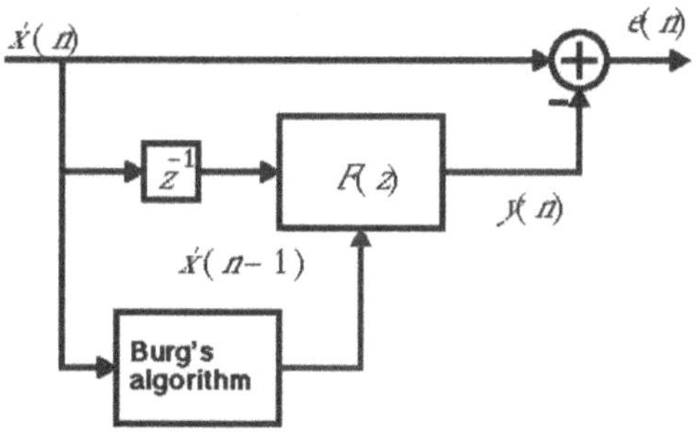

A box labeled "Burg's algorithm" uses one of several methods for calculating the coefficients of the linear predictor each 20ms.

We can check the hypothesis that intelligibility depends on the correlation between samples by introducing the correlation into some random signal that has no speech content. Suppose we start with a white noise signal and filter it with the inverse of the prediction error filter above (changing the filter coefficients every 20ms). The result will be intelligible whispered speech. The block diagram used to create this synthetic speech is as follows:

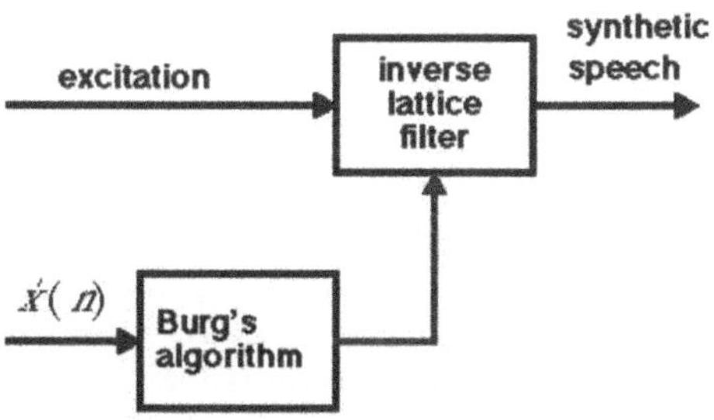

Burg's algorithm is used again to analyze each 20ms segment of speech, but now the results of the analysis are loaded into an "inverse lattice filter," which implements the *inverse* of the filter above that produced the prediction error.

Notice that since the result is intelligible, information about intelligibility is almost entirely in the results produced by Burg's algorithm. Thus, such an algorithm can (and often does) form the front end of any device that analyzes speech, such as speech recognition system or a speech encoder.
The whispered speech effect above, while intelligible, sounds, well ... whispered. The problem here is that the excitation, white noise, does not match well what the human vocal cords do. The human vocal cords, which provide an excitation signal in natural speech, vibrate at a frequency that depends on the speaker (and whether the speaker is male or female) and on the inflection intended by the speaker. A naive way to try to replicate the effect of the vocal cords is to use a sinusoidal excitation instead of white noise. The result is completely unintelligible. There is simply not enough spectral richness in a sinusoid.
An alternative excitation that is more spectrally rich is a periodic sequence of impulses, which looks like this:

If we set the period at 40 samples (5ms, or 39 zero-valued samples for every non-zero sample), then the excitation has a perceptual pitch of 200Hz, but obviously no discernable speech content. Filtering it with the inverse lattice filter yields intelligible if mechanical sounding speech. Increasing the period to 80 samples results in speech with a lower tone.
With a periodic pulse excitation, speech sounds very mechanical. A slightly better result comes from combining white noise with periodic pulses. More sophisticated techniques, such as those used today in digital cellular phones, analyze the speech further to construct much better excitation signals.
Since the intelligibility information is contained in the coefficients produced by Burg's algorithm, we can manipulate the speed of the speech by manipulating these coefficients. For example, if we use every set of coefficients to reconstruct 40ms worth of speech rather than 20ms, the result is slow speech. Note that we could also get slow speech by using every speech *sample* twice, but the result is very different, having the overall pitch shifted down by a factor of two in addition to having the speech slowed down.
We can similarly speed up the speech by using each set of coefficients to reconstruct 10ms worth of speech rather than 20ms, the result is fast speech. Note that we could also get fast speech by discarding every second speech *sample*, but the result is very different, having the overall pitch shifted up by a factor of two in addition to having the speech speeded up.
Finally, synthesizing the speech from a musical excitation in this case the first few bars of *Passio Domini nostri* by Arvo Part, yields a particularly interesting result.
Automatic Speech Recognition (ASR)
In this chapter, we examine the process of speech recognition by machine, which is in essence the inverse of the text-to-speech problem. The driving factor behind research in machine recognition of speech has been the potentially huge payoff of providing services where humans interact solely with machines, thereby eliminating the cost of live agents and significantly reducing the cost of providing services. Interestingly, as a side benefit, this process often provides users with a natural and convenient way of accessing information and services.
The Problem of Automatic Speech Recognition The goal of an ASR system is to accurately and efficiently convert a speech signal into a text message transcription of the spoken words, independent of the device used to record the speech (i.e., the transducer or microphone), the speaker's accent, or the acoustic environment in which the speaker is located (e.g., quiet office, noisy room, outdoors). That is, the ultimate goal, which has not yet been achieved, is to perform as well as a human listener. It is assumed that the speaker intends to express some thought as part of a process of conversing with another human or with a machine. To express that thought, the speaker must compose a linguistically meaningful sentence, W, in the form of a sequence of words (possibly with pauses and other acoustic events such as uh's, um's, er's etc.). Once the words are chosen, the speaker sends appropriate control signals to the articulatory speech organs which form a speech utterance whose sounds are those required to speak the desired sentence, resulting in the speech waveform s[n]. We refer to the process of creating the speech waveform from the speaker's intention as the Speaker Model since it reflects the speaker's accent and choice of words to express a given thought or request. The processing steps of the Speech Recognizer and consist of an acoustic processor which analyzes the speech signal and converts it into a set of acoustic (spectral, temporal) features, X, which efficiently characterize the speech sounds, followed by a linguistic decoding process which makes a best (maximum likelihood) estimate of the words of the spoken sentence, resulting in the recognized sentence W^ . This is in essence a digital

simulation of the lower part of the speech chain diagram the overall speech recognition system. The input speech signal, s[n], is converted to the sequence of feature vectors, X = {x1, x2, xT}, by the feature analysis block (also denoted spectral analysis). The feature vectors are computed on a frame-by-frame basis using the techniques discussed in the earlier chapters. In particular, the mel frequency cepstrum coefficients are widely used to represent the short-time spectral characteristics. The pattern classification block (also denoted as the decoding and search block) decodes the sequence of feature vectors into a symbolic representation that is the maximum likelihood string, W^ that could have produced the input sequence of feature vectors. The pattern recognition system uses a set of acoustic models (represented as hidden Markov models) and a word lexicon to provide the acoustic match score for each proposed string. Also, an N-gram language model is used to compute a language model score for each proposed word string. The final block in the process is a confidence scoring process (also denoted as an utterance verification block), which is used to provide a confidence score for each individual word in the recognized string.

Building a Speech Recognition System

The steps in building and evaluating a speech recognition system are the following: (1) choose the feature set and the associated signal processing for representing the properties of the speech signal over time.

(2) choose the recognition task, including the recognition word vocabulary (the lexicon), the basic speech sounds to represent the vocabulary (the speech units), the task syntax or language model, and the task semantics (if any) (3) train the set of speech acoustic and language models (4) evaluate performance of the resulting speech recognition system. Each of these steps may involve many choices and can involve significant research and development effort. Some of the important issues are summarized in this section.

Recognition Feature Set

There is no "standard" set of features for speech recognition. Instead, various combinations of acoustic, articulatory, and auditory features have been utilized in a range of speech recognition systems. The most popular acoustic features have been the (LPC-derived) mel-frequency cepstrum coefficients and their derivatives. A block diagram of the signal processing used in most modern large vocabulary speech recognition systems is shown in Figure . The analog speech signal is sampled and quantized at rates between 8000 up to 20,000 samples/s. A first order (highpass) pre-emphasis network (1 − αz−1) is used to compensate for the speech spectral falloff at higher frequencies and approximates the inverse to the mouth transmission frequency response. The pre-emphasized signal is next blocked into frames of N samples, with adjacent frames spaced M samples apart. Typical values for N and M correspond to frames of duration 15–40 ms, with frame shifts of 10 ms being most common; hence adjacent frames overlap by 5–30 ms depending on the chosen values of N and M. A Hamming window is applied to each frame prior to spectral analysis using either standard spectral analysis or LPC methods. Following (optionally used) simple noise removal methods, the spectral coefficients are normalized and converted to mel-frequency cepstral coefficients via standard analysis methods of the type discussed in Chapter 5 [27]. Some type of cepstral bias removal is often used prior to calculation of the first and second order cepstral derivatives.

1 The Recognition Task

Recognition tasks vary from simple word and phrase recognition systems to large vocabulary conversational interfaces to machines. For example, using a digit's vocabulary, the task could be recognition of a string of digits that forms a telephone number, or identification code, or a highly constrained sequence of digits that form a password.

2 Recognition Training There are two aspects to training models for speech recognition, namely acoustic model training and language model training. Acoustic model training requires recording each of the model units (whole words, phonemes) in as many contexts as possible so that the statistical learning method can create accurate distributions for each of the model states. Acoustic training relies on accurately labeled sequences of speech utterances which are segmented according to the transcription, so that training of the acoustic models first involves segmenting the spoken strings into recognition model units (via either a Baum–Welch or Viterbi alignment method), and then using the segmented utterances to simultaneously build model distributions for each state of the vocabulary unit models. The resulting statistical models form the basis for the pattern recognition operations at the heart of the ASR system Language model training requires a sequence of text strings that reflect the syntax of spoken utterances for the task at hand. Generally, such text training sets are created automatically (based on a model of grammar for the recognition task) or by using existing text sources, such as magazine and newspaper articles, or closed caption transcripts of television news broadcasts, etc. Other times, training sets for language models can be created from databases, e.g., valid strings of telephone numbers can be created from existing telephone directories.

Testing and Performance Evaluation

In order to improve the performance of any speech recognition system, there must be a reliable and statistically significant way of evaluating recognition system performance based on an independent test set of labeled utterances. Typically, we measure word error rate and sentence (or task) error rate as a measure of recognizer performance.

The Decision Processes in ASR The heart of any automatic speech recognition system is the pattern classification and decision operations. In this section, we shall give a brief introduction to these important topics Mathematical Formulation of the ASR Problem The problem of automatic speech recognition is represented as a statistical decision problem. Specifically it is formulated as a Bayes maximum a posteriori probability (MAP) decision process where we seek to find the word string W^ (in the task language) that maximizes the a posteriori probability P(W|X) of that string, given the measured feature vector, X, i.e., W^ = argmax W P(W|X). Using Bayes' rule we can rewrite in the form: W^ = argmax W P(X|W) P(W) P(X). Equation shows that the calculation of the a posteriori probability is decomposed into two terms, one that defines the a priori probability of the word sequence, W, namely P(W), and the other that defines the likelihood that the word string, W, produced the feature vector, X, namely P(X|W). For all future calculations we disregard the denominator term, P(X), since it is independent of the word sequence W which is being optimized. The term P(X|W) is known as the "acoustic model" and is generally denoted as PA(X|W) to emphasize the acoustic nature of this term. The term P(W) is known as the "language model" and is generally denoted as PL(W) to emphasize the linguistic nature of this term. The probabilities associated with PA(X|W) and PL(W) are estimated or learned from a set of training data that have been labeled by a knowledge source, usually a human expert, where the training set is as large as reasonably possible. The recognition decoding process of is often written in the form of a 3-step process, i.e., W^ = argmax W | {z } Step 3 PA(X|W) | {z } Step 1 PL(W) | {z } where Step 1 is the computation of the probability associated with the acoustic model of the speech sounds in the sentence W, Step 2 is the computation of the probability associated with the linguistic model of the words in the utterance, and Step 3 is the computation associated with the search through all valid sentences in the task language for the maximum likelihood sentence. In order to be more explicit about the signal processing and computations associated with each of the three steps of we need to more explicit about the relationship between the feature vector, X, and the word sequence W. As discussed above, the feature vector, X, is a sequence of acoustic observations corresponding to each of T frames of the speech, of the form: X = {x1,x2,...,xT }, (9.4) where the speech signal duration is T frames (i.e., T times the frame shift in ms) and each frame, xt , t = 1,2,...,T is an acoustic feature vector of the form: xt = (xt1,xt2,...,xtD) (9.5) that characterizes the spectral/temporal properties of the speech signal at time t and D is the number of acoustic features in each frame. Similarly, we can express the optimally decoded word sequence, W, as: W = w1, w2, wM, (9.6) where there are assumed to be exactly M words in the decoded string.

The Hidden Markov Model

The most widely used method of building acoustic models (for both phonemes and words) is the use of a statistical characterization known as Hidden Markov Models (HMMs) , a simple Q = 5-state HMM for modeling a whole word. Each HMM state is characterized by a mixture density Gaussian distribution that characterizes the statistical behavior of the feature vectors within the states of the model [61, 62]. In addition to the statistical feature densities within states, the HMM is also characterized by an explicit set of state transitions, aij , which specify the probability of making a transition from state i to state j at each frame, thereby defining the time sequence of the feature vectors over the duration of the word. Usually the self-transitions, aii are large (close to 1.0), and the jump transitions, a12, a23, a34, a45, in the model, are small (close to 0) The complete HMM characterization of a Q-state word model (or a sub-word unit like a phoneme model) is generally written as $\lambda(A,B,\pi)$ with state transition matrix $A = \{aij ,1 \leq i, j \leq Q\}$, state observation probability density, $B = \{bj (xt),1 \leq j \leq Q\}$, and initial state distribution, $\pi = \{\pi i ,1 \leq i \leq Q\}$ with $\pi 1$ set to 1 for the "left-to-right" models of the type shown in Figure In order to train the HMM (i.e., learn the optimal model parameters) for each word (or sub-word) unit, a labeled training set of sentences (transcribed into words and sub-word units) is used to guide an efficient training procedure known as the Baum–Welch algorithm. This algorithm aligns each of the various words (or subword units) with the spoken inputs and then estimates the appropriate means, covariances and mixture gains for the distributions in each model state. The Baum–Welch method is a hill-climbing algorithm and is iterated until a stable alignment of models and speech is obtained. The details of the Baum–Welch procedure are beyond the scope of this chapter but can be found in several references on Speech Recognition methods . The heart of the training procedure for re-estimating HMM model parameters using the Baum– Welch procedure is shown in Figure .An initial HMM model is used to begin the training process. The initial model can be randomly chosen or selected based on a priori knowledge of the model parameters. The iteration loop is a simple updating procedure for computing the forward and backward model probabilities based on an input speech database (the training set of utterances) and then optimizing the model parameters to give an updated HMM. This process is iterated until no further improvement in probabilities occurs with each new iteration.

Step 1 — Acoustic Modeling

The function of the acoustic modeling step (Step 1) is to assign probabilities to the acoustic realizations of a sequence of words, given the observed acoustic vectors, i.e., we need to compute the probability that the acoustic vector sequence X = {x1,x2,...,xT } came from the word sequence W = w1,w2,...,wM (assuming each word is represented as an HMM) and perform this computation for all possible word sequences. This calculation can be expressed as: PA(X|W) = PA ({x1, x2, xT} |w1, w2,wM). (9.7) If we make the assumption that each frame, xt , is aligned with word i(t) and HMM model state j(t) via the function w i(t) j(t) and if we assume that each frame is independent of every other frame, we can express as the product PA(X|W) = Y T t=1 PA xt |w i(t) j(t) , where we associate each frame of X with a unique word and state, w i(t) j(t) , in the word sequence. Further, we calculate the local probability PA xt |w i(t) j(t) given that we know the word from which frame t came. The process of assigning individual speech frames to the appropriate word model in an utterance is based on an optimal alignment process between the concatenated sequence of word models and the sequence of feature vectors of the spoken input utterance being recognized. This alignment process is illustrated in Figure which shows the set of T feature vectors (frames) along the horizontal axis, and the set of M words (and word model states) along the vertical axis. The optimal segmentation of these feature vectors (frames) into the M words is shown by the sequence of boxes, each of which corresponds to one of the words in the utterance and its set of optimally matching feature vectors. We assume that each word model is further decomposed into a set of states which reflect the changing statistical properties of the feature vectors over time for the duration of the word. We assume that each word is represented by an N-state HMM model, and we denote the states as Sj, j = 1, 2, N. Within each state of each word there is a probability density that characterizes the statistical properties of the feature vectors in that state. We have seen in the previous section that the probability density of each state, and for each word, is learned during a training phase of the recognizer. Using a mixture of Gaussian densities to characterize the statistical distribution of the feature vectors in each state, j, of the word model, which we denote as bj (xt) we get a state-based probability density of the form: bj (xt) = X K k=1 cjkN[xt ,μjk ,Ujk], (9.9) where K is the number of mixture components in the density function, cjk is the weight of the kth mixture component in state j, with the constraint cjk ≥ 0, and N is a Gaussian density function with mean vector, μjk, for mixture k for state j, and covariance matrix, Ujk, for mixture k in state j. The density constraints are: X K k=1 cjk = 1, 1 ≤ j ≤ N (9.10) Z ∞ −∞ bj (xt)dxt = 1, 1 ≤ j ≤ N. We now return to the issue of the calculation of the probability of frame xt being associated with the j(t)th state of the i(t)th word in The key point is that we assign probabilities to acoustic realizations of a sequence of words by using hidden Markov models of the acoustic feature vectors within words. Using an independent (and orthographically labeled) set of training data, we "train the system" and learn the parameters of the best acoustic models for each word (or more specifically for each sound that comprises each word). The parameters, according to the mixture model of (9.9) are, for each state of the model, the mixture weights, the mean vectors, and the covariance matrix. Although we have been discussing acoustic models for whole words, it should be clear that for any reasonable size speech recognition task, it is impractical to create a separate acoustic model for every possible word in the vocabulary since each word would have to be spoken in every possible context in order to build a statistically reliable model of the density functions of (9.9). Even for modest size vocabularies of about 1000 words, the amount of training data required for word models is excessive. The alternative to word models is to build acoustic-phonetic models for the 40 or so phonemes in the English language and construct the model for a word by concatenating (stringing together sequentially) the models for the constituent phones in the word (as represented in a word dictionary or lexicon). The use of such sub-word acoustic-phonetic models poses no real difficulties in either training or when used to build up word models and hence is the most widely used representation for building word models in a speech recognition system. State-of-theart systems use context-dependent phone models as the basic units of recognition.

Step 2 — The Language Model

The language model assigns probabilities to sequences of words, based on the likelihood of that sequence of words occurring in the context of the task being performed by the speech recognition system. Hence the probability of the text string W = "Call home" for a telephone number identification task is zero since that string makes no sense for the specified task. There are many ways of building Language Models for specific tasks, including: (1) statistical training from text databases transcribed from task-specific dialogs (a learning procedure) (2) rule-based learning of the formal grammar associated with the task (3) enumerating, by hand, all valid text strings in the language and assigning appropriate probability scores to each string. The purpose of the language model, or grammar, is to enable the computation of the a priori probability, PL(W), of a word string, W, consistent with the recognition task. Perhaps the most popular way of constructing the language model is through the use of a statistical N-gram word grammar that is estimated from a large training set of text utterances, either from the task at hand or from a generic database with applicability to a wide range of tasks. We now describe the way in which such a language model is built.

Step 3 — The Search Problem

The third step in the Bayesian approach to automatic speech recognition is to search the space of all valid word sequences from the language model, to find the one with the maximum likelihood of having been spoken. The key problem is that the potential size of the search space can be astronomically large (for large vocabularies and high average word branching factor language models), thereby taking inordinate amounts of computing power to solve by heuristic methods. Fortunately, through the use of methods from the field of Finite State Automata Theory, Finite State Network (FSN) methods have evolved that reduce the computational burden by orders of magnitude, thereby enabling exact maximum likelihood solutions in computationally feasible times, even for very large speech recognition problems.

Challenges in ASR Technology

So far, ASR systems fall far short of human speech perception in all but the simplest, most constrained tasks. Before ASR systems become ubiquitous in society, many improvements will be required in both system performance and operational performance. In the system area we need large improvements in accuracy, efficiency, and robustness in order to utilize the technology for a wide range of tasks, on a wide range of processors, and under a wide range of operating conditions. In the operational area we need better methods of detecting when a person is speaking to a machine and isolating the spoken input from the background, we need to be able to handle users talking over the voice prompts (so-called barge-in conditions), we need more reliable and accurate utterance rejection methods so we can be sure that a word needs to be repeated when poorly recognized the first time, and finally we need better methods of confidence scoring of words, phrases, and even sentences so as to maintain an intelligent dialog with a customer.

Exercise

True Or False

1.Stratified sampling is a technique used to ensure that each class in a dataset is represented proportionally in the sample.

2.Oversampling involves adding more instances of the majority class to balance class distribution.

3.Reinforcement learning is a type of Machine Learning where an agent learns by interacting with an environment to maximize rewards.

4.In reinforcement learning, the primary objective is to minimize the prediction error between model outputs and actual labels.

5.The reward signal in reinforcement learning provides feedback to the agent about the quality of its actions.

6.In reinforcement learning, the policy represents the mapping from states to actions.

7.The value function in reinforcement learning estimates the expected cumulative reward from a given state.

8.Exploration in reinforcement learning refers to exploiting the best-known actions to maximize immediate rewards.

9.True or False: Computer vision is a field of study that focuses on enabling machines to interpret and understand visual information from the world.

10.Image segmentation is a computer vision technique used for converting images into textual descriptions.

11.Speech processing involves converting spoken language into written text or vice versa.

12.The purpose of sampling in Machine Learning is to reduce the complexity of the model.

13.Stratified sampling aims to ensure that each class in a dataset is equally represented in the sample.

14.Reinforcement learning involves a Machine Learning model learning from labeled examples.

15.In reinforcement learning, the agent's goal is to maximize the cumulative reward it receives over time.

16.The components of reinforcement learning include a reward signal, policy, and value function.

17.In the context of reinforcement learning, the value function represents the mapping of states to actions.

18.Computer vision is primarily concerned with understanding and interpreting visual information from the world.

19.Data compression is a common application of computer vision using Machine Learning.

21.Natural language processing (NLP) focuses on analyzing visual data, such as images and videos.

Answer: True, True, True, False, True, True, True, False, True, False, True, False, True, False, True, True, False, True, False, True, False

MCQ

1.What is the primary purpose of a sampling method in Machine Learning?

a) To reduce the size of the dataset

b) To improve the model's performance

c) To select a representative subset of data

d) To increase the complexity of the model

2.In the context of sampling, what is the term "stratified sampling" referring to?

a) A sampling method that focuses on non-uniform data distribution

b) A method for oversampling rare classes in a dataset

c) A technique to randomly select data points without replacement
d) A process of filtering out noisy data from the dataset

3.Which type of learning involves an agent interacting with an environment to maximize cumulative rewards?
a) Supervised learning
b) Unsupervised learning
c) Reinforcement learning
d) Semi-supervised learning

4.What is the main goal of reinforcement learning?
a) Minimize the error between predicted and actual outputs
b) Discover hidden patterns in unlabeled data
c) Optimize a model's parameters using labeled data
d) Learn a policy that maximizes the expected cumulative reward

5.What are the essential components of reinforcement learning?
a) Input, output, and error
b) Reward signal, policy, and value function
c) Features, labels, and predictions
d) Features, coefficients, and residuals
e) Detecting and recognizing objects in images
f) Creating 3D models from images

Question And Answers
Q1: What are the basic sampling methods in advanced learning?
Q2: What is reinforcement learning?
Q3: What are the elements of reinforcement learning?
Q4: How is computer vision applied in Machine Learning?
Q5: What are some applications of computer vision using Machine Learning?
Q6: How is speech processing applied in computer vision using Machine Learning?
Q7: How is natural language processing applied in computer vision using Machine Learning?
Q8: Explain the concept of basic sampling methods in advanced learning and their significance in handling complex probability distributions.
Q9: Describe the principles of reinforcement learning and how it differs from supervised and unsupervised learning.
Q10: Discuss the elements of reinforcement learning, including the role of the agent, environment, state, action, reward function, policy, and value function.
Q11: How is computer vision applied in Machine Learning, and what are some common computer vision tasks?
Q12: Provide examples of applications where computer vision using Machine Learning has made significant advancements.
Q13: How is speech processing applied in computer vision using Machine Learning, and what are its challenges?
Q14: Describe the application of natural language processing in computer vision using Machine Learning, including the generation of image captions.
Q15: How does reinforcement learning work in real-world applications, such as robotics and game playing?
Q16: What are the challenges and limitations of reinforcement learning in practical applications?
Q17: How are advanced learning techniques, such as deep reinforcement learning, used to tackle complex and high-dimensional tasks?
Q18: What are the main components of deep reinforcement learning algorithms?
Q19: Discuss the potential applications of deep reinforcement learning in robotics, autonomous vehicles, and healthcare.
Q20: How can deep reinforcement learning algorithms handle continuous action spaces, and what are some popular algorithms in this context?
Q21: What is transfer learning, and how can it be applied in computer vision tasks?
Q22: Explain the concept of generative models and their role in image generation and data augmentation.
Q23: What are the advantages of unsupervised learning techniques, such as clustering and autoencoders, in exploratory data analysis and anomaly detection?

Q24: Describe the role of deep learning architectures like Convolutional Neural Networks (CNNs) in computer vision tasks and their applications in image recognition and object detection.
Q25: What are the challenges in deploying advanced learning techniques in real-world applications, and how can they be addressed?
Q26: Discuss the impact of advanced learning techniques in personalized recommendation systems, such as movie recommendations and online shopping.
Q27: How is transfer learning used in natural language processing to leverage pre-trained language models for specific tasks like sentiment analysis and text classification?
Q28: Explain the concept of active learning and its role in reducing labeling costs in Machine Learning.
Q29: How does reinforcement learning apply to real-world robotics applications, such as robotic control and manipulation?
Q30: Describe the potential applications of advanced learning techniques in personalized healthcare, disease diagnosis, and medical image analysis.
Q31: How can reinforcement learning be used in game playing, such as playing board games or video games?
Q32: Discuss the challenges and ethical considerations in the use of advanced learning techniques, such as privacy, fairness, and interpretability.
Q33: How can advanced learning techniques, such as Generative Adversarial Networks (GANs), be used for data augmentation in computer vision tasks?
Q34: Explain the concept of meta-learning and its role in facilitating faster learning and adaptation to new tasks.
Q35: How can unsupervised learning techniques, such as autoencoders, be used for data compression and feature extraction in computer vision applications?
Q36: Describe the potential applications of advanced learning techniques in the financial industry, such as fraud detection and algorithmic trading.
Q37: How can reinforcement learning be applied in healthcare for personalized treatment planning and optimization of medical interventions?
Q38: Discuss the role of advanced learning techniques in natural language processing, such as machine translation, sentiment analysis, and chatbots.
Q39: Explain the concept of federated learning and its applications in scenarios where data privacy and security are critical concerns.
Q40: How can advanced learning techniques, such as transfer learning and pre-trained models, be used to improve the performance of Machine Learning models with limited labeled data?

Online Resources

Online Exam Papers
True/False Exam

Link: https://forms.gle/CkNymVoEPXcswi417

QR Code

YouTube Video Playlist Link
Chapter 5
Link: https://www.youtube.com/playlist?list=PLzlh_31VWEFo4U-NXdbbGRiyW0sO7JXGh
QR Code

Chapter- 6: Programming Languages that are used in Machine Learning

6.1 JavaScript

Traditionally, Machine Learning applications are using R or Python. But JavaScript has a great future as an Machine Learning language: JavaScript is well known. All developers can use it. Security is built in. JavaScript cannot access your files. JavaScript is faster than Python.JavaScript can use hardware acceleration. JavaScript runs in the browserJavaScript is Good for Machine Learning

Machine Learning can be math-heavy. The nature of neural networks is highly technical, and the jargon that goes along with it tends to scare people away. This is where JavaScript comes to help, with easy-to-understand software to simplifying the process of creating and training neural networks. With new Machine Learning libraries, JavaScript developers can add Machine Learning and Artificial Intelligence to web applications.

WebGL API

WebGL is a JavaScript API for rendering 2d and 3D graphics in any browser. WebGL can run on both integrated and standalone graphic cards in any PC.

WebGL brings 3D graphics to the web browser. Major browser vendors Apple (Safari), Google (Chrome), Microsoft (Edge), and Mozilla (Firefox) are members of the WebGL Working Group.

JellyFish

JavaScript Machine Learning Libraries

Machine Learning in the Browser means:

Math.js

Math.js is an extensive math library for JavaScript and Node.js.Math.js is powerful and easy to use. It comes with a large set of built-in functions, a flexible expression parser, and solutions to work with many data types like numbers, big numbers, complex numbers, fractions, units, arrays, and matrices.

Brain.js

Brain.js is a JavaScript library that makes it easy to understand Neural Networks because it hides the complexity of the mathematics.Brain.js is simple to use. You do not need to know neural networks in details to work with Brain.js.Brain.js provides multiple neural network implementations as different neural nets can be trained to do different things well.

ml5.js

ml5.js is trying to make Machine Learning more accessible to a wider audience.The ml5 team is working to wrap Machine Learning functionality in friendlier ways.The example below uses only three lines of code to classify an image:

```
<img id="image" src="pic1.jpg" width="100%">
<script>
const classifier = ml5.imageClassifier('MobileNet');
classifier.classify(document.getElementById("image"), gotResult);
function gotResult(error, results) { ... }
</script>
```

TensorFlow

TensorFlow Playground is a web application written in d3.js.With TensorFlow Playground you can learn about Neural Networks (NN) without math.In your own Web Browser you can create a Neural Network and see the result.TensorFlow.js was previously called Tf.js and Deeplearn.js.

Plotting in the Browser

Here is a list of some JavaScript libraries to use for both Machine Learning graphs and other HTML charts: Plotly.js,Chart.js,D3.js,Google Chart

6.2 Other Languages

LISP

LISP is the second oldest programming language in the world (1958), one year younger than Fortran (1957).

The term Artificial Intelligence was made up by John McCarthy who invented LISP.LISP was founded on the theory of Recursive Functions (self modifying functions), and this is very suitable for Machine Learning programs where "self-learning" is an important part of the program.

The R Language

R is a programming language for Graphics and Statistical computing.

R is supported by the R Foundation for Statistical Computing.R comes with a wide set of statistical and graphical techniques for:

Python

Python is a general-purpose coding language. It can be used for all types of programming and software development.

Python is typically used for server development, like building web apps for web servers.Python is also typically used in Data Science.An advantage for using Python is that it comes with some very suitable libraries:NumPy (Library for working with Arrays)

SciPy (Library for Statistical Science)

Matplotlib (Graph Plotting Library)

NLTK (Natural Language Toolkit)

C++

Because of the speed, C++ is a preferred language when programming Computer Games.It provides faster execution and has less response time which is applied in search engines and development of computer games.Google uses C++ in Artificial Intelligence and Machine Learning programs for SEO (Search Engine Optimization).SHARK is a super-fast C++ library with support for supervised learning algorithms, linear regression, neural networks, and clustering.MLPACK is also a super-fast Machine Learning library for C++.

Java

Java is another general-purpose coding language that can be used for all types of software development.

For Machine Learning, Java is mostly used to create algorithms, and neural networks.

SQL

SQL (Structured Query Language) is the most popular language for managing data.

Knowledge of SQL databases, tables and queries helps data scientists when dealing with data.SQL is very convenient for storing, manipulating, and retrieving data in databases.

6.3 Introduction to Python

Machine Learning is a type of artificial intelligence (AI) that provides computers with the ability to learn without being explicitly programmed. Machine Learning focuses on the development of Computer Programs that can change when exposed to new data. In this article, we'll see basics of Machine Learning, and implementation of a simple machine-learning algorithm using python. Machine Learning is a method of teaching computers to learn from data,

without being explicitly programmed. Python is a popular programming language for Machine Learning because it has a large number of powerful libraries and frameworks that make it easy to implement Machine Learning algorithms.To get started with Machine Learning using Python, you will need to have a basic understanding of Python programming and some knowledge of mathematical concepts such as probability, statistics, and linear algebra.There are several libraries and frameworks in Python that can be used for Machine Learning, including:
scikit-learn: This library provides a wide range of Machine Learning algorithms, including supervised and unsupervised learning, and it is built on top of other libraries such as NumPy and SciPy.
TensorFlow: This library is an open-source Machine Learning framework developed by Google, it is widely used for deep learning and other complex Machine Learning tasks.
Keras: A high-level neural networks API, written in Python and capable of running on top of TensorFlow, CNTK, or Theano.
PyTorch: An open-source Machine Learning library for Python, based on Torch library. It provides a seamless integration of computation graph and PyTorch tensors.
Theano: A numerical computation library for Python that allows you to efficiently define, optimize, and evaluate mathematical expressions involving multi-dimensional arrays.
Pandas: A library that provides fast and flexible data structures and data analysis tools for the Python programming language.
To start with Machine Learning, a good way i
Setting up the environmentPython community has developed many modules to help programmers implement Machine Learning. In this article, we will be using numpy, scipy and scikit-learn modules. We can install them using cmd command:
pip install numpy scipy scikit-learn
A better option would be downloading miniconda or anaconda packages for python, which come prebundled with these packages. Follow the instructions given here to use anaconda.
Machine Learning overview-Machine Learning involves a computer to be trained using a given data set, and use this training to predict the properties of a given new data. For example, we can train a computer by feeding it 1000 images of cats and 1000 more images which are not of a cat, and tell each time to the computer whether a picture is cat or not. Then if we show the computer a new image, then from the above training, the computer should be able to tell whether this new image is a cat or not.

The process of training and prediction involves the use of specialized algorithms. We feed the training data to an algorithm, and the algorithm uses this training data to give predictions on a new test data. One such algorithm is K-Nearest-Neighbor classification (KNN classification). It takes a test data, and finds k nearest data values to this data from test data set. Then it selects the neighbor of maximum frequency and gives its properties as the prediction result. For example if the training set is:
petal_sizeflower_type
1a
2b
1a
2b
3c
4d
3c
2b
5a

Now we want to predict flower type for petal of size 2.5 cm. So if we decide no. of neighbors (K)=3, we see that the 3 nearest neighbors of 2.5 are 1, 2 and 3. Their frequencies are 2, 3 and 2 respectively. Therefore the neighbor of maximum frequency is 2 and flower type corresponding to it is b. So for a petal of size 2.5, the prediction will be flower type b.
Implementing KNN- classification algorithm using Python on IRIS datasetHere is a python script which demonstrates knn classification algorithm. Here we use the famous iris flower dataset to train the computer, and then give a new value to the computer to make predictions about it. The data set consists of 50 samples from each of three species of Iris (Iris setosa, Iris virginica and Iris versicolor). Four features are measured from each sample: The length and Width of Sepals & Petals, in centimeters.

We train our program using this dataset, and then use this training to predict species of a iris flower with given measurements.

EX: 1

```
# Python program to demonstrate
# KNN classification algorithm
# on IRIS dataset
from sklearn.datasets import load_iris
from sklearn.neighbors import KNeighborsClassifier
import numpy as np
from sklearn.model_selection import train_test_split
iris_dataset=load_iris()
X_train, X_test, y_train, y_test = train_test_split(iris_dataset["data"], iris_dataset["target"], random_state=0)
kn = KNeighborsClassifier(n_neighbors=1)
kn.fit(X_train, y_train)
x_new = np.array([[5, 2.9, 1, 0.2]])
prediction = kn.predict(x_new)
print("Predicted target value: {}\n".format(prediction))
print("Predicted feature name: {}\n".format
   (iris_dataset["target_names"][prediction]))
print("Test score: {:.2f}".format(kn.score(X_test, y_test)))
```

Output:

```
Predicted target name: [0]
Predicted feature name: ['setosa']
Test score: 0.97
```

Explanation of the program:

Training the Dataset

The first line imports iris data set which is already predefined in sklearn module. Iris data set is basically a table which contains information about various varieties of iris flowers.

We import kNeighbors Classifier algorithm and train_test_split class from sklearn and numpy module for use in this program.

Then we encapsulate load_iris() method in iris_dataset variable. Further we divide the dataset into training data and test data using train_test_split method. The X prefix in variable denotes the feature values (eg. petal length etc) and y prefix denotes target values (eg. 0 for setosa, 1 for virginica and 2 for versicolor).

This method divides dataset into training and test data randomly in ratio of 75:25. Then we encapsulate KNeighborsClassifier method in kn variable while keeping value of k=1. This method contains K Nearest Neighbor algorithm in it.

In the next line, we fit our training data into this algorithm so that computer can get trained using this data. Now the training part is complete.

Testing the Dataset

Now we have dimensions of a new flower in a numpy array called x_new and we want to predict the species of this flower. We do this using the predict method which takes this array as input and spits out predicted target value as output.

So the predicted target value comes out to be 0 which stands for setosa. So this flower has good chances to be of setosa species.

Finally we find the test score which is the ratio of no. of predictions found correct and total predictions made. We do this using the score method which basically compares the actual values of the test set with the predicted values.

BENEFITS:

Here are several benefits to using Python for Machine Learning:

Wide range of libraries and frameworks: Python has a large number of libraries and frameworks available for Machine Learning, such as scikit-learn, TensorFlow, and Keras, which make it easy to implement Machine Learning algorithms and speed up the development process.

1. Easy to learn and use: Python has a simple and easy-to-learn syntax, which makes it accessible to a wide range of users, including those without a background in computer science or programming.

2. Large community and resources: Python has a large and active community, which means there are many resources available for learning and troubleshooting, including tutorials, forums, and documentation.

3. Versatility: Python can be used for a wide range of applications, including data analysis, web development, and scientific computing, making it a versatile tool for Machine Learning projects.

4. High-performance computing: Python is widely used in high-performance computing and data science, which makes it suitable for handling large datasets and complex Machine Learning tasks.

Thus, we saw how Machine Learning works and developed a basic program to implement it using scikit-learn module in python.

6.4 Data representation and visualization of data

Data Representation and Visualization of Data

Data sets and Visualization

Machine Learning is about adapting models to data. For this reason we begin by showing how data can be represented in order to be understood by the computer.

At the beginning of this chapter we quoted Tom Mitchell's definition of Machine Learning: "Well posed Learning Problem: A computer program is said to learn from experience E with respect to some task T and some performance measure P, if its performance on T, as measured by P, improves with experience E." Data is the "raw material" for Machine Learning. It learns from data. In Mitchell's definition, "data" is hidden behind the terms "experience E" and "performance measure P". As mentioned earlier, we need labeled data to learn and test our algorithm.

However, it is recommended that you familiarize yourself with your data before you begin training your classifier. Numpy offers ideal data structures to represent your data and Matplotlib offers great possibilities for visualizing your data.

In the following, we want to show how to do this using the data in the sklearn module.

Iris Dataset, "Hello World" of Machine Learning

What was the first program you saw? I bet it might have been a program giving out "Hello World" in some programming language. Most likely I'm right. Almost every introductory book or tutorial on programming starts with such a program. It's a tradition that goes back to the 1968 book "The C Programming Language" by Brian Kernighan and Dennis Ritchie!

The likelihood that the first dataset you will see in an introductory tutorial on Machine Learning will be the "Iris dataset" is similarly high. The Iris dataset contains the measurements of 150 iris flowers from 3 different species:

1. Iris-Setosa,

2. Iris-Versicolor, and

3. Iris-Virginica.

4. Iris Setosa

5. iris setosa

6. Iris Versicolor

7. iris versicolor

8. Iris Virginica

9. iris virginica

The iris dataset is often used for its simplicity. This dataset is contained in scikit-learn, but before we have a deeper look into the Iris dataset we will look at the other datasets available in scikit-learn.

Loading the Iris Data with Scikit-learn

For example, scikit-learn has a very straightforward set of data on these iris species. The data consist of the following:

Features in the Iris dataset:
1. sepal length in cm

2. sepal width in cm

3. petal length in cm

4. petal width in cm

Target classes to predict:
1. Iris Setosa

2. Iris Versicolour

3. Iris Virginica

4. Sepals and Petals in Iris Flower

scikit-learn embeds a copy of the iris CSV file along with a helper function to load it into numpy arrays:

```
from sklearn.datasets import load_iris
iris = load_iris()
```

The resulting dataset is a Bunch object:

```
type(iris)
```

OUTPUT:

```
sklearn.utils.Bunch
```

You can see what's available for this data type by using the method keys():

```
iris.keys()
```

OUTPUT:

```
dict_keys(['data', 'target', 'frame', 'target_names', 'DESCR', 'feature_names', 'filename'])
```

A Bunch object is similar to a dicitionary, but it additionally allows accessing the keys in an attribute style:

```
print(iris["target_names"])
print(iris.target_names)
```

OUTPUT:

```
['setosa' 'versicolor' 'virginica']
['setosa' 'versicolor' 'virginica']
```

The features of each sample flower are stored in the data attribute of the dataset:

```
n_samples, n_features = iris.data.shape
print('Number of samples:', n_samples)
print('Number of features:', n_features)
# the sepal length, sepal width, petal length and petal width of the first sample (first flower)
print(iris.data[0])
```

OUTPUT:

```
Number of samples: 150
Number of features: 4
[5.1 3.5 1.4 0.2]
```

The feautures of each flower are stored in the data attribute of the data set. Let's take a look at some of the samples:

```
# Flowers with the indices 12, 26, 89, and 114
iris.data[[12, 26, 89, 114]]
```

OUTPUT:

```
array([[4.8, 3. , 1.4, 0.1],
       [5. , 3.4, 1.6, 0.4],
       [5.5, 2.5, 4. , 1.3],
```

```
        [5.8, 2.8, 5.1, 2.4]])
```

The information about the class of each sample, i.e. the labels, is stored in the "target" attribute of the data set:

```
print(iris.data.shape)
print(iris.target.shape)
OUTPUT:
(150, 4)
(150,)
print(iris.target)
OUTPUT:
[0 0 0 0 0 0 0 0 0 0 0 0 0 0 0 0 0 0 0 0 0 0 0 0 0 0 0 0 0 0 0 0 0 0 0 0 0
 0 0 0 0 0 0 0 0 0 0 0 0 0 1 1 1 1 1 1 1 1 1 1 1 1 1 1 1 1 1 1 1 1 1 1 1 1
 1 1 1 1 1 1 1 1 1 1 1 1 1 1 1 1 1 1 1 1 1 1 1 1 1 2 2 2 2 2 2 2 2 2 2 2 2
 2 2 2 2 2 2 2 2 2 2 2 2 2 2 2 2 2 2 2 2 2 2 2 2 2 2 2 2 2 2 2 2 2 2 2 2 2
 2 2]
import numpy as np
np.bincount(iris.target)
OUTPUT:
array([50, 50, 50])
```

Using NumPy's bincount function (above) we can see that the classes in this dataset are evenly distributed - there are 50 flowers of each species, with

class 0: Iris Setosa
class 1: Iris Versicolor
class 2: Iris Virginica

These class names are stored in the last attribute, namely target_names:

```
print(iris.target_names)
OUTPUT:
['setosa' 'versicolor' 'virginica']
```

The information about the class of each sample of our Iris dataset is stored in the target attribute of the dataset:

```
print(iris.target)
OUTPUT:
[0 0 0 0 0 0 0 0 0 0 0 0 0 0 0 0 0 0 0 0 0 0 0 0 0 0 0 0 0 0 0 0 0 0 0 0 0
 0 0 0 0 0 0 0 0 0 0 0 0 0 1 1 1 1 1 1 1 1 1 1 1 1 1 1 1 1 1 1 1 1 1 1 1 1
 1 1 1 1 1 1 1 1 1 1 1 1 1 1 1 1 1 1 1 1 1 1 1 1 1 2 2 2 2 2 2 2 2 2 2 2 2
 2 2 2 2 2 2 2 2 2 2 2 2 2 2 2 2 2 2 2 2 2 2 2 2 2 2 2 2 2 2 2 2 2 2 2 2 2
 2 2]
```

Beside of the shape of the data, we can also check the shape of the labels, i.e. the target.shape:

Each flower sample is one row in the data array, and the columns (features) represent the flower measurements in centimeters. For instance, we can represent this Iris dataset, consisting of 150 samples and 4 features, a 2-dimensional array or matrix

in the following format:

The superscript denotes the ith row, and the subscript denotes the jth feature, respectively.

Generally, we have

rows and

columns:

```
print(iris.data.shape)
print(iris.target.shape)
OUTPUT:
(150, 4)
(150,)
```

bincount of NumPy counts the number of occurrences of each value in an array of non-negative integers. We can use this to check the distribution of the classes in the dataset:

```
import numpy as np
np.bincount(iris.target)
OUTPUT:
array([50, 50, 50])
```

We can see that the classes are distributed uniformly - there are 50 flowers from each species, i.e.

class 0: Iris-Setosa
class 1: Iris-Versicolor
class 2: Iris-Virginica
These class names are stored in the last attribute, namely target_names:

```
print(iris.target_names)
```

OUTPUT:

```
['setosa' 'versicolor' 'virginica']
```

Visualising the Features of the Iris Data Set
The feauture data is four dimensional, but we can visualize one or two of the dimensions at a time using a simple histogram or scatter-plot.

```
from sklearn.datasets import load_iris
iris = load_iris()
print(iris.data[iris.target==1][:5])
print(iris.data[iris.target==1, 0][:5])
```

OUTPUT:

```
[[7.  3.2 4.7 1.4]
 [6.4 3.2 4.5 1.5]
 [6.9 3.1 4.9 1.5]
 [5.5 2.3 4.  1.3]
 [6.5 2.8 4.6 1.5]]
[7.  6.4 6.9 5.5 6.5]
```

Histograms of the features

```
import matplotlib.pyplot as plt
fig, ax = plt.subplots()
x_index = 3
colors = ['blue', 'red', 'green']
for label, color in zip(range(len(iris.target_names)), colors):
    ax.hist(iris.data[iris.target==label, x_index],
            label=iris.target_names[label],
            color=color)
ax.set_xlabel(iris.feature_names[x_index])
ax.legend(loc='upper right')
plt.show()
```

machine-learning/data-representation-and-visualization-data: Graph 0
Scatterplot with two Features
The appearance diagram shows two features in one diagram:

```
import matplotlib.pyplot as plt
fig, ax = plt.subplots()
x_index = 3
y_index = 0
colors = ['blue', 'red', 'green']
for label, color in zip(range(len(iris.target_names)), colors):
    ax.scatter(iris.data[iris.target==label, x_index],
               iris.data[iris.target==label, y_index],
               label=iris.target_names[label],
               c=color)
ax.set_xlabel(iris.feature_names[x_index])
ax.set_ylabel(iris.feature_names[y_index])
ax.legend(loc='upper left')
plt.show()
```

Change x_index and y_index in the above script
Change x_index and y_index in the above script and find a combination of two parameters which maximally separate the three classes.
Generalization
We will now look at all feature combinations in one combined diagram:

```
import matplotlib.pyplot as plt
```

```
n = len(iris.feature_names)
fig, ax = plt.subplots(n, n, figsize=(16, 16))
colors = ['blue', 'red', 'green']
for x in range(n):
   for y in range(n):
      xname = iris.feature_names[x]
      yname = iris.feature_names[y]
      for color_ind in range(len(iris.target_names)):
         ax[x, y].scatter(iris.data[iris.target==color_ind, x],
                          iris.data[iris.target==color_ind, y],
                          label=iris.target_names[color_ind],
                          c=colors[color_ind])
      ax[x, y].set_xlabel(xname)
      ax[x, y].set_ylabel(yname)
      ax[x, y].legend(loc='upper left')
plt.show()
```

machine-learning/data-representation-and-visualization-data 3: Graph 2

Scatterplot 'Matrices

Instead of doing it manually we can also use the scatterplot matrix provided by the pandas module.

Scatterplot matrices show scatter plots between all features in the data set, as well as histograms to show the distribution of each feature.

```
import pandas as pd
   iris_df = pd.DataFrame(iris.data, columns=iris.feature_names)
pd.plotting.scatter_matrix(iris_df,
                         c=iris.target,
                         figsize=(8, 8)
                        );
```

3-Dimensional Visualization

```
import matplotlib.pyplot as plt
from sklearn.datasets import load_iris
from mpl_toolkits.mplot3d import Axes3D
iris = load_iris()
X = []
for iclass in range(3):
   X.append([[], [], []])
   for i in range(len(iris.data)):
      if iris.target[i] == iclass:
         X[iclass][0].append(iris.data[i][0])
         X[iclass][1].append(iris.data[i][1])
         X[iclass][2].append(sum(iris.data[i][2:]))

colours = ("r", "g", "y")
fig = plt.figure()
ax = fig.add_subplot(111, projection='3d')
for iclass in range(3):
   ax.scatter(X[iclass][0], X[iclass][1], X[iclass][2], c=colours[iclass])
plt.show()
```

machine-learning/data-representation-and-visualization-data 5: Graph 4

6.4 Train and Test Sets by Splitting Learn and Test Data

Train and Test datasets in Machine Learning

Machine Learning is one of the booming technologies across the world that enables computers/machines to turn a huge amount of data into predictions. However, these predictions highly depend on the quality of the data, and if we are not using the right data for our model, then it will not generate the expected result. In Machine Learning projects, we generally divide the original dataset into training data and test data. We train our model over a subset of the original dataset, i.e., the training dataset, and then evaluate whether it can generalize well to the new or unseen dataset or test set. Therefore, train and test datasets are the two key concepts of Machine Learning, where the training dataset is used to fit the model, and the test dataset is used to evaluate the model.

In this topic, we are going to discuss train and test datasets along with the difference between both of them. So, let's start with the introduction of the training dataset and test dataset in Machine Learning.

What is Training Dataset?

The training data is the biggest (in -size) subset of the original dataset, which is used to train or fit the Machine Learning model. Firstly, the training data is fed to the ML algorithms, which lets them learn how to make predictions for the given task.

For example, for training a sentiment analysis model, the training data could be as below:

Input	Output (Labels)
The New UI is Great	Positive
Update is really Slow	Negative

The training data varies depending on whether we are using Supervised Learning or Unsupervised Learning Algorithms.

For Unsupervised learning, the training data contains unlabeled data points, i.e., inputs are not tagged with the corresponding outputs. Models are required to find the patterns from the given training datasets in order to make predictions.

On the other hand, for supervised learning, the training data contains labels in order to train the model and make predictions.

The type of training data that we provide to the model is highly responsible for the model's accuracy and prediction ability. It means that the better the quality of the training data, the better will be the performance of the model. Training data is approximately more than or equal to 60% of the total data for an ML project.

What is Test Dataset?

Once we train the model with the training dataset, it's time to test the model with the test dataset. This dataset evaluates the performance of the model and ensures that the model can generalize well with the new or unseen dataset. The test dataset is another subset of original data, which is independent of the training dataset. However, it has some similar types of features and class probability distribution and uses it as a benchmark for model evaluation once the model training is completed. Test data is a well-organized dataset that contains data for each type of scenario for a given problem that the model would be facing when used in the real world. Usually, the test dataset is approximately 20-25% of the total original data for an ML project.

At this stage, we can also check and compare the testing accuracy with the training accuracy, which means how accurate our model is with the test dataset against the training dataset. If the accuracy of the model on training data is greater than that on testing data, then the model is said to have overfitting.

The testing data should:

1. Represent or part of the original dataset.

2. It should be large enough to give meaningful predictions.

3. Need of Splitting dataset into Train and Test set

4. Splitting the dataset into train and test sets is one of the important parts of data pre-processing, as by doing so, we can improve the performance of our model and hence give better predictability.

We can understand it as if we train our model with a training set and then test it with a completely different test dataset, and then our model will not be able to understand the correlations between the features.

Train and Test datasets in Machine Learning

Therefore, if we train and test the model with two different datasets, then it will decrease the performance of the model. Hence it is important to split a dataset into two parts, i.e., train and test set.

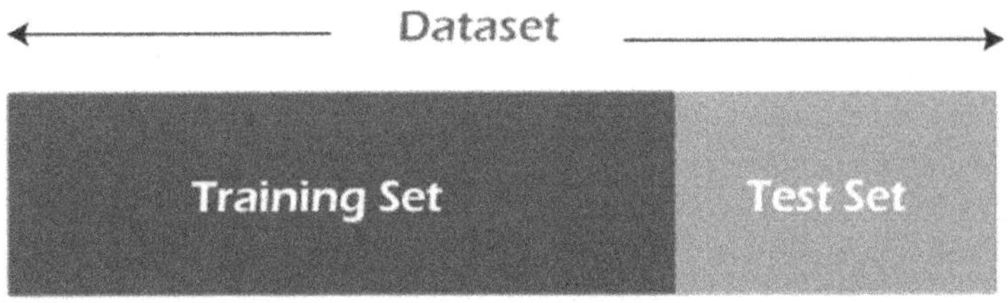

In this way, we can easily evaluate the performance of our model. Such as, if it performs well with the training data, but does not perform well with the test dataset, then it is estimated that the model may be overfitted.
For splitting the dataset, we can use the train_test_split function of scikit-learn.

The bellow line of code can be used to split dataset:

```
from sklearn.model_selection import train_test_split
x_train, x_test, y_train, y_test= train_test_split(x, y, test_size= 0.2, random_state=0)
```

Explanation:

In the first line of the above code, we have imported the train_test_split function from the sklearn library.
In the second line, we have used four variables, which are
x_train: It is used to represent features for the training data
x_test: It is used to represent features for testing data
y_train: It is used to represent dependent variables for training data
y_test: It is used to represent independent variable for testing data
In the train_test_split() function, we have passed four parameters. Which first two are for arrays of data, and test_size is for specifying the size of the test set. The test_size may be .5, .3, or .2, which tells the dividing ratio of training and testing sets.
The last parameter, random_state, is used to set a seed for a random generator so that you always get the same result, and the most used value for this is 42.

Overfitting and Underfitting issues

Overfitting and underfitting are the most common problems that occur in the Machine Learning model.
A model can be said as overfitted when it performs quite well with the training dataset but does not generalize well with the new or unseen dataset. The issue of overfitting occurs when the model tries to cover all the data points and hence starts caching noises present in the data. Due to this, it can't generalize well to the new dataset. Because of these issues, the accuracy and efficiency of the model degrade. Generally, the complex model has a high chance of overfitting. There are various ways by which we can avoid overfitting in the model, such as Using the Cross-Validation method, early stopping the training, or by regularization, etc.On the other hand, the model is said to be under-fitted when it is not able to capture the underlying trend of the data. It means the model shows poor performance even with the training dataset. In most cases, underfitting issues occur when the model is not perfectly suitable for the problem that we are trying to solve. To avoid the overfitting issue, we can either increase the training time of the model or increase the number of features in the dataset.

Training data vs. Testing Data

The main difference between training data and testing data is that training data is the subset of original data that is used to train the Machine Learning model, whereas testing data is used to check the accuracy of the model.
The training dataset is generally larger in size compared to the testing dataset. The general ratios of splitting train and test datasets are 80:20, 70:30, or 90:10.
Training data is well known to the model as it is used to train the model, whereas testing data is like unseen/new data to the model.

How do training and testing data work in Machine Learning?

Machine Learning algorithms enable the machines to make predictions and solve problems on the basis of past observations or experiences. These experiences or observations an algorithm can take from the training data, which is fed to it. Further, one of the great things about ML algorithms is that they can learn and improve over time on their own, as they are trained with the relevant training data.

Once the model is trained enough with the relevant training data, it is tested with the test data. We can understand the whole process of training and testing in three steps, which are as follows:
Feed: Firstly, we need to train the model by feeding it with training input data.
Define: Now, training data is tagged with the corresponding outputs (in Supervised Learning), and the model transforms the training data into text vectors or a number of data features.
Test: In the last step, we test the model by feeding it with the test data/unseen dataset. This step ensures that the model is trained efficiently and can generalize well.
The above process is explained using a flowchart given below:
Train and Test datasets in Machine Learning

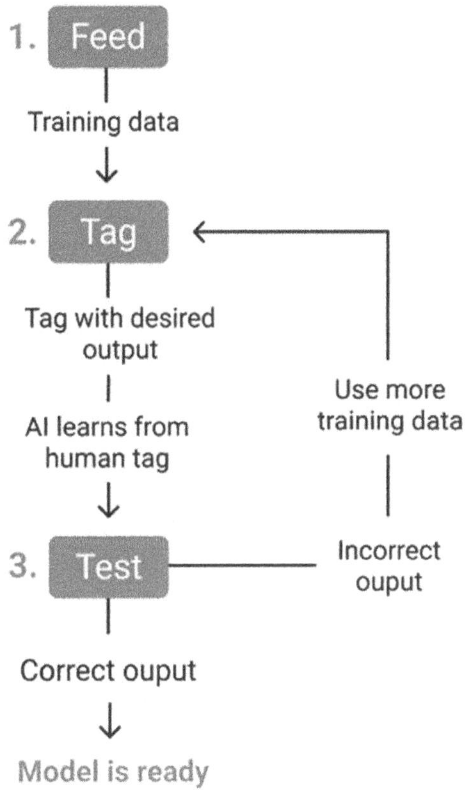

Traits of Quality training data
As the ability to the prediction of an ML model highly depends on how it has been trained, therefore it is important to train the model with quality data. Further, ML works on the concept of "Garbage In, Garbage Out." It means that whatever type of data we will input into our model, it will make the predictions accordingly. For a quality training data, the below points should be considered:
1. Relevant
The very first quality of training data should be relevant to the problem that you are going to solve. It means that whatever data you are using should be relevant to the current problem. For example, if you are building a model to analyze social media data, then data should be taken from different social sites such as Twitter, Facebook, Instagram, etc.
2. Uniform:
There should always be uniformity among the features of a dataset. It means all data for a particular problem should be taken from the same source with the same attributes.
3. Consistency: In the dataset, the similar attributes must always correspond to the similar label in order to ensure uniformity in the dataset.
4. Comprehensive: The training data must be large enough to represent sufficient features that you need to train the model in a better way. With a comprehensive dataset, the model will be able to learn all the edge cases.
Conclusion

Good training data is the backbone of Machine Learning. It is crucial to understand the importance of good training data in Machine Learning, as it ensures that you have data with the right quality and quantity to train your model. The main difference between training data and testing data is that training data is the subset of original data that is used to train the Machine Learning model, whereas testing data is used to check the accuracy of the model.

6.5 k-Nearest Neighbor Classifier in Python

Supervised Learning :

It is the learning where the value or result that we want to predict is within the training data (labeled data) and the value which is in data that we want to study is known as Target or Dependent Variable or Response Variable.

All the other columns in the dataset are known as the Feature or Predictor Variable or Independent Variable.

Supervised Learning is classified into two categories:

Classification: Here our target variable consists of the categories.

Regression: Here our target variable is continuous and we usually try to find out the line of the curve.

As we have understood that to carry out supervised learning we need labeled data. How we can get labeled data? There are various ways to get labeled data:

Historical labeled Data

Experiment to get data: We can perform experiments to generate labeled data like A/B Testing.

Crowd-sourcing

Now it's time to understand algorithms that can be used to solve supervised Machine Learning problem. In this post, we will be using popular scikit-learn package.

Note: There are few other packages as well like TensorFlow, Keras etc to perform supervised learning.

k-nearest neighbor algorithm:

This algorithm is used to solve the classification model problems. K-nearest neighbor or K-NN algorithm basically creates an imaginary boundary to classify the data. When new data points come in, the algorithm will try to predict that to the nearest of the boundary line.

Therefore, larger k value means smother curves of separation resulting in less complex models. Whereas, smaller k value tends to overfit the data and resulting in complex models.

Note: It's very important to have the right k-value when analyzing the dataset to avoid overfitting and underfitting of the dataset.

Using the k-nearest neighbor algorithm we fit the historical data (or train the model) and predict the future.

Example of the k-nearest neighbor algorithm

```
# Import necessary modules
from sklearn.neighbors import KNeighborsClassifier
from sklearn.model_selection import train_test_split
from sklearn.datasets import load_iris
# Loading data
irisData = load_iris()
 Create feature and target arrays
X = irisData.data
y = irisData.target
# Split into training and test set
X_train, X_test, y_train, y_test = train_test_split(
            X, y, test_size = 0.2, random_state=42)
knn = KNeighborsClassifier(n_neighbors=7)
knn.fit(X_train, y_train)
# Predict on dataset which model has not seen before
print(knn.predict(X_test))
```

In the example shown above following steps are performed:

The k-nearest neighbor algorithm is imported from the scikit-learn package.

Create feature and target variables.

Split data into training and test data.

Generate a k-NN model using neighbors value.

Train or fit the data into the model.

Predict the future.

We have seen how we can use K-NN algorithm to solve the supervised Machine Learning problem. But how to measure the accuracy of the model?

Consider an example shown below where we predicted the performance of the above model:

```
# Import necessary modules
from sklearn.neighbors import KNeighborsClassifier
from sklearn.model_selection import train_test_split
from sklearn.datasets import load_iris
 # Loading data
irisData = load_iris()
 # Create feature and target arrays
X = irisData.data
y = irisData.target
 # Split into training and test set
X_train, X_test, y_train, y_test = train_test_split(
          X, y, test_size = 0.2, random_state=42)
 knn = KNeighborsClassifier(n_neighbors=7)
 knn.fit(X_train, y_train)
 # Calculate the accuracy of the model
print(knn.score(X_test, y_test))
```

Model Accuracy:

So far so good. But how to decide the right k-value for the dataset? Obviously, we need to be familiar to data to get the range of expected k-value, but to get the exact k-value we need to test the model for each and every expected k-value. Refer to the example shown below.

```
 # Import necessary modules
from sklearn.neighbors import KNeighborsClassifier
from sklearn.model_selection import train_test_split
from sklearn.datasets import load_iris
import numpy as np
import matplotlib.pyplot as plt
 irisData = load_iris()
 # Create feature and target arrays
X = irisData.data
y = irisData.target
 # Split into training and test set
X_train, X_test, y_train, y_test = train_test_split(
          X, y, test_size = 0.2, random_state=42)
 neighbors = np.arange(1, 9)
train_accuracy = np.empty(len(neighbors))
test_accuracy = np.empty(len(neighbors))
 # Loop over K values
for i, k in enumerate(neighbors):
   knn = KNeighborsClassifier(n_neighbors=k)
   knn.fit(X_train, y_train)
   # Compute training and test data accuracy
   train_accuracy[i] = knn.score(X_train, y_train)
   test_accuracy[i] = knn.score(X_test, y_test)
 # Generate plot
plt.plot(neighbors, test_accuracy, label = 'Testing dataset Accuracy')
plt.plot(neighbors, train_accuracy, label = 'Training dataset Accuracy')
 plt.legend()
plt.xlabel('n_neighbors')
plt.ylabel('Accuracy')
plt.show()
```

Output:

Here in the example shown above, we are creating a plot to see the k-value for which we have high accuracy.

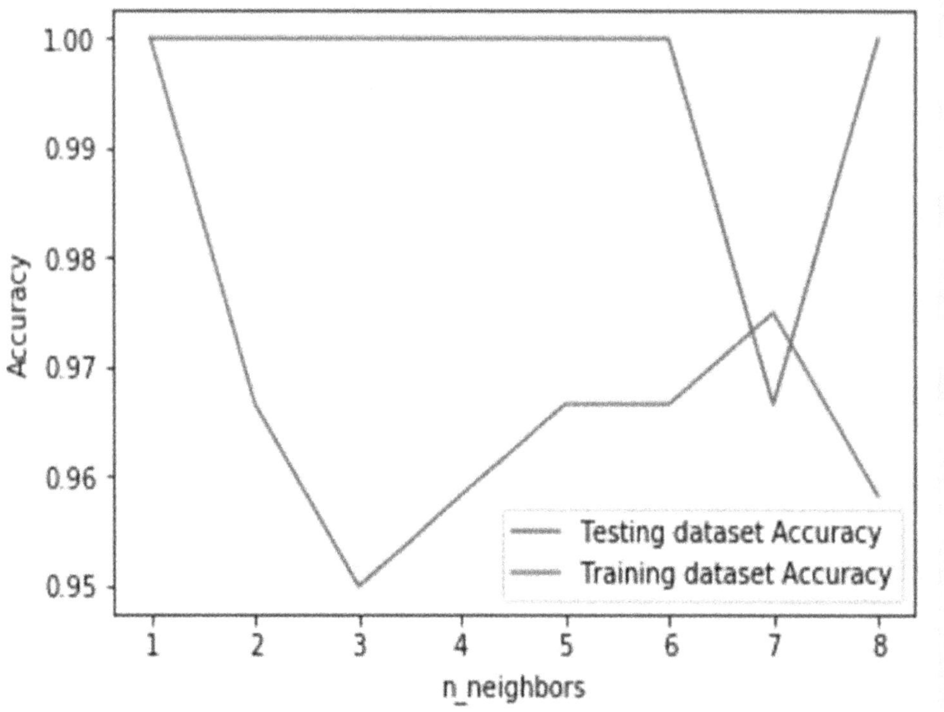

Note: This is a technique which is not used industry-wide to choose the correct value of n_neighbors. Instead, we do hyperparameter tuning to choose the value that gives the best performance.

Exercise

True Or False

1.JavaScript is a commonly used programming language for building Machine Learning models.
2.JavaScript is primarily used for web-based user interfaces and interactions and is not a popular choice for data manipulation in Machine Learning.
3.R is a programming language known for its use in statistical computing and data analysis, making it suitable for Machine Learning tasks.
4.Python and C++ are both commonly used languages for high-performance numerical computations in Machine Learning.
5.Python is favored in Machine Learning because of its extensive libraries and frameworks that facilitate various aspects of the Machine Learning pipeline.
6.Python's weak typing system makes it challenging to work with diverse data types in Machine Learning applications.
7.The purpose of splitting a dataset into training and test sets is to evaluate the model's performance on unseen data.
8.In the train-test split, a larger portion of the data is typically allocated to the test set to ensure accurate model assessment.
9.In the k-Nearest Neighbor (k-NN) algorithm, increasing the value of "k" results in a more flexible and less smooth decision boundary.
10.The k-NN algorithm requires explicit training of a model; it simply stores the entire training dataset for classification.
Answer: False, True , True, True, True, False, True, False, True, True

MCQ

1.Which type of applications is JavaScript commonly used for in the context of Machine Learning?
a) Deep learning models

b) Web-based user interfaces
c) High-performance computing
d) Quantum computing algorithms
Answer: b

2.In Machine Learning, JavaScript is often used for:
a) Data preprocessing and cleaning
b) Model training with neural networks
c) Solving optimization problems
d) Creating virtual reality environments
Answer: a

3.Which language is renowned for its use in statistical computing and data analysis, making it a strong contender for Machine Learning?
a) Ruby
b) Java
c) R
d) Swift
Answer: c

4.For high-performance numerical computations in Machine Learning, which programming language is commonly used?
a) Python
b) C++
c) Perl
d) PHP
Answer: b

5.Python is favored in Machine Learning due to:
a) Its strong typing system
b) Its efficient memory management
c) Its extensive libraries and frameworks
d) Its strict syntax rules
Answer: c

Short Question and Answers
Q1: Is JavaScript a commonly used language for Machine Learning?
Q2: Are there any Machine Learning libraries or frameworks available in JavaScript?
Q3: Besides Python, what are some other programming languages commonly used in Machine Learning?
Q4: Why is Python widely used in Machine Learning?
Q5: What are some popular Python libraries for Machine Learning?
Q6: Why is it important to split data into training and testing sets in Machine Learning?
Q7: What is the common practice for splitting data into training and testing sets?
Q8: How can data be split into training and testing sets using Python?
Q9: What is the purpose of the random_state parameter in the train_test_split function?
Q10: How can we evaluate the performance of a Machine Learning model using the test set?

Online Resources

Online Exam Papers
True/False Exam

Link

https://forms.gle/7kaE7Fr7DQ1Hzrhw5

QR Code

YouTube Video Playlist Link

Chapter 6
Link
https://www.youtube.com/playlist?list=PLzlh_31VWEFoBaaSxMx4782wb82nztpGE
QR Code

Chapter 7: Model Evaluation and Selection

Model Selection and Evaluation is a hugely important procedure in the Machine Learning workflow. This is the section of our workflow in which we will analyse our model. We look at more insightful statistics of its performance and decide what actions to take in order to improve this model. This step is usually the difference between a model that performs well and a model that performs very well. When we evaluate our model, we gain a greater insight into what it predicts well and what it doesn't and this helps us turn it from a model that predicts our dataset with a 65% accuracy level to closer to 80% or 90%.
Metrics and Scoring
Let's say we have two hypothesis for a task, h(x) and h'(x). How would we know which one is better. Well from a high level perspective, we might take the following steps:
Measure the accuracy of both hypotheses
Determine whether there is any statistical significance between the two results. If there is, select the better performing hypothesis. If not, we cannot say with any statistical certainty that either h(x) or h'(x) is better.
When we have a classification task, we will consider the accuracy of our model by its ability to assign an instance to its correct class. Consider this on a binary level. We have two classes, 1 and 0. We would classify a correct prediction therefore as being when the model classifies a class 1 instance as class 1, or a class 0 instance as class 0. Assuming our 1 class as being the 'Positive class' and the 0 class being the 'Negative class', we can build a table that outlines all the possibilities our model might produce.

7.1 Training, Validation, and Test Sets
Data splitting is one of the simplest preprocessing techniques we can use in a Machine Learning/Deep Learning task. The original dataset is split into subsets like training, test, and validation sets. One of the prime reasons this is done is to tackle the problem of overfitting. However, there are other benefits as well. Let's have a brief understanding of these terms and see how they are useful.
Training Set
The training set is used to fit or train the model. These data points are used to learn the parameters of the model. This is the biggest of all sets in terms of size. The training set includes the features and well as labels in the case of supervised learning. In the case of unsupervised learning, it can simply be the feature sets. These labels are used in the training phase to get the training accuracy score. The training set is usually taken as 70% of the original dataset but can be changed per the use case or available data.
For example

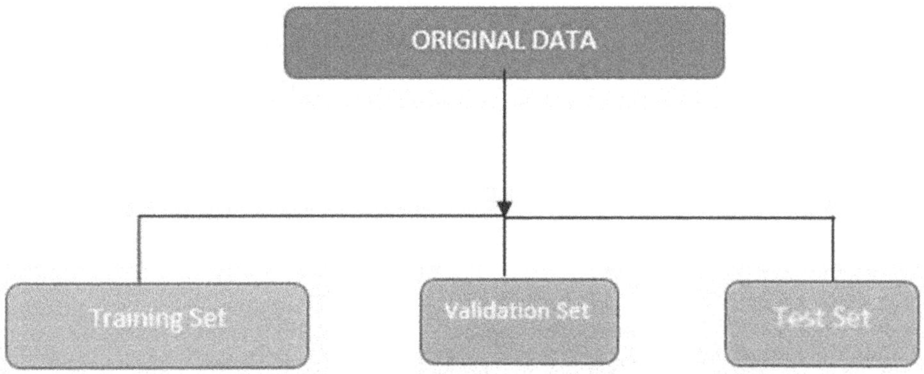

Fig. General representation of training, validation, and testing datasets

While using Linear Regression, the points in the training set are used to draw the line of best fit.

In K-Nearest Neighbors, the points in the training set are the points that could be the neighbors.

Applications of Train Set

Training sets are used in supervised learning procedures in data mining (i.e., classification of records or prediction of continuous target values.)

Example

Let's consider a dataset containing 20 points

Dataset1 = [1,5,6,7,8,6,4,5,6,7,23,45,12,34,45,1,7,7,8,0]

Train set can be taken as 60 % of the original Dataset1

The train set will contain 12 data points [8,6,4,5,6,7,23,45,12,34,1,5]

Validation Set

The validation set is used to provide an unbiased evaluation of the model fit during hyperparameter tuning of the model. It is the set of examples that are used to change learning process parameters. Optimal values of hyperparameters are tested against the model trained using the training set. In Machine Learning or Deep Learning, we generally need to test multiple models with different hyperparameters and check which model gives the best result. This process is carried out with the help of a validation set.

For example, in deep LSTM networks, a validation set is used to find the number of hidden layers, number of nodes, Dense units, etc.

Applications of Validation Set

Validations sets are used for Hyperparameter tuning of AI models. Domains include Healthcare, Analytics, Cyber Security, etc.

Example

Let's consider a dataset containing 20 points

Dataset2 = [1,5,6,7,8,6,4,5,6,7,23,45,12,34,45,1,7,7,8,0]

The validation set can be taken as 20 % of the original Dataset2.

The validation set will contain 4 data points [45,1,7,7]

Testing Set

Once we have the model trained with the training set and the hyperparameter tuned using the validation set, we need to test whether the model can generalize well on unseen data. To accomplish this, a test set is used. Here we can check and compare the training and test accuracies. To ensure that the model is not overfitting or underfitting, test accuracies are highly useful. If there is a large difference in train and test accuracies, overfitting might have occurred.

While choosing the test set the below points should be kept in mind:

The test should contain the same characteristics as of the train set.

It should be large enough to yield statistically significant results

Applications of Test Set

Test sets are used for evaluating metrics like:

Precision, Recall, AUC - ROC Curve, F1-Score

Example

Let's consider a data set containing 20 points

Dataset3 = [1,5,6,7,8,6,4,5,6,7,23,45,12,34,45,1,7,7,8,0]

The test set can be taken as 20 % of the original Dataset2

The test set will contain 4 data points [6,7,8,0]

Why do we need a train, validation, and test sets?

The training set is necessary to train the model and learn the parameters. Almost all Machine Learning/Deep Learning tasks should contain at least a training set.

The validation set and test sets are optional but highly recommended to use because only then can a trained model's legibility and accuracy can be verified. The validation set can be omitted if we do not choose to perform hyperparameter tuning or model selection. In such cases, a train set and test set will do the job.

A smart way to evaluate a model is to use K-Fold cross-validation.

The below table summarizes Training, Validation, and Testing sets

Training Set	Validation Set	Testing Set
It is used to fit the model to learn the parameters of the model	It is used to provide an unbiased evaluation of the model fit during hyperparameter tuning of the model	It is used to test whether the model can generalize well on unseen data.
Larger in size as compared to validation and test sets	Smaller in size.	Smaller in size as compared to the train set.
In the case of supervised learning, it comprises features and labels. In unsupervised learning, it includes only features	Contains both features and labels in supervised learning and only features in supervised learning	Contains both features and labels in supervised learning and only features in supervised learning
Slower on larger datasets but the job can be run in parallel using multiprocessing	Usually slower on a single core, if hyperparameters under observation are large. Can be run in parallel.	Faster than both train and validation sets. Used to get the metrics on test data based on the trained model

7.2 Cross-Validation

In Machine Learning, we couldn't fit the model on the training data and can't say that the model will work accurately for the real data. For this, we must assure that our model got the correct patterns from the data, and it is not getting up too much noise. For this purpose, we use the cross-validation technique.

Cross validation is a technique used in Machine Learning to evaluate the performance of a model on unseen data. It involves dividing the available data into multiple folds or subsets, using one of these folds as a validation set, and training the model on the remaining folds. This process is repeated multiple times, each time using a different fold as the validation set. Finally, the results from each validation step are averaged to produce a more robust estimate of the model's performance.

The main purpose of cross validation is to prevent overfitting, which occurs when a model is trained too well on the training data and performs poorly on new, unseen data. By evaluating the model on multiple validation sets, cross validation provides a more realistic estimate of the model's generalization performance, i.e., its ability to perform well on new, unseen data.

There are several types of cross validation techniques, including k-fold cross validation, leave-one-out cross validation, and stratified cross validation. The choice of technique depends on the size and nature of the data, as well as the specific requirements of the modeling problem.

In summary, cross validation is an important step in the Machine Learning process and helps to ensure that the model selected for deployment is robust and generalizes well to new data.

Cross-Validation

Cross-validation is a technique in which we train our model using the subset of the data-set and then evaluate using the complementary subset of the data-set. The three steps involved in cross-validation are as follows :

Methods of Cross Validation

Validation In this method, we perform training on the 50% of the given data-set and rest 50% is used for the testing purpose. The major drawback of this method is that we perform training on the 50% of the dataset, it may possible that the remaining 50% of the data contains some important information which we are leaving while training our model i.e higher bias. LOOCV (Leave One Out Cross Validation) In this method, we perform training on the whole data-set but leaves only one data-point of the available data-set and then iterates for each data-point. It has some advantages as well as disadvantages also. An advantage of using this method is that we make use of all data points and hence it is low bias. The major drawback of this method is that it leads to higher variation in the testing model as we are testing against one data point. If the data point is an outlier it can lead to higher variation. Another drawback is it takes a lot of execution time as it iterates over 'the number of data points' times. K-Fold Cross Validation In this

method, we split the data-set into k number of subsets(known as folds) then we perform training on the all the subsets but leave one(k-1) subset for the evaluation of the trained model. In this method, we iterate k times with a different subset reserved for testing purpose each time.
It is always suggested that the value of k should be 10 as the lower value
of k is takes towards validation and higher value of k leads to LOOCV method.
Example The diagram below shows an example of the training subsets and evaluation subsets generated in k-fold cross-validation. Here, we have total 25 instances. In first iteration we use the first 20 percent of data for evaluation, and the remaining 80 percent for training([1-5] testing and [5-25] training) while in the second iteration we use the second subset of 20 percent for evaluation, and the remaining three subsets of the data for training([5-10] testing and [1-5 and 10-25] training), and so on.
Total instances: 25
Value of k : 5

No. Iteration	Training set observations	Testing set observations
1	[5 6 7 8 9 10 11 12 13 14 15 16 17 18 19 20 21 22 23 24]	[0 1 2 3 4]
2	[0 1 2 3 4 10 11 12 13 14 15 16 17 18 19 20 21 22 23 24]	[5 6 7 8 9]
3	[0 1 2 3 4 5 6 7 8 9 15 16 17 18 19 20 21 22 23 24]	[10 11 12 13 14]
4	[0 1 2 3 4 5 6 7 8 9 10 11 12 13 14 20 21 22 23 24]	[15 16 17 18 19]
5	[0 1 2 3 4 5 6 7 8 9 10 11 12 13 14 15 16 17 18 19]	[20 21 22 23 24]

Comparison of train/test split to cross-validation

Advantages of train/test split:
This runs K times faster than Leave One Out cross-validation because K-fold cross-validation repeats the train/test split K-times.
Simpler to examine the detailed results of the testing process.

Advantages of cross-validation:
More accurate estimate of out-of-sample accuracy.
More "efficient" use of data as every observation is used for both training and testing.

Advantages of Cross Validation:
- **Overcoming Overfitting:** Cross validation helps to prevent overfitting by providing a more robust estimate of the model's performance on unseen data.

- **Model Selection:** Cross validation can be used to compare different models and select the one that performs the best on average.

- **Hyperparameter tuning:** Cross validation can be used to optimize the hyperparameters of a model, such as the regularization parameter, by selecting the values that result in the best performance on the validation set.

- **Data Efficient:** Cross validation allows the use of all the available data for both training and validation, making it a more data-efficient method compared to traditional validation techniques.

Disadvantages of Cross Validation:
- **Computationally Expensive:** Cross validation can be computationally expensive, especially when the number of folds is large or when the model is complex and requires a long time to train.

- **Time-Consuming:** Cross validation can be time-consuming, especially when there are many hyperparameters to tune or when multiple models need to be compared.

- **Bias-Variance Tradeoff:** The choice of the number of folds in cross validation can impact the bias-variance tradeoff, i.e., too few folds may result in high variance, while too many folds may result in high bias.

7.3 Performance Metrics

After doing the usual Feature Engineering, Selection, and of course, implementing a model and getting some output in forms of a probability or a class, the next step is to find out how effective is the model based on some metric using test datasets. Different performance metrics are used to evaluate different Machine Learning Algorithms. For now, we will be focusing on the ones used for Classification problems. We can use classification performance metrics such as Log-Loss, Accuracy, AUC(Area under Curve) etc. Another example of metric for evaluation of Machine Learning algorithms is precision, recall, which can be used for sorting algorithms primarily used by search engines. The metrics that you choose to evaluate your Machine Learning model is very important. Choice of metrics influences how the performance of Machine Learning algorithms is measured and compared. Before wasting any more time, let's jump right in and see what those metrics are.

1. Confusion Matrix:

The Confusion matrix is one of the most intuitive and easiest (unless of course, you are not confused)metrics used for finding the correctness and accuracy of the model. It is used for Classification problem where the output can be of two or more types of classes.

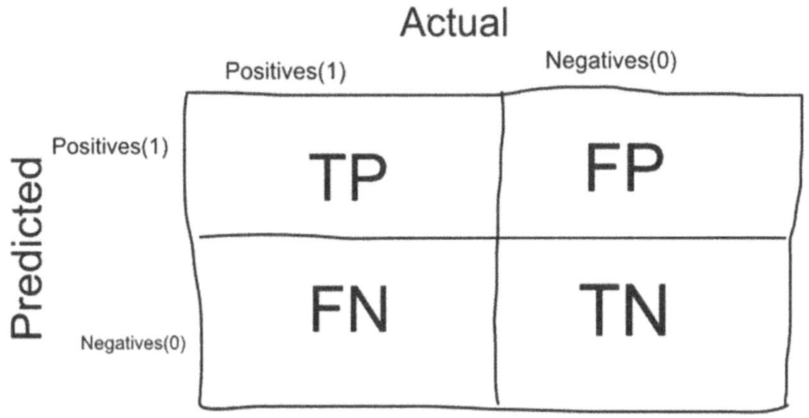

Before diving into what the confusion matrix is all about and what it conveys, Let's say we are solving a classification problem where we are predicting whether a person is having cancer or not.

Let's give a label of to our target variable:

1: When a person is having cancer 0: When a person is NOT having cancer.

Alright! Now that we have identified the problem, the confusion matrix, is a table with two dimensions ("Actual" and "Predicted"), and sets of "classes" in both dimensions. Our Actual classifications are columns and Predicted ones are Rows.

Confusion Matrix

The Confusion matrix in itself is not a performance measure as such, but almost all of the performance metrics are based on Confusion Matrix and the numbers inside it.

Terms associated with Confusion matrix:

1. **True Positives (TP)**: True positives are the cases when the actual class of the data point was 1(True) and the predicted is also 1(True)

Ex: The case where a person is actually having cancer(1) and the model classifying his case as cancer(1) comes under True positive.

2. **True Negatives (TN):** True negatives are the cases when the actual class of the data point was 0(False) and the predicted is also 0(False

Ex: The case where a person NOT having cancer and the model classifying his case as Not cancer comes under True Negatives.

3. **False Positives (FP):** False positives are the cases when the actual class of the data point was 0(False) and the predicted is 1(True). False is because the model has predicted incorrectly and positive because the class predicted was a positive one. (1)

Ex: A person NOT having cancer and the model classifying his case as cancer comes under False Positives.

4. **False Negatives (FN)**: False negatives are the cases when the actual class of the data point was 1(True) and the predicted is 0(False). False is because the model has predicted incorrectly and negative because the class predicted was a negative one. (0)

Ex: A person having cancer and the model classifying his case as No-cancer comes under False Negatives.

The ideal scenario that we all want is that the model should give 0 False Positives and 0 False Negatives. But that's not the case in real life as any model will NOT be 100% accurate most of the times.

When to minimise what?

We know that there will be some error associated with every model that we use for predicting the true class of the target variable. This will result in False Positives and False Negatives(i.e Model classifying things incorrectly as compared to the actual class).

There's no hard rule that says what should be minimised in all the situations. It purely depends on the business needs and the context of the problem you are trying to solve. Based on that, we might want to minimise either False Positives or False negatives.

1. Minimising False Negatives:

Let's say in our cancer detection problem example, out of 100 people, only 5 people have cancer. In this case, we want to correctly classify all the cancerous patients as even a very BAD model(Predicting everyone as NON-Cancerous) will give us a 95% accuracy(will come to what accuracy is). But, in order to capture all cancer cases, we might end up making a classification when the person actually NOT having cancer is classified as Cancerous. This might be okay as it is less dangerous than NOT identifying/capturing a cancerous patient since we will anyway send the cancer cases for further examination and reports. But missing a cancer patient will be a huge mistake as no further examination will be done on them.

2. Minimising False Positives:

For better understanding of False Positives, let's use a different example where the model classifies whether an email is spam or not

Let's say that you are expecting an important email like hearing back from a recruiter or awaiting an admit letter from a university. Let's assign a label to the target variable and say, 1: "Email is a spam" and 0:"Email is not a spam"

Suppose the Model classifies that important email that you are desperately waiting for, as Spam(case of False positive). Now, in this situation, this is pretty bad than classifying a spam email as important or not spam since in that case, we can still go ahead and manually delete it and it's not a pain if it happens once a while. So in case of Spam email classification, minimising False positives is more important than False Negatives.

3. Accuracy:

Accuracy in classification problems is the number of correct predictions made by the model over all kinds predictions made.

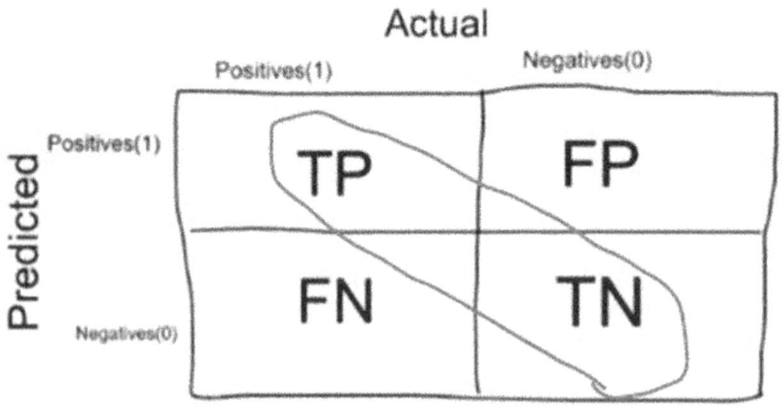

$$\text{Accuracy} = \frac{TP + TN}{TP + FP + FN + TN}$$

Accuracy

In the Numerator, are our correct predictions (True positives and True Negatives)(Marked as red in the fig above) and in the denominator, are the kind of all predictions made by the algorithm(Right as well as wrong ones).

When to use Accuracy:

Accuracy is a good measure when the target variable classes in the data are nearly balanced.
Ex:60% classes in our fruits images data are apple and 40% are oranges.
A model which predicts whether a new image is Apple or an Orange, 97% of times correctly is a very good measure in this example.
When NOT to use Accuracy:
Accuracy should NEVER be used as a measure when the target variable classes in the data are a majority of one class.
Ex: In our cancer detection example with 100 people, only 5 people has cancer. Let's say our model is very bad and predicts every case as No Cancer. In doing so, it has classified those 95 non-cancer patients correctly and 5 cancerous patients as Non-cancerous. Now even though the model is terrible at predicting cancer, The accuracy of such a bad model is also 95%.
3. Precision:
Let's use the same confusion matrix as the one we used before for our cancer detection example.

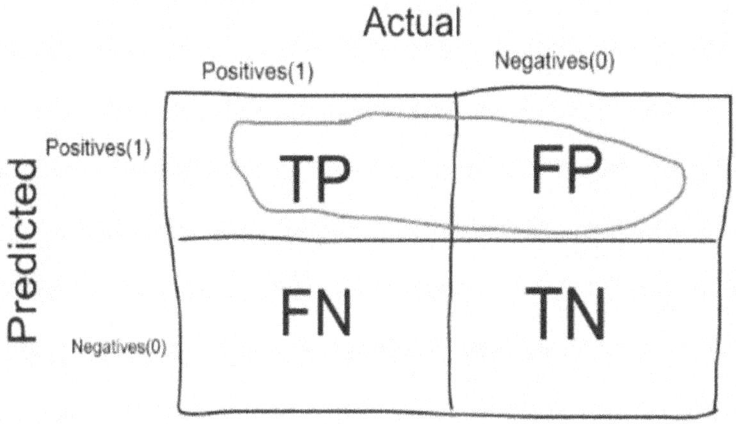

$$\text{Precision} = \frac{TP}{TP + FP}$$

7.3.1 Precision
Precision is a measure that tells us what proportion of patients that we diagnosed as having cancer, actually had cancer. The predicted positives (People predicted as cancerous are TP and FP) and the people actually having a cancer are TP.
Ex: In our cancer example with 100 people, only 5 people have cancer. Let's say our model is very bad and predicts every case as Cancer. Since we are predicting everyone as having cancer, our denominator(True positives and False Positives) is 100 and the numerator, person having cancer and the model predicting his case as cancer is 5. So in this example, we can say that Precision of such model is 5%.
4. Recall or Sensitivity:
Recall or Sensitivity
Recall is a measure that tells us what proportion of patients that actually had cancer was diagnosed by the algorithm as having cancer. The actual positives (People having cancer are TP and FN) and the people diagnosed by the model having a cancer are TP. (Note: FN is included because the Person actually had a cancer even though the model predicted otherwise).
Ex: In our cancer example with 100 people, 5 people actually have cancer. Let's say that the model predicts every case as cancer.
So our denominator(True positives and False Negatives) is 5 and the numerator, person having cancer and the model predicting his case as cancer is also 5(Since we predicted 5 cancer cases correctly). So in this example, we can say that the Recall of such model is 100%. And Precision of such a model(As we saw above) is 5%

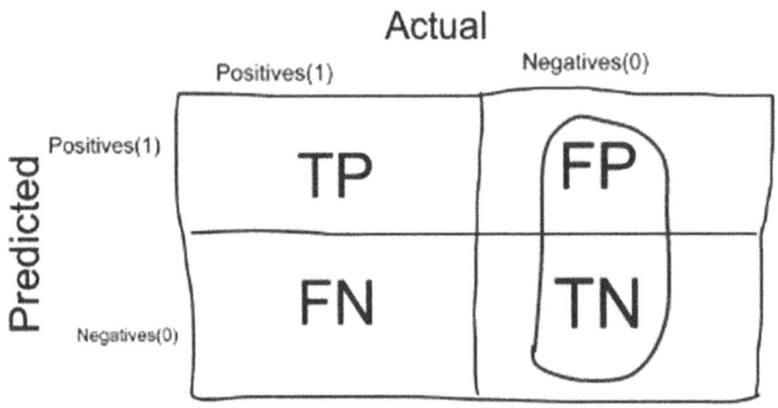

$$\text{Specificity} = \frac{TN}{TN + FP}$$

When to use Precision and When to use Recall?:

It is clear that recall gives us information about a classifier's performance with respect to false negatives (how many did we miss), while precision gives us information about its performance with respect to false positives (how many did we caught).

Precision is about being precise. So even if we managed to capture only one cancer case, and we captured it correctly, then we are 100% precise.

Recall is not so much about capturing cases correctly but more about capturing all cases that have "cancer" with the answer as "cancer". So if we simply always say every case as "cancer", we have 100% recall.

So basically if we want to focus more on minimising False Negatives, we would want our Recall to be as close to 100% as possible without precision being too bad and if we want to focus on minimising False positives, then our focus should be to make Precision as close to 100% as possible.

5. Specificity:

Specificity is a measure that tells us what proportion of patients that did NOT have cancer, were predicted by the model as non-cancerous. The actual negatives (People actually NOT having cancer are FP and TN) and the people diagnosed by us not having cancer are TN. (Note: FP is included because the Person did NOT actually have cancer even though the model predicted otherwise).

Specificity is the exact opposite of Recall.

Ex: In our cancer example with 100 people, 5 people actually have cancer. Let's say that the model predicts every case as cancer.

So our denominator(False positives and True Negatives) is 95 and the numerator, person not having cancer and the model predicting his case as no cancer is 0 (Since we predicted every case as cancer). So in this example, we can that that Specificity of such model is 0%.

6. F1 Score:

We don't really want to carry both Precision and Recall in our pockets every time we make a model for solving a classification problem. So it's best if we can get a single score that kind of represents both Precision(P) and Recall(R).

One way to do that is simply taking their arithmetic mean. i.e (P + R) / 2 where P is Precision and R is Recall. But that's pretty bad in some situations.

Suppose we have 100 credit card transactions, of which 97 are legit and 3 are fraud and let's say we came up a model that predicts everything as fraud. (Horrendous right!?)

Precision and Recall for the example is shown in the fig below.

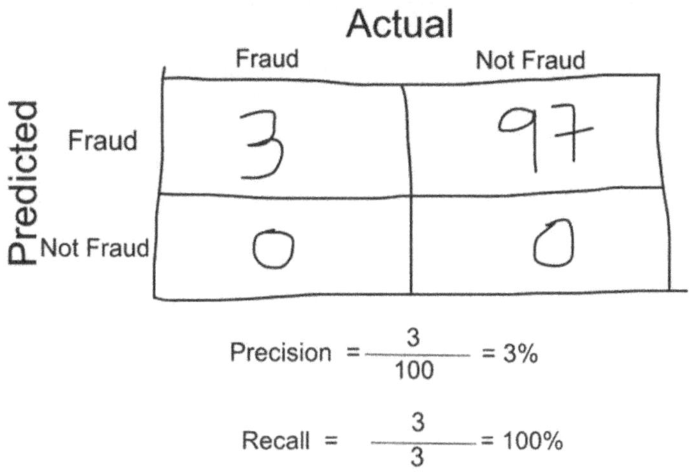

Precision and Recall for Credit Card example
Now, if we simply take arithmetic mean of both, then it comes out to be nearly 51%. We shouldn't be giving such a moderate score to a terrible model since it's just predicting every transaction as fraud.
So, we need something more balanced than the arithmetic mean and that is harmonic mean.

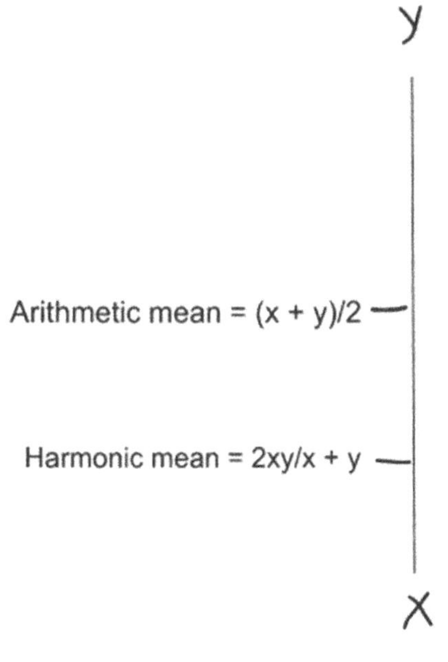

Arithmetic Mean vs Harmonic Mean
The Harmonic mean is given by the formula shown in the figure on the left.

Harmonic mean is kind of an average when x and y are equal. But when x and y are different, then it's closer to the smaller number as compared to the larger number.
For our previous example, F1 Score = Harmonic Mean(Precision, Recall)
F1 Score = 2 * Precision * Recall / (Precision + Recall) = 2*3*100/103 = 5%
So if one number is really small between precision and recall, the F1 Score kind of raises a flag and is more closer to the smaller number than the bigger one, giving the model an appropriate score rather than just an arithmetic mean.
So far, we have seen what the Confusion matrix is, what is Accuracy, Precision, Recall (or Sensitivity), Specificity and F1-score for a classification problem. In the next post, I will be discussing the other metrics that can be used in Classification problems like the AUC-ROC Curve, Log loss, F-Beta score etc.

7.3.2 ROC and AUC

You might have come across the terms ROC and AUC associated with artificial intelligence, deep learning, and convolutional neural networks (CNNs). So what exactly are they?
An ROC curve, or receiver operating characteristic curve, is like a graph that shows how well a classification model performs. It helps us see how the model makes decisions at different levels of certainty. The curve has two lines: one for how often the model correctly identifies positive cases (true positives) and another for how often it mistakenly identifies negative cases as positive (false positives). By looking at this graph, we can understand how good the model is and choose the threshold that gives us the right balance between correct and incorrect predictions.

The Receiver Operator Characteristic (ROC) curve is an evaluation metric for binary classification problems. It is a probability curve that plots the TPR against FPR at various threshold values and essentially separates the 'signal' from the 'noise.' In other words, it shows the performance of a classification model at all classification thresholds. The Area Under the Curve (AUC) is the measure of the ability of a binary classifier to distinguish between classes and is used as a summary of the ROC curve. The higher the AUC, the better the model's performance at distinguishing between the positive and negative classes.

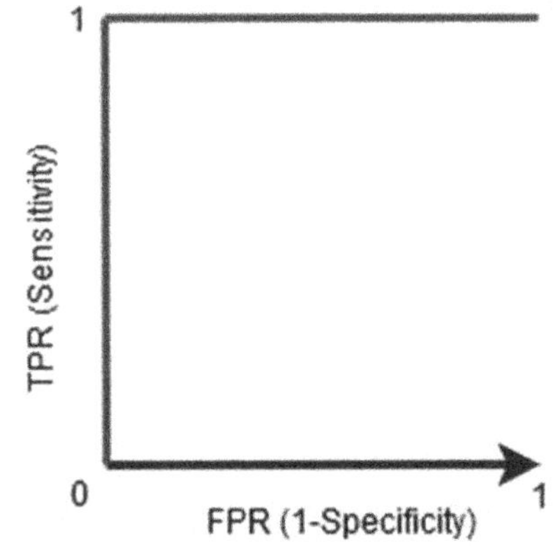

When AUC = 1, the classifier can correctly distinguish between all the Positive and the Negative class points. If, however, the AUC had been 0, then the classifier would predict all Negatives as Positives and all Positives as Negatives.

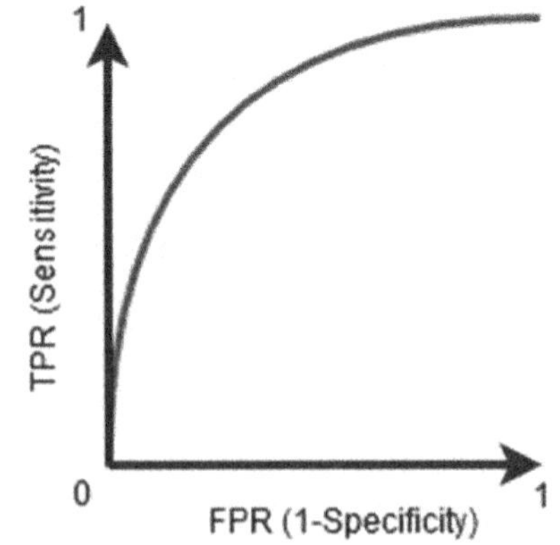

When 0.5<AUC<1, there is a high chance that the classifier will be able to distinguish the positive class values from the negative ones. This is so because the classifier is able to detect more numbers of True positives and True negatives than False negatives and False positives.

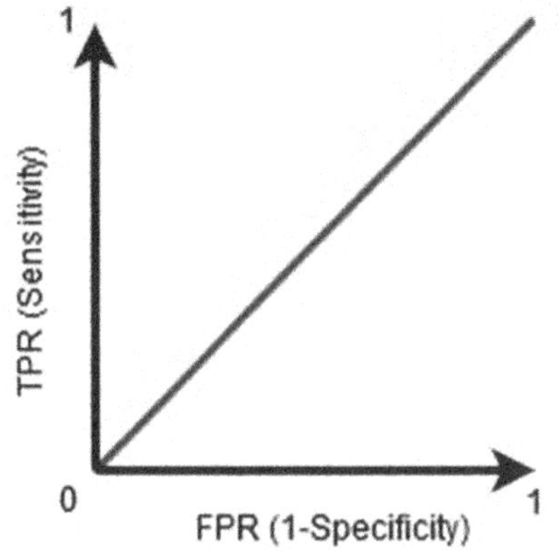

When AUC=0.5, then the classifier is not able to distinguish between Positive and Negative class points. Meaning that the classifier either predicts a random class or a constant class for all the data points.

So, the higher the AUC value for a classifier, the better its ability to distinguish between positive and negative classes.

How Does the AUC-ROC Curve Work?

In a ROC curve, a higher X-axis value indicates a higher number of False positives than True negatives. While a higher Y-axis value indicates a higher number of True positives than False negatives. So, the choice of the threshold depends on the ability to balance False positives and False negatives.

Let's dig a bit deeper and understand what our ROC curve would look like for different threshold values and how the specificity and sensitivity would vary.

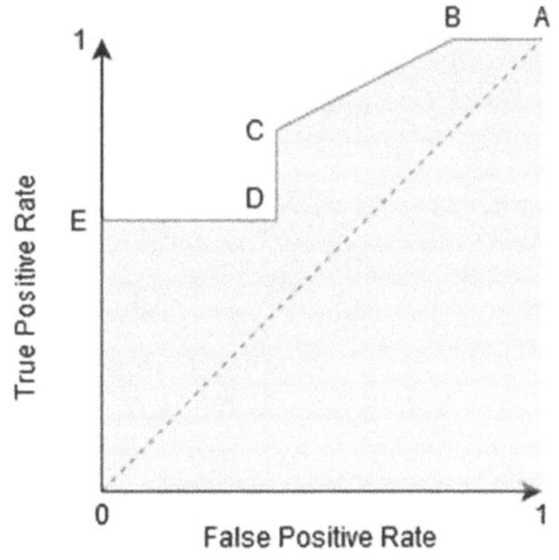

We can try and understand this graph by generating a confusion matrix for each point corresponding to a threshold and talk about the performance of our classifier:

Predicted \ Actual	+ve	-ve
+ve	5	5
-ve	0	0

Point A is where the Sensitivity is the highest and Specificity the lowest. This means all the Positive class points are classified correctly, and all the Negative class points are classified incorrectly.

In fact, any point on the blue line corresponds to a situation where the True Positive Rate is equal to False Positive Rate.

All points above this line correspond to the situation where the proportion of correctly classified points belonging to the Positive class is greater than the proportion of incorrectly classified points belonging to the Negative class.

Actual

Predicted	+ve	-ve
+ve	5	4
-ve	0	1

Although Point B has the same Sensitivity as Point A, it has a higher Specificity. Meaning the number of incorrectly Negative class points is lower than the previous threshold. This indicates that this threshold is better than the previous one.

Point C

Actual

Predicted	+ve	-ve
+ve	4	2
-ve	1	3

TPR/Sensitivity = 0.8
FPR = 0.4
Specificity = 1-FPR = 0.6

Point D

Actual

Predicted	+ve	-ve
+ve	3	2
-ve	2	3

TPR/Sensitivity = 0.6
FPR = 0.4
Specificity = 1-FPR = 0.6

Between points C and D, the Sensitivity at point C is higher than point D for the same Specificity. This means, for the same number of incorrectly classified Negative class points, the classifier predicted a higher number of Positive class points. Therefore, the threshold at point C is better than point D.

Now, depending on how many incorrectly classified points we want to tolerate for our classifier, we would choose between point B or C to predict whether you can defeat me in PUBG or not.

Point E

Actual

Predicted	+ve	-ve
+ve	3	0
-ve	2	5

TPR/Sensitivity = 0.6
FPR = 0
Specificity = 1-FPR = 1

Point E is where the Specificity becomes highest. Meaning the model classifies no False Positives. The model can correctly classify all the Negative class points! We would choose this point if our problem was to give perfect song recommendations to our users.

Going by this logic, can you guess where the point corresponding to a perfect classifier would lie on the graph? Yes! It would be on the top-left corner of the ROC graph corresponding to the coordinate (0, 1) in the cartesian plane. Here, both the Sensitivity and Specificity would be the highest, and the classifier would correctly classify all the Positive and Negative class points.

7.4 Overfitting and Underfitting

Overfitting and Underfitting are the two main problems that occur in Machine Learning and degrade the performance of the Machine Learning models.

The main goal of each Machine Learning model is to generalize well. Here generalization defines the ability of an ML model to provide a suitable output by adapting the given set of unknown input. It means after providing training on the dataset, it can produce reliable and accurate output. Hence, the underfitting and overfitting are the two terms that need to be checked for the performance of the model and whether the model is generalizing well or not.

Before understanding the overfitting and underfitting, let's understand some basic term that will help to understand this topic well:
- **Signal:** It refers to the true underlying pattern of the data that helps the Machine Learning model to learn from the data.

- **Noise:** Noise is unnecessary and irrelevant data that reduces the performance of the model.

- **Bias:** Bias is a prediction error that is introduced in the model due to oversimplifying the Machine Learning algorithms. Or it is the difference between the predicted values and the actual values.

- **Variance:** If the Machine Learning model performs well with the training dataset, but does not perform well with the test dataset, then variance occurs.

Overfitting

Overfitting occurs when our Machine Learning model tries to cover all the data points or more than the required data points present in the given dataset. Because of this, the model starts caching noise and inaccurate values present in the dataset, and all these factors reduce the efficiency and accuracy of the model. The overfitted model has low bias and high variance.

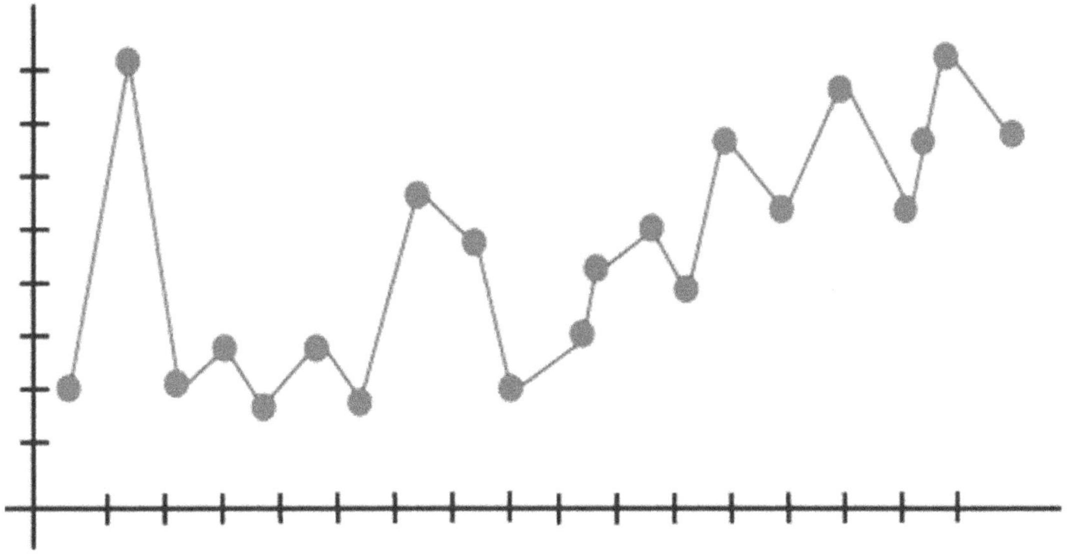

The chances of occurrence of overfitting increase as much we provide training to our model. It means the more we train our model, the more chances of occurring the overfitted model.
Overfitting is the main problem that occurs in supervised learning.
Example: The concept of the overfitting can be understood by the below graph of the linear regression output:
Overfitting and Underfitting in Machine Learning
As we can see from the above graph, the model tries to cover all the data points present in the scatter plot. It may look efficient, but in reality, it is not so. Because the goal of the regression model to find the best fit line, but here we have not got any best fit, so, it will generate the prediction errors.

How to avoid the Overfitting in Model

Both overfitting and underfitting cause the degraded performance of the Machine Learning model. But the main cause is overfitting, so there are some ways by which we can reduce the occurrence of overfitting in our model.
- Cross-Validation

- Training with more data

- Removing features

- Early stopping the training

- Regularization

- Ensembling

Underfitting
Underfitting occurs when our Machine Learning model is not able to capture the underlying trend of the data. To avoid the overfitting in the model, the fed of training data can be stopped at an early stage, due to which the model may not learn enough from the training data. As a result, it may fail to find the best fit of the dominant trend in the data.
In the case of underfitting, the model is not able to learn enough from the training data, and hence it reduces the accuracy and produces unreliable predictions.
An underfitted model has high bias and low variance.
Example: We can understand the underfitting using below output of the linear regression model:

Overfitting and Underfitting in Machine Learning
As we can see from the above diagram, the model is unable to capture the data points present in the plot.

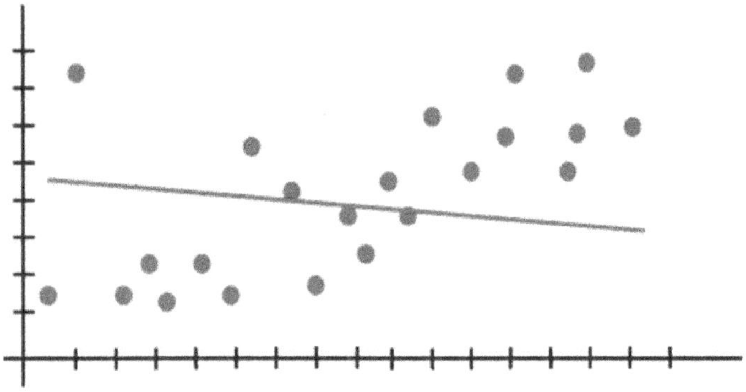

How to avoid underfitting:
- By increasing the training time of the model.

- By increasing the number of features.

Goodness of Fit
The "Goodness of fit" term is taken from the statistics, and the goal of the Machine Learning models to achieve the goodness of fit. In statistics modeling, it defines how closely the result or predicted values match the true values of the dataset.
The model with a good fit is between the underfitted and overfitted model, and ideally, it makes predictions with 0 errors, but in practice, it is difficult to achieve it.
As when we train our model for a time, the errors in the training data go down, and the same happens with test data. But if we train the model for a long duration, then the performance of the model may decrease due to the overfitting, as the model also learn the noise present in the dataset. The errors in the test dataset start increasing, so the point, just before the raising of errors, is the good point, and we can stop here for achieving a good model.
There are two other methods by which we can get a good point for our model, which are the resampling method to estimate model accuracy and validation dataset.

7.5 Hyperparameter Tuning
When you're training Machine Learning models, each dataset and model needs a different set of hyperparameters, which are a kind of variable. The only way to determine these is through multiple experiments, where you pick a set

of hyperparameters and run them through your model. This is called hyperparameter tuning. In essence, you're training your model sequentially with different sets of hyperparameters. This process can be manual, or you can pick one of several automated hyperparameter tuning methods.

Whichever method you use, you need to track the results of your experiments. You'll have to apply some form of statistical analysis, such as the loss function, to determine which set of hyperparameters gives the best result. Hyperparameter tuning is an important and computationally intensive process.

What are hyperparameters?

Hyperparameters are external configuration variables that data scientists use to manage Machine Learning model training. Sometimes called model hyperparameters, the hyperparameters are manually set before training a model. They're different from parameters, which are internal parameters automatically derived during the learning process and not set by data scientists.

Examples of hyperparameters include the number of nodes and layers in a neural network and the number of branches in a decision tree. Hyperparameters determine key features such as model architecture, learning rate, and model complexity.

How do you identify hyperparameters?

Selecting the right set of hyperparameters is important in terms of model performance and accuracy. Unfortunately, there are no set rules on which hyperparameters work best nor their optimal or default values. You need to experiment to find the optimum hyperparameter set. This activity is known as hyperparameter tuning or hyperparameter optimization.

Why is hyperparameter tuning important?

Hyperparameters directly control model structure, function, and performance. Hyperparameter tuning allows data scientists to tweak model performance for optimal results. This process is an essential part of Machine Learning, and choosing appropriate hyperparameter values is crucial for success.

For example, assume you're using the learning rate of the model as a hyperparameter. If the value is too high, the model may converge too quickly with suboptimal results. Whereas if the rate is too low, training takes too long and results may not converge. A good and balanced choice of hyperparameters results in accurate models and excellent model performance.

How does hyperparameter tuning work?

As previously stated, hyperparameter tuning can be manual or automated. While manual tuning is slow and tedious, a benefit is that you better understand how hyperparameter weightings affect the model. But in most instances, you would normally use one of the well-known hyperparameter learning algorithms.

The process of hyperparameter tuning is iterative, and you try out different combinations of parameters and values. You generally start by defining a target variable such as accuracy as the primary metric, and you intend to maximize or minimize this variable. It's a good idea to use cross-validation techniques, so your model isn't centered on a single portion of your data.

Exercise

True Or False

1.The training set is used to fine-tune model hyperparameters.

2.A validation set helps prevent overfitting by assessing the model's performance on unseen data.

3.Cross-validation involves training the model on the entire dataset and evaluating its performance on a separate test set.

4.K-Fold cross-validation creates k subsets of the data, using each as the test set exactly once.

5.Precision is the ratio of true positive predictions to the total number of positive instances.

6.The F1 score is the harmonic mean of precision and recall.

8.A higher AUC value indicates a model that is performing worse in terms of discrimination between positive and negative classes.

9.Overfitting occurs when a model captures noise in the training data and performs poorly on unseen data.

10.Underfitting occurs when a model is too complex and fits the training data perfectly, but fails to generalize.

Answer: False, True, False, True, False, True, True, False, True, False

MCQ

1.What is the purpose of a validation set in Machine Learning?
a) To assess a model's performance on unseen data
b) To fine-tune model hyperparameters
c) To train the model on a larger dataset
d) To create ensembles of models

2.How should the training, validation, and test sets be split for model evaluation?
a) 70% training, 15% validation, 15% test
b) 60% training, 20% validation, 20% test
c) 80% training, 10% validation, 10% test
d) Equal split among all sets

3.Cross-validation helps address which potential issue in model evaluation?
a) Overfitting
b) Underfitting
c) Model bias
d) Feature engineering

4.Which cross-validation technique involves dividing the dataset into k subsets and using each as a test set while the rest are used for training?
a) Leave-One-Out
b) Holdout
c) K-Fold
d) Random Split

5.Which performance metric is calculated as the ratio of correctly predicted positive instances to the total predicted positive instances?
a) Precision
b) Recall
c) Accuracy
d) F1 Score

Short Question And Answers

1. Q: Why is it important to split a dataset into training, validation, and test sets?
2. Q: What is the purpose of the validation set in model development?
3. Q: How does cross-validation address the limitations of a single train-test split?
4. Q: What is K-fold cross-validation, and why is it useful?
5. Q: How does stratified cross-validation address imbalanced class distributions?
6. Q: Define precision and recall. How do they differ from each other?
7. Q: What is the F1 score, and why is it useful in evaluating models?
8. Q: Describe the ROC curve and its components.
9. Q: How is AUC calculated, and what does it represent?
10. Q: What is overfitting, and how does it affect model performance?
11. Q: How can regularization techniques help prevent overfitting?
12. Q: Describe underfitting and its characteristics.
13. Q: How can underfitting be addressed in model development?
14. Q: What are hyperparameters, and why do they require tuning?
15. Q: Explain the concept of grid search for hyperparameter tuning.
16. Q: How does random search differ from grid search in hyperparameter tuning?
17. Q: What is cross-validation used for during hyperparameter tuning?
18. Q: How does Bayesian optimization contribute to efficient hyperparameter tuning?
19. Q: How does the choice of performance metric influence model evaluation and selection?
20. Q: Summarize the role of model evaluation and selection in the Machine Learning workflow.

Online Resources

Online Exam Papers
True/False Exam

Link

https://forms.gle/XJRw797mcjiELcReA

QR Code

YouTube Video Playlist Link

Chapter 7
Link
https://www.youtube.com/playlist?list=PLzlh_31VWEFq5-MUdQUQDfxkff0IOMLSH
QR Code

Chapter 8: Ensemble Learning

Ensemble Learning is a powerful Machine Learning technique that combines multiple individual models (learners) to improve overall predictive performance and robustness. The idea behind ensemble learning is that by combining multiple models, each with its own strengths and weaknesses, the ensemble can achieve better results than any single model alone.

Ensemble methods work on the principle of "wisdom of the crowd," where diverse opinions from different models contribute to a more accurate and reliable prediction. Some common ensemble learning methods include:Bagging (Bootstrap Aggregating): In bagging, multiple instances of the same model are trained on different subsets of the training data, created through bootstrapping (random sampling with replacement). These models then vote on the final prediction, and the majority vote is considered the ensemble's prediction. Random Forest is a popular ensemble method based on bagging and decision trees.

Boosting: Boosting focuses on training weak learners sequentially, where each learner corrects the errors of the previous one. The key idea is to give more weight to misclassified instances, making the subsequent models focus on these challenging cases. The final prediction is usually weighted by the contributions of each weak learner. Gradient Boosting Machines (GBM) and AdaBoost are well-known boosting algorithms.

Stacking: Stacking involves training multiple diverse models and using their predictions as inputs to train a higher-level model (meta-model). The meta-model learns to combine the outputs of the base models, effectively learning from the strengths of each base model. Stacking can often outperform individual models and even traditional ensembles.

Ensemble learning can be applied to various types of Machine Learning algorithms, including decision trees, support vector machines, neural networks, and more. The primary advantages of ensemble learning are improved generalization, reduced overfitting, and increased model stability. However, it's worth noting that ensemble methods may be computationally more expensive due to training multiple models. Nonetheless, their effectiveness makes them a widely used technique in the field of Machine Learning.

8.1 Bagging

Bagging (Bootstrap Aggregating) is an ensemble learning technique that aims to improve the performance and robustness of Machine Learning models. It involves creating multiple instances of the same model, each trained on different subsets of the training data. The subsets are generated by random sampling with replacement, a process known as bootstrapping.

Here's a brief overview of how bagging works:

Bootstrap Sampling: Given a dataset of size N, bagging randomly selects N samples (with replacement) from the original dataset to create a new subset. Some samples may appear multiple times, while others may be left out. This process creates a diverse set of training subsets.

Model Training: Each subset is used to train a separate instance of the same model. For example, in bagging with decision trees, several decision trees are trained, each using one of the bootstrapped subsets.

Voting: When making predictions, all the trained models vote on the final output. In a classification problem, each model votes for a class, and the majority class is selected as the ensemble prediction. In a regression problem, the models' predictions are averaged to form the final prediction.

The key advantages of bagging are:

- **Reducing Overfitting:** By training models on different subsets of data, bagging helps to reduce overfitting and increase the model's generalization performance on unseen data.

- **Improved Accuracy:** Bagging often leads to improved accuracy compared to training a single model, especially when the base model tends to be unstable or sensitive to small changes in the training data.

- **Robustness:** Bagging makes the ensemble more robust against outliers and noisy data points since different subsets will be affected differently by such instances.

One popular ensemble method based on bagging is the Random Forest algorithm. Random Forest uses decision trees as base models and aggregates their predictions using bagging. It is widely used due to its high accuracy, robustness, and ability to handle large datasets with high dimensionality.

8.2 Boosting

Boosting is another ensemble learning technique that aims to improve the performance of Machine Learning models by combining the strengths of multiple weak learners (simple and relatively low-performing models) to create a strong learner with high predictive accuracy.

Here's a brief overview of how boosting works:

- **Sequential Training:** Boosting trains a sequence of weak learners one after the other, with each learner focused on correcting the mistakes of its predecessor. Unlike bagging, where models are trained independently, boosting is a sequential process.

- **Weighted Data:** During each iteration, the misclassified instances from the previous learner are given higher weights to increase their importance. This process allows subsequent models to concentrate on the challenging instances that the previous models struggled with.

- **Weighted Voting:** When making predictions, each weak learner's prediction is weighted based on its performance, and the weighted votes are combined to produce the final ensemble prediction.

The key characteristics of boosting are:

- **Adaptive Learning:** Boosting adapts and learns from its mistakes. As the iterations progress, the ensemble becomes increasingly focused on difficult examples, leading to better overall performance.

- **Reduction of Bias and Variance:** Boosting helps reduce both bias and variance, enhancing the model's ability to capture complex patterns in the data while still avoiding overfitting.

- **Focus on Data Points:** Weak learners are designed to be slightly better than random guessing, and boosting ensures that they concentrate on the problematic data points, thus improving the model's overall accuracy.

Some popular boosting algorithms include:

- **AdaBoost (Adaptive Boosting):** One of the earliest and most well-known boosting algorithms, AdaBoost assigns weights to misclassified instances, and subsequent weak learners are trained to pay more attention to these weighted instances.

- **Gradient Boosting Machines (GBM):** GBM builds weak learners in a stage-wise manner, each one fitting the negative gradient of the loss function to reduce errors. It is a general framework that can be used with various loss functions and base models.

- **XGBoost (Extreme Gradient Boosting):** XGBoost is an optimized version of gradient boosting that includes additional features like regularization, handling missing values, and tree pruning to enhance performance and efficiency.

- **Boosting algorithms** are widely used in various Machine Learning tasks, including classification, regression, and ranking problems, and they often achieve state-of-the-art results in many applications.

8.3 Stacking

Stacking, also known as stacked generalization, is an advanced ensemble learning technique that combines multiple diverse base models to create a more powerful and accurate meta-model. It goes beyond simple averaging or voting used in bagging and boosting by leveraging the diverse opinions of multiple models to make predictions.

Here's a brief overview of how stacking works:

- **Base Models:** Stacking involves training several different base models, each with its own strengths and weaknesses. These base models can be of different types or built using different algorithms.

- **Data Splitting:** The original training dataset is split into multiple subsets. Each base model is trained on a different subset of the data.

- **Level 1 Predictions:** Once the base models are trained, they make predictions on the validation (or test) dataset that they have not seen during training.

- **Meta-Model:** The level 1 predictions from the base models become the input features for a higher-level meta-model. The meta-model is typically a simple model, like a linear regression, logistic regression, or another Machine Learning algorithm.

- **Meta-Model Training:** The meta-model is trained using the level 1 predictions as input features and the actual target labels as the target variable.

- **Final Prediction:** For making predictions on new data, the base models first generate level 1 predictions, which are then fed into the trained meta-model to obtain the final ensemble prediction.

The key advantages of stacking are:

- **Improved Performance:** Stacking can often outperform individual base models and traditional ensembles because it learns to combine the diverse predictions of the base models effectively.

- **Better Generalization:** By combining multiple base models, stacking can reduce overfitting and improve generalization performance on unseen data.

- **Flexibility:** Stacking is flexible and can work with various base models and meta-models, allowing practitioners to mix and match different algorithms to find the optimal combination.

However, stacking also comes with some challenges, such as the potential risk of overfitting at the meta-model level and increased computational complexity due to training multiple models.
To use stacking effectively, it's essential to select a diverse set of base models, ensuring that they make different types of errors on the data, and carefully tune the meta-model to avoid overfitting.

Exercise

True Or False

1.Bagging involves training multiple models and combining their predictions to make a final decision.
2.In bagging, each model is trained on the entire dataset without any modifications.
3.Boosting aims to combine multiple weak models to create a single strong model
4.In boosting, the weights of misclassified data points are decreased to focus on them less.
5.Stacking involves training multiple models independently and averaging their predictions.
6.Stacking uses a meta-model to combine predictions from base models.
7.Bagging and boosting both focus on reducing model variance and overfitting.
8.Stacking is generally a simpler ensemble technique compared to bagging and boosting
9.One advantage of ensemble learning is that it always guarantees better model performance.
Answer: True, False, True, False, False, True, True, False, False

MCQ

1.What is bagging in ensemble learning?
a) A technique for creating ensembles of models using boosting algorithms
b) A method for aggregating the predictions of multiple models to improve accuracy
c) A way to reduce the variance of a single model by using bootstrap samples
d) A process of feature engineering to improve model performance

2.Bagging involves training multiple models on:
a) The same subset of the training data
b) Different subsets of the training data
c) The test data
d) The validation data

3.What is the main idea behind boosting in ensemble learning?

a) Combining multiple weak models to create a strong model
b) Reducing the complexity of individual models for better generalization
c) Training multiple models independently and averaging their predictions
d) Creating an ensemble by stacking models on top of each other

4.In boosting, which data points are assigned higher weights during the training process?
a) Misclassified data points
b) Correctly classified data points
c) Validation data points
d) Test data points

5.Stacking involves:
a) Training multiple models independently and averaging their predictions
b) Combining the predictions of multiple models using weighted averages
c) Creating an ensemble of models by using bagging techniques
d) Training a meta-model on the predictions of base models

6.What is a meta-model in stacking?
a) The first model trained in the ensemble
b) A model used for feature selection
c) A model trained on the original dataset
d) A model trained on the predictions of base models

7.Which ensemble technique focuses on reducing variance and improving stability?
a) Bagging
b) Boosting
c) Stacking
d) Regularization

8.Which ensemble technique is known to have a higher risk of overfitting due to its iterative nature?
a) Bagging
b) Boosting
c) Stacking
d) Random Forest

9.What is an advantage of ensemble learning?
a) It always guarantees improved model performance
b) It is computationally less expensive than training a single model
c) It can capture complex relationships in the data by combining multiple models
d) It eliminates the need for hyperparameter tuning

10.One disadvantage of ensemble learning is:
a) It requires a small amount of training data
b) It is not suitable for handling categorical features
c) It may increase the risk of overfitting if not properly tuned
d) It is limited to a single type of base model

11.What does "bagging" stand for in ensemble learning?
a) Boosted Aggregation of Grouped Inputs
b) Bagging and Grouping
c) Bootstrap Aggregating
d) Boosted Aggregation of Gradient Inputs
Answer: c

12.Bagging involves training multiple models and combining their predictions using:
a) A weighted average

b) A linear combination
c) A majority voting scheme
d) A gradient descent algorithm
Answer: c

13.In boosting, what is the primary objective of each subsequent model?
a) To independently make predictions
b) To minimize the training error of the previous model
c) To introduce randomization in the ensemble
d) To maximize the validation accuracy
Answer: b

14.What happens to the weights of misclassified data points in boosting?
a) They are increased to emphasize their importance
b) They remain the same throughout the boosting process
c) They are decreased to reduce their impact
d) They are set to zero and excluded from training
Answer: a

15.Stacking in ensemble learning involves:
a) Training multiple models independently and selecting the best one
b) Combining the predictions of base models using majority voting
c) Sequentially training models, each correcting the errors of the previous one
d) Training a meta-model on predictions of base models
Answer: d

Question And Answers

Q1.What is ensemble learning?
Q2.What's the main idea behind ensemble learning?
Q3.What is the principle behind the "wisdom of the crowd" in ensemble learning?
Q4.What is bagging, and what does the acronym stand for?
Q5.How does bagging reduce overfitting in models?
Q6.What is an example of a bagging algorithm?
Q7.What is boosting in ensemble learning?
Q8.How does boosting differ from bagging?
Q9.What is the role of adaptive boosting (AdaBoost) in boosting?
Q10.What is stacking in ensemble learning?
Q11.What is a level-0 model in stacking?
Q12.How does stacking address the limitations of individual models?
Q13.What are the benefits of ensemble learning over using a single model?
Q14.Can ensemble methods be used for both classification and regression tasks?
Q15.How can ensemble methods be used to handle imbalanced datasets?
Q16.Give an example of a real-world application where ensemble learning is particularly effective.
Q17.What are some challenges in implementing ensemble learning?
Q18.Are there cases where ensemble learning might not be suitable?
Q19.How does ensemble learning impact model interpretability?

Online Resources
Online Exam Papers
True/False Exam

Link

https://forms.gle/hHnc5uGsNEZxCv5JA

QR Code

YouTube Video Playlist Link

Chapter 8
Link
https://www.youtube.com/playlist?list=PLzlh_31VWEFoRPdSlkRBu9A2BUOWx2lkM
QR Code

Chapter 9: Neural Networks and Deep Learning

Neural Networks and Deep Learning is a free online book. The book will teach you about:

1. Neural networks, a beautiful biologically-inspired programming paradigm which enables a computer to learn from observational data

2. Deep learning, a powerful set of techniques for learning in neural networks

Neural networks and deep learning currently provide the best solutions to many problems in image recognition, speech recognition, and natural language processing. This book will teach you many of the core concepts behind neural networks and deep learning.

9.1 Basics of Neural Networks

Neural networks are used to mimic the basic functioning of the human brain and are inspired by how the human brain interprets information. It is used to solve various real-time tasks because of its ability to perform computations quickly and its fast responses.

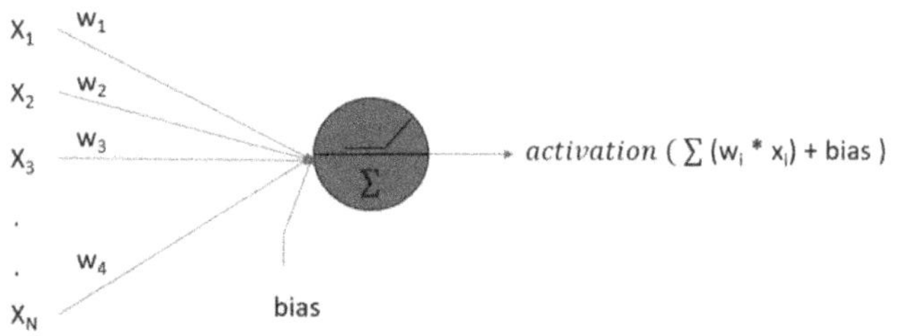

A single neuron shown with X_i inputs with their respective weights W_i and a bias term and applied activation function

An Artificial Neural Network model contains various components that are inspired by the biological nervous system.Artificial Neural Network has a huge number of interconnected processing elements, also known as Nodes. These nodes are connected with other nodes using a connection link. The connection link contains weights, these weights contain the information about the input signal. Each iteration and input in turn leads to updation of these weights. After inputting all the data instances from the training data set, the final weights of the Neural Network along with its architecture is known as the Trained Neural Network. This process is called Training of Neural Networks. This trained neural network is used to solve specific problems as defined in the problem statement.

Types of tasks that can be solved using an artificial neural network include Classification problems, Pattern Matching, Data Clustering, etc. We use artificial neural networks because they learn very efficiently and adaptively. They have the capability to learn "how" to solve a specific problem from the training data it receives. After learning, it can be used to solve that specific problem very quickly and efficiently with high accuracy.Some real-life applications of neural networks include Air Traffic Control, Optical Character Recognition as used by some scanning apps like Google Lens, Voice Recognition, etc.

Types of Neural Networks

(i) ANN– It is also known as an artificial neural network. It is a feed-forward neural network because the inputs are sent in the forward direction. It can also contain hidden layers which can make the model even denser. They have a fixed length as specified by the programmer. It is used for Textual Data or Tabular Data. A widely used real-life application is Facial Recognition. It is comparatively less powerful than CNN and RNN.

(ii) CNN– It is also known as Convolutional Neural Networks. It is mainly used for Image Data. It is used for Computer Vision. Some of the real-life applications are object detection in autonomous vehicles. It contains a combination of convolutional layers and neurons. It is more powerful than both ANN and RNN.

(iii) RNN–

It is also known as Recurrent Neural Networks. It is used to process and interpret time series data. In this type of model, the output from a processing node is fed back into nodes in the same or previous layers. The most known types of RNN are LSTM (Long Short Term Memory) Networks

Now that we know the basics about Neural Networks, We know that Neural Networks' learning capability is what makes it interesting.

There are 3 types of learnings in Neural networks, namely

1. Supervised Learning

2. Unsupervised Learning

3. Reinforcement Learning

Supervised Learning: As the name suggests, it is a type of learning that is looked after by a supervisor. It is like learning with a teacher. There are input training pairs that contain a set of input and the desired output. Here the output from the model is compared with the desired output and an error is calculated, this error signal is sent back into the network for adjusting the weights. This adjustment is done till no more adjustments can be made and the output of the model matches the desired output. In this, there is feedback from the environment to the model.

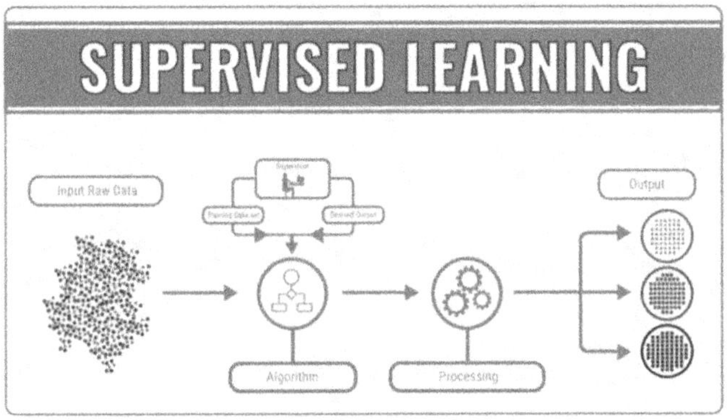

Unsupervised Learning: Unlike supervised learning, there is no supervisor or a teacher here. In this type of learning, there is no feedback from the environment, there is no desired output and the model learns on its own. During the training phase, the inputs are formed into classes that define the similarity of the members. Each class contains similar input patterns. On inputting a new pattern, it can predict to which class that input belongs based on similarity with other patterns. If there is no such class, a new class is formed.

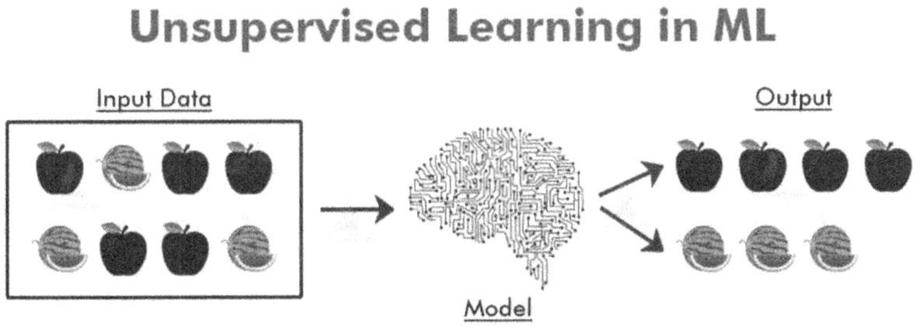

Reinforcement Learning: It gets the best of both worlds, that is, the best of both Supervised learning and Unsupervised learning. It is like learning with a critique. Here there is no exact feedback from the environment, rather there is critique feedback. The critique tells how close our solution is. Hence the model learns on its own based on the critique information. It is similar to supervised learning in that it receives feedback from the environment, but it is different in that it does not receive the desired output information, rather it receives critique information.

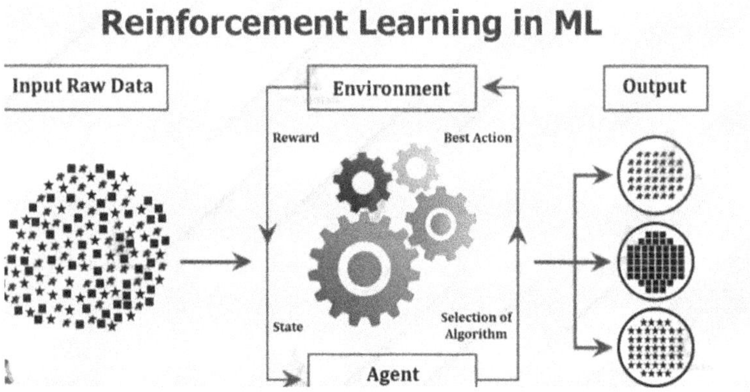

How does a Neural Network work?

According to Arthur Samuel, one of the early American pioneers in the field of computer gaming and artificial intelligence, he defined Machine Learning as:

Suppose we arrange for some automatic means of testing the effectiveness of any current weight assignment in terms of actual performance and provide a mechanism for altering the weight assignment so as to maximize the performance. We need not go into the details of such a procedure to see that it could be made entirely automatic and to see that a machine so programmed would "learn" from its experience.

Let's see what we can take out of this quote:

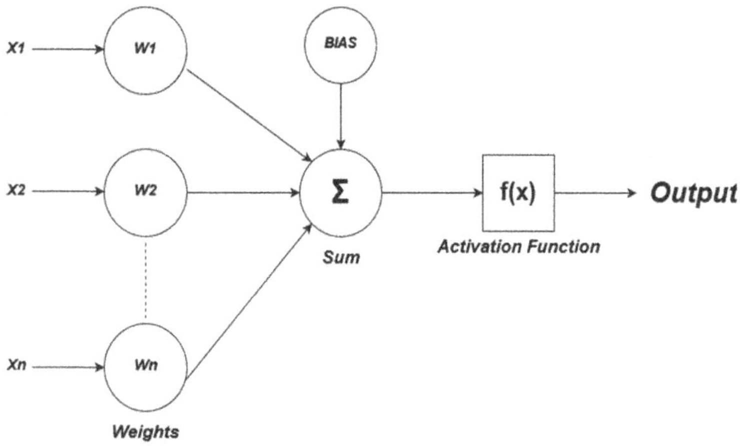

An artificial neuron can be thought of as a simple or multiple linear regression model with an activation function at the end. A neuron from layer i will take the output of all the neurons from the later i-1 as inputs calculate the weighted sum and add bias to it. After this is sent to an activation function as we saw in the previous diagram.

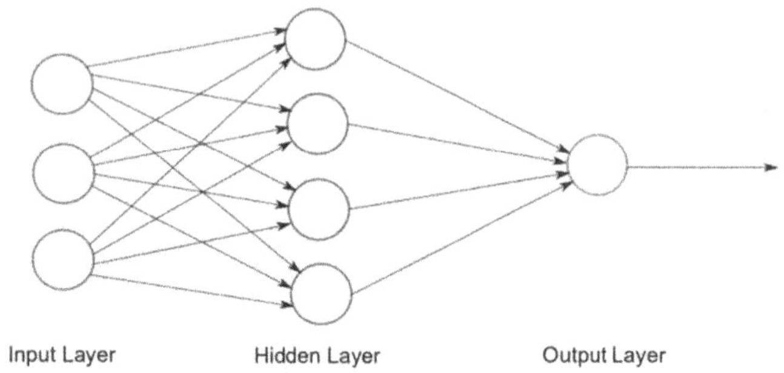

The first neuron from the first layer is connected to all the inputs from the previous layer, Similarly, the second neuron from the first hidden layer will also be connected to all the inputs from the previous layer and so on for all the neurons in the first hidden layer.

For neurons in the second hidden layer (outputs of the previously hidden layer) are considered as inputs and each of these neurons are connected to previous neurons, likewise. This whole process is called Forward propagation.
After this, there is an interesting thing that happens. Once we have predicted the output it is then compared to the actual output. We then calculate the loss and try to minimize it. But how can we minimize this loss? For this, there comes another concept which is known as Back Propagation. We will understand more about this in another article. I will tell you how it works. First, the loss is calculated then weights and biases are adjusted in such a way that they try to minimize the loss. Weights and biases are updated with the help of another algorithm called gradient descent. We will understand more about gradient descent in a later section. We basically move in the direction opposite to the gradient.

9.2 Activation Functions

is recommended to understand Neural Networks before reading this article. In the process of building a neural network, one of the choices you get to make is what Activation Function to use in the hidden layer as well as at the output layer of the network. This article discusses some of the choices.

- **Elements of a Neural Network Input Layer:** This layer accepts input features. It provides information from the outside world to the network, no computation is performed at this layer, nodes here just pass on the information(features) to the hidden layer.

- **Hidden Layer:** Nodes of this layer are not exposed to the outer world, they are part of the abstraction provided by any neural network. The hidden layer performs all sorts of computation on the features entered through the input layer and transfers the result to the output layer.

- **Output Layer**: This layer bring up the information learned by the network to the outer world.

What is an activation function and why use them?

The activation function decides whether a neuron should be activated or not by calculating the weighted sum and further adding bias to it. The purpose of the activation function is to introduce non-linearity into the output of a neuron.

Explanation: We know, the neural network has neurons that work in correspondence with weight, bias, and their respective activation function. In a neural network, we would update the weights and biases of the neurons on the basis of the error at the output. This process is known as back-propagation. Activation functions make the back-propagation possible since the gradients are supplied along with the error to update the weights and biases.

Why do we need Non-linear activation function?

A neural network without an activation function is essentially just a linear regression model. The activation function does the non-linear transformation to the input making it capable to learn and perform more complex tasks.
Mathematical proof

Suppose we have a Neural net like this :-

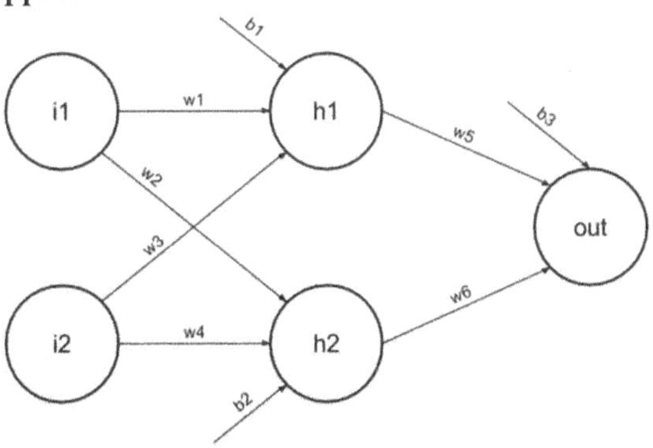

Elements of the diagram are as follows:
Hidden layer i.e. layer 1:

z(1) = W(1)X + b(1) a(1)

Here,

1. z(1) is the vectorized output of layer 1

2. W(1) be the vectorized weights assigned to neurons of hidden layer i.e. w1, w2, w3 and w4

3. X be the vectorized input features i.e. i1 and i2

4. b is the vectorized bias assigned to neurons in hidden layer i.e. b1 and b2

5. a(1) is the vectorized form of any linear function.

*(**Note:** We are not considering activation function here)*

Layer 2 i.e. output layer :-

Note : *Input for layer 2 is output from layer 1*

z(2) = W(2)a(1) + b(2)

a(2) = z(2)

Calculation at Output layer

*z(2) = (W(2) * [W(1)X + b(1)]) + b(2)*

*z(2) = [W(2) * W(1)] * X + [W(2)*b(1) + b(2)]*

Let,

*[W(2) * W(1)] = W*

*[W(2)*b(1) + b(2)] = b*

*Final output : z(2) = W*X + b*

which is again a linear function

This observation results again in a linear function even after applying a hidden layer, hence we can conclude that, doesn't matter how many hidden layer we attach in neural net, all layers will behave same way because ***the composition of two linear function is a linear function itself***. Neuron can not learn with just a linear function attached to it. A non-linear activation function will let it learn as per the difference w.r.t error. **Hence we need an activation function.**

Variants of Activation Function

Linear Function

1. Equation : Linear function has the equation similar to as of a straight line i.e. **y = x**

2. No matter how many layers we have, if all are linear in nature, the final activation function of last layer is nothing but just a linear function of the input of first layer.

3. Range : -inf to +inf

4. Uses : Linear activation function is used at just one place i.e. output layer.

5. Issues : If we will differentiate linear function to bring non-linearity, result will no more depend on *input "x"* and function will become constant, it won't introduce any ground-breaking behavior to our algorithm.

> **For example :** Calculation of price of a house is a regression problem. House price may have any big/small value, so we can apply linear activation at output layer. Even in this case neural net must have any non-linear function at hidden layers.

Sigmoid Function

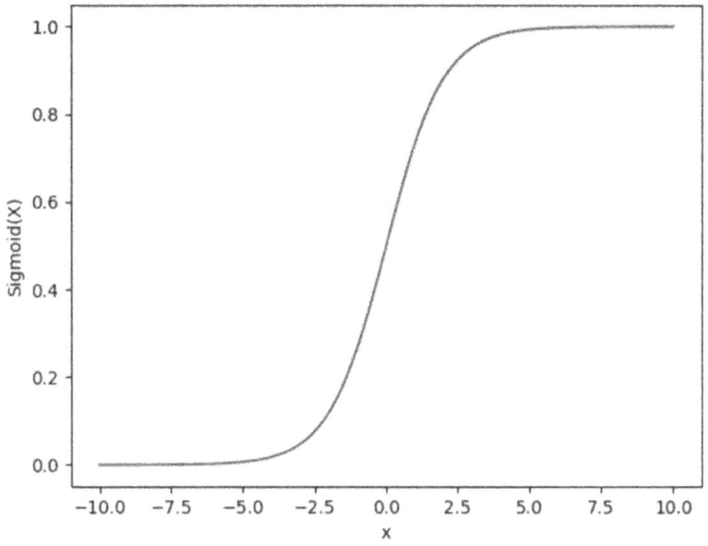

1. It is a function which is plotted as **'S'** shaped graph.

2. Equation : A = $1/(1 + e^{-x})$

3. Nature : Non-linear. Notice that X values lies between -2 to 2, Y values are very steep. This means, small changes in x would also bring about large changes in the value of Y.

4. Value Range : 0 to 1

5. Uses : Usually used in output layer of a binary classification, where result is either 0 or 1, as value for sigmoid function lies between 0 and 1 only so, result can be predicted easily to be ***1*** if value is greater than **0.5** and ***0*** otherwise.

Tanh Function

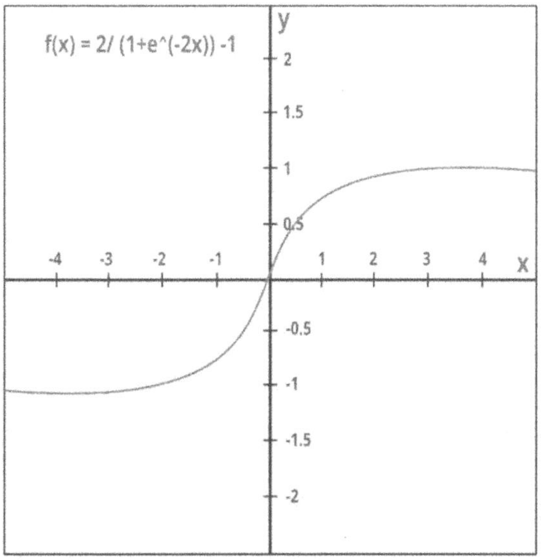

1. The activation that works almost always better than sigmoid function is Tanh function also known as **Tangent**

Hyperbolic function. It's actually mathematically shifted version of the sigmoid function. Both are similar and can be derived from each other.

1. Equation :-

$$f(x) = tanh(x) = \frac{2}{1+e^{-2x}} - 1$$

Value Range :- -1 to +1

2. Nature :- non-linear

3. Uses :- Usually used in hidden layers of a neural network as it's values lies between **-1 to 1** hence the mean for the hidden layer comes out be 0 or very close to it, hence helps in *centering the data* by bringing mean close to 0. This makes learning for the next layer much easier.

RELU Function

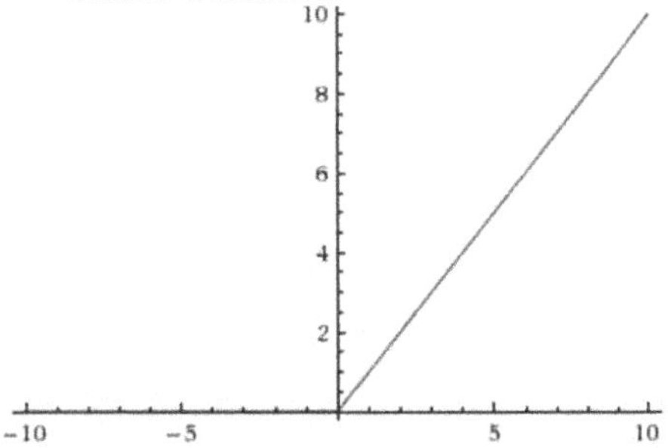

It Stands for *Rectified linear unit*. It is the most widely used activation function. Chiefly implemented in *hidden layers* of Neural network.

1. Equation :- ***A(x) = max(0,x)***. It gives an output x if x is positive and 0 otherwise.

2. Value Range :- [0, inf)

3. Nature :- non-linear, which means we can easily backpropagate the errors and have multiple layers of neurons being activated by the ReLU function.

4. Uses :- ReLu is less computationally expensive than tanh and sigmoid because it involves simpler mathematical operations. At a time only a few neurons are activated making the network sparse making it efficient and easy for computation.

In simple words, RELU learns *much faster* than sigmoid and Tanh function.

Softmax Function

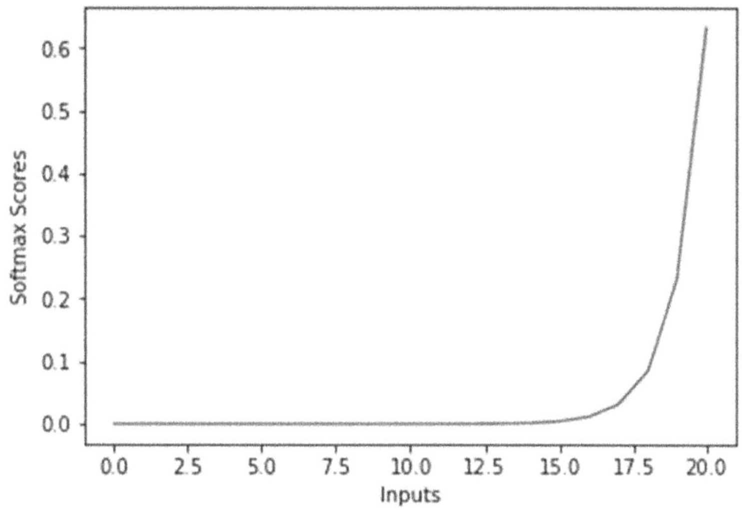

The softmax function is also a type of sigmoid function but is handy when we are trying to handle multi- class classification problems.

1. Nature :- non-linear

2. Uses :- Usually used when trying to handle multiple classes. the softmax function was commonly found in the output layer of image classification problems.The softmax function would squeeze the outputs for each class between 0 and 1 and would also divide by the sum of the outputs.

3. Output:- The softmax function is ideally used in the output layer of the classifier where we are actually trying to attain the probabilities to define the class of each input.

4. The basic rule of thumb is if you really don't know what activation function to use, then simply use *RELU* as it is a general activation function in hidden layers and is used in most cases these days.

5. If your output is for binary classification then, *sigmoid function* is very natural choice for output layer.

6. If your output is for multi-class classification then, Softmax is very useful to predict the probabilities of each classes.

7. It is recommended to understand Neural Networks before reading this article.

In the process of building a neural network, one of the choices you get to make is what Activation Function to use in the hidden layer as well as at the output layer of the network. This article discusses some of the choices.

9.3 Gradient Descent and Backpropagation

Backpropagation is an algorithm used in Machine Learning that works by calculating the gradient of the loss function, which points us in the direction of the value that minimizes the loss function. It relies on the chain rule of calculus to calculate the gradient backward through the layers of a neural network. Using gradient descent, we can iteratively move closer to the minimum value by taking small steps in the direction given by the gradient.

In other words, backpropagation and gradient descent are two different methods that form a powerful combination in the learning process of neural networks.

For the rest of this post, I assume that you know how forward propagation in a neural network works and have a basic understanding of matrix multiplication.

Why We Need Backpropagation

During forward propagation, we use weights, biases, and nonlinear activation functions to calculate a prediction y hat from the input x that should match the expected output y as closely as possible (which is given together with the input data x). We use a cost function to quantify the difference between the expected output y and the calculated output y hat.

$J=n1i=1\sum nL(y\hat{},y)$

The goal of backpropagation is to adjust the weights and biases throughout the neural network based on the calculated cost so that the cost will be lower in the next iteration. Ultimately, we want to find a minimum value for the cost function. But how exactly does that work?

. Difference between Backpropagation and Gradient Descent

Following table summarizes the differences between Backpropagation and Gradient Descent

POINT	BACKPROPAGATION	GRADIENT DESCENT
Definition	the algorithm that is used to calculate the gradient of the loss function with respect to parameters of the neural network.	the optimisation algorithm that is used to find parameters that minimise the loss function.
Dependencies	Calculus and Chain rules	Backpropagation
Type of method	This is not a learning method	first order optimizer
Input size	Calculate the gradient for each single input-output example	may be Stochastic, batch or mini-batch
Sequence	come first	must be after backpropagation
Problems	None	may have some problems such as local minima and saddle point

Moving forward, we will understand the two concepts deeper so that the above points in the table will make much more sense.

2. How NN works:

First of all, i'd like to name neural network as baby 'basiclly your baby' who you try your best to learn him well and of course he will learn through his all life by trial and correction his faults, exactly like your neural network.

You have input data and want to train your model on it but how ?
Let's say each sample of your data has 3 features and only one label (y)(of two classes), how the model will find the pattern between them?

Magically the answer will be backpropagation and gradient descent.
You will input your features into your model as (X1 ,X2, X3) and each neurons of your model will randomly create weights multiplying them to Xs, adding bias,perform activation function and calculate outputs which enter the next layer of neurons, and this process occurs till the output layer where your model out a predicted label (y-hat).

This what is called feed Forward.

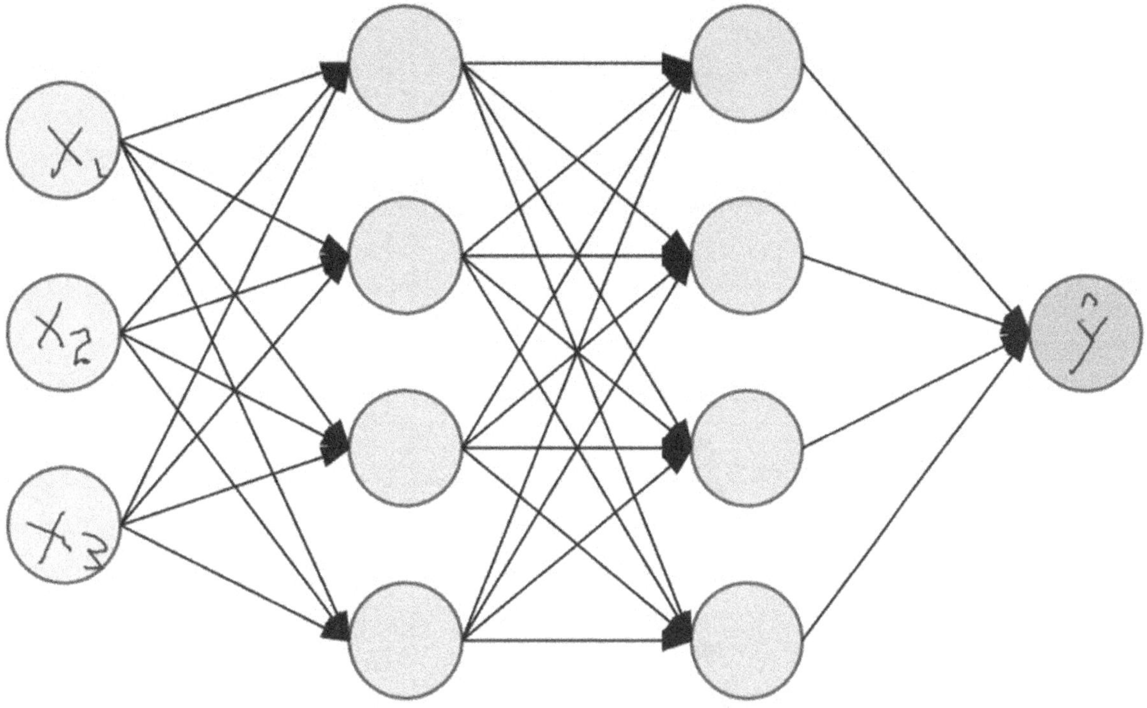

3. Backpropagation algorithm:
But what if your model predicted label (y-hat) away from the true label (y) of your data (and of course it's a normal phenomenon as your model at the first place *randomly* creates weights for its neurons). here role of loss function will come which calculate the difference between y and y-hat. Then the model now knows how much the difference between them and want to upgrade the weights of each neurons to decrease this difference. here the role of backpropagation will come which calculate how much exactly our weights need to be upgraded which we call it the gradient (how our loss will change in respect of the weights) and now it all about calculus but you don't need to be a genius in math to calculate it as now there are many frameworks that remove this hassle off your shoulder (like TensorFlow and PyTourch).
But if you want to dive into, so be with this:
This what NN does...
1. z1 = W1.X + b1 (W is the weight, b is the bias)

2. a1 = relu(z1) (relu is the activation function, a1 output of fist layer)

3. z2 = W2.a1 +b2

4. a2 = relu(z2)

5. z3 = W3.a2 +b3

6. y-hat = sigmoid(z3) (sigmoid is another activation function for binary classification as in our case)

7. Loss (y-hat,y)

So we need to know what is the derivative of loss with respect to the weights so we can update the weight to improve the loss(decrease it) (dL/dW).
First we will use what is called the chain rule :

1. dL/d(y-hat)

2. dL/dz3 = dL/d(y-hat). d(y-hat)/dz3 (calculs of sigmoid equal yhat(1-yhat))

3. dL/da2 = dL/dz3 . dz3/da2 (also *dL/dW3 = dL/dz3.dz3/dW3*(dz3/dW3 = a2))

4. dL/dz2 = dL/da2 . da2/dz2

5. dL/da1 = dL/dz2 . dz2/da1 (also *dL/dW2 = dL/dz2.dz2/dW2*(dz2/dW2 = a1))

6. dL/dz1 = dL/da1 . da1/dz1

7. dL/dW1 = dL/dz1 . dz1/dW1 (we can say dL/dW1 as dW1) till now you probably know why it call backpropagation as we letterly back each step in feed forward propagation.

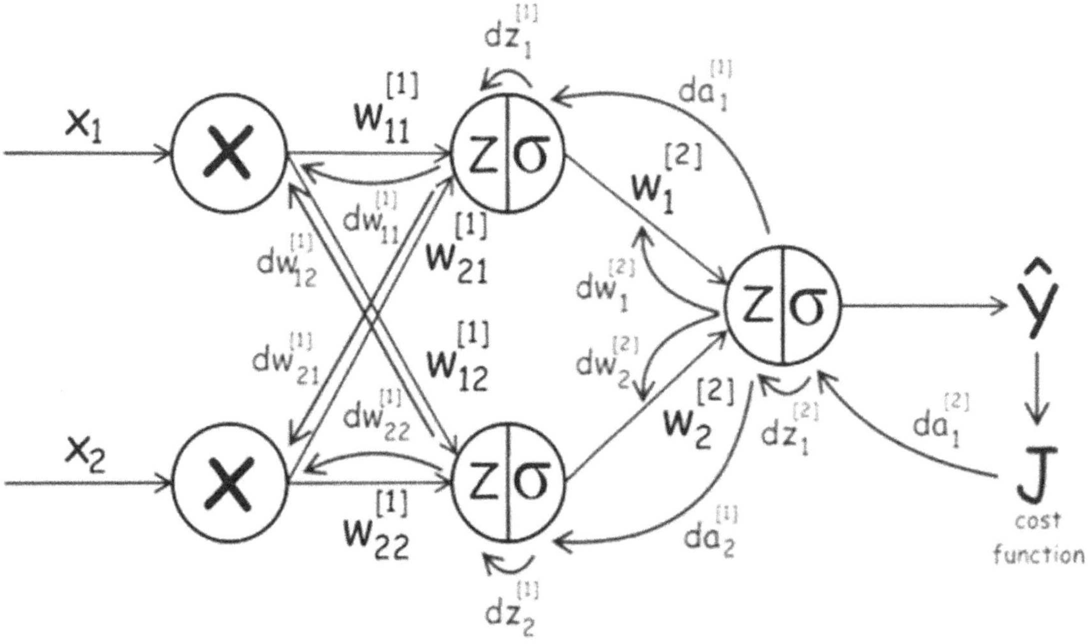

J(cost function) is another name of L(loss function)

Gradient Descent algorithm:

After we found our gradient, we will update our weights in the opposite direction to the gradient for our loss function to find the minimum value.
so W := W - learning rate * dW.
and b := b - learning rate * db.

We can say that the Gradient Descent algorithm is the optimization algorithm which tries to find the minimum value of the cost or loss function by taking steps in the opposite direction of the gradients. So if the gradient is positive, the model will decrease the weights where the gradient is negative, the model will increase the weights in order to decrease the tot.

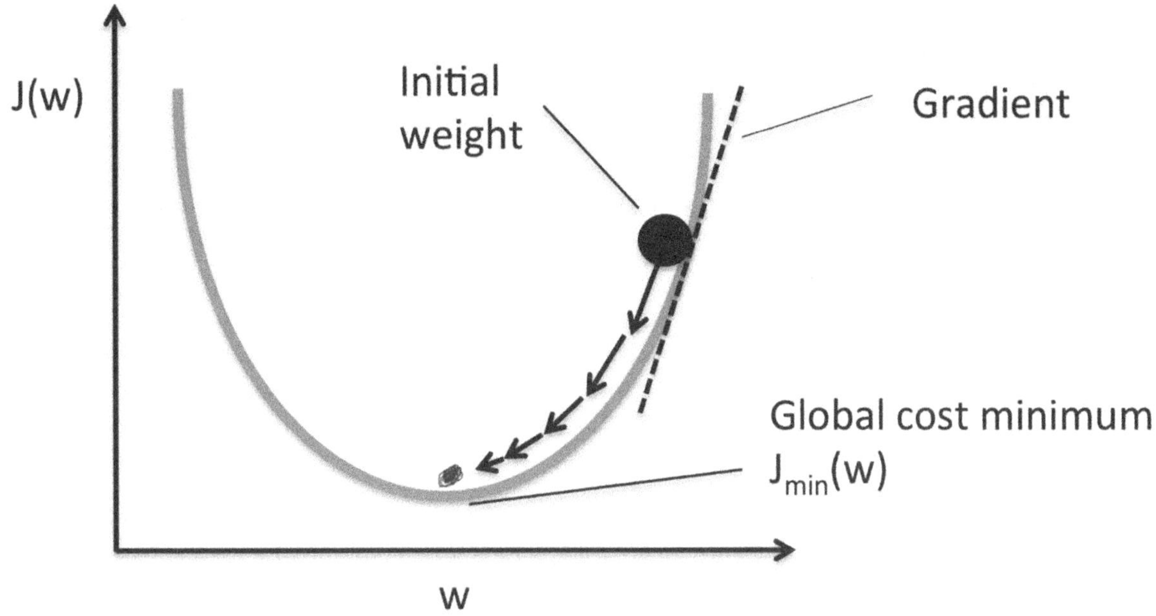

the model updates the weights of neurons after calculating the gradient of each single example. So the process will be :

1. Take an example
2. Feed Forward it to Neural Network
3. Calculate its gradient
4. Use the gradient we calculated in step 3 to update the weights
5. Repeat steps 1–4 for all the examples in the training dataset.

So this type is fast and will be good in huge datasets, but not computationally effective in many cases.
Mini-batch Gradient Descent:
On the other hand, Batch Gradient Descent considers all the training examples before updating the weights. it takes the average of the gradients of all the training examples and then uses that mean gradient to update our parameters. It is located in the middle of SGD and Batch Gradient Descent. Neither we use all the dataset all at once nor we use the single example at a time. Mini-batch divide the the training examples into batches, then calculate the average gradient for them. So the process will be :

1. Pick a mini-batch
2. Feed Forward it to Neural Network
3. Calculate the average gradient of the mini-batch
4. Use the average gradient we calculated in step 3 to update the parameters
5. Repeat steps 1–4 for the mini-batches we created.

9.4 Convolutional Neural Networks (CNN)

A Convolutional Neural Network (CNN) is a type of Deep Learning neural network architecture commonly used in Computer Vision. Computer vision is a field of Artificial Intelligence that enables a computer to understand and interpret the image or visual data.
When it comes to Machine Learning, Artificial Neural Networks perform really well. Neural Networks are used in various datasets like images, audio, and text. Different types of Neural Networks are used for different purposes, for example for predicting the sequence of words we use Recurrent Neural Networks more precisely an

LSTM, similarly for image classification we use Convolution Neural networks. In this blog, we are going to build a basic building block for CNN.

In a regular Neural Network there are three types of layers:

Input Layers: It's the layer in which we give input to our model. The number of neurons in this layer is equal to the total number of features in our data (number of pixels in the case of an image).

Hidden Layer: The input from the Input layer is then feed into the hidden layer. There can be many hidden layers depending upon our model and data size. Each hidden layer can have different numbers of neurons which are generally greater than the number of features. The output from each layer is computed by matrix multiplication of output of the previous layer with learnable weights of that layer and then by the addition of learnable biases followed by activation function which makes the network nonlinear.

Output Layer: The output from the hidden layer is then fed into a logistic function like sigmoid or softmax which converts the output of each class into the probability score of each class.

The data is fed into the model and output from each layer is obtained from the above step is called feedforward, we then calculate the error using an error function, some common error functions are cross-entropy, square loss error, etc. The error function measures how well the network is performing. After that, we backpropagate into the model by calculating the derivatives. This step is called Backpropagation which basically is used to minimize the loss. Convolution Neural Network

Convolutional Neural Network (CNN) is the extended version of artificial neural networks (ANN) which is predominantly used to extract the feature from the grid-like matrix dataset. For example visual datasets like images or videos where data patterns play an extensive role.

CNN architecture

Convolutional Neural Network consists of multiple layers like the input layer, Convolutional layer, Pooling layer, and fully connected layers.

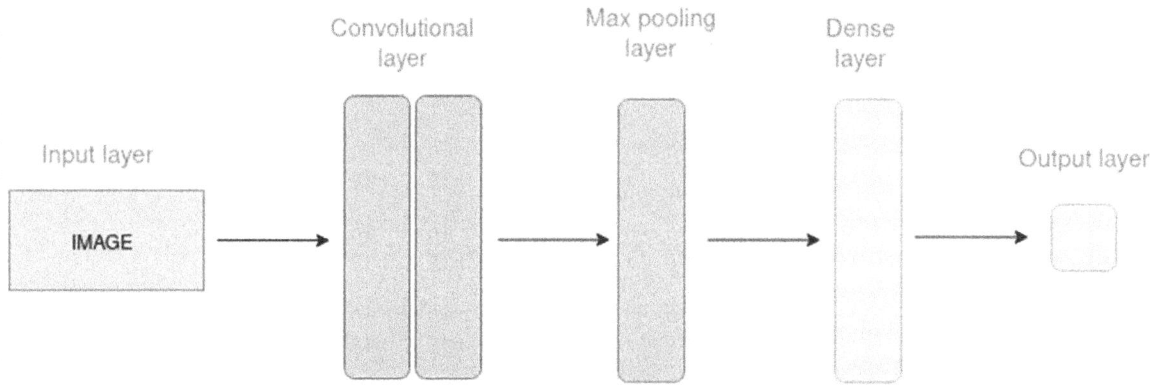

The Convolutional layer applies filters to the input image to extract features, the Pooling layer downsamples the image to reduce computation, and the fully connected layer makes the final prediction. The network learns the optimal filters through backpropagation and gradient descent.

How Convolutional Layers works

Convolution Neural Networks or covnets are neural networks that share their parameters. Imagine you have an image. It can be represented as a cuboid having its length, width (dimension of the image), and height (i.e the channel as images generally have red, green, and blue channels).

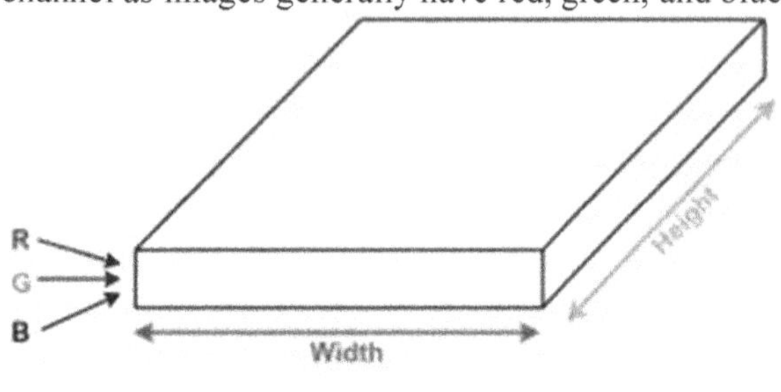

Now imagine taking a small patch of this image and running a small neural network, called a filter or kernel on it, with say, K outputs and representing them vertically. Now slide that neural network across the whole image, as a result, we will get another image with different widths, heights, and depths. Instead of just R, G, and B channels now we have more channels but lesser width and height. This operation is called **Convolution.** If the patch size is the same as that of the image it will be a regular neural network. Because of this small patch, we have fewer weights.

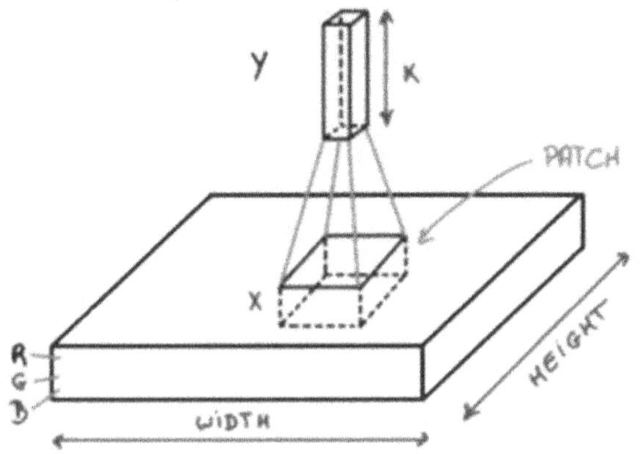

Now let's talk about a bit of mathematics that is involved in the whole convolution process.

1. Convolution layers consist of a set of learnable filters (or kernels) having small widths and heights and the same depth as that of input volume (3 if the input layer is image input).

2. For example, if we have to run convolution on an image with dimensions 34x34x3. The possible size of filters can be axax3, where 'a' can be anything like 3, 5, or 7 but smaller as compared to the image dimension.

3. During the forward pass, we slide each filter across the whole input volume step by step where each step is called **stride** (which can have a value of 2, 3, or even 4 for high-dimensional images) and compute the dot product between the kernel weights and patch from input volume.

4. As we slide our filters we'll get a 2-D output for each filter and we'll stack them together as a result, we'll get output volume having a depth equal to the number of filters. The network will learn all the filters.

Layers used to build ConvNets

A complete Convolution Neural Networks architecture is also known as covnets. A covnets is a sequence of layers, and every layer transforms one volume to another through a differentiable function.

Types of layers: datasets

Let's take an example by running a covnets on of image of dimension 32 x 32 x 3.

- **Input Layers:** It's the layer in which we give input to our model. In CNN, Generally, the input will be an image or a sequence of images. This layer holds the raw input of the image with width 32, height 32, and depth 3.

- **Convolutional Layers:** This is the layer, which is used to extract the feature from the input dataset. It applies a set of learnable filters known as the kernels to the input images. The filters/kernels are smaller matrices usually 2×2, 3×3, or 5×5 shape. It slides over the input image data and computes the dot product between kernel weight and the corresponding input image patch. The output of this layer is referred ad feature maps. Suppose we use a total of 12 filters for this layer we'll get an output volume of dimension 32 x 32 x 12.

- **Activation Layer:** By adding an activation function to the output of the preceding layer, activation layers add nonlinearity to the network. It will apply an element-wise activation function to the output of the convolution layer. Some common activation functions are **RELU**: max(0, x), **Tanh**, **Leaky RELU**, etc. The volume remains unchanged hence output volume will have dimensions 32 x 32 x 12.

- **Pooling layer**: This layer is periodically inserted in the covnets and its main function is to reduce the size of volume which makes the computation fast reduces memory and also prevents overfitting. Two common types of pooling layers are **max pooling** and **average pooling**. If we use a max pool with 2 x 2 filters and stride 2, the resultant volume will be of dimension 16x16x12.

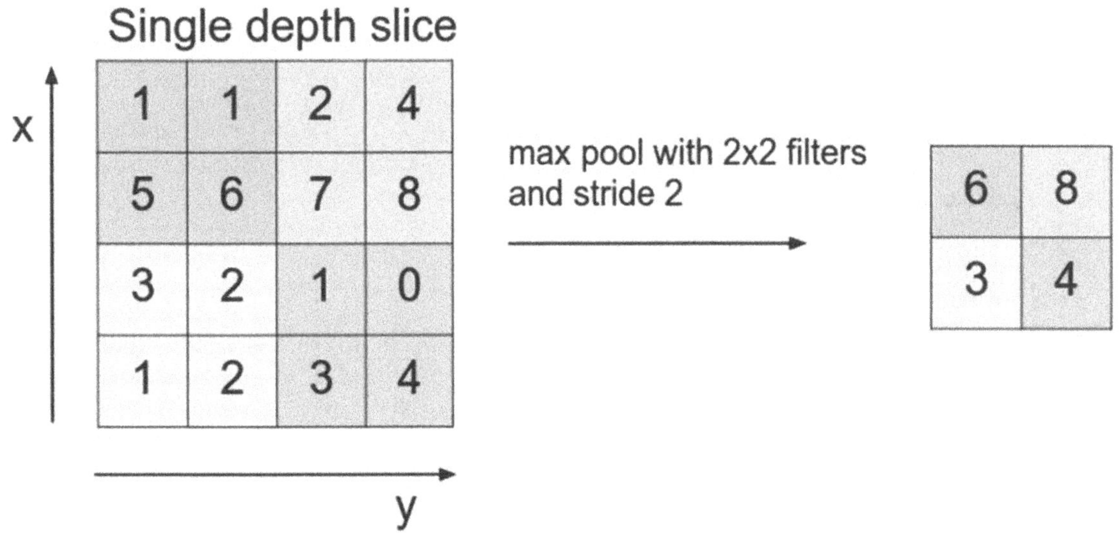

1. Flattening: The resulting feature maps are flattened into a one-dimensional vector after the convolution and pooling layers so they can be passed into a completely linked layer for categorization or regression.

2. Fully Connected Layers: It takes the input from the previous layer and computes the final classification or regression task.

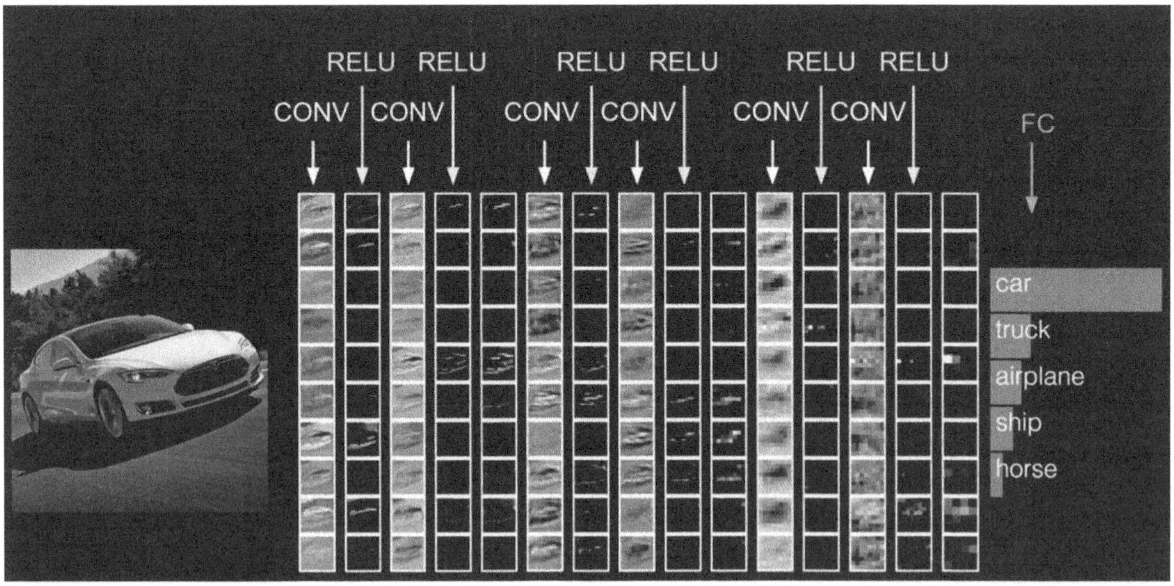

1. Output Layer: The output from the fully connected layers is then fed into a logistic function for classification tasks like sigmoid or softmax which converts the output of each class into the probability score of each class.

Advantages of Convolutional Neural Networks (CNNs):

1. Good at detecting patterns and features in images, videos, and audio signals.

2. Robust to translation, rotation, and scaling invariance.

3. End-to-end training, no need for manual feature extraction.

4. Can handle large amounts of data and achieve high accuracy.

5. Disadvantages of Convolutional Neural Networks (CNNs):

6. Computationally expensive to train and require a lot of memory.

7. Can be prone to overfitting if not enough data or proper regularization is used.

8. Requires large amounts of labeled data.

9. Interpretability is limited, it's hard to understand what the network has learned.

9.5 Recurrent Neural Networks (RNN)

A recurrent neural network (RNN) is a type of artificial neural network which uses sequential data or time series data. These deep learning algorithms are commonly used for ordinal or temporal problems, such as language translation, natural language processing (nlp), speech recognition, and image captioning; they are incorporated into popular applications such as Siri, voice search, and Google Translate. Like feedforward and convolutional neural networks (CNNs), recurrent neural networks utilize training data to learn. They are distinguished by their "memory" as they take information from prior inputs to influence the current input and output. While traditional deep neural networks assume that inputs and outputs are independent of each other, the output of recurrent neural networks depend on the prior elements within the sequence. While future events would also be helpful in determining the output of a given sequence, unidirectional recurrent neural networks cannot account for these events in their predictions.

Let's take an idiom, such as "feeling under the weather", which is commonly used when someone is ill, to aid us in the explanation of RNNs. In order for the idiom to make sense, it needs to be expressed in that specific order. As a result, recurrent networks need to account for the position of each word in the idiom and they use that information to predict the next word in the sequence.

Another distinguishing characteristic of recurrent networks is that they share parameters across each layer of the network. While feedforward networks have different weights across each node, recurrent neural networks share the same weight parameter within each layer of the network. That said, these weights are still adjusted in the through the processes of backpropagation and gradient descent to facilitate reinforcement learning.

Recurrent neural networks leverage backpropagation through time (BPTT) algorithm to determine the gradients, which is slightly different from traditional backpropagation as it is specific to sequence data. The principles of BPTT are the same as traditional backpropagation, where the model trains itself by calculating errors from its output layer to its input layer. These calculations allow us to adjust and fit the parameters of the model appropriately. BPTT differs from the traditional approach in that BPTT sums errors at each time step whereas feedforward networks do not need to sum errors as they do not share parameters across each layer.

Through this process, RNNs tend to run into two problems, known as exploding gradients and vanishing gradients. These issues are defined by the size of the gradient, which is the slope of the loss function along the error curve. When the gradient is too small, it continues to become smaller, updating the weight parameters until they become insignificant—i.e. 0. When that occurs, the algorithm is no longer learning. Exploding gradients occur when the gradient is too large, creating an unstable model. In this case, the model weights will grow too large, and they will eventually be represented as NaN. One solution to these issues is to reduce the number of hidden layers within the neural network, eliminating some of the complexity in the RNN model.

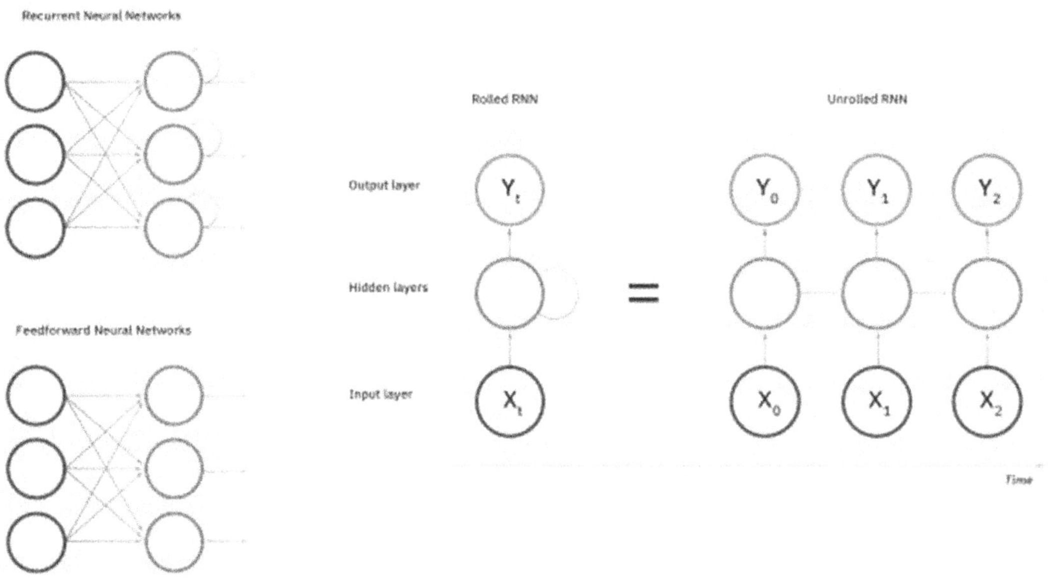

Types of recurrent neural networks

Feedforward networks map one input to one output, and while we've visualized recurrent neural networks in this way in the above diagrams, they do not actually have this constraint. Instead, their inputs and outputs can vary in length, and different types of RNNs are used for different use cases, such as music generation, sentiment classification, and machine translation.

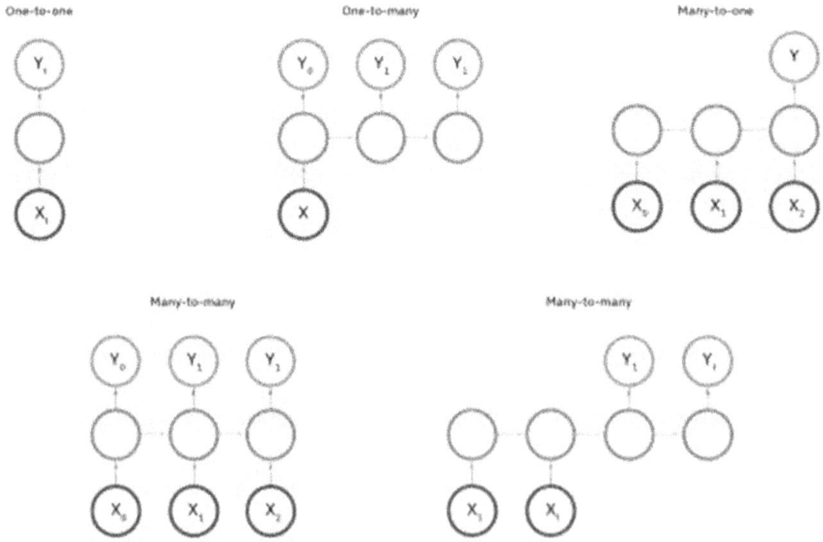

Common activation functions

As discussed in the Learn article on Neural Networks, an activation function determines whether a neuron should be activated. The nonlinear functions typically convert the output of a given neuron to a value between 0 and 1 or -1 and 1.

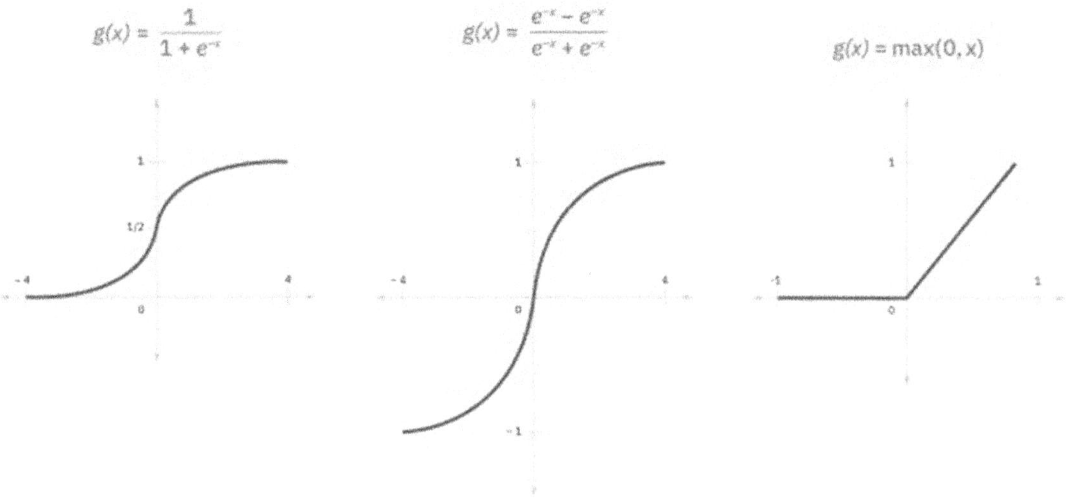

Variant RNN architectures

Bidirectional recurrent neural networks (BRNN): These are a variant network architecture of RNNs. While unidirectional RNNs can only drawn from previous inputs to make predictions about the current state, bidirectional RNNs pull in future data to improve the accuracy of it. If we return to the example of "feeling under the weather" earlier in this article, the model can better predict that the second word in that phrase is "under" if it knew that the last word in the sequence is "weather."

Long short-term memory (LSTM): This is a popular RNN architecture, which was introduced by Sepp Hochreiter and Juergen Schmidhuber as a solution to vanishing gradient problem, they work to address the problem of long-term dependencies. That is, if the previous state that is influencing the current prediction is not in the recent past, the RNN model may not be able to accurately predict the current state. As an example, let's say we wanted to predict the italicized words in following, "Alice is allergic to nuts. She can't eat *peanut butter*." The context of a nut allergy can help us anticipate that the food that cannot be eaten contains nuts. However, if that context was a few sentences prior, then it would make it difficult, or even impossible, for the RNN to connect the information. To remedy this, LSTMs have "cells" in the hidden layers of the neural network, which have three gates–an input gate, an output gate, and a forget gate. These gates control the flow of information which is needed to predict the output in the network. For example, if gender pronouns, such as "she", was repeated multiple times in prior sentences, you may exclude that from the cell state.

Gated recurrent units (GRUs): This RNN variant is similar the LSTMs as it also works to address the short-term memory problem of RNN models. Instead of using a "cell state" regulate information, it uses hidden states, and instead of three gates, it has two—a reset gate and an update gate. Similar to the gates within LSTMs, the reset and update gates control how much and which information to retain.

9.6 Transfer Learning

Transfer learning, used in Machine Learning, is the reuse of a pre-trained model on a new problem. In transfer learning, a machine exploits the knowledge gained from a previous task to improve generalization about another. For example, in training a classifier to predict whether an image contains food, you could use the knowledge it gained during training to recognize drinks. What Is Transfer Learning?

In transfer learning, the knowledge of an already trained Machine Learning model is applied to a different but related problem. For example, if you trained a simple classifier to predict whether an image contains a backpack, you could use the knowledge that the model gained during its training to recognize other objects like sunglasses. With transfer learning, we basically try to exploit what has been learned in one task to improve generalization in another. We transfer the weights that a network has learned at "task A" to a new "task B."

The general idea is to use the knowledge a model has learned from a task with a lot of available labeled training data in a new task that doesn't have much data. Instead of starting the learning process from scratch, we start with patterns learned from solving a related task.

Transfer learning is mostly used in computer vision and natural language processing tasks like sentiment analysis due to the huge amount of computational power required.

Transfer learning isn't really a Machine Learning technique, but can be seen as a "design methodology" within the field, for example, active learning. It is also not an exclusive part or study-area of Machine Learning. Nevertheless, it has become quite popular in combination with neural networks that require huge amounts of data and computational power.

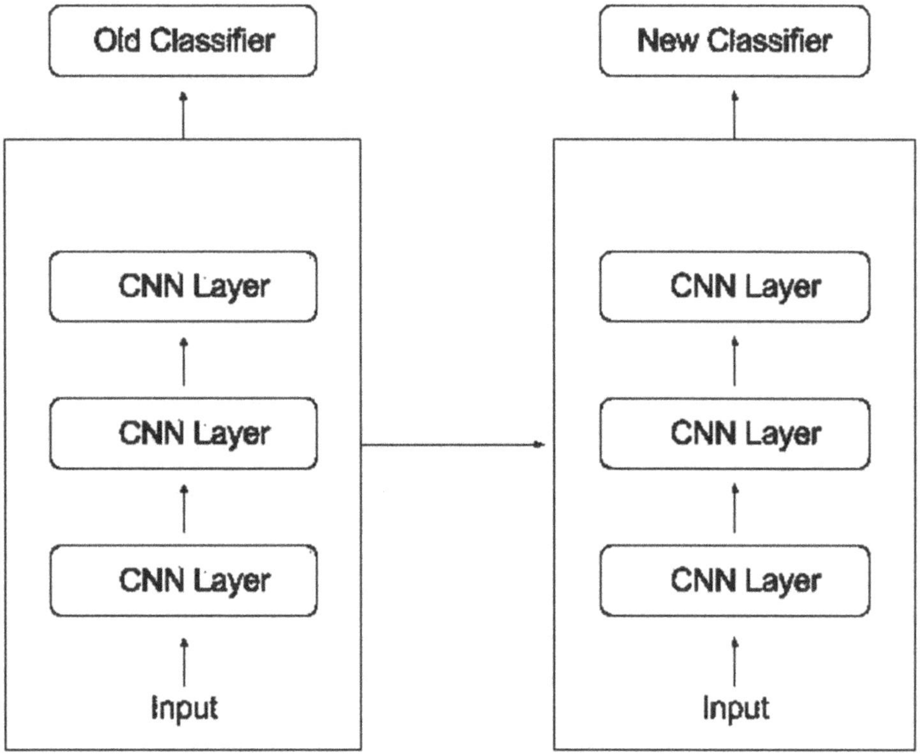

How Transfer Learning Works

In computer vision, for example, neural networks usually try to detect edges in the earlier layers, shapes in the middle layer and some task-specific features in the later layers. In transfer learning, the early and middle layers are used and we only retrain the latter layers. It helps leverage the labeled data of the task it was initially trained on.

Let's go back to the example of a model trained for recognizing a backpack on an image, which will be used to identify sunglasses. In the earlier layers, the model has learned to recognize objects, because of that we will only retrain the latter layers so it will learn what separates sunglasses from other objects.

classifiers transfer learning

In transfer learning, we try to transfer as much knowledge as possible from the previous task the model was trained on to the new task at hand. This knowledge can be in various forms depending on the problem and the data. For example, it could be how models are composed, which allows us to more easily identify novel objects.

Why Use Transfer Learning

Transfer learning has several benefits, but the main advantages are saving training time, better performance of neural networks (in most cases), and not needing a lot of data.

Usually, a lot of data is needed to train a neural network from scratch but access to that data isn't always available — this is where transfer learning comes in handy. With transfer learning a solid Machine Learning model can be built with comparatively little training data because the model is already pre-trained. This is especially valuable in natural language processing because mostly expert knowledge is required to create large labeled data sets. Additionally, training time is reduced because it can sometimes take days or even weeks to train a deep neural network from scratch on a complex task.

According to DeepMind CEO Demis Hassabis, transfer learning is also one of the most promising techniques that could lead to artificial general intelligence (AGI) someday:

AGI transfer learning

When to Use Transfer Learning

As is always the case in Machine Learning, it is hard to form rules that are generally applicable, but here are some guidelines on when transfer learning might be used:

There isn't enough labeled training data to train your network from scratch.

There already exists a network that is pre-trained on a similar task, which is usually trained on massive amounts of data.

When task 1 and task 2 have the same input.

If the original model was trained using an open-source library like TensorFlow, you can simply restore it and retrain some layers for your task. Keep in mind, however, that transfer learning only works if the features learned from the first task are general, meaning they can be useful for another related task as well. Also, the input of the model needs to have the same size as it was initially trained with. If you don't have that, add a pre-processing step to resize your input to the needed size.

Approaches to Transfer Learning

1. TRAINING A MODEL TO REUSE IT

Imagine you want to solve task A but don't have enough data to train a deep neural network. One way around this is to find a related task B with an abundance of data. Train the deep neural network on task B and use the model as a starting point for solving task A. Whether you'll need to use the whole model or only a few layers depends heavily on the problem you're trying to solve.

If you have the same input in both tasks, possibly reusing the model and making predictions for your new input is an option. Alternatively, changing and retraining different task-specific layers and the output layer is a method to explore.

2. USING A PRE-TRAINED MODEL

The second approach is to use an already pre-trained model. There are a lot of these models out there, so make sure to do a little research. How many layers to reuse and how many to retrain depends on the problem.

Keras, for example, provides numerous pre-trained models that can be used for transfer learning, prediction, feature extraction and fine-tuning. You can find these models, and also some brief tutorials on how to use them, here. There are also many research institutions that release trained models.

This type of transfer learning is most commonly used throughout deep learning.

1. FEATURE EXTRACTION

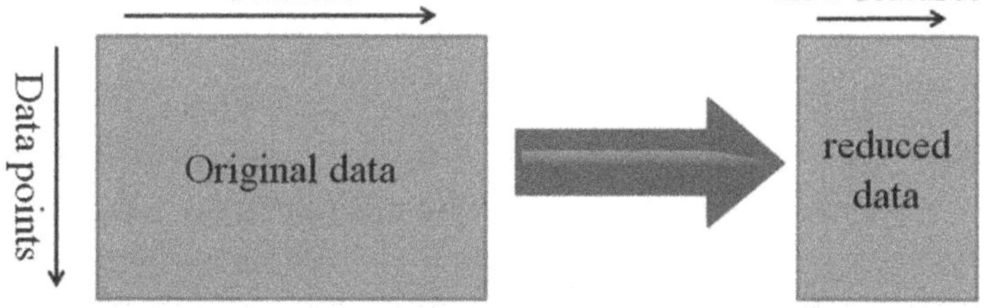

Another approach is to use deep learning to discover the best representation of your problem, which means finding the most important features. This approach is also known as representation learning, and can often result in a much better performance than can be obtained with hand-designed representation.

feature extraction transfer learning

In Machine Learning, features are usually manually hand-crafted by researchers and domain experts. Fortunately, deep learning can extract features automatically. Of course, this doesn't mean feature engineering and domain knowledge isn't important anymore — you still have to decide which features you put into your network. That said, neural networks have the ability to learn which features are really important and which ones aren't. A

representation learning algorithm can discover a good combination of features within a very short timeframe, even for complex tasks which would otherwise require a lot of human effort.
The learned representation can then be used for other problems as well. Simply use the first layers to spot the right representation of features, but don't use the output of the network because it is too task-specific. Instead, feed data into your network and use one of the intermediate layers as the output layer. This layer can then be interpreted as a representation of the raw data.
This approach is mostly used in computer vision because it can reduce the size of your dataset, which decreases computation time and makes it more suitable for traditional algorithms, as well.

Exercise

True Or False

1.Neural networks are computational models inspired by the structure and function of the human brain.
2.The input layer of a neural network is responsible for processing and transforming the input data.
3.A hidden layer in a neural network refers to a layer that is not directly connected to the input or output.
4.An activation function introduces non-linearity to the neural network, enabling it to model complex relationships.
5.The sigmoid activation function can suffer from the vanishing gradient problem, which can hinder training.
6.ReLU (Rectified Linear Activation) is an activation function that outputs a negative value for negative inputs.
7.Gradient descent is an optimization algorithm used to adjust the model's parameters to minimize the loss function.
8.Backpropagation is the process of propagating gradients from the output layer to the input layer to update weights.
9.Backpropagation ensures that the model learns from the training data by updating weights in the correct direction.
10.CNNs are particularly well-suited for image processing tasks due to their ability to capture spatial hierarchies.
11.A pooling layer in a CNN is responsible for learning feature representations through convolutional operations.
12.The kernel in a convolutional layer is used to perform element-wise multiplication on the input data.
13.RNNs are designed to handle sequential data by capturing temporal dependencies and patterns.
14.The vanishing gradient problem in RNNs occurs when gradients become too large, causing instability.
15.A recurrent layer in an RNN allows information to be passed from one time step to the next.
16.Transfer learning involves using a pre-trained model on a new task with little or no modification.
17.Fine-tuning involves adjusting all layers of a pre-trained model to fit the new task's requirements.
18.Transfer learning is especially useful when you have a small amount of labeled data for the new task.
19.A pre-trained model's base network typically includes all layers except the input layer.
20.CNNs are well-suited for processing sequential data, such as time series or text.
21.An activation function preprocesses the input data before passing it to the next layer.
22.Gradient descent is an algorithm used to maximize the loss function.
23.A convolutional layer is responsible for reducing the spatial dimensions of input data.
24.CNNs and RNNs have the same architectural structure.
25.Backpropagation involves propagating gradients from the input layer to the output layer.
26.Transfer learning is a technique where a neural network learns to transfer knowledge between different tasks.
27.Data augmentation is a type of transfer learning.
28.In transfer learning, fine-tuning involves adjusting only the output layer of the pre-trained model.
Answer: True, False, True, True, True, False, True, True, True, True, False, False, True, False, True, False, False, True, True, False, False, False, False, False, False, True, False, False

MCQ

1.What is the primary challenge when applying transfer learning to a new task?
a) Ensuring the pre-trained model is exactly the same as the new task's requirements
b) Dealing with overfitting due to excessive knowledge transfer
c) Finding an appropriate pre-trained model for the new task
d) Lack of compatibility between different neural network architectures
Answer: c

2.Which type of transfer learning involves using a pre-trained model as a feature extractor?
a) Soft transfer
b) Hard transfer
c) Fine-tuning
d) Coarse transfer
Answer: b

3.In transfer learning, what is the "base network" typically referring to?
a) The output layer of the pre-trained model
b) The input layer of the pre-trained model
c) All layers except the last one in the pre-trained model
d) The activation functions in the pre-trained model
Answer: c

4.Which type of neural network is well-suited for handling sequential data, such as time series or text?
a) Convolutional Neural Networks (CNNs)
b) Recurrent Neural Networks (RNNs)
c) Feedforward Neural Networks (FNNs)
d) Radial Basis Function Networks (RBFNs)
Answer: b

5.What is the purpose of the activation function in a neural network?
a) To define the number of layers in the network
b) To preprocess the input data
c) To introduce non-linearity into the model
d) To reduce the computational complexity
Answer: c

6.Which algorithm is used to adjust the model's weights during training by minimizing the loss function?
a) Gradient Boosting
b) K-Means
c) Gradient Descent
d) Principal Component Analysis (PCA)
Answer: c

7.Which type of neural network layer is responsible for extracting features from input data through learned filters?
a) Fully Connected Layer
b) Activation Layer
c) Pooling Layer
d) Convolutional Layer
Answer: d

8.What is the main difference between a CNN and an RNN?
a) CNNs can handle sequential data, while RNNs can handle image data.
b) CNNs are more efficient for image data, while RNNs are specialized for sequential data.
c) CNNs use convolutional layers, while RNNs use recurrent layers.
d) CNNs are shallow networks, while RNNs are deep networks.
Answer: b

9.What does the term "backpropagation" refer to in neural network training?
a) The process of calculating gradients for model parameters

b) The process of calculating the forward pass through the network
c) The process of reducing the number of layers in the network
d) The process of selecting the optimal activation function
Answer: a

10.Which technique involves using a pre-trained model on a large dataset and fine-tuning it for a specific task?
a) Transfer Learning
b) Data Augmentation
c) Ensemble Learning
d) Dropout Regularization
Answer: a

11.What is the primary advantage of using transfer learning?
a) It allows the model to learn from scratch on the new task.
b) It guarantees optimal performance on any task.
c) It requires a large amount of labeled data.
d) It can significantly speed up the training process.
Answer: d

12.Which layer type is commonly used for reducing the spatial dimensions of feature maps in a CNN?
a) Fully Connected Layer
b) Pooling Layer
c) Convolutional Layer
d) Activation Layer
Answer: b

13.What is a neural network?
a) A network of interconnected neurons in the human brain
b) A computational model inspired by the human brain's structure and function
c) A type of regression model
d) A database management system
Answer: b

14.What is the primary purpose of an input layer in a neural network?
a) To make predictions
b) To process hidden features
c) To receive and represent input data
d) To apply activation functions
Answer: c

15.Which of the following is NOT a common layer type in a neural network?
a) Input layer
b) Output layer
c) Activation layer
d) Hidden layer
Answer: c

17.What is the role of an activation function in a neural network?
a) It defines the architecture of the network
b) It computes the sum of input values
c) It introduces non-linearity to the network
d) It performs gradient descent optimization

Answer: c

18. Which activation function is often used for binary classification tasks?
a) ReLU (Rectified Linear Activation)
b) Sigmoid
c) Tanh (Hyperbolic Tangent)
d) Softmax
Answer: b

19. What is a drawback of the Sigmoid activation function?
a) It can lead to vanishing gradients
b) It is computationally expensive
c) It is not differentiable
d) It has a limited output range
Answer: a

20. What is the main goal of gradient descent in neural network training?
a) To maximize the model's accuracy
b) To minimize the loss function
c) To prevent overfitting
d) To speed up convergence
Answer: b

21. Which step of neural network training involves updating the model's weights based on the calculated gradients?
a) Forward propagation
b) Activation function
c) Gradient descent
d) Backpropagation
Answer: d

22. What is backpropagation?
a) The process of propagating gradients from the output layer to the input layer
b) The process of propagating data through convolutional layers
c) The process of choosing the optimal activation function
d) The process of randomly initializing weights in a neural network
Answer: a

23. What is the primary advantage of using Convolutional Neural Networks (CNNs) for image processing?
a) They have fewer layers than traditional neural networks
b) They can automatically label images
c) They capture spatial hierarchies and patterns in images
d) They require less computational power
Answer: c

24. Which layer in a CNN is responsible for reducing the spatial dimensions of the input?
a) Convolutional layer
b) Pooling layer
c) Fully connected layer
d) Activation layer
Answer: b

25.What is the purpose of the kernel in a convolutional layer?
a) To compute gradients
b) To apply an activation function
c) To perform element-wise multiplication
d) To extract features from the input
Answer: d

26.What makes Recurrent Neural Networks (RNNs) well-suited for sequential data?
a) Their ability to handle images efficiently
b) Their deep architecture
c) Their ability to capture temporal dependencies
d) Their fast training process
Answer: c

Short Question And Answers

Q1. What is a neural network?
Q2. What are the main components of a neural network?
Q3. Explain the feedforward process in a neural network.
Q4. What is an activation function in a neural network?
Q5. Name and describe some common activation functions.
Q6. What is gradient descent?
Q7. What is backpropagation?
Q8. How does gradient descent and backpropagation work together in training a neural network?
Q9. What are convolutional neural networks (CNNs)?
Q10. Explain the concept of convolution in CNNs.
Q11. How do pooling layers contribute to the architecture of CNNs?
Q12. What is a recurrent neural network (RNN)?
Q14. How do long short-term memory (LSTM) networks address the vanishing gradient problem?
Q15. What is transfer learning in the context of deep learning?
Q16. How can transfer learning benefit model training?
Q17. Describe the process of fine-tuning a pre-trained model for a new task.
Q18. When might transfer learning not be suitable for a particular task?
Q19. How can CNNs and RNNs be combined to handle both image and sequential data in a single model?

Online Resources
Online Exam Papers
True/False Exam

Link: https://forms.gle/qBw9Lu9Zxn6aDKWE8

QR Code

YouTube Video Playlist Link

Chapter 9
Link
https://www.youtube.com/playlist?list=PLzlh_31VWEFqTsAnVKeNEV90e6sorM9xw
QR Code

Chapter 10: Natural Language Processing (NLP)

What is natural language processing?

Natural language processing (NLP) is the ability of a computer program to understand human language as it is spoken and written -- referred to as natural language. It is a component of artificial intelligence (AI). NLP has existed for more than 50 years and has roots in the field of linguistics. It has a variety of real- world applications in a number of fields, including medical research, search engines and business intelligence.

How does natural language processing work?

NLP enables computers to understand natural language as humans do. Whether the language is spoken or written, natural language processing uses artificial intelligence to take real-world input, process it, and make sense of it in a way a computer can understand. Just as humans have different sensors -- such as ears to hear and eyes to see -- computers have programs to read and microphones to collect audio. And just as humans have a brain to process that input, computers have a program to process their respective inputs. At some point in processing, the input is converted to code that the computer can understand.

There are two main phases to natural language processing: data preprocessing and algorithm development.

Data preprocessing involves preparing and "cleaning" text data for machines to be able to analyze it. preprocessing puts data in workable form and highlights features in the text that an algorithm can work with. There are several ways this can be done, including:

- Tokenization: This is when text is broken down into smaller units to work with.
- Stop word removal: This is when common words are removed from text so unique words that offer the most information about the text remain.
- Lemmatization and stemming: This is when words are reduced to their root forms to process.
- Part-of-speech tagging: This is when words are marked based on the part-of speech they are -- such as nouns, verbs and adjectives.

Once the data has been preprocessed, an algorithm is developed to process it. There are many different natural language processing algorithms, but two main types are commonly used:

- Rules-based system: This system uses carefully designed linguistic rules. This approach was used early on in the development of natural language processing, and is still used.
- Machine Learning-based system: Machine Learning algorithms use statistical methods. They learn to perform tasks based on training data they are fed, and adjust their methods as more data is processed. Using a combination of Machine Learning, deep learning and neural networks, natural language processing algorithms hone their own rules through repeated processing and learning.

Why is natural language processing important?

Businesses use massive quantities of unstructured, text-heavy data and need a way to efficiently process it. A lot of the information created online and stored in databases is natural human language, and until recently, businesses could not effectively analyze this data. This is where natural language processing is useful.

The advantage of natural language processing can be seen when considering the following two statements: "Cloud computing insurance should be part of every service-level agreement," and, "A good SLA ensures an easier night's sleep -- even in the cloud." If a user relies on natural language processing for search, the program will recognize that cloud computing is an entity, that cloud is an abbreviated form of cloud computing and that SLA is an industry acronym for service-level agreement.

NLP uses diagram

These are some of the key areas in which a business can use natural language processing (NLP).

These are the types of vague elements that frequently appear in human language and that Machine Learning algorithms have historically been bad at interpreting. Now, with improvements in deep learning and Machine Learning methods, algorithms can effectively interpret them. These improvements expand the breadth and depth of data that can be analyzed.

Techniques and methods of natural language processing

Syntax and semantic analysis are two main techniques used with natural language processing

Syntax is the arrangement of words in a sentence to make grammatical sense. NLP uses syntax to assess meaning from a language based on grammatical rules. Syntax techniques include:

- Parsing: This is the grammatical analysis of a sentence. Example: A natural language processing algorithm is fed the sentence, "The dog barked." Parsing involves breaking this sentence into parts of speech -- i.e., dog = noun, barked = verb. This is useful for more complex downstream processing tasks.
- Word segmentation: This is the act of taking a string of text and deriving word forms from it. Example: A person scans a handwritten document into a computer. The algorithm would be able to analyze the page and recognize that the words are divided by white spaces.
- Sentence breaking: This places sentence boundaries in large texts. Example: A natural language processing algorithm is fed the text, "The dog barked. I woke up." The algorithm can recognize the period that splits up the sentences using sentence breaking.
- Morphological segmentation: This divides words into smaller parts called morphemes. Example: The word un test ably would be broken into [[un[[test]able]]ly], where the algorithm recognizes "un," "test," "able" and "ly" as morphemes. This is especially useful in machine translation and speech recognition.
- Stemming: This divides words with inflection in them to root forms. Example: In the sentence, "The dog barked," the algorithm would be able to recognize the root of the word "barked" is "bark." This would be useful if a user was analyzing a text for all instances of the word bark, as well as all of its conjugations. The algorithm can see that they are essentially the same word even though the letters are different.
- Semantics involves the use of and meaning behind words. Natural language processing applies algorithms to understand the meaning and structure of sentences. Semantics techniques include:
- Word sense disambiguation: This derives the meaning of a word based on context. Example: Consider the sentence, "The pig is in the pen." The word pen has different meanings. An algorithm using this method can understand that the use of the word pen here refers to a fenced-in area, not a writing implement.
- Named entity recognition: This determines words that can be categorized into groups. Example: An algorithm using this method could analyze a news article and identify all mentions of a certain company or product. Using the semantics of the text, it would be able to differentiate between entities that are visually the same. For instance, in the sentence, "Daniel McDonald's son went to McDonald's and ordered a Happy Meal," the algorithm could recognize the two instances of "McDonald's" as two separate entities -- one a restaurant and one a person.
- Natural language generation: This uses a database to determine semantics behind words and generate new text. Example: An algorithm could automatically write a summary of findings from a business intelligence platform, mapping certain words and phrases to features of the data in the BI platform. Another example would be automatically generating news articles or tweets based on a certain body of text used for training.

Current approaches to natural language processing are based on deep learning, a type of AI that examines and uses patterns in data to improve a program's understanding. Deep learning models require massive amounts of labeled data for the natural language processing algorithm to train on and identify relevant correlations, and assembling this kind of big data set is one of the main hurdles to natural language processing.

Earlier approaches to natural language processing involved a more rules-based approach, where simpler Machine Learning algorithms were told what words and phrases to look for in text and given specific responses when those phrases appeared. But deep learning is a more flexible, intuitive approach in which algorithms learn to identify speakers' intent from many examples -- almost like how a child would learn human language.

Three tools used commonly for natural language processing include Natural Language Toolkit (NLTK),Gen sim and Intel natural language processing Architect. NLTK is an open source Python module with data sets and tutorials. Gen sim is a Python library for topic modeling and document indexing. Intel NLP Architect is another Python library for deep learning topologies and techniques.

What is natural language processing used for?

Some of the main functions that natural language processing algorithms perform are:
- Text classification. This involves assigning tags to texts to put them in categories. This can be useful for sentiment analysis, which helps the natural language processing algorithm determine the sentiment, or emotion behind a text. For example, when brand A is mentioned in X number of texts, the algorithm can determine how many of those mentions were positive and how many were negative. It can also be useful for intent detection, which helps predict what the speaker or writer may do based on the text they are producing.
- Text extraction. This involves automatically summarizing text and finding important pieces of data. One example of this is keyword extraction, which pulls the most important words from the text, which can be useful for search engine optimization. Doing this with natural language processing requires some programming -- it is not completely automated. However, there are plenty of simple keyword extraction tools

that automate most of the process -- the user just has to set parameters within the program. For example, a tool might pull out the most frequently used words in the text. Another example is named entity recognition, which extracts the names of people, places and other entities from text.

- Machine translation. This is the process by which a computer translates text from one language, such as English, to another language, such as French, without human intervention.
- Natural language generation. This involves using natural language processing algorithms to analyze unstructured data and automatically produce content based on that data. One example of this is in language models such as GPT3, which are able to analyze an unstructured text and then generate believable articles based on the text.

The functions listed above are used in a variety of real-world applications, including:

customer feedback analysis -- where AI analyzes social media reviews;

a. customer service automation -- where voice assistants on the other end of a customer service phone line are able to use speech recognition to understand what the customer is saying, so that it can direct the call correctly;

b. automatic translation -- using tools such as Google Translate, Bing Translator and Translate Me;

academic research and analysis -- where AI is able to analyze huge amounts of academic material and research papers not just based on the metadata of the text, but the text itself;

c. analysis and categorization of medical records -- where AI uses insights to predict, and ideally prevent, disease;

d. word processors used for plagiarism and proofreading -- using tools such as Grammarly and Microsoft Word;

e. stock forecasting and insights into financial trading -- using AI to analyze market history and 10-K documents, which contain comprehensive summaries about a company's financial performance;

f. talent recruitment in human resources; and

g. automation of routine litigation tasks -- one example is the artificially intelligent attorney.

h. Research being done on natural language processing revolves around search, especially Enterprise search. This involves having users query data sets in the form of a question that they might pose to another person. The machine interprets the important elements of the human language sentence, which correspond to specific features in a data set, and returns an answer.

- NLP can be used to interpret free, unstructured text and make it analyzable. There is a tremendous amount of information stored in free text files, such as patients' medical records. Before deep learning-based NLP models, this information was inaccessible to computer-assisted analysis and could not be analyzed in any systematic way. With NLP analysts can sift through massive amounts of free text to find relevant information.
- Sentiment analysis is another primary use case for NLP. Using sentiment analysis, data scientists can assess comments on social media to see how their business's brand is performing, or review notes from customer service teams to identify areas where people want the business to perform better.

Benefits of natural language processing

- The main benefit of NLP is that it improves the way humans and computers communicate with each other. The most direct way to manipulate a computer is through code -- the computer's language. By enabling computers to understand human language, interacting with computers becomes much more intuitive for humans.

Other benefits include:

- improved accuracy and efficiency of documentation;
- ability to automatically make a readable summary of a larger, more complex original text;
- useful for personal assistants such as Alexa, by enabling it to understand spoken word;
- enables an organization to use chatbots for customer support;
- easier to perform sentiment analysis; and
- provides advanced insights from analytics that were previously unreachable due to data volume.

Challenges of natural language processing

- There are a number of challenges of natural language processing and most of them boil down to the fact that natural language is ever-evolving and always somewhat ambiguous. They include:
    - Precision. Computers traditionally require humans to "speak" to them in a programming language that is precise, unambiguous and highly structured -- or through a limited number of clearly enunciated voice commands. Human speech, however, is not always precise; it is often ambiguous

and the linguistic structure can depend on many complex variables, including slang, regional dialects and social context.

- Tone of voice and inflection. Natural language processing has not yet been perfected. For example, semantic analysis can still be a challenge. Other difficulties include the fact that the abstract use of language is typically tricky for programs to understand. For instance, natural language processing does not pick up sarcasm easily. These topics usually require understanding the words being used and their context in a conversation. As another example, a sentence can change meaning depending on which word or syllable the speaker puts stress on. NLP algorithms may miss the subtle, but important, tone changes in a person's voice when performing speech recognition. The tone and inflection of speech may also vary between different accents, which can be challenging for an algorithm to parse.
- Evolving use of language. Natural language processing is also challenged by the fact that language -- and the way people use it -- is continually changing. Although there are rules to language, none are written in stone, and they are subject to change over time. Hard computational rules that work now may become obsolete as the characteristics of real-world language change over time.

The evolution of natural language processing

NLP draws from a variety of disciplines, including computer science and computational linguistics developments dating back to the mid-20th century. Its evolution included the following major milestones:

1950s. Natural language processing has its roots in this decade, when Alan Turing developed the Turing Test to determine whether or not a computer is truly intelligent. The test involves automated interpretation and the generation of natural language as criterion of intelligence.

1950s-1990s. NLP was largely rules-based, using handcrafted rules developed by linguists to determine how computers would process language.

1990s. The top-down, language-first approach to natural language processing was replaced with a more statistical approach, because advancements in computing made this a more efficient way of developing NLP technology. Computers were becoming faster and could be used to develop rules based on linguistic statistics without a linguist creating all of the rules. Data-driven natural language processing became mainstream during this decade. Natural language processing shifted from a linguist-based approach to an engineer-based approach, drawing on a wider variety of scientific disciplines instead of delving into linguistics.

2000-2020s. Natural language processing saw dramatic growth in popularity as a term. With advances in computing power, natural language processing has also gained numerous real-world applications. Today, approaches to NLP involve a combination of classical linguistics and statistical methods.

Natural language processing plays a vital part in technology and the way humans interact with it. It is used in many real-world applications in both the business and consumer spheres, including chatbots, cybersecurity, search engines and big data analytics. Though not without its challenges, NLP is expected to continue to be an important part of both industry and everyday life.Although there are doubts, natural language processing is making significant strides in the medical imaging field.

10.1 Text Preprocessing

- Text data derived from natural language is unstructured and noisy. Text preprocessing involves transforming text into a clean and consistent format that can then be fed into a model for further analysis and learning.
- Text preprocessing techniques may be general so that they are applicable to many types of applications, or they can be specialized for a specific task. For example, the methods for processing scientific documents with equations and other mathematical symbols can be quite different from those for dealing with user comments on social media.
- However, some steps, such as sentence segmentation, tokenization, spelling corrections, and stemming, are common to both.

Here's what you need to know about text preprocessing to improve your natural language processThe NLP Preprocessing Pipeline

A natural language processing system for textual data reads, processes, analyzes, and interprets text. As a first step, the system preprocesses the text into a more structured format using several different stages. The output from one stage becomes an input for the next—hence the name "preprocessing pipeline."

An NLP pipeline for document classification might include steps such as sentence segmentation, word tokenization, lowercasing, stemming or lemmatization, stop word removal, and spelling correction. Some or all of these commonly used text prepr.ocessing stages are used in typical NLP systems, although the order can vary depending on the application.

Segmentation

Segmentation involves breaking up text into corresponding sentences. While this may seem like a trivial task, it has a few challenges. For example, in the English language, a period normally indicates the end of a sentence, but many abbreviations, including "Inc.," "Calif.," "Mr.," and "Ms.," and all fractional numbers contain periods and introduce uncertainty unless the end-of-sentence rules accommodate those exceptions.

Tokenization

The tokenization stage involves converting a sentence into a stream of words, also called "tokens." Tokens are the basic building blocks upon which analysis and other methods are built.

Many NLP toolkits allow users to input multiple criteria based on which word boundaries are determined. For example, you can use a whitespace or punctuation to determine if one word has ended and the next one has started. Again, in some instances, these rules might fail. For example, don't, it's, etc. are words themselves that contain punctuation marks and have to be dealt with separately.

Change Case

Changing the case involves converting all text to lowercase or uppercase so that all word strings follow a consistent format. Lowercasing is the more frequent choice in NLP software.

Spell Correction

Many NLP applications include a step to correct the spelling of all words in the text.

Stop-Words Removal

"Stop words" are frequently occurring words used to construct sentences. In the English language, stop words include is, the, are, of, in, and For some NLP applications, such as document categorization, sentiment analysis, and spam filtering, these words are redundant, and so are removed at the preprocessing stage.

Stemming

The term word stem is borrowed from linguistics and used to refer to the base or root form of a word. For example, learn is a base word for its variants such as learn, learns, learning, and learned.

Stemming is the process of converting all words to their base form, or stem. Normally, a lookup table is used to find the word and its corresponding stem. Many search engines apply stemming for retrieving documents that match user queries. Stemming is also used at the preprocessing stage for applications such as emotion identification and text classification.

Lemmatization

Lemmatization is a more advanced form of stemming and involves converting all words to their corresponding root form, called "lemma." While stemming reduces all words to their stem via a lookup table, it does not employ any knowledge of the parts of speech or the context of the word. This means stemming can't distinguish which meaning of the word right is intended in the sentences "Please turn right at the next light" and "She is always right."

The stemmer would stem right to right in both sentences; the lemmatizer would treat right differently based upon its usage in the two phrases.

A lemmatizer also converts different word forms or inflections to a standard form.For example, it would convert less to little ,wrote to write, slept to sleep, etc.

A lemmatizer works with more rules of the language and contextual information than does a stemmer. It also relies on a dictionary to look up matching words. Because of that, it requires more processing power and time than a stemmer to generate output. For these reasons, some NLP applications only use a stemmer and not a lemmat

Text Normalization

Text normalization is the preprocessing stage that converts text to a canonical representation. A common application is the processing of social media posts, where input text is shortened or words are spelled in different ways. For example, hello might be written as hello or something might appear as smth, and different people might choose to write real time, real-time, or real time. Text normalization cleans the text and ideally replaces all words with their corresponding canonical representation. In the last example, all three forms would be converted to real time. Many text normalization stages also replace emojis in text with a corresponding word. For example, :-) is replaced by happy face.

Parts of Speech Tagging

One of the more advanced text preprocessing techniques is parts of speech (POS) tagging. This step augments the input text with additional information about the sentence's grammatical structure. Each word is, therefore, inserted into one of the predefined categories such as a noun, verb, adjective, etc. This step is also sometimes referred to as grammatical tagging.

Is Text Preprocessing Really Necessary?

The simple answer is yes. Text preprocessing improves the performance of an NLP system. For tasks such as sentiment analysis, document categorization, document retrieval based upon user queries, and more, adding a text preprocessing layer provides more accuracy.

Stages such as stemming, lemmatization, and text normalization make the vocabulary size more manageable and transform the text into a more standard form across a variety of documents acquired from different sources.

Once you have a clear idea of the type of application you are developing and the source and nature of text data, you can decide on which preprocessing stages can be added to your NLP pipeline. Most of the NLP toolkits on the market include options for all of the preprocessing stages discussed above.

10.2 Word Embedding.

Representing text as numbers

Machine Learning models take vectors (arrays of numbers) as input. When working with text, the first thing you must do is come up with a strategy to convert strings to numbers (or to "vectorize" the text) before feeding it to the model. In this section, you will look at three strategies for doing so.

One-hot encodings

As a first idea, you might "one-hot" encode each word in your vocabulary. Consider the sentence "The cat sat on the mat". The vocabulary (or unique words) in this sentence is (cat, mat, on, sat, the). To represent each word, you will create a zero vector with length equal to the vocabulary, then place a one in the index that corresponds to the word. This approach is shown in the following diagram.

Diagram of one-hot encodings

To create a vector that contains the encoding of the sentence, you could then concatenate the one-hot vectors for each word.

Key Point: This approach is inefficient. A one-hot encoded vector is sparse (meaning, most indices are zero). Imagine you have 10,000 words in the vocabulary. To one-hot encode each word, you would create a vector where 99.99% of the elements are zero.

Encode each word with a unique number

A second approach you might try is to encode each word using a unique number. Continuing the example above, you could assign 1 to "cat", 2 to "mat", and so on. You could then encode the sentence "The cat sat on the mat" as a dense vector like [5, 1, 4, 3, 5, 2]. This approach is efficient. Instead of a sparse vector, you now have a dense one (where all elements are full).

There are two downsides to this approach, however:

The integer-encoding is arbitrary (it does not capture any relationship between words).

An integer-encoding can be challenging for a model to interpret. A linear classifier, for example, learns a single weight for each feature. Because there is no relationship between the similarity of any two words and the similarity of their encodings, this feature-weight combination is not meaningful.

Word embeddings

Word embeddings give us a way to use an efficient, dense representation in which similar words have a similar encoding. Importantly, you do not have to specify this encoding by hand. An embedding is a dense vector of floating point values (the length of the vector is a parameter you specify). Instead of specifying the values for the embedding manually, they are trainable parameters (weights learned by the model during training, in the same way a model learns weights for a dense layer). It is common to see word embeddings that are 8-dimensional (for small datasets), up to 1024-dimensions when working with large datasets. A higher dimensional embedding can capture fine-grained relationships between words, but takes more data to learn.

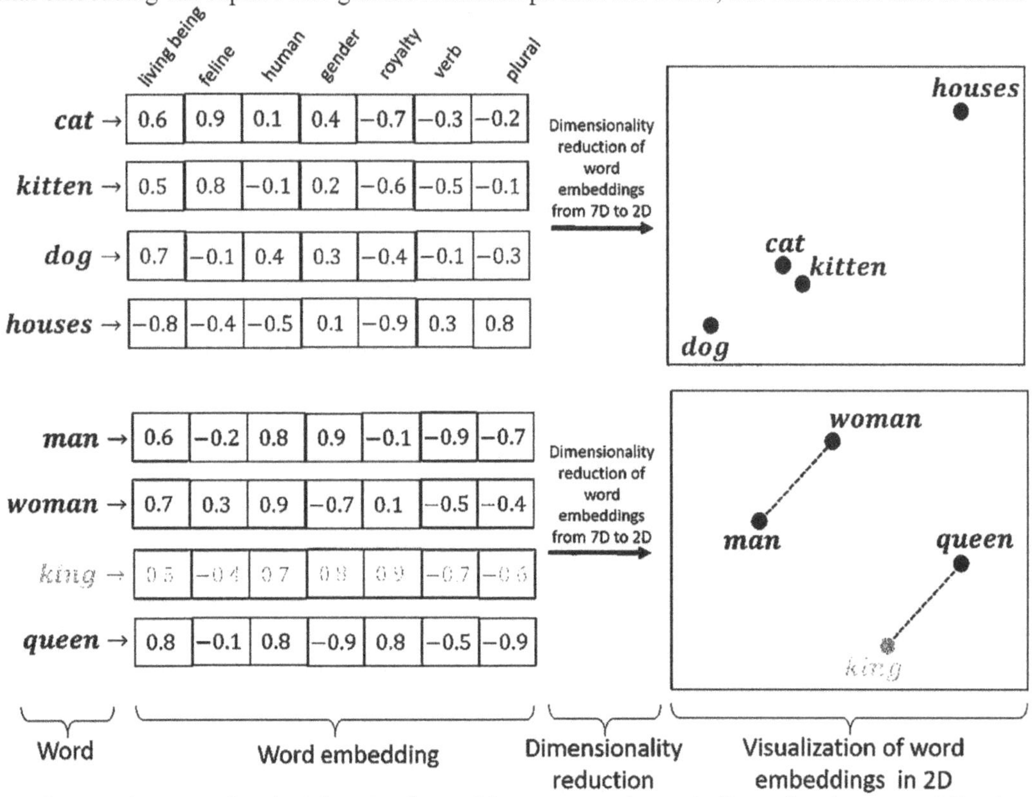

Above is a diagram for a word embedding. Each word is represented as a 4-dimensional vector of floating point values. Another way to think of an embedding is as "lookup table". After these weights have been learned, you can encode each word by looking up the dense vector it corresponds to in the table.

Setup

```
import io
import os
import re
import shutil
import string
import tensorflow as tf

    from tensorflow.keras import Sequential
    from tensorflow.keras.layers import Dense, Embedding, GlobalAveragePooling1D
    from tensorflow.keras.layers import TextVectorization


    url = "https://ai.stanford.edu/~amaas/data/sentiment/aclImdb_v1.tar.gz"

    dataset = tf.keras.utils.get_file("aclImdb_v1.tar.gz", url,
                                      untar=True, cache_dir='.',
                                      cache_subdir='')
```

```
dataset_dir = os.path.join(os.path.dirname(dataset), 'aclImdb')
os.listdir(dataset_dir)
```

```
Downloading data from https://ai.stanford.edu/~amaas/data/sentiment/aclImdb_v1.tar.gz
84125825/84125825 [==============================] - 3s 0us/step
['test', 'imdb.vocab', 'README', 'train', 'imdbEr.txt']
```

Take a look at the train/ directory. It has pos and neg folders with movie reviews labelled as positive and negative respectively. You will use reviews from pos and neg folders to train a binary classification model.

```
train_dir = os.path.join(dataset_dir, 'train')
os.listdir(train_dir)
```

```
['pos',
 'neg',
 'unsupBow.feat',
 'urls_pos.txt',
 'unsup',
 'urls_neg.txt',
 'urls_unsup.txt',
 'labeledBow.feat']
```

The train directory also has additional folders which should be removed before creating training dataset.

```
remove_dir = os.path.join(train_dir, 'unsup')
shutil.rmtree(remove_dir)
```

Next, create a tf.data.Dataset using tf.keras.utils.text_dataset_from_directory. You can read more about using this utility in this text classification tutorial.

Use the train directory to create both train and validation datasets with a split of 20% for validation.

```
batch_size = 1024
seed = 123
train_ds = tf.keras.utils.text_dataset_from_directory(
   'aclImdb/train', batch_size=batch_size, validation_split=0.2,
   subset='training', seed=seed)
val_ds = tf.keras.utils.text_dataset_from_directory(
   'aclImdb/train', batch_size=batch_size, validation_split=0.2,
   subset='validation', seed=seed)
```

```
Found 25000 files belonging to 2 classes.
Using 20000 files for training.
Found 25000 files belonging to 2 classes.
Using 5000 files for validation.
```

Take a look at a few movie reviews and their labels (1: positive, 0: negative) from the train dataset.

```
for text_batch, label_batch in train_ds.take(1):
  for i in range(5):
    print(label_batch[i].numpy(), text_batch.numpy()[i])
```

These are two important methods you should use when loading data to make sure that I/O does not become blocking.

.cache() keeps data in memory after it's loaded off disk. This will ensure the dataset does not become a bottleneck while training your model. If your dataset is too large to fit into memory, you can also use this method to create a performant on-disk cache, which is more efficient to read than many small files.

.prefetch() overlaps data preprocessing and model execution while training.

You can learn more about both methods, as well as how to cache data to disk in the data performance guide.

```
AUTOTUNE = tf.data.AUTOTUNE

train_ds = train_ds.cache().prefetch(buffer_size=AUTOTUNE)
val_ds = val_ds.cache().prefetch(buffer_size=AUTOTUNE)
```

Using the Embedding layer

Keras makes it easy to use word embeddings. Take a look at the Embedding layer.

The Embedding layer can be understood as a lookup table that maps from integer indices (which stand for specific words) to dense vectors (their embeddings). The dimensionality (or width) of the embedding is a parameter you can experiment with to see what works well for your problem, much in the same way you would experiment with the number of neurons in a Dense layer.

```
# Embed a 1,000 word vocabulary into 5 dimensions.
embedding_layer = tf.keras.layers.Embedding(1000, 5)
```

When you create an Embedding layer, the weights for the embedding are randomly initialized (just like any other layer). During training, they are gradually adjusted via backpropagation. Once trained, the learned word embeddings will roughly encode similarities between words (as they were learned for the specific problem your model is trained on).

If you pass an integer to an embedding layer, the result replaces each integer with the vector from the embedding table:

```
result = embedding_layer(tf.constant([1, 2, 3]))
result.numpy()

array([[ 0.03135875,  0.03640932, -0.00031054,  0.04873694, -0.03376802],
       [ 0.00243857, -0.02919209, -0.01841091, -0.03684188,  0.02765827],
       [-0.01245669, -0.01057661, -0.04422194, -0.0317696 , -0.00031216]],
      dtype=float32)
```

For text or sequence problems, the Embedding layer takes a 2D tensor of integers, of shape (samples, sequence_length), where each entry is a sequence of integers. It can embed sequences of variable lengths. You could feed into the embedding layer above batches with shapes (32, 10) (batch of 32 sequences of length 10) or (64, 15) (batch of 64 sequences of length 15).

The returned tensor has one more axis than the input, the embedding vectors are aligned along the new last axis. Pass it a (2, 3) input batch and the output is (2, 3, N)

```
result = embedding_layer(tf.constant([[0, 1, 2], [3, 4, 5]]))
result.shape

TensorShape([2, 3, 5])
```

When given a batch of sequences as input, an embedding layer returns a 3D floating point tensor, of shape (samples, sequence_length, embedding_dimensionality). To convert from this sequence of variable length to a fixed representation there are a variety of standard approaches. You could use an RNN, Attention, or pooling layer before passing it to a Dense layer. This tutorial uses pooling because it's the simplest. The Text Classification with an RNN tutorial is a good next step.

Text preprocessing

Next, define the dataset preprocessing steps required for your sentiment classification model. Initialize a TextVectorization layer with the desired parameters to vectorize movie reviews. You can learn more about using this layer in the Text Classification tutorial.

```
# Create a custom standardization function to strip HTML break tags '<br />'.
def custom_standardization(input_data):
  lowercase = tf.strings.lower(input_data)
  stripped_html = tf.strings.regex_replace(lowercase, '<br />', ' ')
  return tf.strings.regex_replace(stripped_html,
                                  '[%s]' % re.escape(string.punctuation), '')


# Vocabulary size and number of words in a sequence.
vocab_size = 10000
sequence_length = 100

# Use the text vectorization layer to normalize, split, and map strings to
# integers. Note that the layer uses the custom standardization defined above.
# Set maximum_sequence length as all samples are not of the same length.
vectorize_layer = TextVectorization(
    standardize=custom_standardization,
    max_tokens=vocab_size,
    output_mode='int',
    output_sequence_length=sequence_length)

# Make a text-only dataset (no labels) and call adapt to build the vocabulary.
text_ds = train_ds.map(lambda x, y: x)
vectorize_layer.adapt(text_ds)
```

The TextVectorization layer transforms strings into vocabulary indices. You have already initialized vectorize_layer as a TextVectorization layer and built its vocabulary by calling adapt on text_ds. Now vectorize_layer can be used as the first layer of your end-to-end classification model, feeding transformed strings into the Embedding layer.

The Embedding layer takes the integer-encoded vocabulary and looks up the embedding vector for each word-index. These vectors are learned as the model trains. The vectors add a dimension to the output array. The resulting dimensions are: (batch, sequence, embedding).

The GlobalAveragePooling1D layer returns a fixed-length output vector for each example by averaging over the sequence dimension. This allows the model to handle input of variable length, in the simplest way possible.

The fixed-length output vector is piped through a fully-connected (Dense) layer with 16 hidden units.

The last layer is densely connected with a single output node.

Caution: This model doesn't use masking, so the zero-padding is used as part of the input and hence the padding length may affect the output. To fix this, see the masking and padding guide.

```
embedding_dim=16
```

```
model = Sequential([
  vectorize_layer,
  Embedding(vocab_size, embedding_dim, name="embedding"),
  GlobalAveragePooling1D(),
  Dense(16, activation='relu'),
  Dense(1)
])
```

Compile and train the model

You will use TensorBoard to visualize metrics including loss and accuracy. Create a tf.keras.callbacks.TensorBoard.

```
tensorboard_callback = tf.keras.callbacks.TensorBoard(log_dir="logs")
```

Compile and train the model using the Adam optimizer and BinaryCrossentropy loss.

```
model.compile(optimizer='adam',
          loss=tf.keras.losses.BinaryCrossentropy(from_logits=True),
          metrics=['accuracy'])

model.fit(
   train_ds,
   validation_data=val_ds,
   epochs=15,
   callbacks=[tensorboard_callback])
```

```
Epoch 1/15
20/20 [==============================] - 7s 206ms/step - loss: 0.6920 - accuracy: 0.5028 - val_loss: 0.6904 - val_accuracy: 0.4886
Epoch 2/15
20/20 [==============================] - 1s 50ms/step - loss: 0.6879 - accuracy: 0.5028 - val_loss: 0.6856 - val_accuracy: 0.4886
Epoch 3/15
20/20 [==============================] - 1s 48ms/step - loss: 0.6815 - accuracy: 0.5028 - val_loss: 0.6781 - val_accuracy: 0.4886
Epoch 4/15
20/20 [==============================] - 1s 51ms/step - loss: 0.6713 - accuracy: 0.5028 - val_loss: 0.6663 - val_accuracy: 0.4886
Epoch 5/15
20/20 [==============================] - 1s 49ms/step - loss: 0.6566 - accuracy: 0.5028 - val_loss: 0.6506 - val_accuracy: 0.4886
Epoch 6/15
20/20 [==============================] - 1s 49ms/step - loss: 0.6377 - accuracy: 0.5028 - val_loss: 0.6313 - val_accuracy: 0.4886
Epoch 7/15
20/20 [==============================] - 1s 49ms/step - loss: 0.6148 - accuracy: 0.5057 - val_loss: 0.6090 - val_accuracy: 0.5068
Epoch 8/15
20/20 [==============================] - 1s 48ms/step - loss: 0.5886 - accuracy: 0.5724 - val_loss: 0.5846 - val_accuracy: 0.5864
Epoch 9/15
20/20 [==============================] - 1s 48ms/step - loss: 0.5604 - accuracy: 0.6427 - val_loss: 0.5596 - val_accuracy: 0.6368
Epoch 10/15
20/20 [==============================] - 1s 49ms/step - loss: 0.5316 - accuracy: 0.6967 - val_loss: 0.5351 - val_accuracy: 0.6758
```

```
Epoch 11/15
20/20 [==============================] - 1s 50ms/step - loss: 0.5032 - accuracy: 0.7372 - val_loss: 0.5121 - val_accuracy: 0.7102
Epoch 12/15
20/20 [==============================] - 1s 48ms/step - loss: 0.4764 - accuracy: 0.7646 - val_loss: 0.4912 - val_accuracy: 0.7344
Epoch 13/15
20/20 [==============================] - 1s 48ms/step - loss: 0.4516 - accuracy: 0.7858 - val_loss: 0.4727 - val_accuracy: 0.7492
Epoch 14/15
20/20 [==============================] - 1s 48ms/step - loss: 0.4290 - accuracy: 0.8029 - val_loss: 0.4567 - val_accuracy: 0.7584
Epoch 15/15
20/20 [==============================] - 1s 49ms/step - loss: 0.4085 - accuracy: 0.8163 - val_loss: 0.4429 - val_accuracy: 0.7674
<keras.callbacks.History at 0x7f5095954190>
```

With this approach the model reaches a validation accuracy of around 78% (note that the model is overfitting since training accuracy is higher).

```
model.summary()
```

```
Model: "sequential"
_________________________________________________________________
 Layer (type)                Output Shape              Param #
=================================================================
 text_vectorization (TextVec  (None, 100)              0
 torization)

 embedding (Embedding)       (None, 100, 16)           160000

 global_average_pooling1d (G  (None, 16)               0
 lobalAveragePooling1D)

 dense (Dense)               (None, 16)                272

 dense_1 (Dense)             (None, 1)                 17

=================================================================
Total params: 160,289
Trainable params: 160,289
Non-trainable params: 0
_________________________________________________________________
```

Visualize the model metrics in TensorBoard.

```
#docs_infra: no_execute
%load_ext tensorboard
%tensorboard --logdir logs
```

embeddings_classifier_accuracy.png

Retrieve the trained word embeddings and save them to disk

Next, retrieve the word embeddings learned during training. The embeddings are weights of the Embedding layer in the model. The weights matrix is of shape (vocab_size, embedding_dimension).

Obtain the weights from the model using get_layer() and get_weights(). The get_vocabulary() function provides the vocabulary to build a metadata file with one token per line.

```
weights = model.get_layer('embedding').get_weights()[0]
vocab = vectorize_layer.get_vocabulary()
```

Write the weights to disk. To use the Embedding Projector, you will upload two files in tab separated format: a file of vectors (containing the embedding), and a file of meta data (containing the words).

```
out_v = io.open('vectors.tsv', 'w', encoding='utf-8')
out_m = io.open('metadata.tsv', 'w', encoding='utf-8')

for index, word in enumerate(vocab):
  if index == 0:
    continue # skip 0, it's padding.
  vec = weights[index]
  out_v.write('\t'.join([str(x) for x in vec]) + "\n")
  out_m.write(word + "\n")
out_v.close()
out_m.close()
```

10.3 Sequence-to-Sequence Models

Google first released sequence-to-sequence models for machine translation. Before it, the translation operated in an extremely ignorant manner. It was automatically translated into its intended language without considering the syntax or sentence structure of each word you typed. Sequence-to-sequence models used deep learning to transform the translation process. When translating, it considers the current word or input and its surroundings.

It is employed in many applications, including text summarization, conversational modeling, and image captioning.

Introduction to sequence-to-sequence Model

The many-to-many architecture of an RNN is what the sequence-to-sequence model (seq2seq) uses. Its ability to transfer arbitrary-length input sequences to arbitrary-length output sequences has made it useful for various applications. Some of the uses are Language translation, music creation, speech creation, and chatbots are all included in the sequence-to-sequence models concept.

In most cases, the length of the input and output differ. For example, if we take a translation task. Let's assume we need to convert a sentence from English to French.

Consider the sentence "I am doing good" to be mapped to "Je vais bien". We can see that the input feed has four words, but where in the output, we would see only three words. Hence, this algorithm handles these scenarios with varying input and output sequence lengths.

The architecture of the sequence-to-sequence model comprises two components:

Encoder

Decoder

The Encoder learns the embeddings of the input sentence. Embeddings are vectors comprising the meaning of the sentence. Then the Decoder takes the embedding vectors as input and tries constructing the target sentence.

In simple words, in a translation task, the Encoder takes the English sentence as input, learns the embedding from it, and feeds the embeddings to the decider. The Decoder generates the target French sentence using embedding fed.

Use Cases of the Sequence to Sequence Models

Many of the technologies you use every day are based on sequence-to-sequence models. For instance, voice-activated gadgets, online chatbots, and services like Google Translate are all powered by the sequence-to-sequence model architecture. Among the applications are the following:

Machine translation - The seq2seq model predicts a word from the user's input, after which each subsequent word is predicted using the likelihood that the first word will appear.
Video captioning - To understand the temporal structure of the sequence of frames and the sequence model of the generated sentences with RNNs, a sequence-to-sequence model for Video captioning was developed.
Text summarization - Using neural sequence-to-sequence models, an effective novel method for abstractive text summarization has been made available (not restricted to selecting and rearranging passages from the original text)
Example

Any sequence-based problem can be solved using this technique, especially if the inputs and outputs come in various sizes and classifications.

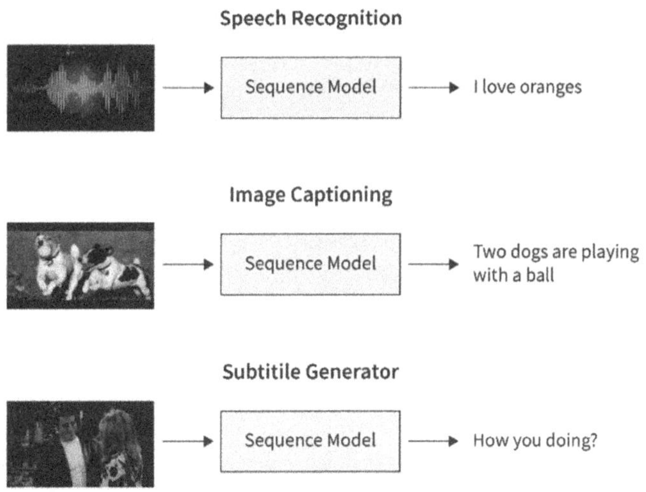

Any sequence-based problem can be solved using this technique, especially if the inputs and outputs come in various sizes and classifications.

Encoder-Decoder Architecture
An overview of the model is illustrated in the diagram below. Both have the Decoder on the right and the Encoder on the left. The Encoder and decoder output are combined to predict the following word at each time step.

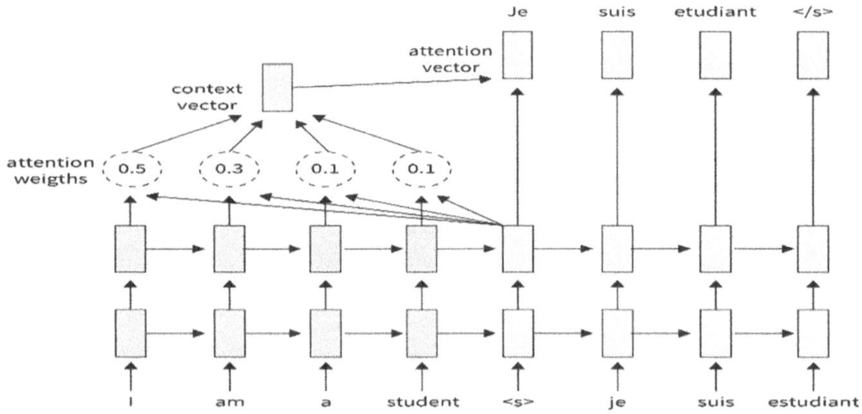

One sequence is converted into another via sequence to sequence model (sequence transformation). It uses a recurrent neural network (RNN) or, more frequently, an LSTM or GRU to get over the vanishing gradient issue. The output from the preceding stage serves as the context for each item. One Encoder and one decoder network make up the main parts. First, the Encoder converts each item into a corresponding hidden vector that includes the item and its context. Then, with the previous output as the input context, the Decoder reverses the process and produces the vector as an output item.

Encoder- Transforms the input words into matching hidden vectors using deep neural network layers. Each vector represents the current word and its context.

Decoder- To create the following hidden vector and ultimately predict the following word, it uses the current word, its hidden states, and the hidden vector created by the Encoder as input. Apart from these two, numerous optimizations must result in the following additional sequence-to-sequence model components.

Attention- The input to the Decoder is a single vector that must contain all of the context-related data. Large sequences cause difficulty with this. As a result, the attention mechanism lets the decoder focus on specific input sequences and generate an attention vector.

Beam Search- The Decoder chooses the word with the highest probability as the output. But because greedy algorithms are the root of the issue, this does not necessarily produce the optimal outcomes. As a result, beam search is used, suggesting potential translations at each stage. A tree of the top k-results is created to do this.

Bucketing- Because both the input and the output of a sequence-to-sequence model are padded with zeroes, variable-length sequences are conceivable. However, if we put the maximum length at 100 and the sentence is just three words long, there will be a significant loss of space. So, we apply the bucketing concept. First, we create buckets of varying sizes, such as (4, 8), (8, 15), and so forth, where 4 is the maximum input length and 8 is the maximum output length.

Input and Output Sequences of Equal Length

You can easily create similar models with a Keras LSTM or GRU layer when the input and output sequences are the same lengths.

This strategy has a drawback because it presumes you can generate target[...t] for given input[...t]. Unfortunately, the whole input sequence is usually required before generating the target sequence. That works in a few situations (such as adding strings of digits), but it could be more effective for most use cases.

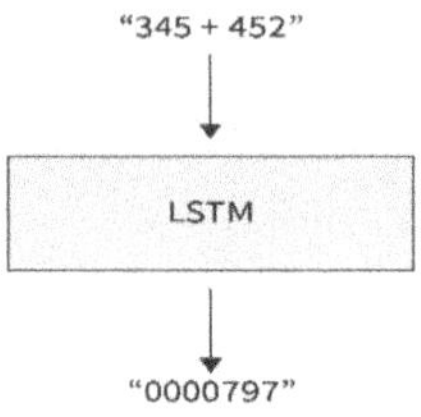

Language Translation Using the seq2seq Mode

As discussed above, let's learn how the encoder and decoder work to handle tasks that map input and output of different lengths.

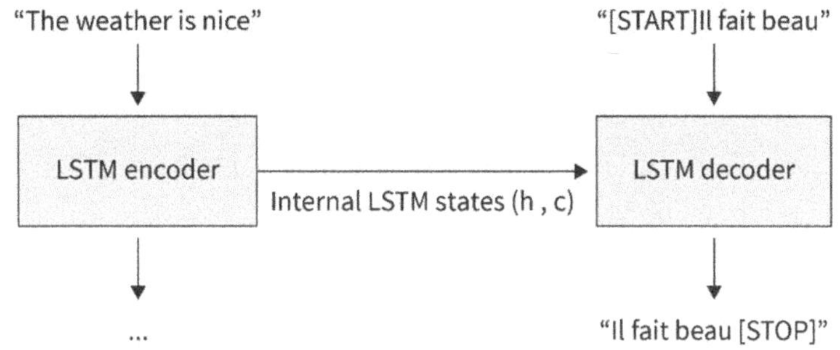

We try to translate a sentence from English to French. Let the sentence be, "The weather is nice."
Encoder
The basic structure of an encoder is an RNN with LSTM or GRU cells(control what information to keep or what to throw). Another option is a bidirectional RNN. Instead of using the output from the Encoder, we feed the input sentence into it, and we use the hidden state from the last time step as the embeddings.

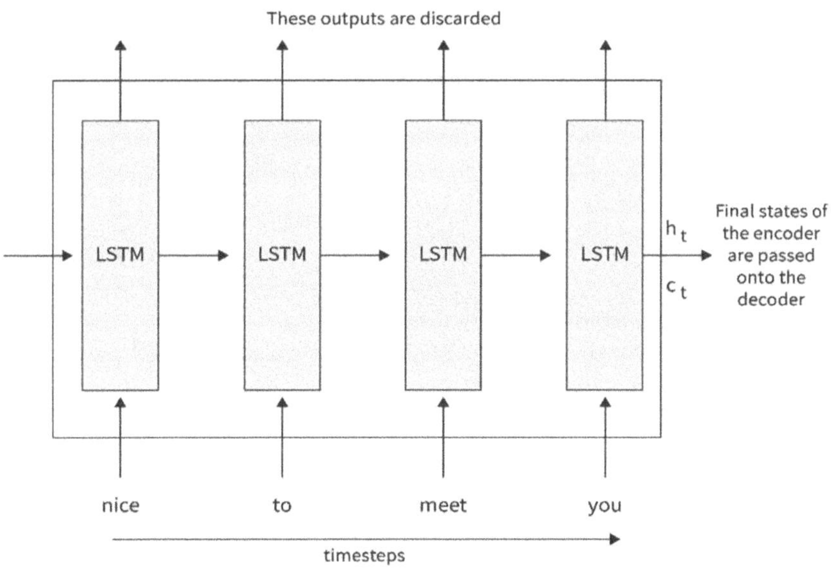

As a first step at a time steps t=0, To the LSTM cell, we pass the input xo, which is the first word from the source sentence. The model randomly initialized the hidden state with the input(hi); the LSTM cell computes the first hidden state, $h0$, as:

$h0 = LSTM(x0,hi)$

In the next step at time t=1, we pass the input, $x1$, the next word from the sentence "weather", to the Encoder. Along with this, we also pass the previously hidden state $h0$ to the cell and compute the hidden state $h1$:

$h1 = LSTM(x1,h0)$

The process repeated all over the source sentence. Thus the final hidden layer captures the context of all the words from the source sentence. Here the English sentence "The weather is nice" is the source. The words processed in the layers would be "The,", "Weather", "is", and "nice".
Since the final hidden layers hold context, this forms the embedding Ct, which is otherwise known as the context vector:

$Ct= ht$

Decoder

A decoder is an RNN with LSTM OR GRU cells. The Decoder aims to generate the output from the given input sentence. Now, we will learn about the working of the Decoder to generate the output using the vector Z generated by the Encoder

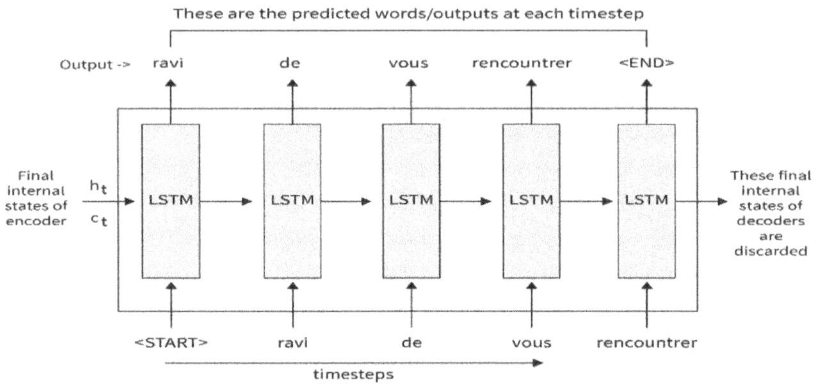

We provide the Decoder with <sos>, which denotes the beginning of the sentence, as input. So, after receiving <sos>, the decode attempts to guess the target sentence's first word.

We initialize the first hidden state of the Decoder with the vector generated by the Encoder instead of initializing them with a random value. Next, we feed the predicted output and the hidden state from the previous time step as input to the Decoder at the current time step and then predict the current output.

We need to predict the output sentence, a French sentence mapping the English sentence that feeds as input to the model. Then, we feed the Decoder hidden state, which returns the scores of all the words in our vocabulary to the corresponding input.

We convert them into probabilities and use the softmax function, which squashes the values between 0 to 1. Then, we select the high-probability valued word for the mapping to the input.

Thus, the sequence-to-sequence model changes the source sentence into the destination sentence in this manner.

Drawbacks of Encoder-Decoder Models

This architecture has two main disadvantages, both of which are length-related.

First off, its architecture has considerably less memory. You're attempting to squeeze the full sentence to translate into that last hidden state of the LSTM. Typically, They only have a few hundred units (or floating-point integers); the more you try to fit into this restricted dimensions vector, the lossier the neural network is compelled to be. It can be quite helpful to think of neural networks regarding the "lossy compression" that must be done.

Second, a neural network is more challenging to train the deeper it goes. For recurrent neural networks, the sequence length determines how far the network extends over time. As a result, the gradient signal from the recurrent neural network learns vanishes as it moves backward, resulting in vanishing gradients. Hence this remains a basic issue even with RNNs designed to help prevent disappearing gradients, like the LSTM.

10.4 Sentiment Analysis

What Is Sentiment Analysis?

Sentiment analysis is the process of detecting positive or negative sentiment in text. It's often used by businesses to detect sentiment in social data, gauge brand reputation, and understand customers.

Types of Sentiment Analysis

Sentiment analysis focuses on the polarity of a text (positive, negative, neutral) but it also goes beyond polarity to detect specific feelings and emotions (angry, happy, sad, etc), urgency (urgent, not urgent) and even intentions (interested v. not interested).

Depending on how you want to interpret customer feedback and queries, you can define and tailor your categories to meet your sentiment analysis needs. In the meantime, here are some of the most popular types of sentiment analysis:

Graded Sentiment Analysis

If polarity precision is important to your business, you might consider expanding your polarity categories to include different levels of positive and negative:

Very positive
Positive
Neutral
Negative
Very negative
This is usually referred to as graded or fine-grained sentiment analysis, and could be used to interpret 5-star ratings in a review, for example:

Very Positive = 5 stars
Very Negative = 1 star
Emotion detection
Emotion detection sentiment analysis allows you to go beyond polarity to detect emotions, like happiness, frustration, anger, and sadness.

Many emotion detection systems use lexicons (i.e. lists of words and the emotions they convey) or complex Machine Learning algorithms.

One of the downsides of using lexicons is that people express emotions in different ways. Some words that typically express anger, like bad or kill (e.g. your product is so bad or your customer support is killing me) might also express happiness (e.g. this is bad ass or you are killing it).

Aspect-based Sentiment Analysis
Usually, when analyzing sentiments of texts you'll want to know which particular aspects or features people are mentioning in a positive, neutral, or negative way.

That's where aspect-based sentiment analysis can help, for example in this product review: "The battery life of this camera is too short", an aspect-based classifier would be able to determine that the sentence expresses a negative opinion about the battery life of the product in question.

Multilingual sentiment analysis
Multilingual sentiment analysis can be difficult. It involves a lot of preprocessing and resources. Most of these resources are available online (e.g. sentiment lexicons), while others need to be created (e.g. translated corpora or noise detection algorithms), but you'll need to know how to code to use them.

Alternatively, you could detect language in texts automatically with a language classifier, then train a custom sentiment analysis model to classify texts in the language of your choice.

Why Is Sentiment Analysis Important?
Since humans express their thoughts and feelings more openly than ever before, sentiment analysis is fast becoming an essential tool to monitor and understand sentiment in all types of data.

Automatically analyzing customer feedback, such as opinions in survey responses and social media conversations, allows brands to learn what makes customers happy or frustrated, so that they can tailor products and services to meet their customers' needs.

For example, using sentiment analysis to automatically analyze 4,000+ open-ended responses in your customer satisfaction surveys could help you discover why customers are happy or unhappy at each stage of the customer journey.

Maybe you want to track brand sentiment so you can detect disgruntled customers immediately and respond as soon as possible. Maybe you want to compare sentiment from one quarter to the next to see if you need to take action. Then you could dig deeper into your qualitative data to see why sentiment is falling or rising.

The overall benefits of sentiment analysis include:

Sorting Data at Scale
Can you imagine manually sorting through thousands of tweets, customer support conversations, or surveys? There's just too much business data to process manually. Sentiment analysis helps businesses process huge amounts of unstructured data in an efficient and cost-effective way.

Real-Time Analysis
Sentiment analysis can identify critical issues in real-time, for example is a PR crisis on social media escalating? Is an angry customer about to churn? Sentiment analysis models can help you immediately identify these kinds of situations, so you can take action right away.

Consistent criteria
It's estimated that people only agree around 60-65% of the time when determining the sentiment of a particular text. Tagging text by sentiment is highly subjective, influenced by personal experiences, thoughts, and beliefs.

By using a centralized sentiment analysis system, companies can apply the same criteria to all of their data, helping them improve accuracy and gain better insights.

The applications of sentiment analysis are endless. So, to help you understand how sentiment analysis could benefit your business, let's take a look at some examples of texts that you could analyze using sentiment analysis.

Then, we'll jump into a real-world example of how Chewy, a pet supplies company, was able to gain a much more nuanced (and useful!) understanding of their reviews through the application of sentiment analysis.

Sentiment Analysis Examples
To understand the goal and challenges of sentiment analysis, here are some examples:

Basic examples of sentiment analysis data

Netflix has the best selection of films
Hulu has a great UI
I dislike like the new crime series
I hate waiting for the next series to come out
More challenging examples of sentiment analysis

I do not dislike horror movies. (phrase with negation)
Disliking horror movies is not uncommon. (negation, inverted word order)
Sometimes I really hate the show. (adverbial modifies the sentiment)
I love having to wait two months for the next series to come out! (sarcasm)
The final episode was surprising with a terrible twist at the end (negative term used in a positive way)
The film was easy to watch but I would not recommend it to my friends. (difficult to categorize)
I LOL'd at the end of the cake scene (often hard to understand new terms)
Now, let's take a look at some real reviews on Trustpilot and see how MonkeyLearn's sentiment analysis tools fare when it comes to recognizing and categorizing sentiment.

Case Study: Sentiment analysis on TrustPilot Reviews
Chewy is a pet supplies company – an industry with no shortage of competition, so providing a superior customer experience (CX) to their customers can be a massive difference maker.

For this reason, online reviews can be an extremely valuable source of information to gain customer insights to improve their CX. Chewy has thousands of reviews in TrustPilot, this is what their review archive looks like:

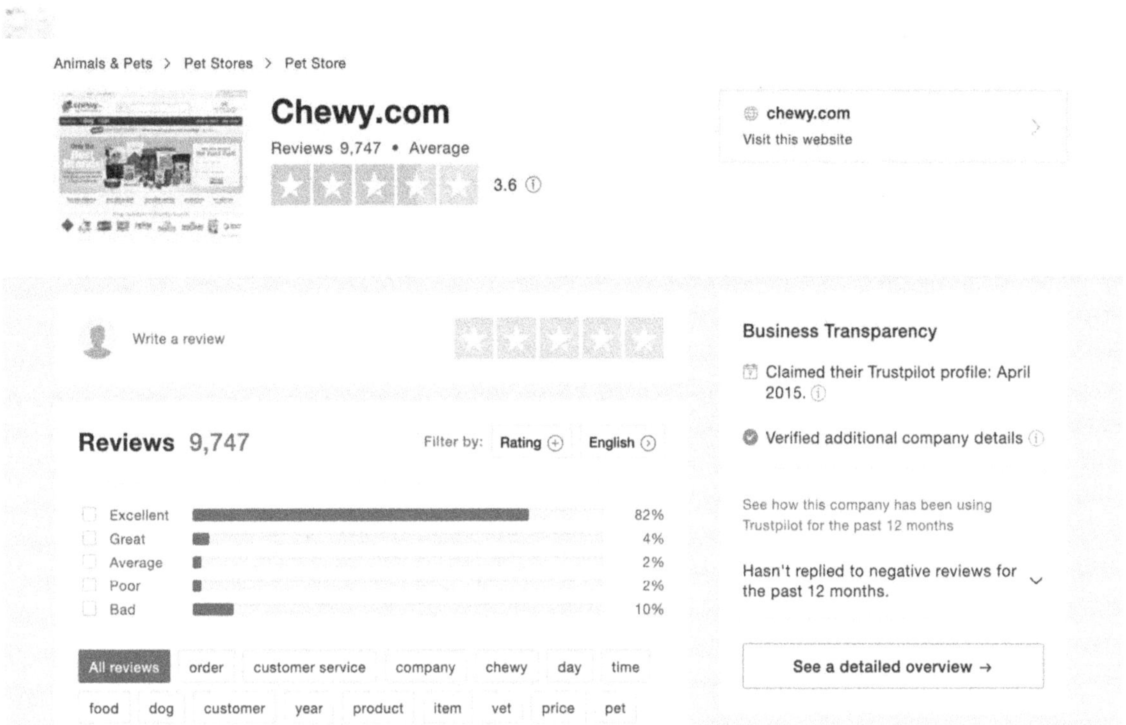

It is easy to draw a general conclusion about Chewy's relative success from this alone - 82% of responses being excellent is a great starting place.

But TrustPilot's results alone fall short if Chewy's goal is to improve its services. This perfunctory overview fails to provide actionable insight, the cornerstone, and end goal, of effective sentiment analysis.

If Chewy wanted to unpack the what and why behind their reviews, in order to further improve their services, they would need to analyze each and every negative review at a granular level.

But with sentiment analysis tools, Chewy could plug in their 5,639 (at the time) TrustPilot reviews to gain instant sentiment analysis insights.

We uploaded and analyzed Chewy's reviews to MonkeyLearn's all-in-one data analysis and visualization studio to generate the following dashboard:

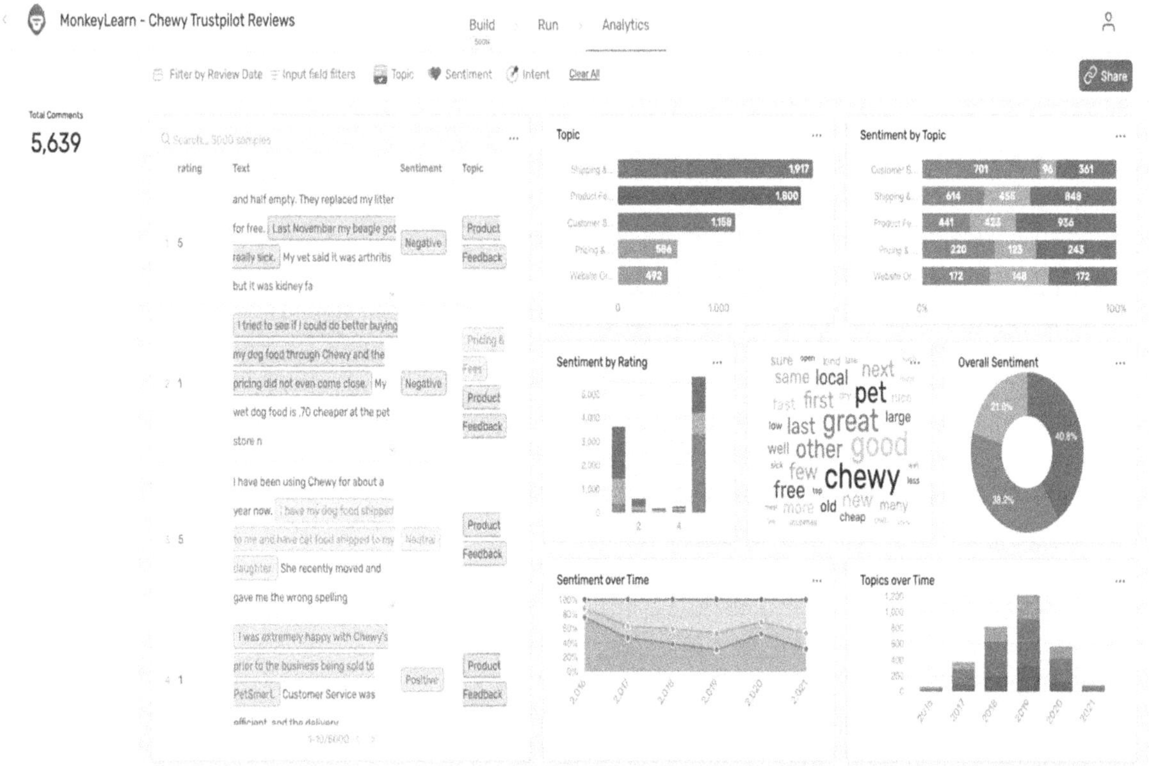

While there is a ton more to explore, in this breakdown we are going to focus on four sentiment analysis data visualization results that the dashboard has visualized for us.

1. Overall Sentiment

2. Sentiment over Time

3. Sentiment by Rating

4. Sentiment by Topic

1. Overall sentiment

We'll begin by pulling the relevant graphic from the above dashboard.

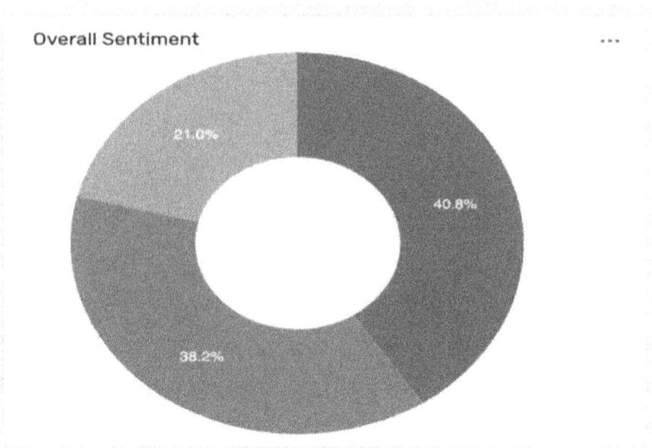

You'll notice that these results are very different from TrustPilot's overview (82% excellent, etc). This is because MonkeyLearn's sentiment analysis AI performs advanced sentiment analysis, parsing through each review sentence by sentence, word by word.

What you are left with is an accurate assessment of everything customers have written, rather than a simple tabulation of stars. This analysis can point you towards friction points much more accurately and in much more detail.
Read up on the mechanics of how sentiment analysis works below.
2. Sentiment over time
Here's our handy-dandy sentiment over time graph, blown up:

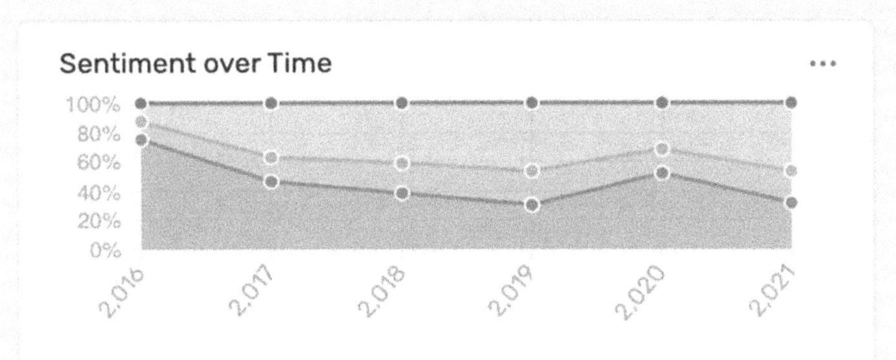

This data visualization sample is classic temporal datavis, a datavis type that tracks results and plots them over a period of time.
This graph expands on our Overall Sentiment data - it tracks the overall proportion of positive, neutral, and negative sentiment in the reviews from 2016 to 2021.
This graph informs the gradual change in the content of their written reviews over this five year period. For instance, negative responses went down from 2019-2020, then jumped back up to previous levels in 2021.
3. Sentiment by rating

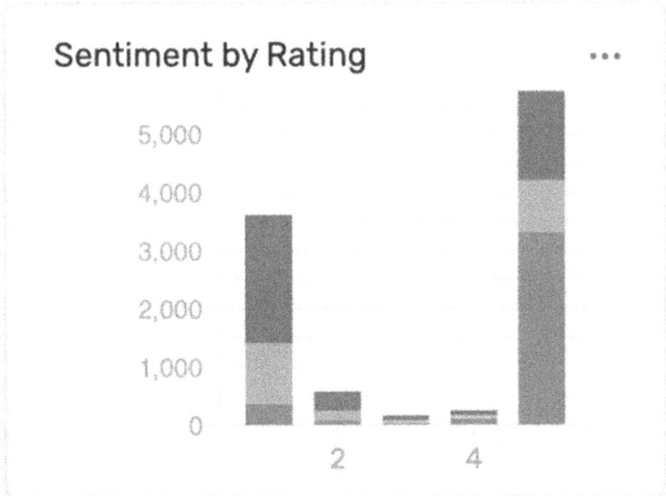

Now we jump to something that anchors our text-based sentiment to TrustPilot's earlier results.
By taking each TrustPilot category from 1-Bad to 5-Excellent, and breaking down the text of the written reviews from the scores you can derive the above graphic.
Looking at the results, and courtesy of taking a deeper look at the reviews via sentiment analysis, we can draw a couple interesting conclusions right off the bat.
TrustPilots results aren't useless - the better reviews have higher proportions of positive sentiment and the worse reviews have more negative sentiment. But, all reviews contain a little bit of all types of sentiment - we've learned that our reviews are nuanced and thus likely have even more hidden insight for us!
Our reviews are polarized. They skew in amounts towards 5 and 1.

These quick takeaways point us towards goldmines for future analysis. Namely, the positive sentiment sections of negative reviews and the negative section of positive ones, and the 2 - 4 reviews (why do they feel the way they do, how could we improve their scores?).

4. Sentiment by Topic

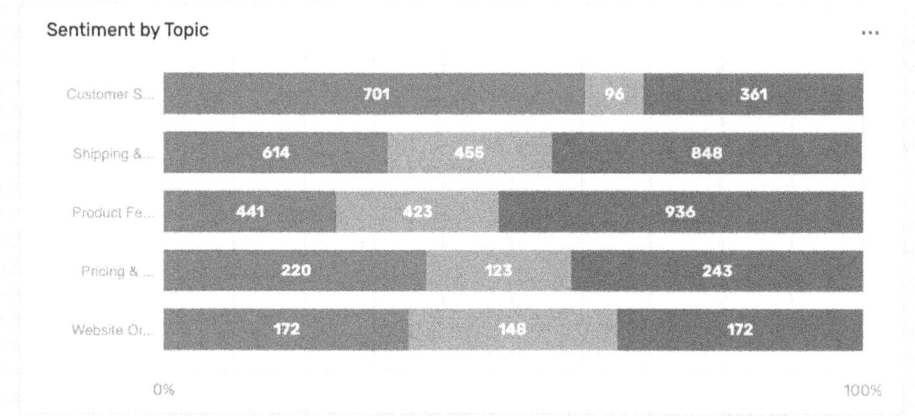

Finally, we can take a look at Sentiment by Topic to begin to illustrate how sentiment analysis can take us even further into our data.
The above chart applies product-linked text classification in addition to sentiment analysis to pair given sentiment to product/service specific features, this is known as aspect-based sentiment analysis.
This means we can know how our customers feel about what, helping us zero in and fix specific pain points or issues.
These are all great jumping off points designed to visually demonstrate the value of sentiment analysis - but they only scratch the surface of its true power.

Read on for a step-by-step walkthrough of how sentiment analysis works.

How Does Sentiment Analysis Work?
Rule-based: these systems automatically perform sentiment analysis based on a set of manually crafted rules.
Automatic: systems rely on Machine Learning techniques to learn from data.
Hybrid systems combine both rule-based and automatic approaches.
Rule-based Approaches
Usually, a rule-based system uses a set of human-crafted rules to help identify subjectivity, polarity, or the subject of an opinion.
These rules may include various NLP techniques developed in computational linguistics, such as:
Stemming, tokenization, part-of-speech tagging and parsing.
Lexicons (i.e. lists of words and expressions).
Here's a basic example of how a rule-based system works:
Defines two lists of polarized words (e.g. negative words such as bad, worst, ugly, etc and positive words such as good, best, beautiful, etc).
Counts the number of positive and negative words that appear in a given text.
If the number of positive word appearances is greater than the number of negative word appearances, the system returns a positive sentiment, and vice versa. If the numbers are even, the system will return a neutral sentiment.
Rule-based systems are very naive since they don't take into account how words are combined in a sequence. Of course, more advanced processing techniques can be used, and new rules added to support new expressions and vocabulary. However, adding new rules may affect previous results, and the whole system can get very complex. Since rule-based systems often require fine-tuning and maintenance, they'll also need regular investments.
Automatic Approaches

Automatic methods, contrary to rule-based systems, don't rely on manually crafted rules, but on Machine Learning techniques. A sentiment analysis task is usually modeled as a classification problem, whereby a classifier is fed a text and returns a category, e.g. positive, negative, or neutral.
Here's how a Machine Learning classifier can be implemented:

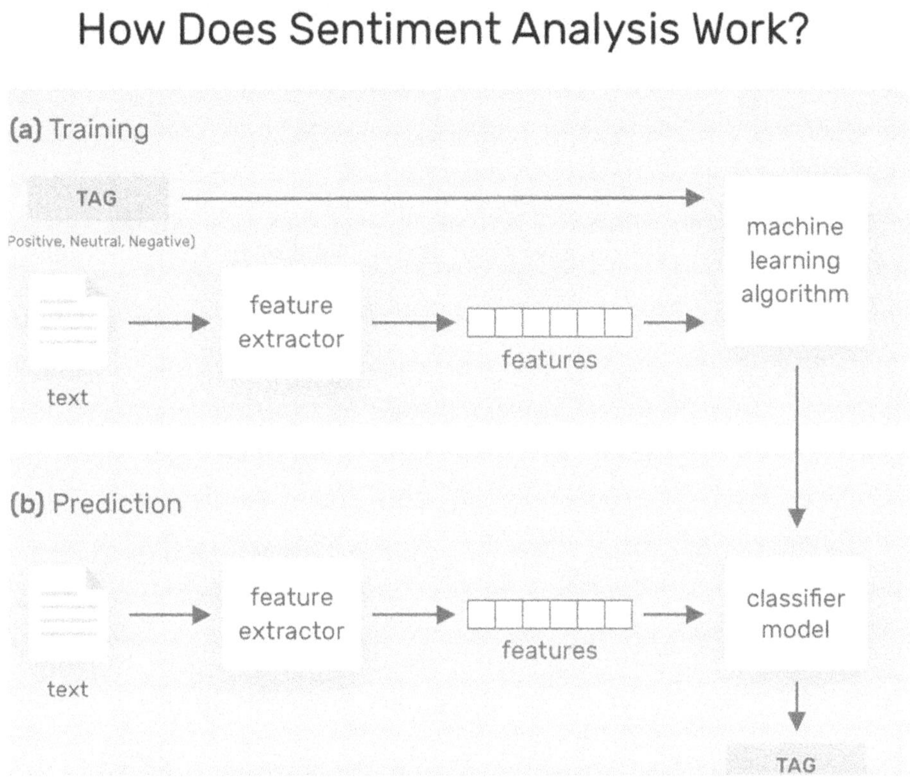

The Training and Prediction Processes
In the training process (a), our model learns to associate a particular input (i.e. a text) to the corresponding output (tag) based on the test samples used for training. The feature extractor transfers the text input into a feature vector. Pairs of feature vectors and tags (e.g. positive, negative, or neutral) are fed into the Machine Learning algorithm to generate a model.
In the prediction process (b), the feature extractor is used to transform unseen text inputs into feature vectors. These feature vectors are then fed into the model, which generates predicted tags (again, positive, negative, or neutral).

Feature Extraction from Text
The first step in a Machine Learning text classifier is to transform the text extraction or text vectorization, and the classical approach has been bag-of-words or bag-of-ngrams with their frequency.

More recently, new feature extraction techniques have been applied based on word embeddings (also known as word vectors). This kind of representations makes it possible for words with similar meaning to have a similar representation, which can improve the performance of classifiers.
Classification Algorithms
The classification step usually involves a statistical model like Naïve Bayes, Logistic Regression, Support Vector Machines, or Neural Networks:
Naïve Bayes: a family of probabilistic algorithms that uses Bayes's Theorem to predict the category of a text.
Linear Regression: a very well-known algorithm in statistics used to predict some value (Y) given a set of features (X).
Support Vector Machines: a non-probabilistic model which uses a representation of text examples as points in a multidimensional space. Examples of different categories (sentiments) are mapped to distinct regions

within that space. Then, new texts are assigned a category based on similarities with existing texts and the regions they're mapped to.
Deep Learning: a diverse set of algorithms that attempt to mimic the human brain, by employing artificial neural networks to process data.
Hybrid Approaches
Hybrid systems combine the desirable elements of rule-based and automatic techniques into one system. One huge benefit of these systems is that results are often more accurate.

Sentiment Analysis Challenges
Sentiment analysis is one of the hardest tasks in natural language processing because even humans struggle to analyze sentiments accurately.

Data scientists are getting better at creating more accurate sentiment classifiers, but there's still a long way to go. Let's take a closer look at some of the main challenges of machine-based sentiment analysis:

Subjectivity & Tone
Context & Polarity
Irony & Sarcasm
Comparisons
Emojis
Defining Neutral
Human Annotator Accuracy
Subjectivity and Tone
There are two types of text: subjective and objective. Objective texts do not contain explicit sentiments, whereas subjective texts do. Say, for example, you intend to analyze the sentiment of the following two texts:

The package is nice.

The package is red.

Most people would say that sentiment is positive for the first one and neutral for the second one, right? All predicates (adjectives, verbs, and some nouns) should not be treated the same with respect to how they create sentiment. In the examples above, nice is more subjective than red.

Context and Polarity
All utterances are uttered at some point in time, in some place, by and to some people, you get the point. All utterances are uttered in context. Analyzing sentiment without context gets pretty difficult. However, machines cannot learn about contexts if they are not mentioned explicitly. One of the problems that arise from context is changes in polarity. Look at the following responses to a survey:

Everything about it.

Absolutely nothing!

Imagine the responses above come from answers to the question What did you like about the event? The first response would be positive and the second one would be negative, right? Now, imagine the responses come from answers to the question What did you DISlike about the event? The negative in the question will make sentiment analysis change altogether.

A good deal of preprocessing or postprocessing will be needed if we are to take into account at least part of the context in which texts were produced. However, how to preprocess or postprocess data in order to capture the bits of context that will help analyze sentiment is not straightforward.

Irony and Sarcasm

When it comes to irony and sarcasm, people express their negative sentiments using positive words, which can be difficult for machines to detect without having a thorough understanding of the context of the situation in which a feeling was expressed.

For example, look at some possible answers to the question, Did you enjoy your shopping experience with us?

Yeah, sure. So smooth!

Not one, but many!

What sentiment would you assign to the responses above? The first response with an exclamation mark could be negative, right? The problem is there is no textual cue that will help a machine learn, or at least question that sentiment since yeah and sure often belong to positive or neutral texts.

How about the second response? In this context, sentiment is positive, but we're sure you can come up with many different contexts in which the same response can express negative sentiment.

Comparisons
How to treat comparisons in sentiment analysis is another challenge worth tackling. Look at the texts below:

This product is second to none.

This is better than older tools.

This is better than nothing.

The first comparison doesn't need any contextual clues to be classified correctly. It's clear that it's positive.

The second and third texts are a little more difficult to classify, though. Would you classify them as neutral, positive, or even negative? Once again, context can make a difference. For example, if the 'older tools' in the second text were considered useless, then the second text is pretty similar to the third text.

Emojis
There are two types of emojis according to Guibon et al.. Western emojis (e.g. :D) are encoded in only one or two characters, whereas Eastern emojis (e.g. ¯\(ツ)/¯) are a longer combination of characters of a vertical nature. Emojis play an important role in the sentiment of texts, particularly in tweets.

You'll need to pay special attention to character-level, as well as word-level, when performing sentiment analysis on tweets. A lot of preprocessing might also be needed. For example, you might want to preprocess social media content and transform both Western and Eastern emojis into tokens and whitelist them (i.e. always take them as a feature for classification purposes) in order to help improve sentiment analysis performance.

Here's a quite comprehensive list of emojis and their unicode characters that may come in handy when preprocessing.

Defining Neutral
Defining what we mean by neutral is another challenge to tackle in order to perform accurate sentiment analysis. As in all classification problems, defining your categories -and, in this case, the neutral tag- is one of the most important parts of the problem. What you mean by neutral, positive, or negative does matter when you train sentiment analysis models. Since tagging data requires that tagging criteria be consistent, a good definition of the problem is a must.

Here are some ideas to help you identify and define neutral texts:

Objective texts. So called objective texts do not contain explicit sentiments, so you should include those texts into the neutral category.
Irrelevant information. If you haven't preprocessed your data to filter out irrelevant information, you can tag it neutral. However, be careful! Only do this if you know how this could affect overall performance. Sometimes, you will be adding noise to your classifier and performance could get worse.
Texts containing wishes. Some wishes like, I wish the product had more integrations are generally neutral. However, those including comparisons like, I wish the product were better are pretty difficult to categorize
Human Annotator Accuracy
Sentiment analysis is a tremendously difficult task even for humans. On average, inter-annotator agreement (a measure of how well two (or more) human labelers can make the same annotation decision) is pretty low when it comes to sentiment analysis. And since machines learn from labeled data, sentiment analysis classifiers might not be as precise as other types of classifiers.

Still, sentiment analysis is worth the effort, even if your sentiment analysis predictions are wrong from time to time. analysis model, you can expect correct predictions about 70-80% of the time you submit your texts for classification.

If you are new to sentiment analysis, then you'll quickly notice improvements. For typical use cases, such as ticket routing, brand monitoring, and VoC analysis, you'll save a lot of time and money on tedious manual tasks.

Sentiment Analysis Use Cases & Applications

The applications of sentiment analysis are endless and can be applied to any industry, from finance and retail to hospitality and technology. Below, we've listed some of the most popular ways that sentiment analysis is being used in business:

1. Social Media Monitoring

2. Brand Monitoring

3. Voice of customer (VoC)

4. Customer Service

5. Market Research

6. Social Media Monitoring

Sentiment analysis is used in social media monitoring, allowing businesses to gain insights about how customers feel about certain topics, and detect urgent issues in real time before they spiral out of control.

On the fateful evening of April 9th, 2017, United Airlines forcibly removed a passenger from an overbooked flight. The nightmare-ish incident was filmed by other passengers on their smartphones and posted immediately. One of the videos, posted to Facebook, was shared more than 87,000 times and viewed 6.8 million times by 6pm on Monday, just 24 hours later.

The fiasco was only magnified by the company's dismissive response. On Monday afternoon, United's CEO tweeted a statement apologizing for "having to re-accommodate customers."

This is exactly the kind of PR catastrophe you can avoid with sentiment analysis. It's an example of why it's important to care, not only about if people are talking about your brand, but how they're talking about it. More mentions don't equal positive mentions.

Brands of all shapes and sizes have meaningful interactions with customers, leads, even their competition, all across social media. By monitoring these conversations you can understand customer sentiment in real time and over time, so you can detect disgruntled customers immediately and respond as soon as possible.

Most marketing departments are already tuned into online mentions as far as volume – they measure more chatter as more brand awareness. But businesses need to look beyond the numbers for deeper insights.

Brand Monitoring

Not only do brands have a wealth of information available on social media, but across the internet, on news sites, blogs, forums, product reviews, and more. Again, we can look at not just the volume of mentions, but the individual and overall quality of those mentions.

In our United Airlines example, for instance, the flare-up started on the social media accounts of just a few passengers. Within hours, it was picked up by news sites and spread like wildfire across the US, then to China and Vietnam, as United was accused of racial profiling against a passenger of Chinese-Vietnamese descent. In China, the incident became the number one trending topic on Weibo, a microblogging site with almost 500 million users.

And again, this is all happening within mere hours of the incident.

Brand monitoring offers a wealth of insights from conversations happening about your brand from all over the internet. Analyze news articles, blogs, forums, and more to gauge brand sentiment, and target certain demographics or regions, as desired. Automatically categorize the urgency of all brand mentions and route them instantly to designated team members.

Get an understanding of customer feelings and opinions, beyond mere numbers and statistics. Understand how your brand image evolves over time, and compare it to that of your competition. You can tune into a specific point in time to follow product releases, marketing campaigns, IPO filings, etc., and compare them to past events.

Real-time sentiment analysis allows you to identify potential PR crises and take immediate action before they become serious issues. Or identify positive comments and respond directly, to use them to your benefit.

Example: Expedia Canada

Around Christmas time, Expedia Canada ran a classic "escape winter" marketing campaign. All was well, except for the screeching violin they chose as background music. Understandably, people took to social media, blogs, and forums. Expedia noticed right away and removed the ad.

Then, they created a series of follow-up spin-off videos: one showed the original actor smashing the violin; another invited a real negative Twitter user to rip the violin out of the actor's hands on screen. Though their original campaign was a flop, Expedia were able to redeem themselves by listening to their customers and responding.

Sentiment analysis allows you to automatically monitor all chatter around your brand and detect and address this type of potentially-explosive scenario while you still have time to defuse it.

Voice of Customer (VoC)

Social media and brand monitoring offer us immediate, unfiltered, and invaluable information on customer sentiment, but you can also put this analysis to work on surveys and customer support interactions.

Net Promoter Score (NPS) surveys are one of the most popular ways for businesses to gain feedback with the simple question: Would you recommend this company, product, and/or service to a friend or family member? These result in a single score on a number scale.

Businesses use these scores to identify customers as promoters, passives, or detractors. The goal is to identify overall customer experience, and find ways to elevate all customers to "promoter" level, where they, theoretically, will buy more, stay longer, and refer other customers.

Numerical (quantitative) survey data is easily aggregated and assessed. But the next question in NPS surveys, asking why survey participants left the score they did, seeks open-ended responses, or qualitative data.

Open-ended survey responses were previously much more difficult to analyze, but with sentiment analysis these texts can be classified into positive and negative (and everywhere in between) offering further insights into the Voice of Customer (VoC).

Sentiment analysis can be used on any kind of survey – quantitative and qualitative – and on customer support interactions, to understand the emotions and opinions of your customers. Tracking customer sentiment over time adds depth to help understand why NPS scores or sentiment toward individual aspects of your business may have changed.

You can use it on incoming surveys and support tickets to detect customers who are 'strongly negative' and target them immediately to improve their service. Zero in on certain demographics to understand what works best and how you can improve.

Real-time analysis allows you to see shifts in VoC right away and understand the nuances of the customer experience over time beyond statistics and percentages.

Discover how we analyzed the sentiment of thousands of Facebook reviews, and transformed them into actionable insights.

Example: McKinsey City Voices project

In Brazil, federal public spending rose by 156% from 2007 to 2015, while satisfaction with public services steadily decreased. Unhappy with this counterproductive progress, the Urban Planning Department recruited McKinsey to help them focus on user experience, or "citizen journeys," when delivering services. This citizen-centric style of governance has led to the rise of what we call Smart Cities.

McKinsey developed a tool called City Voices, which conducts citizen surveys across more than 150 metrics, and then runs sentiment analysis to help leaders understand how constituents live and what they need, in order to better inform public policy. By using this tool, the Brazilian government was able to uncover the most urgent needs – a safer bus system, for instance – and improve them first.

If this can be successful on a national scale, imagine what it can do for your company.

Customer Service

We already looked at how we can use sentiment analysis in terms of the broader VoC, so now we'll dial in on customer service teams.

We all know the drill: stellar customer experiences means a higher rate of returning customers. Leading companies know that how they deliver is just as, if not more, important as what they deliver. Customers expect their experience with companies to be immediate, intuitive, personal, and hassle-free. If not, they'll leave and do business elsewhere. Did you know that one in three customers will leave a brand after just one bad experience?

You can use sentiment analysis and text classification to automatically organize incoming support queries by topic and urgency to route them to the correct department and make sure the most urgent are handled right away.

Analyze customer support interactions to ensure your employees are following appropriate protocol. Increase efficiency, so customers aren't left waiting for support. Decrease churn rates; after all it's less hassle to keep customers than acquire new ones.

Market Research

Sentiment analysis empowers all kinds of market research and competitive analysis. Whether you're exploring a new market, anticipating future trends, or seeking an edge on the competition, sentiment analysis can make all the difference.

You can analyze online reviews of your products and compare them to your competition. Maybe your competitor released a new product that landed as a flop. Find out what aspects of the product performed most negatively and use it to your advantage.

Follow your brand and your competition in real time on social media. Locate new markets where your brand is likely to succeed. Uncover trends just as they emerge, or follow long-term market leanings through analysis of formal market reports and business journals.

You'll tap into new sources of information and be able to quantify otherwise qualitative information. With social data analysis you can fill in gaps where public data is scarce, like emerging markets.

Discover how to analyze the sentiment of hotel reviews on TripAdvisor or perform sentiment analysis on Yelp restaurant reviews.

Sentiment Analysis Tools & Tutorials

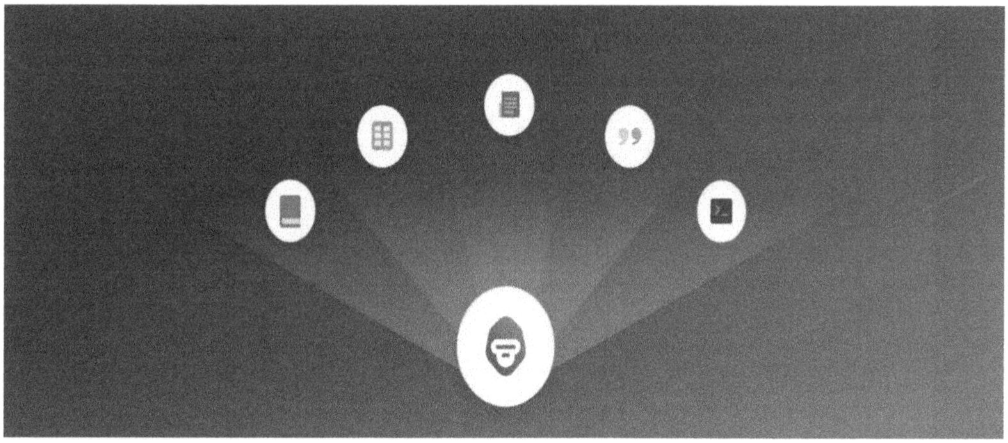

Sentiment analysis is a vast topic, and it can be intimidating to get started. Luckily, there are many useful resources, from helpful tutorials to all kinds of free online tools, to help you take your first steps.

Free Online Sentiment Analysis Tools
A good start to your journey is to simply play around with a sentiment analysis tool. A little first-hand experience will help you understand how it works

Next, to take your sentiment analysis further, you'll want to try out MonkeyLearn's sentiment analysis and keyword template. First, you'll need sign up, then walk through the following steps:

1. Choose Keyword + Sentiment Analysis template

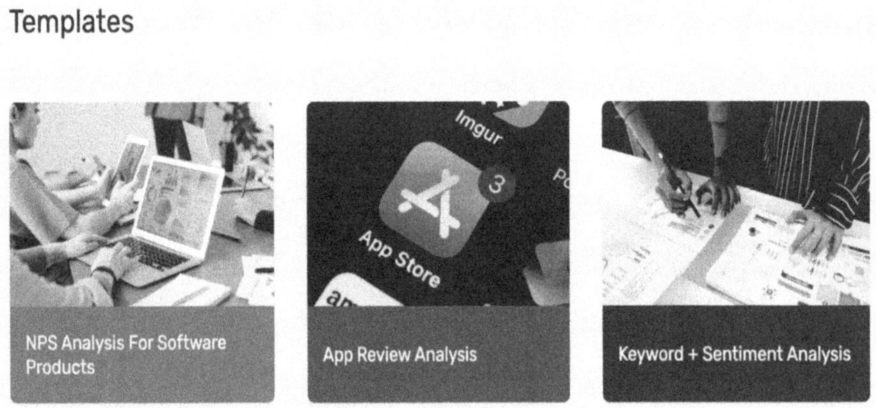

2. Upload your data

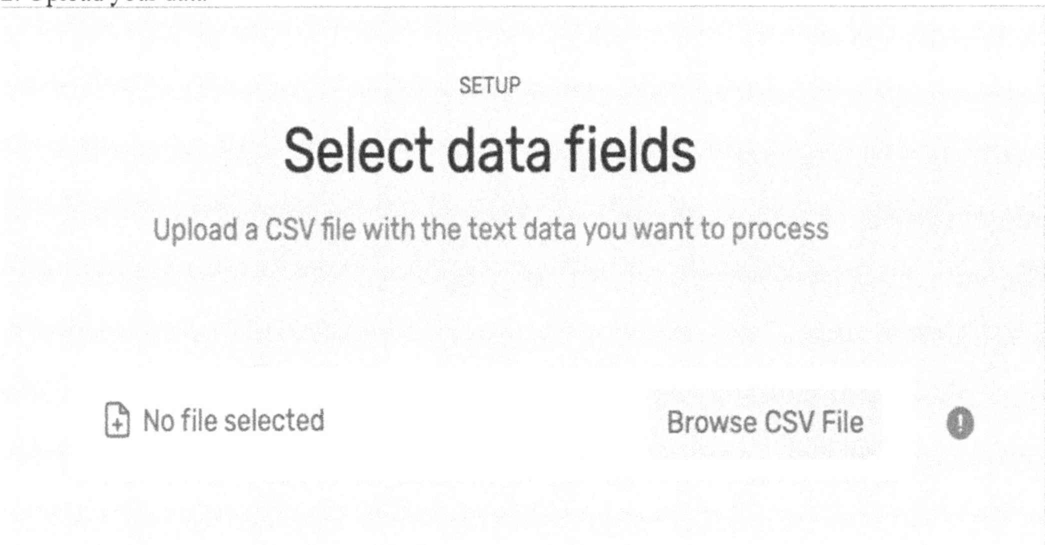

If you don't have a CSV, you can use our sample dataset.

3. Match the CSV columns to the dashboard fields

In this template, there is only one field: text. If you have more than one column in your dataset, choose the column that has the text you would like to analyze.

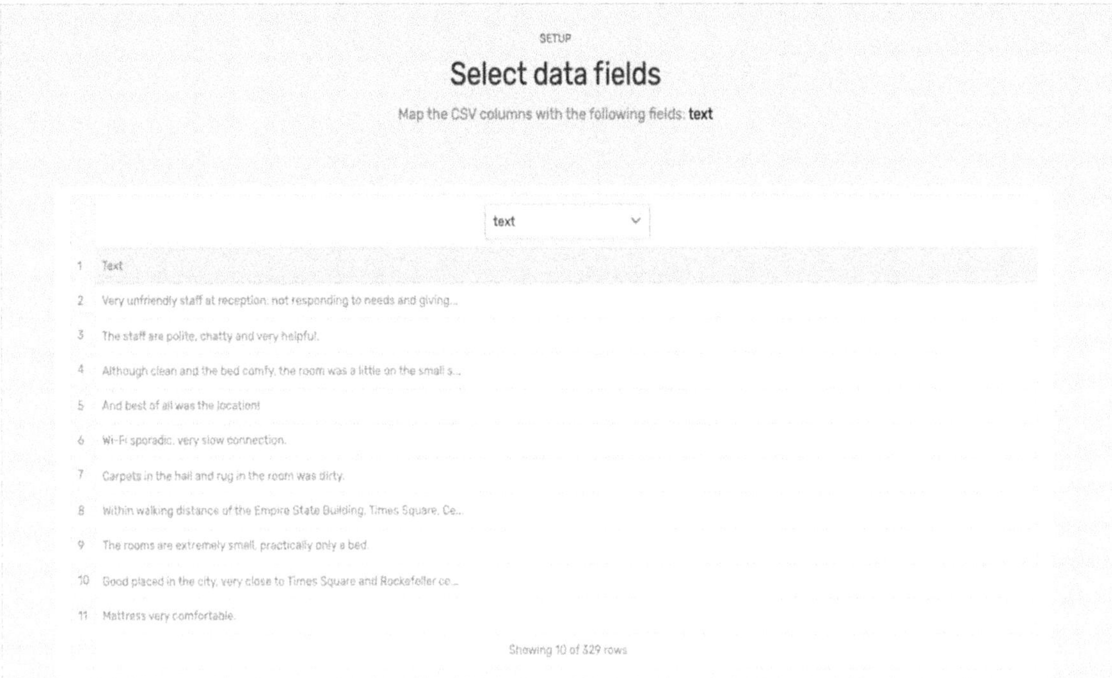

4. Name your workflow

5. Wait for your data to import

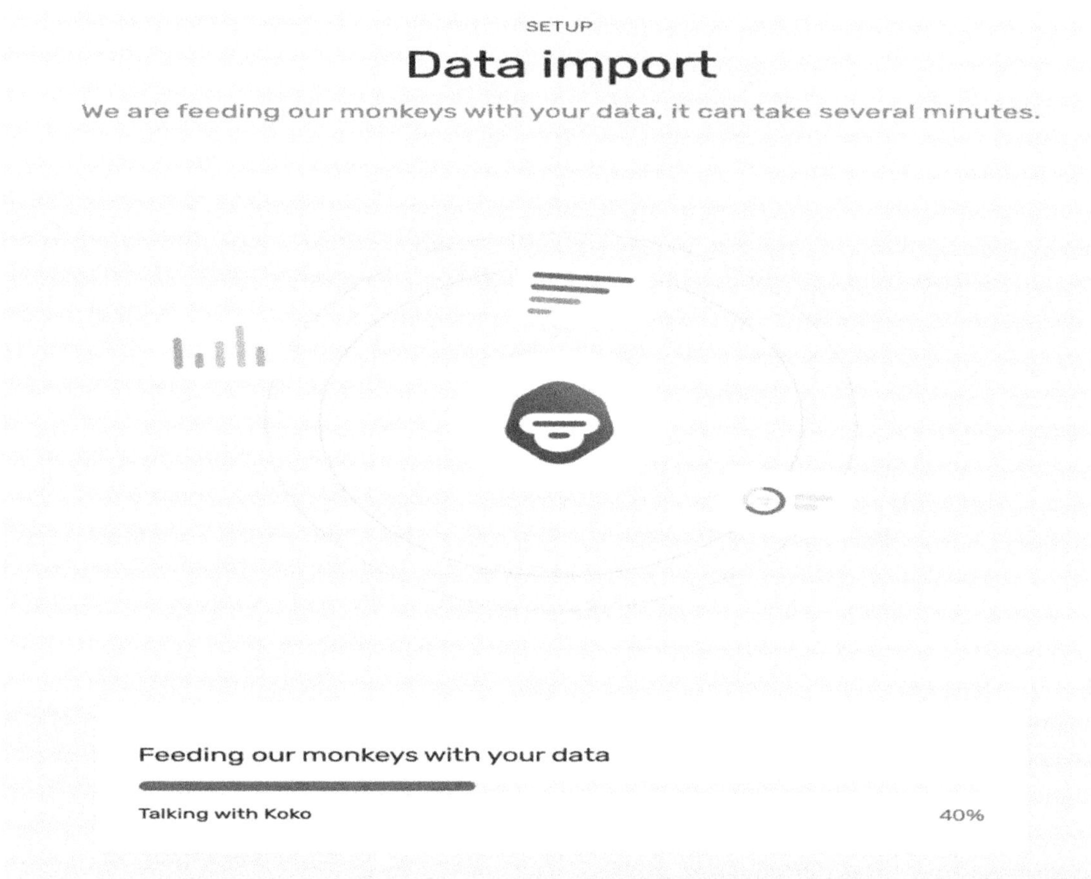

6. Explore your dashboard!

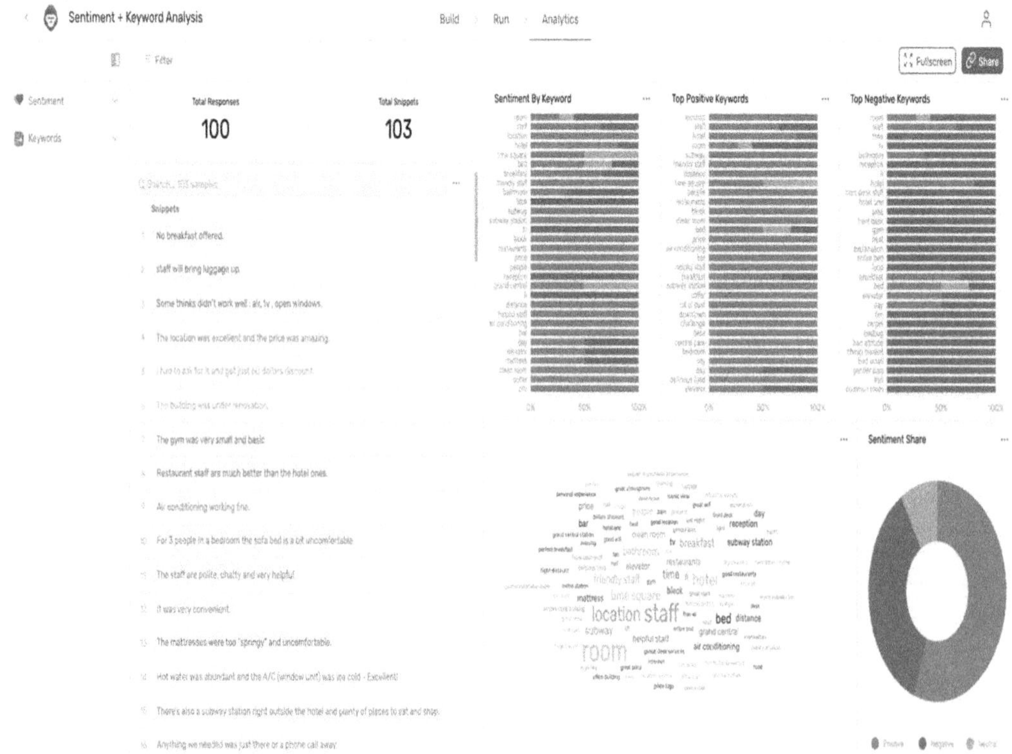

Emojis as representations of sentiments: positive, neutral, and negative to show how sentiment analysis works. Text reads 'my experience so far has been fantastic!' (positive), 'The product is ok, I guess' (neutral), and 'your support team is useless' (negative).

Sentiment analysis (or opinion mining) is a natural language processing (NLP) technique used to determine whether data is positive, negative or neutral. Sentiment analysis is often performed on textual data to help businesses monitor brand and product sentiment in customer feedback, and understand customer needs.

Types of Sentiment Analysis

Sentiment analysis focuses on the polarity of a text (positive, negative, neutral) but it also goes beyond polarity to detect specific feelings and emotions (angry, happy, sad, etc), urgency (urgent, not urgent) and even intentions (interested v. not interested).

Depending on how you want to interpret customer feedback and queries, you can define and tailor your categories to meet your sentiment analysis needs. In the meantime, here are some of the most popular types of sentiment analysis:

Graded Sentiment Analysis

If polarity precision is important to your business, you might consider expanding your polarity categories to include different levels of positive and negative:

Very positive
Positive
Neutral
Negative
Very negative

This is usually referred to as graded or fine-grained sentiment analysis, and could be used to interpret 5-star ratings in a review, for example:

Very Positive = 5 stars
Very Negative = 1 star

Emotion detection

Emotion detection sentiment analysis allows you to go beyond polarity to detect emotions, like happiness, frustration, anger, and sadness.

Many emotion detection systems use lexicons (i.e. lists of words and the emotions they convey) or complex Machine Learning algorithms.

One of the downsides of using lexicons is that people express emotions in different ways. Some words that typically express anger, like bad or kill (e.g. your product is so bad or your customer support is killing me) might also express happiness (e.g. this is bad ass or you are killing it).

Aspect-based Sentiment Analysis

Usually, when analyzing sentiments of texts you'll want to know which particular aspects or features people are mentioning in a positive, neutral, or negative way.

That's where aspect-based sentiment analysis can help, for example in this product review: "The battery life of this camera is too short", an aspect-based classifier would be able to determine that the sentence expresses a negative opinion about the battery life of the product in question.

Multilingual sentiment analysis

Multilingual sentiment analysis can be difficult. It involves a lot of preprocessing and resources. Most of these resources are available online (e.g. sentiment lexicons), while others need to be created (e.g. translated corpora or noise detection algorithms), but you'll need to know how to code to use them.

Alternatively, you could detect language in texts automatically with a language classifier, then train a custom sentiment analysis model to classify texts in the language of your choice.

Why Is Sentiment Analysis Important?

Since humans express their thoughts and feelings more openly than ever before, sentiment analysis is fast becoming an essential tool to monitor and understand sentiment in all types of data.

Automatically analyzing customer feedback, such as opinions in survey responses and social media conversations, allows brands to learn what makes customers happy or frustrated, so that they can tailor products and services to meet their customers' needs.

For example, using sentiment analysis to automatically analyze 4,000+ open-ended responses in your customer satisfaction surveys could help you discover why customers are happy or unhappy at each stage of the customer journey.

Maybe you want to track brand sentiment so you can detect disgruntled customers immediately and respond as soon as possible. Maybe you want to compare sentiment from one quarter to the next to see if you need to take action. Then you could dig deeper into your qualitative data to see why sentiment is falling or rising.
The overall benefits of sentiment analysis include:
Sorting Data at Scale
Can you imagine manually sorting through thousands of tweets, customer support conversations, or surveys? There's just too much business data to process manually. Sentiment analysis helps businesses process huge amounts of unstructured data in an efficient and cost-effective way.
Sentiment analysis can identify critical issues in real-time, for example is a PR crisis on social media escalating? Is an angry customer about to churn? Sentiment analysis models can help you immediately identify these kinds of situations, so you can take action right away.
Consistent criteria
It's estimated that people only agree around 60-65% of the time when determining the sentiment of a particular text. Tagging text by sentiment is highly subjective, influenced by personal experiences, thoughts, and beliefs.
By using a centralized sentiment analysis system, companies can apply the same criteria to all of their data, helping them improve accuracy and gain better insights.
The applications of sentiment analysis are endless. So, to help you understand how sentiment analysis could benefit your business, let's take a look at some examples of texts that you could analyze using sentiment analysis.
Then, we'll jump into a real-world example of how Chewy, a pet supplies company, was able to gain a much more nuanced (and useful!) understanding of their reviews through the application of sentiment analysis.
Sentiment Analysis Examples
To understand the goal and challenges of sentiment analysis, here are some examples:
Basic examples of sentiment analysis data
Netflix has the best selection of films
Hulu has a great UI
I dislike like the new crime series
I hate waiting for the next series to come out
More challenging examples of sentiment analysis
I do not dislike horror movies. (phrase with negation)
Disliking horror movies is not uncommon. (negation, inverted word order)
Sometimes I really hate the show. (adverbial modifies the sentiment)
I love having to wait two months for the next series to come out! (sarcasm)
The final episode was surprising with a terrible twist at the end (negative term used in a positive way)
The film was easy to watch but I would not recommend it to my friends. (difficult to categorize)
I LOL'd at the end of the cake scene (often hard to understand new terms)
Now, let's take a look at some real reviews on Trustpilot and see how MonkeyLearn's sentiment analysis tools fare when it comes to recognizing and categorizing sentiment.
Case Study: Sentiment analysis on TrustPilot Reviews
Chewy is a pet supplies company – an industry with no shortage of competition, so providing a superior customer experience (CX) to their customers can be a massive difference maker.
For this reason, online reviews can be an extremely valuable source of information to gain customer insights to improve their CX. Chewy has thousands of reviews in TrustPilot, this is what their review archive looks like:
The overall star rating of Chewy reviews on Trustpilot: 3.6 star rating from over 9,000 reviews, with 82% leaving a score of 'excellent'.
Via TrustPilot

It is easy to draw a general conclusion about Chewy's relative success from this alone - 82% of responses being excellent is a great starting place.
But TrustPilot's results alone fall short if Chewy's goal is to improve its services. This perfunctory overview fails to provide actionable insight, the cornerstone, and end goal, of effective sentiment analysis.
If Chewy wanted to unpack the what and why behind their reviews, in order to further improve their services, they would need to analyze each and every negative review at a granular level.

But with sentiment analysis tools, Chewy could plug in their 5,639 (at the time) TrustPilot reviews to gain instant sentiment analysis insights.
We uploaded and analyzed Chewy's reviews to MonkeyLearn's all-in-one data analysis and visualization studio to generate the following dashboard:
MonkeyLearn data visualization dashboard showing how reviews have been filtered by topic and sentiment. An example of aspect-based sentiment analysis in the form of graphs, pie charts, word clouds, and tagged data.
Chewy TrustPilot Reviews Sample
Feel free to click this link to peruse the results at your leisure - as this sample dashboard is a public demo, you can click through and explore the inputs and filters at work yourself.
While there is a ton more to explore, in this breakdown we are going to focus on four sentiment analysis data visualization results that the dashboard has visualized for us.
Overall Sentiment
Sentiment over Time
Sentiment by Rating
Sentiment by Topic
1. Overall sentiment
We'll begin by pulling the relevant graphic from the above dashboard.
Overall sentiment of Chewy's reviews, split by positive (38.2%), negative (40.8%), and neutral (21%) sentiment in a pie chart.
You'll notice that these results are very different from TrustPilot's overview (82% excellent, etc). This is because MonkeyLearn's sentiment analysis AI performs advanced sentiment analysis, parsing through each review sentence by sentence, word by word.
What you are left with is an accurate assessment of everything customers have written, rather than a simple tabulation of stars. This analysis can point you towards friction points much more accurately and in much more detail.
Read up on the mechanics of how sentiment analysis works below.
2. Sentiment over time
Here's our handy-dandy sentiment over time graph, blown up:
Temporal dataviz example that plots the gradual change in sentiment of reviews over a period of time. It tracks the overall proportion of positive, neutral, and negative sentiment in review language from 2016 to 2021. Negative responses went down from 2019-2020, then jumped back up to previous levels in 2021.
This data visualization sample is classic temporal datavis, a datavis type that tracks results and plots them over a period of time.
This graph expands on our Overall Sentiment data - it tracks the overall proportion of positive, neutral, and negative sentiment in the reviews from 2016 to 2021.
This graph informs the gradual change in the content of their written reviews over this five year period. For instance, negative responses went down from 2019-2020, then jumped back up to previous levels in 2021.
3. Sentiment by rating
The number of reviews and proportion of sentiment broken down by rating.
Now we jump to something that anchors our text-based sentiment to TrustPilot's earlier results.
By taking each TrustPilot category from 1-Bad to 5-Excellent, and breaking down the text of the written reviews from the scores you can derive the above graphic.

Looking at the results, and courtesy of taking a deeper look at the reviews via sentiment analysis, we can draw a couple interesting conclusions right off the bat.
TrustPilots results aren't useless - the better reviews have higher proportions of positive sentiment and the worse reviews have more negative sentiment. But, all reviews contain a little bit of all types of sentiment - we've learned that our reviews are nuanced and thus likely have even more hidden insight for us!
Our reviews are polarized. They skew in amounts towards 5 and 1.
These quick takeaways point us towards goldmines for future analysis. Namely, the positive sentiment sections of negative reviews and the negative section of positive ones, and the 2 - 4 reviews (why do they feel the way they do, how could we improve their scores?).
4. Sentiment by Topic
Number of reviews and proportion of sentiment broken down by topics: customer support, shipping, product, pricing, and website

Finally, we can take a look at Sentiment by Topic to begin to illustrate how sentiment analysis can take us even further into our data.

The above chart applies product-linked text classification in addition to sentiment analysis to pair given sentiment to product/service specific features, this is known as aspect-based sentiment analysis.

This means we can know how our customers feel about what, helping us zero in and fix specific pain points or issues.

These are all great jumping off points designed to visually demonstrate the value of sentiment analysis - but they only scratch the surface of its true power.

Read on for a step-by-step walkthrough of how sentiment analysis works.

How Does Sentiment Analysis Work?

How Does Sentiment Analysis Work?

Sentiment analysis, otherwise known as opinion mining, works thanks to natural language processing (NLP) and Machine Learning algorithms, to automatically determine the emotional tone behind online conversations.

There are different algorithms you can implement in sentiment analysis models, depending on how much data you need to analyze, and how accurate you need your model to be. We'll go over some of these in more detail, below.

Sentiment analysis algorithms fall into one of three buckets:

Rule-based: these systems automatically perform sentiment analysis based on a set of manually crafted rules.

Automatic: systems rely on Machine Learning techniques to learn from data.

Hybrid systems combine both rule-based and automatic approaches.

Rule-based Approaches

Usually, a rule-based system uses a set of human-crafted rules to help identify subjectivity, polarity, or the subject of an opinion.

These rules may include various NLP techniques developed in computational linguistics, such as:

Stemming, tokenization, part-of-speech tagging and parsing.

Lexicons (i.e. lists of words and expressions).

Here's a basic example of how a rule-based system works:

Defines two lists of polarized words (e.g. negative words such as bad, worst, ugly, etc and positive words such as good, best, beautiful, etc).

Counts the number of positive and negative words that appear in a given text.

If the number of positive word appearances is greater than the number of negative word appearances, the system returns a positive sentiment, and vice versa. If the numbers are even, the system will return a neutral sentiment.

Rule-based systems are very naive since they don't take into account how words are combined in a sequence. Of course, more advanced processing techniques can be used, and new rules added to support new expressions and vocabulary. However, adding new rules may affect previous results, and the whole system can get very complex. Since rule-based systems often require fine-tuning and maintenance, they'll also need regular investments.

Automatic Approaches

Automatic methods, contrary to rule-based systems, don't rely on manually crafted rules, but on Machine Learning techniques. A sentiment analysis task is usually modeled as a classification problem, whereby a classifier is fed a text and returns a category, e.g. positive, negative, or neutral.

Here's how a Machine Learning classifier can be implemented:

How does Sentiment Analysis Work

The Training and Prediction Processes

In the training process (a), our model learns to associate a particular input (i.e. a text) to the corresponding output (tag) based on the test samples used for training. The feature extractor transfers the text input into a feature vector. Pairs of feature vectors and tags (e.g. positive, negative, or neutral) are fed into the Machine Learning algorithm to generate a model.

In the prediction process (b), the feature extractor is used to transform unseen text inputs into feature vectors. These feature vectors are then fed into the model, which generates predicted tags (again, positive, negative, or neutral).

Feature Extraction from Text

The first step in a Machine Learning text classifier is to transform the text extraction or text vectorization, and the classical approach has been bag-of-words or bag-of-ngrams with their frequency.

More recently, new feature extraction techniques have been applied based on word embeddings (also known as word vectors). This kind of representations makes it possible for words with similar meaning to have a similar representation, which can improve the performance of classifiers.

Classification Algorithms

The classification step usually involves a statistical model like Naïve Bayes, Logistic Regression, Support Vector Machines, or Neural Networks:

Naïve Bayes: a family of probabilistic algorithms that uses Bayes's Theorem to predict the category of a text.

Linear Regression: a very well-known algorithm in statistics used to predict some value (Y) given a set of features (X).

Support Vector Machines: a non-probabilistic model which uses a representation of text examples as points in a multidimensional space. Examples of different categories (sentiments) are mapped to distinct regions within that space. Then, new texts are assigned a category based on similarities with existing texts and the regions they're mapped to.

Deep Learning: a diverse set of algorithms that attempt to mimic the human brain, by employing artificial neural networks to process data.

Hybrid Approaches

Hybrid systems combine the desirable elements of rule-based and automatic techniques into one system. One huge benefit of these systems is that results are often more accurate.

Sentiment Analysis Challenges

Sentiment analysis is one of the hardest tasks in natural language processing because even humans struggle to analyze sentiments accurately.

Data scientists are getting better at creating more accurate sentiment classifiers, but there's still a long way to go. Let's take a closer look at some of the main challenges of machine-based sentiment analysis:

Subjectivity & Tone

Context & Polarity

Irony & Sarcasm

Comparisons

Emojis

Defining Neutral

Human Annotator Accuracy

Subjectivity and Tone

There are two types of text: subjective and objective. Objective texts do not contain explicit sentiments, whereas subjective texts do. Say, for example, you intend to analyze the sentiment of the following two texts:

The package is nice.

The package is red.

Most people would say that sentiment is positive for the first one and neutral for the second one, right? All predicates (adjectives, verbs, and some nouns) should not be treated the same with respect to how they create sentiment. In the examples above, nice is more subjective than red.

Context and Polarity

All utterances are uttered at some point in time, in some place, by and to some people, you get the point. All utterances are uttered in context. Analyzing sentiment without context gets pretty difficult. However, machines cannot learn about contexts if they are not mentioned explicitly. One of the problems that arise from context is changes in polarity. Look at the following responses to a survey:

Everything about it.

Absolutely nothing!

Imagine the responses above come from answers to the question What did you like about the event? The first response would be positive and the second one would be negative, right? Now, imagine the responses come from answers to the question What did you DISlike about the event? The negative in the question will make sentiment analysis change altogether.

A good deal of preprocessing or postprocessing will be needed if we are to take into account at least part of the context in which texts were produced. However, how to preprocess or postprocess data in order to capture the bits of context that will help analyze sentiment is not straightforward.

Irony and Sarcasm

When it comes to irony and sarcasm, people express their negative sentiments using positive words, which can be difficult for machines to detect without having a thorough understanding of the context of the situation in which a feeling was expressed.

For example, look at some possible answers to the question, Did you enjoy your shopping experience with us?

Yeah, sure. So smooth!

Not one, but many!

What sentiment would you assign to the responses above? The first response with an exclamation mark could be negative, right? The problem is there is no textual cue that will help a machine learn, or at least question that sentiment since yeah and sure often belong to positive or neutral texts.

How about the second response? In this context, sentiment is positive, but we're sure you can come up with many different contexts in which the same response can express negative sentiment.

Comparisons

How to treat comparisons in sentiment analysis is another challenge worth tackling. Look at the texts below:

This product is second to none.

This is better than older tools.

This is better than nothing.

The first comparison doesn't need any contextual clues to be classified correctly. It's clear that it's positive. The second and third texts are a little more difficult to classify, though. Would you classify them as neutral, positive, or even negative? Once again, context can make a difference. For example, if the 'older tools' in the second text were considered useless, then the second text is pretty similar to the third text.

Emojis

There are two types of emojis according to Guibon et al.. Western emojis (e.g. :D) are encoded in only one or two characters, whereas Eastern emojis (e.g. ¯\(ツ)/¯) are a longer combination of characters of a vertical nature. Emojis play an important role in the sentiment of texts, particularly in tweets.

You'll need to pay special attention to character-level, as well as word-level, when performing sentiment analysis on tweets. A lot of preprocessing might also be needed. For example, you might want to preprocess social media content and transform both Western and Eastern emojis into tokens and whitelist them (i.e. always take them as a feature for classification purposes) in order to help improve sentiment analysis performance.

Here's a quite comprehensive list of emojis and their unicode characters that may come in handy when preprocessing.

Defining Neutral

Defining what we mean by neutral is another challenge to tackle in order to perform accurate sentiment analysis. As in all classification problems, defining your categories -and, in this case, the neutral tag- is one of the most important parts of the problem. What you mean by neutral, positive, or negative does matter when you train sentiment analysis models. Since tagging data requires that tagging criteria be consistent, a good definition of the problem is a must.

Here are some ideas to help you identify and define neutral texts:

Objective texts. So called objective texts do not contain explicit sentiments, so you should include those texts into the neutral category.

Irrelevant information. If you haven't preprocessed your data to filter out irrelevant information, you can tag it neutral. However, be careful! Only do this if you know how this could affect overall performance. Sometimes, you will be adding noise to your classifier and performance could get worse.

Texts containing wishes. Some wishes like, I wish the product had more integrations are generally neutral. However, those including comparisons like, I wish the product were better are pretty difficult to categorize

Human Annotator Accuracy

Sentiment analysis is a tremendously difficult task even for humans. On average, inter-annotator agreement (a measure of how well two (or more) human labelers can make the same annotation decision) is pretty low when it comes to sentiment analysis. And since machines learn from labeled data, sentiment analysis classifiers might not be as precise as other types of classifiers.

Still, sentiment analysis is worth the effort, even if your sentiment analysis predictions are wrong from time to time. By using MonkeyLearn's sentiment analysis model, you can expect correct predictions about 70-80% of the time you submit your texts for classification.

If you are new to sentiment analysis, then you'll quickly notice improvements. For typical use cases, such as ticket routing, brand monitoring, and VoC analysis, you'll save a lot of time and money on tedious manual tasks.

Sentiment Analysis Use Cases & Applications

Sentiment Analysis Applications and Examples

The applications of sentiment analysis are endless and can be applied to any industry, from finance and retail to hospitality and technology. Below, we've listed some of the most popular ways that sentiment analysis is being used in business:

Social Media Monitoring
Brand Monitoring
Voice of customer (VoC)
Customer Service
Market Research

Social Media Monitoring

Sentiment analysis is used in social media monitoring, allowing businesses to gain insights about how customers feel about certain topics, and detect urgent issues in real time before they spiral out of control.

On the fateful evening of April 9th, 2017, United Airlines forcibly removed a passenger from an overbooked flight. The nightmare-ish incident was filmed by other passengers on their smartphones and posted immediately. One of the videos, posted to Facebook, was shared more than 87,000 times and viewed 6.8 million times by 6pm on Monday, just 24 hours later.

The fiasco was only magnified by the company's dismissive response. On Monday afternoon, United's CEO tweeted a statement apologizing for "having to re-accommodate customers."

This is exactly the kind of PR catastrophe you can avoid with sentiment analysis. It's an example of why it's important to care, not only about if people are talking about your brand, but how they're talking about it. More mentions don't equal positive mentions.

Brands of all shapes and sizes have meaningful interactions with customers, leads, even their competition, all across social media. By monitoring these conversations you can understand customer sentiment in real time and over time, so you can detect disgruntled customers immediately and respond as soon as possible.

Most marketing departments are already tuned into online mentions as far as volume – they measure more chatter as more brand awareness. But businesses need to look beyond the numbers for deeper insights.

Brand Monitoring

Not only do brands have a wealth of information available on social media, but across the internet, on news sites, blogs, forums, product reviews, and more. Again, we can look at not just the volume of mentions, but the individual and overall quality of those mentions.

In our United Airlines example, for instance, the flare-up started on the social media accounts of just a few passengers. Within hours, it was picked up by news sites and spread like wildfire across the US, then to China and Vietnam, as United was accused of racial profiling against a passenger of Chinese-Vietnamese descent.

In China, the incident became the number one trending topic on Weibo, a microblogging site with almost 500 million users.

And again, this is all happening within mere hours of the incident.

Brand monitoring offers a wealth of insights from conversations happening about your brand from all over the internet. Analyze news articles, blogs, forums, and more to gauge brand sentiment, and target certain demographics or regions, as desired. Automatically categorize the urgency of all brand mentions and route them instantly to designated team members.

Get an understanding of customer feelings and opinions, beyond mere numbers and statistics. Understand how your brand image evolves over time, and compare it to that of your competition. You can tune into a specific point in time to follow product releases, marketing campaigns, IPO filings, etc., and compare them to past events.

Real-time sentiment analysis allows you to identify potential PR crises and take immediate action before they become serious issues. Or identify positive comments and respond directly, to use them to your benefit.

Example: Expedia Canada

Around Christmas time, Expedia Canada ran a classic "escape winter" marketing campaign. All was well, except for the screeching violin they chose as background music. Understandably, people took to social media, blogs, and forums. Expedia noticed right away and removed the ad.

Then, they created a series of follow-up spin-off videos: one showed the original actor smashing the violin; another invited a real negative Twitter user to rip the violin out of the actor's hands on screen. Though their original campaign was a flop, Expedia were able to redeem themselves by listening to their customers and responding.

Sentiment analysis allows you to automatically monitor all chatter around your brand and detect and address this type of potentially-explosive scenario while you still have time to defuse it.

Voice of Customer (VoC)
Social media and brand monitoring offer us immediate, unfiltered, and invaluable information on customer sentiment, but you can also put this analysis to work on surveys and customer support interactions.

Net Promoter Score (NPS) surveys are one of the most popular ways for businesses to gain feedback with the simple question: Would you recommend this company, product, and/or service to a friend or family member? These result in a single score on a number scale.

Businesses use these scores to identify customers as promoters, passives, or detractors. The goal is to identify overall customer experience, and find ways to elevate all customers to "promoter" level, where they, theoretically, will buy more, stay longer, and refer other customers.
Numerical (quantitative) survey data is easily aggregated and assessed. But the next question in NPS surveys, asking why survey participants left the score they did, seeks open-ended responses, or qualitative data.
Open-ended survey responses were previously much more difficult to analyze, but with sentiment analysis these texts can be classified into positive and negative (and everywhere in between) offering further insights into the Voice of Customer (VoC).

Sentiment analysis can be used on any kind of survey – quantitative and qualitative – and on customer support interactions, to understand the emotions and opinions of your customers. Tracking customer sentiment over time adds depth to help understand why NPS scores or sentiment toward individual aspects of your business may have changed.
You can use it on incoming surveys and support tickets to detect customers who are 'strongly negative' and target them immediately to improve their service. Zero in on certain demographics to understand what works best and how you can improve.

Real-time analysis allows you to see shifts in VoC right away and understand the nuances of the customer experience over time beyond statistics and percentages.

Discover how we analyzed the sentiment of thousands of Facebook reviews, and transformed them into actionable insights.

Example: McKinsey City Voices project

In Brazil, federal public spending rose by 156% from 2007 to 2015, while satisfaction with public services steadily decreased. Unhappy with this counterproductive progress, the Urban Planning Department recruited McKinsey to help them focus on user experience, or "citizen journeys," when delivering services. This citizen-centric style of governance has led to the rise of what we call Smart Cities.

McKinsey developed a tool called City Voices, which conducts citizen surveys across more than 150 metrics, and then runs sentiment analysis to help leaders understand how constituents live and what they need, in order to better inform public policy. By using this tool, the Brazilian government was able to uncover the most urgent needs – a safer bus system, for instance – and improve them first.

If this can be successful on a national scale, imagine what it can do for your company.

10.5 Named Entity Recognition (NER)

Named entity recognition (NER) — sometimes referred to as entity chunking, extraction, or identification — is the task of identifying and categorizing key information (entities) in text. An entity can be any word or series of words that consistently refers to the same thing. Every detected entity is classified into a predetermined category. For example, an NER Machine Learning (ML) model might detect the word "super.AI" in a text and classify it as a "Company".

NER is a form of natural language processing (NLP), a subfield of artificial intelligence. NLP is concerned with computers processing and analyzing natural language, i.e., any language that has developed naturally, rather than artificially, such as with computer coding languages.

This post explores the basics of how NER works, along with some high-level use cases and how you can apply it in your business or project.

How NER works

At the heart of any NER model is a two step process:

Step one involves detecting a word or string of words that form an entity. Each word represents a token: "The Great Lakes" is a string of three tokens that represents one entity. Inside-outside-beginning tagging is a common way of indicating where entities begin and end.

The second step requires the creation of entity categories. Here are some common entity categories:

Person

E.g., Elvis Presley, Audrey Hepburn, David Beckham

Organization

E.g., Google, Mastercard, University of Oxford

Time

E.g., 2006, 16:34, 2am

Location

E.g., Trafalgar Square, MoMA, Machu Picchu

Work of art

E.g., Hamlet, Guernica, Exile on Main St.

These are just a few examples. You can create your own entity categories to suit your task, as well as provide granular rules for which entities belong to which categories in instances of ambiguity or task-specific ontologies.

To learn what is and is not a relevant entity and how to categorize them, a model requires training data. The more relevant that training data is to the task, the more accurate the model will be at completing said task. Train your model on Victorian gothic literature, and it will probably struggle to navigate Twitter.

Once you have defined your entities and your categories, you can use these to label data and create a training dataset (our named entity recognition data program can do this for you automatically). You then use this training dataset to train an algorithm to label your text predictively.

How is NER used?

NER is suited to any situation in which a high-level overview of a large quantity of text is helpful. With NER, you can, at a glance, understand the subject or theme of a body of text and quickly group texts based on their relevancy or similarity.

Some notable NER use cases include:

Human resources
Speed up the hiring process by summarizing applicants' CVs; improve internal workflows by categorizing employee complaints and questions
Customer support
Improve response times by categorizing user requests, complaints and questions and filtering by priority keywords
Search and recommendation engines
Improve the speed and relevance of search results and recommendations by summarizing descriptive text, reviews, and discussions
Booking.com is a notable success story here
Content classification
Surface content more easily and gain insights into trends by identifying the subjects and themes of blog posts and news articles
Health care
Improve patient care standards and reduce workloads by extracting essential information from lab reports
Roche is doing this with pathology and radiology reports
Academia
Enable students and researchers to find relevant material faster by summarizing papers and archive material and highlighting key ters, topics, and themes
The EU's digital platform for cultural heritage, Europeana, is using NER to make historical newspapers searchable
How can I use NER?
If you think that your business or project could benefit from NER, it's pretty easy to start out. There are a number of excellent open-source libraries that can get you going, including NLTK, SpaCy, and Stanford NER. Each has its own pros and cons, which we'll be exploring in more detail soon.
But before you begin using one of these libraries to build a model, you will need to produce a relevant labeled dataset to train the model on. That's where super.AI is there to help. Using our named entity recognition data program, you provide us your raw text and desired entities and categories. We'll label the text you send and return a high quality training dataset that you can take to train and tailor your NER model.
If you're interested in learning more or have a specialized use case, reach out to us. You can also stay tuned to our blog, where we'll be running a series of posts covering different aspects of NLP over the coming months.

Exercise

True Or False

1.Text preprocessing in NLP is the process of converting unstructured text into a structured format suitable for analysis.
2.Tokenization involves splitting text into paragraphs for better readability.
3.Stopword removal is a step in text preprocessing where common words like "the" and "is" are removed from the text.
4.Word embeddings represent words as vectors in a continuous space, capturing semantic relationships between words.
5.Word2Vec is a technique used to visualize textual data using 2D scatter plots.
6.Word embeddings are primarily used for representing words in a one-hot encoded format.
7.Sequence-to-sequence models are commonly used for tasks like machine translation and text summarization.
8.Sequence-to-sequence models handle only fixed-length sequences of input and output data.
9.Recurrent Neural Networks (RNNs) are not suitable for sequence-to-sequence tasks.
10.Sentiment analysis involves analyzing the grammatical structure of text.
11.Sentiment analysis can help determine whether a text expresses a positive, negative, or neutral sentiment.
12.Sentiment analysis is limited to analyzing written text and cannot be applied to other forms of data.

13.Named Entity Recognition (NER) is the process of extracting and categorizing entities like names, dates, and locations from text.
14.NER is not useful for tasks such as information retrieval and question answering.
15.NER is solely concerned with identifying common nouns in text.
16.Text preprocessing is the final step in the NLP pipeline.
17.Word embeddings can be used to measure the semantic similarity between words.
18.Sequence-to-sequence models are typically used for single-task applications and cannot handle multiple tasks simultaneously.
Answer- True, False, True, True, False, False, True, False, False, False, True ,False, True, False, False, False, True , False

MCQ
1.What is the primary goal of text preprocessing in NLP?
a) Enhancing the aesthetics of the text
b) Transforming text into a structured format for analysis
c) Removing all the words except keywords
d) Adding irrelevant information to the text
Answer: b

2.Which of the following is NOT a common text preprocessing step?
a) Tokenization
b) Lemmatization
c) Capitalization
d) Stopword removal
Answer: c

3.What is tokenization?
a) Assigning a token or reward for each word in the text
b) Converting text to uppercase letters
c) Removing punctuation marks from the text
d) Splitting text into individual words or tokens
Answer: d

4.What is the purpose of word embeddings in NLP?
a) Converting words to images
b) Representing words as vectors in a continuous space
c) Replacing words with emojis for better understanding
d) Generating new words from existing ones
Answer: b

5.Which method is commonly used to train word embeddings on large text corpora?
a) Reinforcement Learning
b) Word Counting
c) Word2Vec
d) Regular Expression
Answer: c

6.What is the main application of sequence-to-sequence models in NLP?
a) Image classification
b) Speech synthesis
c) Predicting stock prices
d) Text preprocessing

Answer: b

7.What are sequence-to-sequence models designed to handle?
a) Single input and single output sequences of different lengths
b) Single input sequences only
c) Single output sequences only
d) Pairs of input and output sequences of the same length
Answer: a

8.Which architecture is commonly used in sequence-to-sequence models?
a) Convolutional Neural Networks (CNNs)
b) Recurrent Neural Networks (RNNs)
c) Feedforward Neural Networks (FNNs)
d) Decision Trees
Answer: b

9.What is the primary goal of sentiment analysis?
a) Analyzing the grammatical structure of sentences
b) Identifying the author of a text
c) Determining the emotional tone of a text
d) Counting the number of words in a text
Answer: c

10.Which type of sentiment analysis involves classifying the sentiment as positive, negative, or neutral?
a) Polarity-based sentiment analysis
b) Emotion-based sentiment analysis
c) Aspect-based sentiment analysis
d) Intent-based sentiment analysis
Answer: a

11.What is Named Entity Recognition (NER) in NLP?
a) Recognizing names of famous authors in text
b) Identifying words with more than three syllables
c) Extracting entities such as names, dates, and locations from text
d) Detecting grammatical errors in sentences
Answer: c

12.Which of the following is an example of a named entity?
a) Verb
b) Pronoun
c) Adjective
d) Organization
Answer: d

Short Question And Answers

Q1.What is text preprocessing in NLP?
Q2.Why is text tokenization important in NLP?
Q3.What is stop-word removal, and why is it useful?
Q4.What are word embeddings?
Q5.How do word embeddings capture semantic meaning?
Q6.Name a popular algorithm used to generate word embeddings.

Q7.What are sequence-to-sequence models in NLP?
Q8.How does attention mechanism enhance sequence-to-sequence models?
Q9.What is sentiment analysis in NLP?
Q10.How can Machine Learning be used for sentiment analysis?
Q11.What are some challenges in sentiment analysis?
Q12.What is Named Entity Recognition (NER)?
Q13.How does NER contribute to information extraction from text?
Q14.Compare rule-based and Machine Learning-based approaches for NER.
Q15.How are word embeddings used in sentiment analysis?
Q16.Give an example of a real-world application where sequence-to-sequence models are utilized.
Q18.What are some challenges in developing accurate sentiment analysis models?
Q19.What are some potential future directions for NLP research and applications?
Q20.What are some ethical considerations in NLP, especially regarding sentiment analysis and NER?
Q21.What are some limitations in word embeddings and their interpretability?

Online Resources

Online Exam Papers
True/False Exam

Link

https://forms.gle/pBWjHSdLqxic8JvB8

QR Code

YouTube Video Playlist Link

Chapter 10
Link
https://www.youtube.com/playlist?list=PLzlh_31VWEFqTgiDaY80qF20LmqP_OowB
QR Code

Chapter 11: Reinforcement Learning

Reinforcement learning is an area of Machine Learning. It is about taking suitable action to maximize reward in a particular situation. It is employed by various software and machines to find the best possible behavior or path it should take in a specific situation. Reinforcement learning differs from supervised learning in a way that in supervised learning the training data has the answer key with it so the model is trained with the correct answer itself whereas in reinforcement learning, there is no answer but the reinforcement agent decides what to do to perform the given task. In the absence of a training dataset, it is bound to learn from its experience.

Reinforcement Learning (RL) is the science of decision making. It is about learning the optimal behavior in an environment to obtain maximum reward. In RL, the data is accumulated from Machine Learning systems that use a trial-and-error method. Data is not part of the input that we would find in supervised or unsupervised Machine Learning.

Reinforcement learning uses algorithms that learn from outcomes and decide which action to take next. After each action, the algorithm receives feedback that helps it determine whether the choice it made was correct, neutral or incorrect. It is a good technique to use for automated systems that have to make a lot of small decisions without human guidance.

Reinforcement learning is an autonomous, self-teaching system that essentially learns by trial and error. It performs actions with the aim of maximizing rewards, or in other words, it is learning by doing in order to achieve the best outcomes.

Example:

The problem is as follows: We have an agent and a reward, with many hurdles in between. The agent is supposed to find the best possible path to reach the reward. The following problem explains the problem more easily.

The above image shows the robot, diamond, and fire. The goal of the robot is to get the reward that is the diamond and avoid the hurdles that are fired. The robot learns by trying all the possible paths and then choosing the path which gives him the reward with the least hurdles. Each right step will give the robot a reward and each wrong step will subtract the reward of the robot. The total reward will be calculated when it reaches the final reward that is the diamond.

Main points in Reinforcement learning –

Input: The input should be an initial state from which the model will start

Output: There are many possible outputs as there are a variety of solutions to a particular problem

Training: The training is based upon the input, The model will return a state and the user will decide to reward or punish the model based on its output.
The model keeps continues to learn.
The best solution is decided based on the maximum reward.

Difference between Reinforcement learning and Supervised learning:

Reinforcement learning	**Supervised learning**
1. Reinforcement learning is all about making decisions sequentially. In simple words, we can say that the output depends on the state of the current input and the next input depends on the output of the previous input	2. In Supervised learning, the decision is made on the initial input or the input given at the start
1. In Reinforcement learning decision is dependent, So we give labels to sequences of dependent decisions	2. In supervised learning the decisions are independent of each other so labels are given to each decision.
1. Example: Chess game, text summarization	2. Example: Object recognition, spam detection

Types of Reinforcement:
There are two types of Reinforcement:

Positive: Positive Reinforcement is defined as when an event, occurs due to a particular behavior, increases the strength and the frequency of the behavior. In other words, it has a positive effect on behavior.

Advantages of reinforcement learning are:
- Maximizes Performance
- Sustain Change for a long period of time
- Too much Reinforcement can lead to an overload of states which can diminish the results
- Negative: Negative Reinforcement is defined as strengthening of behavior because a negative condition is stopped or avoided.

Advantages of reinforcement learning:
- Increases Behavior
- Provide defiance to a minimum standard of performance
- It Only provides enough to meet up the minimum behavior
- Elements of Reinforcement Learning

Reinforcement learning elements are as follows:

Policy
Reward function
Value function
Model of the environment

Policy: Policy defines the learning agent behavior for given time period. It is a mapping from perceived states of the environment to actions to be taken when in those states.
Reward function: Reward function is used to define a goal in a reinforcement learning problem.A reward function is a function that provides a numerical score based on the state of the environment
Value function: Value functions specify what is good in the long run. The value of a state is the total amount of reward an agent can expect to accumulate over the future, starting from that state.

Model of the environment: Models are used for planning.
Credit assignment problem: Reinforcement learning algorithms learn to generate an internal value for the intermediate states as to how good they are in leading to the goal. The learning decision maker is called the agent. The agent interacts with the environment that includes everything outside the agent.
The agent has sensors to decide on its state in the environment and takes action that modifies its state.
The reinforcement learning problem model is an agent continuously interacting with an environment. The agent and the environment interact in a sequence of time steps. At each time step t, the agent receives the state of the environment and a scalar numerical reward for the previous action, and then the agent then selects an action.
Reinforcement learning is a technique for solving Markov decision problems.
Reinforcement learning uses a formal framework defining the interaction between a learning agent and its environment in terms of states, actions, and rewards. This framework is intended to be a simple way of representing essential features of the artificial intelligence problem.

Various Practical Applications of Reinforcement Learning –
RL can be used in robotics for industrial automation.
RL can be used in Machine Learning and data processing
RL can be used to create training systems that provide custom instruction and materials according to the requirement of students.

Application of Reinforcement Learnings
1. Robotics: Robots with pre-programmed behavior are useful in structured environments, such as the assembly line of an automobile manufacturing plant, where the task is repetitive in nature.
2. A master chess player makes a move. The choice is informed both by planning, anticipating possible replies and counter replies.
3. An adaptive controller adjusts parameters of a petroleum refinery's operation in real time.
RL can be used in large environments in the following situations:

A model of the environment is known, but an analytic solution is not available;
Only a simulation model of the environment is given (the subject of simulation-based optimization)
The only way to collect information about the environment is to interact with it.

Advantages and Disadvantages of Reinforcement Learning
Advantages of Reinforcement learning
1. Reinforcement learning can be used to solve very complex problems that cannot be solved by conventional techniques.
2. The model can correct the errors that occurred during the training process.
3. In RL, training data is obtained via the direct interaction of the agent with the environment
4. Reinforcement learning can handle environments that are non-deterministic, meaning that the outcomes of actions are not always predictable. This is useful in real-world applications where the environment may change over time or is uncertain.
5. Reinforcement learning can be used to solve a wide range of problems, including those that involve decision making, control, and optimization.
6. Reinforcement learning is a flexible approach that can be combined with other Machine Learning techniques, such as deep learning, to improve performance.

Disadvantages of Reinforcement learning

1. Reinforcement learning is not preferable to use for solving simple problems.
2. Reinforcement learning needs a lot of data and a lot of computation
3. Reinforcement learning is highly dependent on the quality of the reward function. If the reward function is poorly designed, the agent may not learn the desired behavior.
4. Reinforcement learning can be difficult to debug and interpret. It is not always clear why the agent is behaving in a certain way, which can make it difficult to diagnose and fix problems.
Implementation:

```
import gym
```

```
import numpy as np

# Define the Q-table and learning rate
q_table = np.zeros((state_size, action_size))
alpha = 0.8
gamma = 0.95

# Train the Q-Learning algorithm
for episode in range(num_episodes):
state = env.reset()
done = False
while not done:
# Choose an action
action = np.argmax(
q_table[state, :] + np.random.randn(1, action_size) * (1. / (episode + 1)))

# Take the action and observe the new state and reward
next_state, reward, done, _ = env.step(action)

# Update the Q-table
q_table[state, action] = (1 - alpha) * q_table[state, action] + \
alpha * (reward + gamma * np.max(q_table[next_state, :]))

state = next_state

# Test the trained Q-Learning algorithm
state = env.reset()
done = False
while not done:
# Choose an action
action = np.argmax(q_table[state, :])

# Take the action
state, reward, done, _ = env.step(action)
env.render()
```

11.1 Markov Decision Processes (MDP)

A Markov decision process (MDP) is defined as a stochastic decision-making process that uses a mathematical framework to model the decision-making of a dynamic system in scenarios where the results are either random or controlled by a decision maker, which makes sequential decisions over time. This article explains MDP with the help of some real-world examples.

Markov decision process (MDP) is defined as a stochastic decision-making process that uses a mathematical framework to model the decision-making of a dynamic system in scenarios where the results are either random or controlled by a decision maker, which makes sequential decisions over time. This article explains MDP with the help of some real-world examples.

A Markov decision process (MDP) refers to a stochastic decision-making process that uses a mathematical framework to model the decision-making of a dynamic system. It is used in scenarios where the results are either random or controlled by a decision maker, which makes sequential decisions over time. MDPs evaluate which actions the decision maker should take considering the current state and environment of the system.

A MDPs rely on variables such as the environment, agent's actions, and rewards to decide the system's next optimal action. They are classified into four types — finite, infinite, continuous, or discrete — depending on various factors such as sets of actions, available states, and the decision-making frequency.

MDPs have been around since the early part of the 1950s. The name Markov refers to the Russian mathematician Andrey Markov who played a pivotal role in shaping stochastic processes. In its initial days, MDPs were known to solve issues related to inventory management and control, queuing optimization, and routing matters. Today, MDPs find applications in studying optimization problems via dynamic programming, robotics, automatic control, economics, manufacturing, etc.

In artificial intelligence, MDPs model sequential decision-making scenarios with probabilistic dynamics. They are used to design intelligent machines or agents that need to function longer in an environment where actions can yield uncertain results.

MDP models are typically popular in two sub-areas of AI: probabilistic planning and reinforcement learning (RL).

Probabilistic planning is the discipline that uses known models to accomplish an agent's goals and objectives. While doing so, it emphasizes guiding machines or agents to make decisions while enabling them to learn how to behave to achieve their goals.
Reinforcement learning allows applications to learn from the feedback the agents receive from the environment.
Let's understand this through a real-life example:

Consider a hungry antelope in a wildlife sanctuary looking for food in its environment. It stumbles upon a place with a mushroom on the right and a cauliflower on the left. If the antelope eats the mushroom, it receives water as a reward. However, if it opts for the cauliflower, the nearby lion's cage opens and sets the lion free in the sanctuary. With time, the antelope learns to choose the side of the mushroom, as this choice offers a valuable reward in return.

In the above MDP example, two important elements exist — agent and environment. The agent here is the antelope, which acts as a decision-maker. The environment reveals the surrounding (wildlife sanctuary) in which the antelope resides. As the agent performs different actions, different situations emerge. These situations are labeled as states. For example, when the antelope performs an action of eating the mushroom, it receives the reward (water) in correspondence with the action and transitions to another state. The agent (antelope) repeats the process over a period and learns the optimal action at each state.

In the context of MDP, we can formalize that the antelope knows the optimal action to perform (eat the mushroom). Therefore, it does not prefer eating the cauliflower as it generates a reward that can harm its survival. The example illustrates that MDP is essential in capturing the dynamics of RL problems.

How Does the Markov Decision Process Work?
The MDP model operates by using key elements such as the agent, states, actions, rewards, and optimal policies. The agent refers to a system responsible for making decisions and performing actions. It operates in an environment that details the various states that the agent is in while it transitions from one state to another. MDP defines the mechanism of how certain states and an agent's actions lead to the other states. Moreover, the agent receives rewards depending on the action it performs and the state it attains (current state). The policy for the MDP model reveals the agent's following action depending on its current state.

The MDP framework has the following key components:
S: states ($s \in S$)
A: Actions ($a \in A$)
P ($St+1|st.at$): Transition probabilities
R (s): Reward
The graphical representation of the MDP model is as follows:

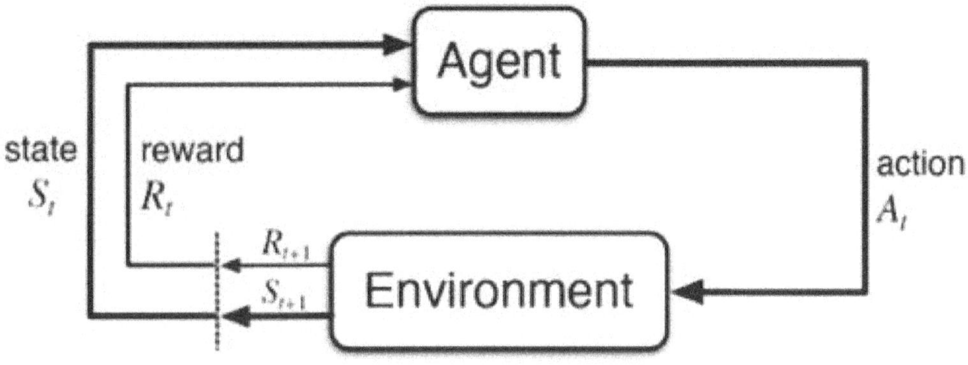

The MDP model uses the Markov Property, which states that the future can be determined only from the present state that encapsulates all the necessary information from the past. The Markov Property can be evaluated by using this equation:

P[St+1|St] = P[St+1 |S1,S2,S3……St]

According to this equation, the probability of the next state (P[St+1]) given the present state (St) is given by the next state's probability (P[St+1]) considering all the previous states (S1,S2,S3……St). This implies that MDP uses only the present/current state to evaluate the next actions without any dependencies on previous states or actions.

The policy and value function
The policy (Π) is known to determine the agent's optimal action given the current state so that it gains the maximum reward. In simple words, it associates actions with states.

Π: S –> A

To determine the best policy, it is essential to define the returns that reveal the agent's rewards at every state. As a result, the horizon method is not preferred to focus on short-term or long term-rewards. Instead, a variable termed 'discounted factor (γ)' is introduced. The rule says if γ has values that are closer to zero, then the immediate rewards are prioritized. Subsequently, if γ reveals values closer to one, then the focus shifts to long-term rewards. Hence, the discounted infinite-horizon method is key to revealing the best policy.

The value function V(s) identifies the reward return at each specific state. Its formula is characterized by the expected sum of discounted future rewards:

MDP model1
The value function can be divided into two components: the reward of the current state and the discounted reward value of the next state. This breakdown derives Bellman's equation, as shown below:
MDP model2
Here, it is worth noting that the agent's actions and rewards vary based on the policy. This implies that the value function is specific to a policy.
Optimal value function can be solved with the help of iterative methods such as Monte-Carlo evaluations, dynamic programming, or temporal-difference learning. The policy that chooses the maximum optimal value while considering the present state is referred to as the optimal policy. Mathematically, it is represented by the following equation:
MDP model3
Thus, the policy is a consequence of the current state wherein, at each time step, a new policy is evaluated based on the current state information. It is enabled through several methods, such as policy iteration, Q-learning, value iteration, and linear programming to solve the optimal policy function.
Let's now look at a real-world example to understand the working of MDP better:
We have a problem where we need to decide whether the tribes should go deer hunting or not in a nearby forest to ensure long-term returns. Each deer generates a fixed return. However, if the tribes hunt beyond a limit, it can result in a lower yield next year. Hence, we need to determine the optimum portion of deer that can be caught while maximizing the return over a longer period.

The problem statement can be simplified in this case: whether to hunt a certain portion of deer or not. In the context of MDP, the problem can be expressed as follows:
States: The number of deer available in the forest in the year under consideration. The four states include empty, low, medium, and high, which are defined as follows:
Empty: No deer available to hunt
Low: Available deer count is below a threshold t_1
Medium: Available deer count is between t_1 and t_2
High: Available deer count is above a threshold t_2
Actions: Actions include go_hunt and no_hunting, where go_hunt implies catching certain proportions of deer. It is important to note that for the empty state, the only possible action is no_hunting.
Rewards: Hunting at each state generates rewards of some kind. The rewards for hunting at different states, such as state low, medium, and high, maybe $5K, $50K, and $100k, respectively. Moreover, if the action results in an empty state, the reward is -$200K. This is due to the required e-breeding of new deer, which involves time and money.
State transitions: Hunting in a state causes the transition to a state with fewer deer. Subsequently, the action of no_hunting causes the transition to a state with more deer, except for the 'high' state.

Examples of the Markov Decision Process
MDPs have contributed significantly across several application domains, such as computer science, electrical engineering, manufacturing, operations research, finance and economics, telecommunications, and so on.
Listed here are a few simple examples where MDP continues to play an imminent role:
1. Routing problems
MDP-based sequential decision-making is used to address routing problems such as those revealed in the traveling salesman problem (TSP). TSP can be broken down into the following components:
Salesman = agent,
Routes available = the actions that the agent can take while in the current state,
Rewards = the costs of taking the specific routes, and
Goal = the optimal policy that lowers the overall cost for the entire duration of the trip.
2. Managing maintenance and repair of dynamic systems
The maintenance and repair problems apply to dynamic systems like cars, buses, or trucks that deteriorate over time due to the actions in varied environments. The decisions, in this case, may refer to the act of doing nothing, performing repair tasks, or replacing the critical components of the vehicle. The formulation of this problem under MDP enables the system to choose actions that help minimize the vehicle's maintenance cost over its lifespan.
3. Designing intelligent machines
Advancements in AI and Machine Learning have resulted in the extensive use of MDPs in robotics, complex autonomous systems, autonomous vehicles, automated systems, and so on. MDPs are used within reinforcement learning models that teach robots and machines how to autonomously learn and accomplish specific tasks.
For example, Google's subsidiary, DeepMind Technologies, combines the MDP framework with neural networks and trains computing systems to play Atari games better than humans. The company has further used MDPs to teach machines to play board games such as AlphaGo. DeepMind Technologies has also exploited the MDP framework to teach simulated robots how to walk and run.
4. Designing quiz games
MDPs have been widely used to design quiz games with certain levels. At each level, a question is asked, which, if answered correctly, generates a monetary reward. As the level increases, the questions become tougher and attract higher rewards.
In quiz games, if the participant plays well and answers all questions correctly, then they get the reward for it and also a chance to decide whether to play the quiz from thereon or quit the game. If the participant quits, he can possibly keep all the earned rewards. However, if he chooses to play and fails to answer the question correctly at a certain level, he loses all the accumulated rewards. The goal of such games is to evaluate the actions of playing or quitting while maximizing the rewards.
5. Managing wait time at a traffic intersection
MDPs help in deciding the time duration of traffic lights. The objective here is to maximize the number of vehicles that can pass through traffic intersections while keeping a check on their wait times. It can be a two-way intersection where the traffic can flow in either direction, such as west or south, and so on. It is also assumed that the system has data on the number of vehicles approaching the intersection via sensors. The traffic lights, in this case, are red and

green. Here, each step takes a few seconds (2 or 5). With MDPs, you can decide whether or not to change the traffic lights depending on the vehicles at the intersection and their wait times.
6. Determining the number of patients to admit to a hospital
Every day, a certain number of patients visit the hospital for various reasons. The hospital then has to decide how many patients it can admit while considering factors such as:
the number of patients already admitted,
the number of beds available, and
the total number of patients that recover and get discharged daily.
While determining the number of patients to admit, the hospital also intends to maximize the number of patients that recover over a certain period. Both these objectives can be achieved by formulating MDPs for them.
Apart from the above real-life examples, MDPs are vital for optimizing telecommunication protocols, streamlining stock trading, and fine-tuning queue control in manufacturing sectors.

The Markov decision process is a stochastic decision-making tool based on the Markov Property principle. It is used to make optimal decisions for dynamic systems while considering their current state and the environment in which they operate. MDP is a key component of reinforcement learning applications and is widely employed to design intelligent systems. Several industries, such as robotic process automation, manufacturing, finance & economics, and logistics, use MDPs regularly to carry out their day-to-day tasks.

11.2 Q-Learning
Q-learning is a Machine Learning approach that enables a model to iteratively learn and improve over time by taking the correct action. Q-learning is a type of reinforcement learning.
With reinforcement learning, a Machine Learning model is trained to mimic the way animals or children learn. Good actions are rewarded or reinforced, while bad actions are discouraged and penalized.
With the state-action-reward-state-action form of reinforcement learning, the training regimen follows a model to take the right actions. Q-learning provides a model-free approach to reinforcement learning. There is no model of the environment to guide the reinforcement learning process. The agent -- which is the AI component that acts in the environment -- iteratively learns and makes predictions about the environment on its own.
Q-learning also takes an off-policy approach to reinforcement learning. A Q-learning approach aims to determine the optimal action based on its current state. The Q-learning approach can accomplish this by either developing its own set of rules or deviating from the prescribed policy. Because Q-learning may deviate from the given policy, a defined policy is not needed. Off-policy approach in Q-learning is achieved using Q-values -- also known as action values. The Q-values are the expected future values for action and are stored in the Q-table.
Chris Watkins first discussed the foundations of Q-learning in a 1989 thesis for Cambridge University and further elaborated in a 1992 publication titled Q-learning.

How does Q-learning work?
Q-learning models operate in an iterative process that involves multiple components working together to help train a model. The iterative process involves the agent learning by exploring the environment and updating the model as the exploration continues. The multiple components of Q-learning include the following:
Agents. The agent is the entity that acts and operates within an environment.
States. The state is a variable that identifies the current position in an environment of an agent.
Actions. The action is the agent's operation when it is in a specific state.
Rewards. A foundational concept within reinforcement learning is the concept of providing either a positive or a negative response for the agent's actions.
Episodes. An episode is when an agent can no longer take a new action and ends up terminating.
Q-values. The Q-value is the metric used to measure an action at a particular state.
Here are the two methods to determine the Q-value:
Temporal difference. The temporal difference formula calculates the Q-value by incorporating the value of the current state and action by comparing the differences with the previous state and action.
Bellman's equation. Mathematician Richard Bellman invented this equation in 1957 as a recursive formula for optimal decision-making. In the q-learning context, Bellman's equation is used to help calculate the value of a given state and assess its relative position. The state with the highest value is considered the optimal state.
Q-learning models work through trial-and-error experiences to learn the optimal behavior for a task. The Q-learning process involves modeling optimal behavior by learning an optimal action value function or q-function. This function

represents the optimal long-term value of action a in state s and subsequently follows optimal behavior in every subsequent state.

Bellman's equation

Q(s,a) = Q(s,a) + α * (r + γ * max(Q(s',a')) - Q(s,a))

The equation breaks down as follows:

1. Q(s, a) represents the expected reward for taking action *a* in state *s*.

2. The actual reward received for that action is referenced by *r* while *s'* refers to the next state.

3. The learning rate is *α* and *γ* is the discount factor.

4. The highest expected reward for all possible actions *a'* in state *s'* is represented *by max(Q(s', a'))*.

What is a Q-table?

The Q-table includes columns and rows with lists of rewards for the best actions of each state in a specific environment. A Q-table helps an agent understand what actions are likely to lead to positive outcomes in different situations.

The table rows represent different situations the agent might encounter, and the columns represent the actions it can take. As the agent interacts with the environment and receives feedback in the form of rewards or penalties, the values in the Q-table are updated to reflect what the model has learned.

The purpose of reinforcement learning is to gradually improve performance through the Q-table to help choose actions. With more feedback, the Q-table becomes more accurate so the agent can make better decisions and achieve optimal results.

The Q-table is directly related to the concept of the Q-function. The Q-function is a mathematical equation that looks at the current state of the environment and the action under consideration as inputs. The Q-function then generates outputs along with expected future rewards for that action in the specific state. The Q-table allows the agent to look up the expected future reward for any given state-action pair to move toward an optimized state.

What is the Q-learning algorithm process?

The Q-learning algorithm process is an interactive method where the agent learns by exploring the environment and updating the Q-table based on the rewards received.

The steps involved in the Q-learning algorithm process include the following:

Q-table initialization. The first step is to create the Q-table as a place to track each action in each state and the associated progress.

Observation. The agent needs to observe the current state of the environment.

Action. The agent chooses to act in the environment. Upon completion of the action, the model observes if the action is beneficial in the environment.

Update. After the action has been taken, it's time to update the Q-table with the results.

Repeat. Repeat steps 2-4 until the model reaches a termination state for a desired objective.

What are the advantages of Q-learning?

The Q-learning approach to reinforcement learning can potentially be advantageous for several reasons, including the following:

Model-free. The model-free approach is the foundation of Q-learning and one of the biggest potential advantages for some uses. Rather than requiring prior knowledge about an environment, the Q-learning agent can learn about the environment as it trains. The model-free approach is particularly beneficial for scenarios where the underlying dynamics of an environment are difficult to model or completely unknown.

Off-policy optimization. The model can optimize to get the best possible result without being strictly tethered to a policy that might not enable the same degree of optimization.

Flexibility. The model-free, off-policy approach enables Q-learning flexibility to work across a variety of problems and environments.

Offline training. A Q-learning model can be deployed on pre-collected, offline data sets.

What are the disadvantages of Q-learning?

The Q-learning approach to reinforcement model Machine Learning also has some disadvantages, such as the following:

Exploration vs. exploitation tradeoff. It can be hard for a Q-learning model to find the right balance between trying new actions and sticking with what's already known. It's a dilemma that is commonly referred to as the exploration vs. exploitation tradeoff for reinforcement learning.

Curse of dimensionality. Q-learning can potentially face a Machine Learning risk known as the curse of dimensionality. The curse of dimensionality is a problem with high-dimensional data where the amount of data required to represent the distribution increases exponentially. This can lead to computational challenges and decreased accuracy.

Overestimation. A Q-learning model can sometimes be too optimistic and overestimate how good a particular action or strategy is.

Performance. A Q-learning model can take a long time to figure out the best method if there are several ways to approach a problem.

What are some examples of Q-learning?

Q-learning models can improve processes in various scenarios. Here are a few examples of Q-learning uses:

Energy management. Q-learning models help manage energy for different resources such as electricity, gas and water utilities. A 2022 report from IEEE provides a precise approach for integrating a Q-learning model for energy management.

Finance. A Q-learning-based training model can build models for decision-making assistance, such as determining optimal moments to buy or sell assets.

Gaming. Q-learning models can train gaming systems to achieve an expert level of proficiency in playing a wide range of games as the model learns the optimal strategy to advance.

Recommendation systems. Q-learning models can help optimize recommendation systems, such as advertising platforms. For example, an ad system that recommends products commonly bought together can be optimized based on what users select.

Robotics. Q-learning models can help train robots to execute various tasks, such as object manipulation, obstacle avoidance and transportation.

Self-driving cars. Autonomous vehicles use many different models, and Q-learning models help train models to make driving decisions, such as when to switch lanes or stop.

Supply chain management. The flow of goods and services as part of supply chain management can be improved with Q-learning models to help find the optimized path for products to market.

Q-learning with Python

Python is one of the most common programming languages for Machine Learning. Beginners and experts commonly use Python to apply Q-learning models. For Q-learning and any data science operation in Python, users need Python to write on a system with the NumPy (numerical Python) library that provides support for mathematical functions to use with AI.

With Python and NumPy, Q-learning models are set up with a few basic steps:

Define the environment. Create variables for states and actions to define the environment.

Initialize the Q-table. The initial condition of the Q-table is set to zero.

Set hyperparameters. Set parameters in Python to define the number of episodes, learning and exploration rate.

Execute Q-learning algorithm. The agent selects an action either randomly or based on the highest Q-value for the current state. After the action is taken, the Q-table is updated with the results.

Q-learning application

Before applying a Q-learning model, it's critical to first understand the problem and how Q-learning training can be applied to that problem.

Set up Q-learning in Python with a standard code editor or an integrated development environment to write the code. To apply and test a Q-learning model, use a Machine Learning tool, such as the Farama Foundation's Gymnasium. Other common tools include the open source PyTorch Machine Learning application framework to support reinforcement learning workflows including Q-learning.

11.3 Deep Q Networks (DQN)

This is the architecture of our Deep Q-Learning network:

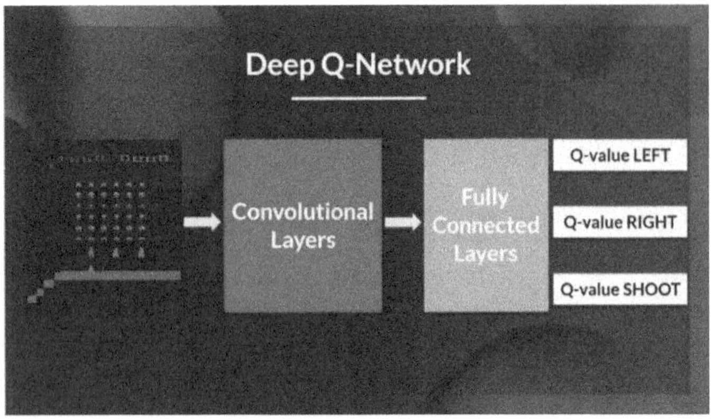

As input, we take a stack of 4 frames passed through the network as a state and output a vector of Q-values for each possible action at that state. Then, like with Q-Learning, we just need to use our epsilon-greedy policy to select which action to take.

When the Neural Network is initialized, the Q-value estimation is terrible. But during training, our Deep Q-Network agent will associate a situation with the appropriate action and learn to play the game well.

Preprocessing the input and temporal limitation

We need to preprocess the input. It's an essential step since we want to reduce the complexity of our state to reduce the computation time needed for training.

To achieve this, we reduce the state space to 84x84 and grayscale it. We can do this since the colors in Atari environments don't add important information. This is a big improvement since we reduce our three color channels (RGB) to 1.

We can also crop a part of the screen in some games if it does not contain important information. Then we stack four frames together.

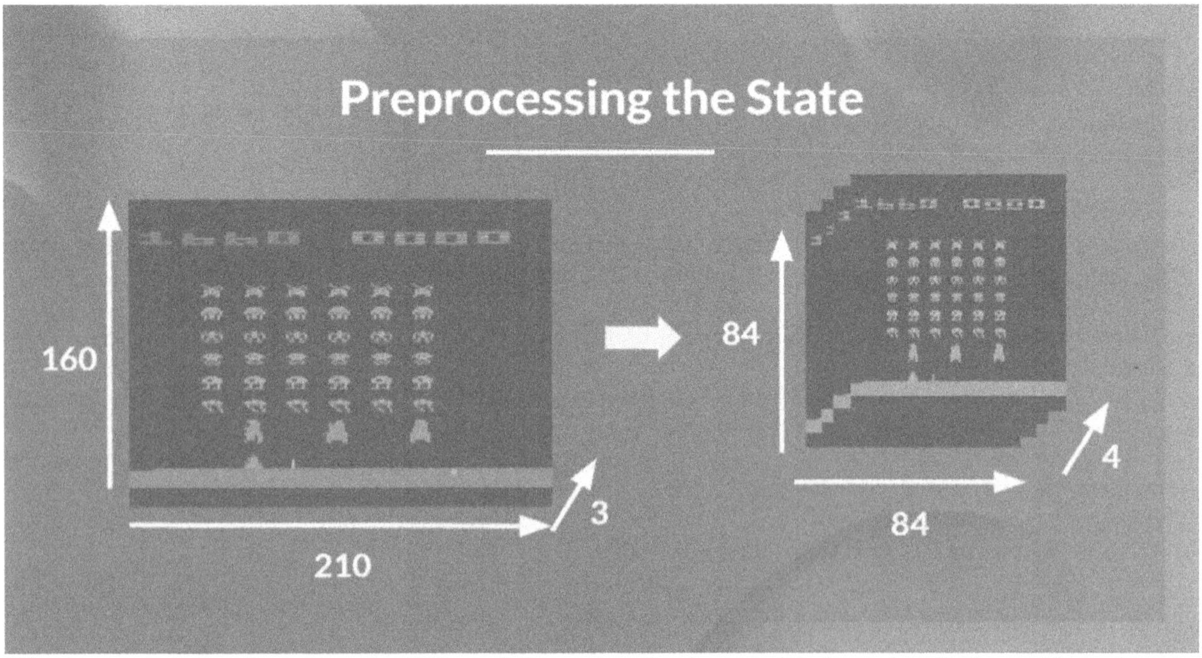

Why do we stack four frames together? We stack frames together because it helps us handle the problem of temporal limitation. Let's take an example with the game of Pong. When you see this frame:

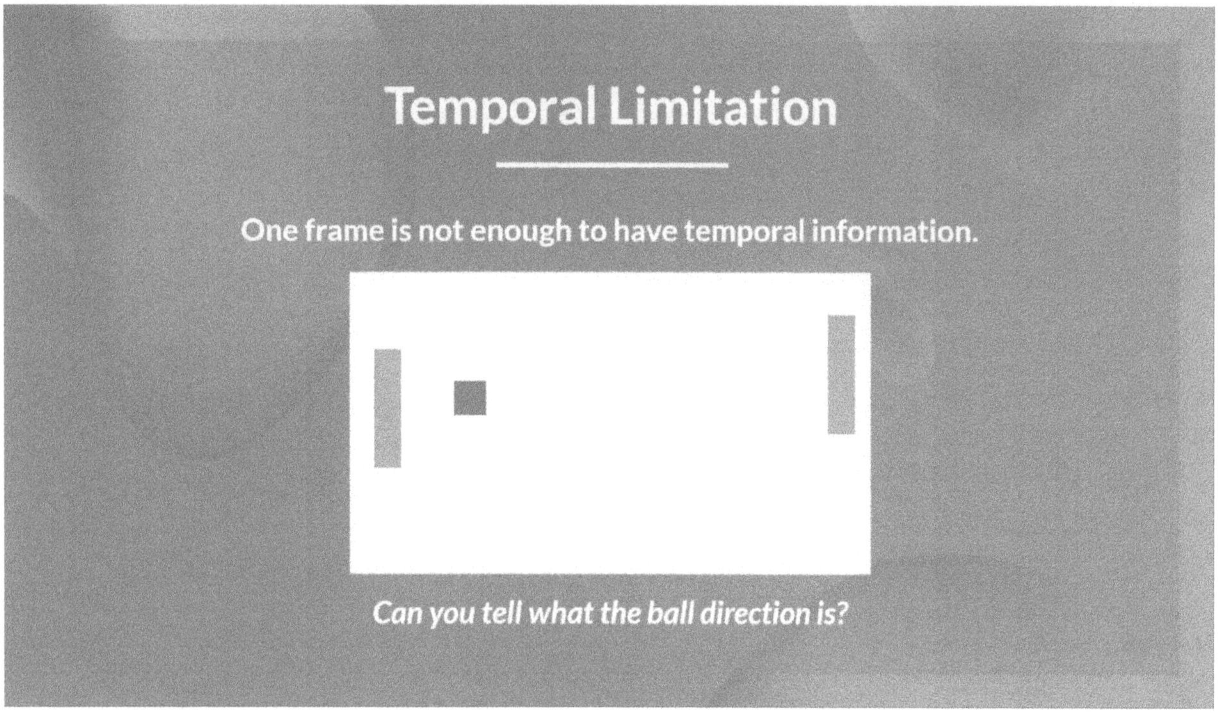

Can you tell me where the ball is going? No, because one frame is not enough to have a sense of motion! But what if I add three more frames? Here you can see that the ball is going to the right.

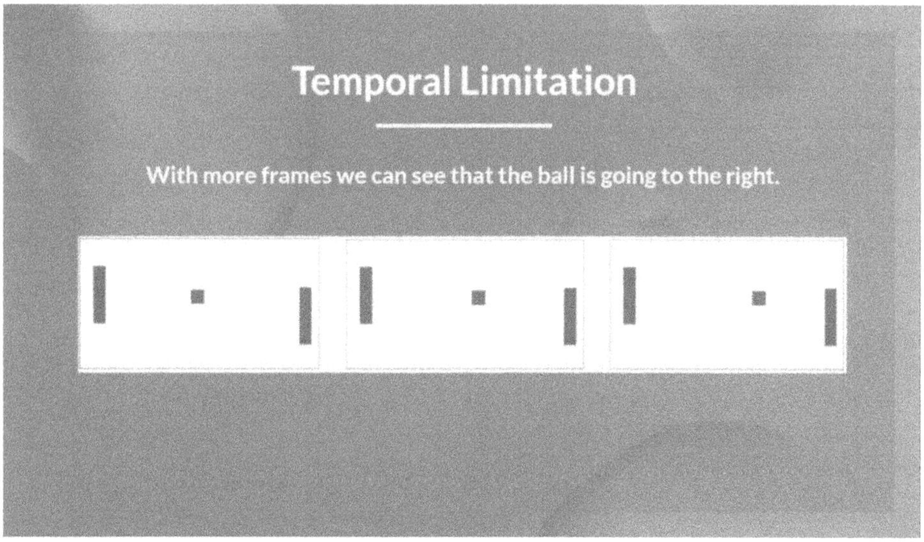

That's why, to capture temporal information, we stack four frames together.

Then the stacked frames are processed by three convolutional layers. These layers allow us to capture and exploit spatial relationships in images. But also, because the frames are stacked together, we can exploit some temporal properties across those frames.

If you don't know what convolutional layers are, don't worry. You can check out Lesson 4 of this free Deep Learning Course by Udacity

Finally, we have a couple of fully connected layers that output a Q-value for each possible action at that state.

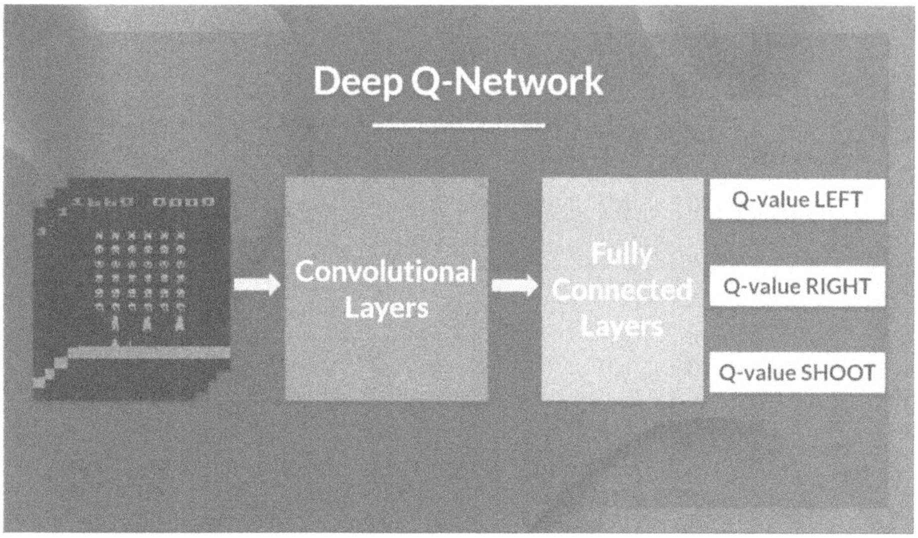

So, we see that Deep Q-Learning uses a neural network to approximate, given a state, the different Q-values for each possible action at that state.

11.4 Policy Gradient Methods

Policy gradient methods are a type of reinforcement learning techniques that rely upon optimizing parametrized policies with respect to the expected return (long-term cumulative reward) by gradient descent. They do not suffer from many of the problems that have been marring traditional reinforcement learning approaches such as the lack of guarantees of a value function, the intractability problem resulting from uncertain state information and the complexity arising from continuous states & actions.

Reinforcement learning is probably the most general framework in which reward-related learning problems of animals, humans or machine can be phrased. However, most of the methods proposed in the reinforcement learning community are not yet applicable to many problems such as robotics, motor control, etc. This inapplicability may result from problems with uncertain state information. Thus, those systems need to be modeled as partially observable Markov decision problems which often results in excessive computational demands. Most traditional reinforcement learning methods have no convergence guarantees and there exist even divergence examples. Continuous states and actions in high dimensional spaces cannot be treated by most off-the-shelf reinforcement learning approaches.

Policy gradient methods differ significantly as they do not suffer from these problems in the same way. For example, uncertainty in the state might degrade the performance of the policy (if no additional state estimator is being used) but the optimization techniques for the policy do not need to be changed. Continuous states and actions can be dealt with in exactly the same way as discrete ones while, in addition, the learning performance is often increased. Convergence at least to a local optimum is guaranteed.

The advantages of policy gradient methods for real world applications are numerous. Among the most important ones are that the policy representations can be chosen so that it is meaningful for the task and can incorporate domain knowledge, that often fewer parameters are needed in the learning process than in value-function based approaches and that there is a variety of different algorithms for policy gradient estimation in the literature which have a rather strong theoretical underpinning. Additionally, policy gradient methods can be used either model-free or model-based as they are a generic formulation.

Of course, policy gradients are not the salvation to all problems but also have significant problems. They are by definition on-policy (note that tricks like importance sampling can slightly alleviate this problem) and need to forget data very fast in order to avoid the introduction of a bias to the gradient estimator. Hence, the use of sampled data is not very efficient. In tabular representations, value function methods are guaranteed to converge to a global maximum while policy gradients only converge to a local maximum and there may be many maxima in discrete problems. Policy gradient methods are often quite demanding to apply, mainly because one has to have considerable knowledge about the system one wants to control to make reasonable policy definitions. Finally, policy gradient methods always have an open parameter, the learning rate, which may decide over the order of magnitude of the speed of convergence, these have led to new approaches inspired by expectation-maximization (see, e.g.,Vlassisetal.,2009;Kober & Peters, 2008).

Nevertheless, due to their advantages stated above, policy gradient methods have become particularly interesting for robotics applications as these have both continuous actions and states. For example, there has been a series of successful applications in robot locomotion, where good policy parametrizations such as CPGs are known. Ben bra him &Franklin (1997) already explored 2D dynamic biped walking, Ted rakee tal.(2004) extended these results to 3D passive dynamics-based walkers and Endo (2005) showed that a full-body gait with sensory feedback can be learned with policy gradients. Kohl & Stone (2004) were able to apply policy gradients to optimize quadruped gaits. There have also been various applications in skill learning starting with the peg-in-a-hole tasks learned by Gull ap allietal .(1994)and ranging to Peters & Schaals' optimizations of discrete movements primitives such as T-Ball swings.
Note that in most applications, there exist many local maxima; for example, if we were told build a high jumping robot, there is a multitude of styles. Current policy gradient methods would be helpful for improving a jumping style of a teacher, let's say the classical straddle jump. However, discovering a fosbery flop when starting with a basic straddle jump policy is probably not possible with policy gradient methods.
Assumptions and Notation
We assume that we can model the control system in a discrete-time manner and we will denote the current time step by k . In order to take possible stochasticity of the plant into account, we denote it using a probability distribution xk+1~p(xk+1|xk,uk) as model where uk ∈RM denotes the current action, and xk , xk+1∈RN denote the current and next state, respectively. We furthermore assume that actions are generated by a policy u_k~πθ(u_k|x_k) which is modeled as a probability distribution in order to incorporate exploratory actions; for some special problems, the optimal solution to a control problem is actually a stochastic controller (Sutton, Mc All ester ,Singh ,and Mansour, 2000). The policy is assumed to be parameterized by K policy parameters θ ∈RK .The sequence of states and actions forms a trajectory denoted by τ=[x0:H,u0:H] where H denotes the horizon which can be infinite. In this article, we will use the words trajectory, history, trial, or roll-out interchangeably. At each instant of time, the learning system receives a reward denoted by r_k=r(x_k,u_k)∈R .
The general goal of policy optimization in reinforcement learning is to optimize the policy parameters θ ∈RK so that the expected return

$$J(\theta)=E\{\sum_{k=1}^{H} a_k r_k\}$$

is optimized where ak denote time-step dependent weighting factors, often set to ak=γk for discounted reinforcement learning (where γ is in [0,1]) or ak=1/H for the average reward case.

For real-world applications, we require that any change to the policy parameterization has to be smooth as drastic changes can be hazardous for the actor as well as useful initializations of the policy based on domain knowledge would otherwise vanish after a single update step. For these reasons, policy gradient methods which follow the steepest descent on the expected return are the method of choice. These methods update the policy parameterization according to the gradient update rule

$$O_h +1=O_h+a_h \nabla o^j |_{o=o_h},|$$

where αh∈R+ denotes a learning rate and h∈{0,1,2,…} the current update number.

The time step k and update number h are two different variables. In actor-critic-based policy gradient methods, the frequency of updates of h can be nearly as high as of k . However, in most episodic methods, the policy update h will be significantly less frequent. Here, cut-off allows updates before the end of the episode (for $a_k=y^k$, it is obvious that there comes a point where any future reward becomes irrelevant; a generically good cut-off point). If the gradient estimate is unbiased and learning rates fulfill $\sum_{h=0}^{\infty} a_h>0$ and $\sum_{h=0}^{\infty} a_h^2$=const , the learning process is guaranteed to converge at least to a local minimum.

The main problem in policy gradient methods is to obtain a good estimator of the policy gradient $\nabla_O J|_{o=o_h}$. In robotics and control, people have traditionally used deterministic model-based methods for obtaining the gradient (Jacobson & Mayne, 1970; Dyer & McReynolds, 1970; Hasdorff, 1976). However, in order to become autonomous we cannot expect to be able to model every detail of the system. Therefore, we need to estimate the policy gradient simply from data generated during the execution of a task, i.e., without the need for a model. In this section, we will study different approaches and discuss their properties.

Approaches to Policy Gradient Estimation

The literature on policy gradient methods has yielded a variety of estimation methods over the last years. The most prominent approaches, which have been applied to robotics are finite-difference and likelihood ratio methods, better known as REINFORCE in reinforcement learning.

Finite-difference Methods

Finite-difference methods are among the oldest policy gradient approaches; they originated from the stochastic simulation community and are quite straightforward to understand. The policy parameterization is varied I times by small increments ΔO_i,i=1…I and for each policy parameter variation O_h+ΔO_iroll-outs (or trajectories) are performed which generate estimates ΔJ^$_i$≈J(O_h+ΔO_i)− $J_{ref}$of the expected return. There are different ways of choosing the reference value Jref , e.g. forward-difference estimators with J_{ref} =J(O_h) and central-difference estimators with J_{ref}=J(O_h−ΔO_i) . The policy gradient estimate g_{FD}≈∇_0J$|_{0=0_h}|$ can be estimated by regression yielding

g_{FD}=($\mathbf{\Delta O^T \Delta \Theta})^{-1}\mathbf{\Delta O^T \Delta}$J^,

where ΔΘ=[Δ0_1,…,Δ0_I]T and ΔJ^=[ΔJ^$_1$,…,ΔJ^$_I$)^T|denote the I samples.This approach can be highly efficient in simulation optimization of deterministic systems (Spall, 2003) or when a common history of random numbers (Glynn, 1987) is being used (the latter is known as PEGASUS in reinforcement learning (Ng & Jordan, 2000)), and the error of the gradient estimate can get close to O($I^{1/2}$) (Glynn, 1987). However, the uncertainty of real systems will result in stochasticity and an artificial common history of random numbers can no longer be applied. Hence, when used on a real system, the performance degrades in a gradient estimate error ranging between O($I^{-1/4}$) to O($I^{-2/5}$) depending on the chosen reference value (Glynn, 1987). An implementation of this algorithm is shown below.

```
input: policy parameterization o_h
for i=1 to  I do
   generate policy variation Δθi
   estimate J^I ≈J(θh+Δθi)=⟨∑\begin{matrix}H\\k=O\ \\\end{matrix}a_{k\ }T_k⟩ from roll-out
   estimate J^ref , e.g., J^ ref=J(o_h −Δ \mathbit{o}_\mathbit{i}) from roll-out
   compute ΔJ^I ≈ J(o_h +Δ\mathbit{o}_\mathbit{i})−J_{ref}
end for
return            gradient            estimate            g_{FD}=(Δ\mathbf{0}^\mathbit{T}ΔΘ)^{-\mathbf{1}}Δ\mathbf{0}^\mathbit{T}ΔJ^
```

Note that an alternative implementation would keep increasing I until the gradient estimate converges. The choice of I can be essential; empirically it can be observed that taking I as twice the number of parameters yields very accurate gradient estimates.

Due to the simplicity of this approach, such methods have been successfully applied to numerous applications. However, the straightforward application is not without peril as the generation of the $\Delta 0_i$ requires proper knowledge of the system, as badly chosen $\Delta 0_i$ can destabilize the policy so that the system becomes instable and the gradient estimation process is prone to fail. If the parameters differ highly in scale, significant difficulties could be the consequences.

Advantages of this approach: Finite-difference methods require very little skill and can usually be implemented out of the box. They work both with stochastic and deterministic policies without any change. It is highly efficient in simulation with a set of common histories of random numbers and on totally deterministic systems.

Disadvantages of this approach: The perturbation of the parameters is a very difficult problem often with disastrous impact on the learning process when the system goes unstable. In the presence of noise on a real system, the gradient estimate error decreases much slower than for the following methods. Performance depends highly on the chosen policy parametrization.

Likelihood Ratio Methods and REINFORCE

Likelihood ratio methods are driven by a different important insight. Assume that trajectories τ are generated from a system by roll-outs, i.e., $\tau \sim p_o(\tau)$ = p(τ/θ)| with return $r(\tau)=\sum_{k=0}^{H} a_k r_k$ which leads to $J(\theta) = E\{r(\tau)\}=\int_T p_o(\tau) r(\tau) d\tau$.| In this case, the policy gradient can be estimated using the likelihood ratio (see e.g. Glynn, 1987;Aleksandrov,Sysoyev, and Shemeneva,1968) better known as REINFORCE (Williams, 1992) trick, i.e., by using

$$\nabla_o p_o(\tau)= p_o(\tau)\nabla_o \log p\theta(\tau)$$

from standard differential calculus ($\nabla_o \log p_o(\tau) = \nabla_o p_o((\tau)/ p_o(\tau))$, we obtain

$$\nabla_o J(\theta)=\int_T p_o(\tau)r(\tau)d\tau =\int_T p_o(\tau)\nabla_o \log p_o(\tau)r(\tau)\, d\tau = E\{\nabla_o \log p_o(\tau)r(\tau)\}.|$$

As the expectation $E\{\cdot\}$| can be replaced by sample averages, denoted by $\langle\cdot\rangle$, only the derivative $\nabla_o \log P_o(\tau)$ is needed for the estimator. Importantly, this derivative can be computed without knowledge of the generating distribution $P_o(\tau)$ as

$$P_o(\tau)=p(x_o)\prod_{k=0}^{H} p(x_{k+1}|x_k,u_k)n_o(u_k|x_k)|$$

implies that

$$\nabla_o \log p_o(\tau)=\sum_{K=0}^{H} \nabla_o \log n_o(u_k|x_k)|$$

as only the policy depends on θ .

Thus, the derivatives of $p(x_{k=1}|x_k,u_k)$ do not have to be computed and no model needs to be maintained. However, if we had a deterministic policy u=π(x) instead of a stochastic policy u=π(x)| , computing such a derivative would require the derivative $\nabla_o \log p(x_{k+1}|x_k,u_k)=\nabla_{uk} \log p(x_{k+1}|x_k,u_k)\nabla_o \pi_o(x_k)$ to compute $\nabla_o \log p_o(\tau)$ and, hence, it would require a system model.

In order to reduce the variance of the gradient estimator, a constant baseline can be subtracted from the gradient, i.e.,

$$\nabla_o J(\theta)=E\{\nabla_o \log p_o(\tau)(r(\tau)-b)\},$$

where the baseline b∈R can be chosen arbitrarily (Williams, 1992). It is straightforward to show that this baseline does not introduce bias in the gradient as differentiating $\int_T p_o(\tau)d\tau=1$| implies that

$$\int_T \nabla\theta p_o(\tau)d\,\tau=|0\,,$$

and, hence, the constant baseline will vanish for infinite data while reducing the variance of the gradient estimator for finite data. See Peters & Schaad, 2008 for an overview of how to choose the baseline optimally. Therefore, the general path likelihood ratio estimator or episodic REINFORCE gradient estimator is given by

$$g_{RF}=\langle(\sum_{k=0}^{H} \nabla_0 \log n_o(u_k|x_k))(\sum_{l-0}^{H} a_i r_i - b)\rangle,$$

where $\langle\cdot\rangle$ denotes the average over trajectories. This type of method is guaranteed to converge to the true gradient at the fastest theoretically possible error decrease of $O(I^{1/2})$ where I denote the number of roll-outs (Glynn, 1987) even if the data is generated from a highly stochastic system. An implementation of this algorithm will be shown below together with the estimator for the optimal baseline.

```
input: policy parameterization 0_h
repeat
   perform a trial and obtain x_o:H,u_o:H,r_o:H
   for each  gradient element g_k
      estimate optimal baseline
```

```
        ⟨(∑\begin{matrix}H\\h=0\\\end{matrix}∇o_{k\                                   }log
n_o(u_h||x_h))^2∑\begin{matrix}H\\l=0\\\end{matrix}a_lT_l⟩
                    b=  ----------------------------------
                              ⟨(∑\begin{matrix}H\\h=0\\\end{matrix}∇O_klog n_0(u_h||x_h))^2⟩
     estimate the gradient element
        g_k=⟨(∑\begin{matrix}H\\h=0\\\end{matrix}∇0_k                                  log
\pi_0(u_h|x_h))(∑\begin{matrix}H\\l=0\\\end{matrix}a_ir_i−b)⟩
   end for
until  gradient estimate \mathbf{g}_{RF}=[g_1,…,g_K] converged
return gradient estimate \mathbf{g}_{RF}=[g_1,…,g_K]
```

Advantages of this approach: Besides the theoretically faster convergence rate, likelihood ratio gradient methods have a variety of advantages in comparison to finite difference methods when applied to robotics. As the generation of policy parameter variations is no longer needed, the complicated control of these variables can no longer endanger the gradient estimation process. Furthermore, in practice, already a single roll-out can suffice for an unbiased gradient estimate viable for a good policy update step, thus reducing the amount of roll-outs needed. Finally, this approach has yielded the most real-world robotics results (Peters & Schaal, 2008) and the likelihood ratio gradient is guaranteed to achieve the fastest convergence of the error for a stochastic system.

Disadvantages of this approach: When used with a deterministic policy, likelihood ratio gradients have to maintain a system model. Such a model can be very hard to obtain for continuous states and actions, hence, the simpler finite difference gradients are often superior in this scenario. Similarly, finite difference gradients can still be more useful than likelihood ratio gradients if the system is deterministic and very repetitive. Also, the practical implementation of a likelihood ratio gradient method is much more demanding than the one of a finite difference method.

Natural Policy Gradients

One of the main reasons for using policy gradient methods is that we intend to do just a small change Δθ to the policy πθ while improving the policy. However, the meaning of small is ambiguous. When using the Euclidian metric of ΔO^TΔθ−−−−−−√ , then the gradient is different for every parameterization θ of the policy πθ even if this parameterization is related to each other by a linear transformation (Kakadu, 2002). This problem poses the question of how we can measure the closeness between the current policy and the updated policy based upon the distribution of the paths generated by each of these. In statistics, a variety of distance measures for the closeness of two distributions (e.g., pθ(τ) and $p_0+\Delta\theta^{(T)}$) have been suggested, e.g., the fullback- Leibel divergence $d_{KL}(p_o,p_o+\Delta\theta)$,| the Hellinger distance d_{HD} and others (Su & Gibbs, 2002). Many of these distances (e.g., the previously mentioned ones) can be approximated by its second order Taylor expansion, i.e., by

$d_{KL}(p_o,p_o+\Delta\theta)\approx\Delta o^T F_o\,\Delta\theta$,

where

$F_0=\int T^{P0}(\tau)\nabla\log p_0(\tau)\nabla\log p_0(\tau)^T d\tau=\langle\nabla\log p_0(\tau)\nabla\log p_0(\tau)^T\rangle$

is known as the Fisher-information matrix. Let us now assume that we restrict the change of our policy to $d_{KL}(p_0,p_0+\Delta\theta)\approx\Delta 0^T F_0\Delta\theta=\varepsilon$,| where ε needs to be a very small number (i.e., close to zero).

In that case, the natural gradient is defined by Amari (1998) as the update Δ θ~ that is most similar to the true gradient ∇θJ while the change in our path distribution is limited to ε . Hence, it is given by the program

$$\text{Argmax } \Delta\theta^{\Delta\theta^T}\nabla o^J \ \text{ s .t. } \ \Delta 0^T F_0\,\Delta\,\theta=\varepsilon.$$

The solution to this program is given by

$$\Delta\,\theta \propto F_0^{-1}\nabla o^J,$$

where ∇θJ denotes the regular likelihood ratio policy gradient from the previous section. The update step is unique up to a scaling factor, which is often subsumed into the learning rate. It can be interpreted as follows: determine the maximal improvement Δ θ of the policy for a constant fixed change of the policy $\Delta 0^T F_0\Delta\theta$.

When plotting the expected return landscape for a simple problem such as an 1d linear quadratic regulation, the differences between regular ('vanilla') and natural policy gradients becomes apparent.
This type of approach has its origin in supervised learning (Amari, 1998). It was first suggested in the context of reinforcement learning by Kakade (2002) and has been explored in greater depth in (Bagnell & Schneider, 2003; Peters, Vijayakumar & Schaal, 2003, 2005; Peters & Schaal, 2008). The strongest theoretical advantage of this approach is that its performance no longer depends on the parameterization of the policy and is therefore safe to be used for arbitrary policies. Hence, the regular policy gradient is sometimes referred to as a flavored or vanilla gradient, as it keeps the `vanilla flavor' of the policy. However, a well-chosen policy parametrization can sometimes results in better convergence of the policy gradient than the natural policy gradient. Nevertheless, in practice, a learning process based on natural policy gradients often converges significantly faster for most practical cases. Figure 1 gives an impression of the differences in the learning process: while the regular policy gradient often points to plateaus with little exploration, the natural gradient points to the optimal solution.
One of the fastest general algorithms for estimating natural policy gradients which does not need complex parameterized baselines is the episodic natural actor critic. This algorithm, originally derived in (Peters, Vijayakumar & Schaal, 2003), can be considered the `natural' version of REINFORCE with a baseline optimal for this gradient estimator. However, for steepest descent with respect to a metric, the baseline also needs to minimize the variance with respect to the same metric. In this case, we can minimize the whole covariance matrix of the natural gradient estimate Δθ^ given by

$$\Sigma = \mathrm{Cov}\,\{\Delta\theta\^{}\}F_0 = E\{(\Delta\theta\^{} - F_0^{-1} g_{RF}(b))^T F_0(\Delta\theta\^{} - F_0^{-1} g_{RF}(b))\}$$

,with $g_{RF}(b) = \langle \nabla \log p_0(\tau)(r(\tau) - b)\rangle$

being the REINFORCE gradient with baseline b . The re-weighting with the Fisher information ensures that the best identifiable gradient components get the highest weight. As outlined in (Peters & Schaal, 2008), it can be shown that the minimum-variance unbiased natural gradient estimator can be determined as shown below.

input: policy parameterization \theta_h
repeat
perform M trials and obtain \mathbf{x}_\mathbf{0}:H,\mathbf{u}_0:H,r_0:H for each trial
Obtain the sufficient statistics
Policy derivatives \psi_k=\mathrm{\nabla}_\thetalog \pi_\theta(u_k|x_k)
Fisher matrix F_\theta=⟨(∑\begin{matrix}H\\k=0\\\end{matrix}\psi_k)(∑\begin{matrix}H\\l=0\\\end{matrix}\psi_l)T⟩
Vanilla gradient g=⟨(∑\begin{matrix}H\\k=0\\\end{matrix}\psi_k)(∑\begin{matrix}H\\l=0\\\end{matrix}al rl)⟩
Eligibility ϕ=⟨(∑\begin{matrix}H\\k=0\\\end{matrix}\psi_k)⟩
Average reward r¯=⟨∑\begin{matrix}H\\l=0\\\end{matrix}alrl ⟩
Obtain natural gradient by computing
Baseline b=Q(r¯−\phi^T\mathbit{F}_\mathbf{0}^{-1}g)
with Q=M^{-1}(1+\phi^T(MF_\theta−ϕ\phi^T)\underline{-1}ϕ)
Natural gradient\mathbf{g}_{NG}=F\begin{matrix}-\mathbf{1}\\\mathbit{\theta}\\\end{matrix}(g−ϕb)
until gradient estimate \mathbf{g}_{NG}=[g_1,…,g_h] converged
return gradient estimate \mathbf{g}_{NG}=[g_1,…,g_h]

Advantages of this approach: Natural policy gradients differ in a deciding aspect from both finite difference gradients and regular likelihood ratio gradients, i.e., they are independent from the choice of policy parametrization if the choices have the same representational power. As a result, they can be an order of magnitude faster than the regular gradient. They also profit from most other advantages of the regular policy gradients.
Disadvantages of this approach: In comparison to the regular policy gradient, there are three disadvantages: first, the matrix inversion in the gradient estimators may be numerically brittle and may scale worse (note that there are tricks to alleviate this problem). Second, if we can find a special policy parametrization that trivializes a problem, the natural policy gradient may not make use of it. Third, the natural policy gradient estimators are often much harder to implement.

Exercise

True Or False

1.Markov Decision Processes (MDP) are used to model decision-making problems involving states, actions, rewards, and transitions.

2.In an MDP, the future state only depends on the current state and not on the sequence of past states.

3.The action space in an MDP refers to the set of all possible states that the agent can be in.

4. Q-Learning is a model-free reinforcement learning algorithm used to learn the optimal action-value function.

5.The Bellman equation is used in Q-Learning to update the Q-values based on the current reward and the estimated future rewards.

6.Q-Learning requires complete knowledge of the transition probabilities and rewards in the environment.

7.Deep Q Networks (DQN) use a neural network to approximate the Q-values of state-action pairs

8.Experience replay is a technique used in DQN to store and replay past experiences for more stable learning.

9.The target network in DQN is updated every time a new experience is added to the replay buffer.

10.Policy gradient methods focus on directly optimizing the agent's policy to maximize expected rewards.

11.Policy gradient methods update the policy by using gradient descent to maximize the expected reward.

12.Policy gradient methods can only be applied to problems with discrete action spaces.

13.The action space in a Markov Decision Process (MDP) refers to the set of all possible actions the agent can take.

14.Q-Learning is a type of on-policy reinforcement learning algorithm.

15.Deep Q Networks (DQN) are particularly well-suited for problems with continuous action spaces.

16.Policy gradient methods involve using a neural network to approximate the agent's policy

17.In reinforcement learning, the agent's goal is to minimize immediate rewards in order to achieve a long-term objective.

18.Q-Learning can be used for both episodic and continuous tasks.

Answer: True, True, False, True, True, False, True , True , False , True , False, False , True, False , False, True , False , True

MCQ

1.What is a Markov Decision Process (MDP) in the context of reinforcement learning?

a) A deterministic process without uncertainty

b) A stochastic process with memory

c) A model for decision-making involving states, actions, rewards, and transitions

d) A method for unsupervised learning

Answer: c

2.In an MDP, what is the set of all possible states that the agent can be in?

a) Transition matrix

b) Action space

c) Reward function

d) State space

Answer: d

3.What is the main goal of Q-Learning in reinforcement learning?

a) To estimate the optimal policy directly

b) To calculate the expected rewards for each state-action pair

c) To model the transition probabilities between states

d) To perform clustering of states for better exploration

Answer: b

4.Q-Learning uses an iterative update equation called the:

a) Bellman equation

b) Markov equation

c) Newton's equation

d) Gradient descent equation
Answer: a

5.What is a Deep Q Network (DQN) used for in reinforcement learning?
a) To calculate Q-values directly
b) To approximate Q-values using a neural network
c) To model the state-transition probabilities
d) To perform policy optimization
Answer: b

6.Which key concept is used in DQN to store and replay experiences for more stable learning?
a) Gradient clipping
b) Experience replay
c) Target network
d) Exploration strategy
Answer: b

7.What is the primary goal of policy gradient methods in reinforcement learning?
a) To calculate Q-values
b) To estimate state-transition probabilities
c) To directly optimize the agent's policy
d) To calculate the reward function
Answer: c

Short Question And Answers
Q1. What is the key difference between supervised learning and reinforcement learning?
Q2. What is the exploration-exploitation trade-off in reinforcement learning?
Q3. What is a Markov Decision Process (MDP)?
Q4. What is the Markov property in MDPs?
Q5. What is Q-learning?
Q6. How does Q-learning update the Q-values for state-action pairs?
Q7. What is a Deep Q Network (DQN)?
Q8. How does experience replay benefit DQN training?
Q9. What is target network and how is it used in DQN?
Q10.What are policy gradient methods in reinforcement learning?
Q11.How does the policy gradient algorithm update the policy?
Q12.What is the advantage of policy gradient methods over value-based methods like Q-learning?
Q13.Compare model-free and model-based reinforcement learning.
Q14.What are some real-world applications of reinforcement learning?
Q15.How can reinforcement learning be used for optimizing financial trading strategies?
Q16.What are some challenges in reinforcement learning, especially in real-world applications?
Q17.What are some ethical concerns in using reinforcement learning for decision-making?
Q18.What are some emerging trends in reinforcement learning research?
Q19.What are some open research questions in reinforcement learning?

Online Resources

Online Exam Papers
True/False Exam

Link

https://forms.gle/39mRWSLVkXzMi5618

QR Code

YouTube Video Playlist Link

Chapter 11
Link
https://www.youtube.com/playlist?list=PLzlh_31VWEFoPlkcjztJMUiCV5-u15r3A
QR Code

Chapter 12: Model Deployment and Production

Why and when do you need to deploy a new ML model in production?
ML projects are dynamic systems highly dependent on input data. In contrast to conventional software, most of them degrade over time or become more and more irrelevant. This problem is also known as model staleness. Some of the issues that might happen after the ML model is deployed in production are:
Data drift – when the distribution of input feature i.e., independent variables, changes drastically from what the model has seen in training.
Model or concept drift – when the properties of target variables i.e. dependent variables, change without changing the input features.
Training-serving skew – model in production, doesn't have the same performance as training.
Technical bugs and other similar things.monitoring strategy.

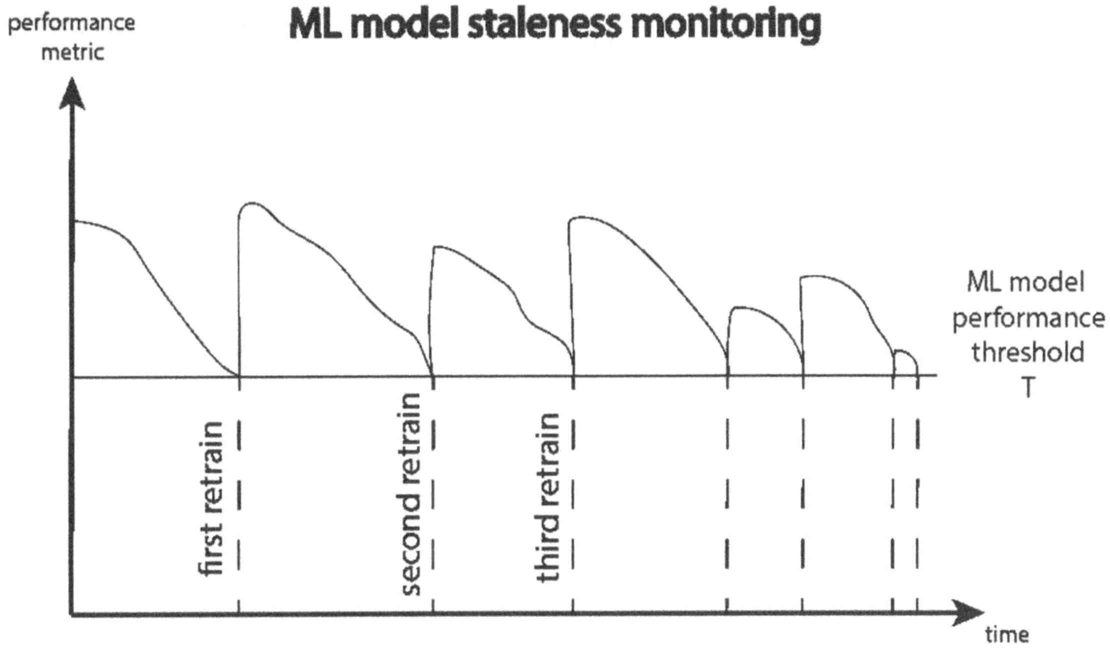

Retrain model if performance is less than T

In addition to monitoring, an antidote to model staleness is the implemented retraining strategy. The time of model retraining depends on the business use case, but in general, there are four different approaches:
•Based on time interval – retrain the model every day, week, month, or similar.
•Performance-based – retrain the model when the performance of the model goes under a predefined threshold.
•Based on data changes – trigger training after significant data shifts or after introducing new features.
•Retrain on demand – manually retrain the model for some other reason. But after all, retraining acts only as the first aid to data and concept drift problems. It's likely that after several retraining iterations, the model won't achieve the maximum performance that it had before. Also, if the retraining logic is based on model performance, the time interval between model retraining might become shorter.
When retraining becomes less and less effective, it's a sign that we need to think about a new model. And the new model needs to be prepared on time because we don't want to wait until the last minute before the model stops performing well at all.
In general, a new model in production can be deployed at any time when the development team is sure that this new model satisfies all requirements to be pushed into production. We don't necessarily need to wait until the old model in production becomes useless.
But before deploying a new model, we need to make sure that it's indeed a better model than the old one. Even if, from every angle, it seems that a new model in development is better than the old one, it wouldn't be safe to just straightforwardly deploy them.

We'll talk about some deployment techniques and best practices for deploying new models in the sections below.
How to compare ML models?
To know which model is "better" is a very challenging task. One big challenge that immediately arises is overfitting. It's the problem when the ML model is too closely fitted to the training data, which leads to poor performance on the new data. This can happen even for experienced Machine Learning practitioners since there is no clear border between an overfit and a good fit. Model evaluation metrics
Before deploying a new model in production, we need to make sure that the new model in development is better than the old one. There are a lot of different evaluation metrics that can be used for comparing models, and choosing the right one is a crucial thing. We will discuss a few popular ones here.
Classification metrics
When it comes to classification metrics, the main factors to consider while choosing metrics are:
The number of classes – binary or multiclass classification.
The number of samples per class – do we have a balanced data set?
Business use case – for example, balancing between precision and recall based on the business use case.
The most used classification metric is accuracy. For more unbalanced data sets, metrics such as F1, precision, and recall are used. All of them and many more can be calculated from the confusion matrix. For multiclass classification, similar metrics are used with slightly different formulas. In order to utilize the probability of the predicted class, metrics such as ROC and AUC are used.
Regression metrics
Regression metrics usually calculate some kind of distance between predicted and ground truth values, which is expressed as an error. The most used regression metrics are:
mean squared error (MSE)
Mean absolute error (MAE)
Root mean squared error (RMSE)
Mean absolute percentage error (MAPE)
R-squared
Recommendation system metrics
On the other hand, ranking algorithms used in recommender systems and search engines have their own set of metrics. Some of them are:

Mean Reciprocal Rank (MRR)
Hit ratio (HR)
Normalized discounted cumulative gain (NDCG)
Mean average precision (MAP)
Similarity metrics
Lastly, similarity metrics are always useful when it comes to unsupervised problems. The most common are:
Euclidean distance
Cosine similarity
Levenshtein distance
Jaccard similarity
There are some other metrics as well which are more related to computer vision projects, such as Intersection over union (IoU) and Structural similarity (SSIM), and some of them are related to NLP, such as Bilingual evaluation understudy (BLEU) and Perplexity (PP).

12.1 Model Serialization and Deserialization

Serialization is a mechanism of converting the state of an object into a byte stream. Deserialization is the reverse process where the byte stream is used to recreate the actual Java object in memory. This mechanism is used to persist the object.

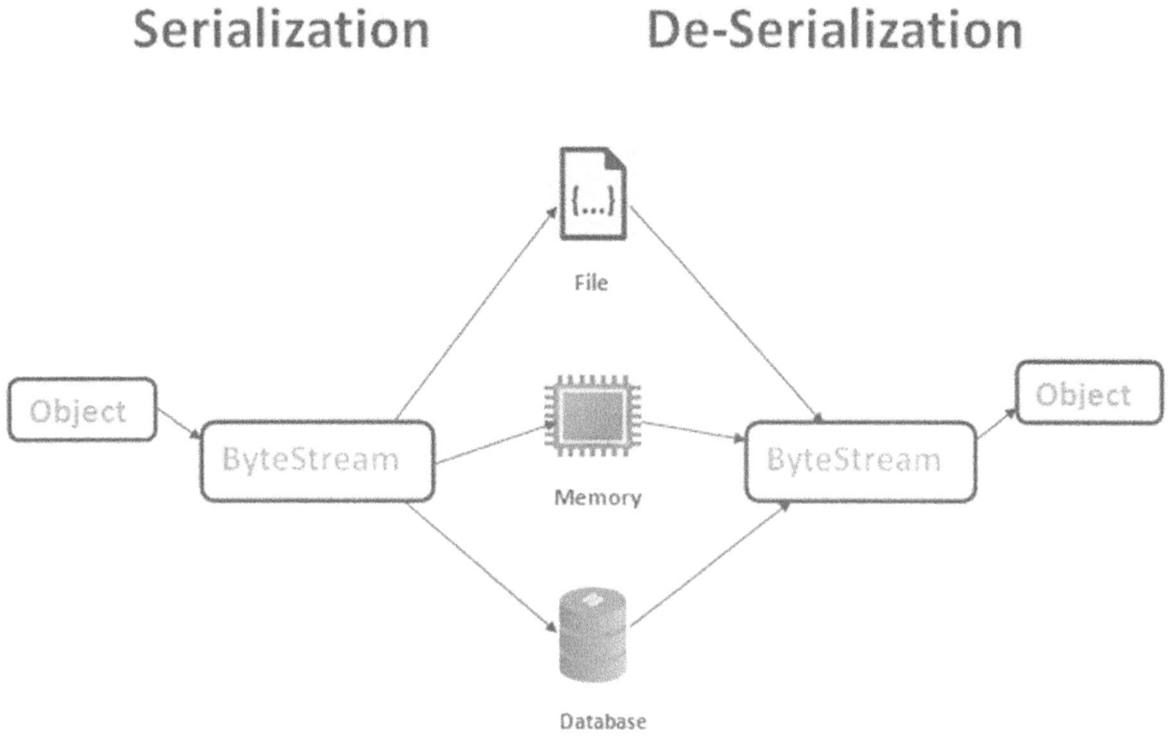

The byte stream created is platform independent. So, the object serialized on one platform can be deserialized on a different platform. To make a Java object serializable we implement the java.io.Serializable interface. The ObjectOutputStream class contains writeObject() method for serializing an Object.

public final void writeObject(Object obj)
throws IOException
The ObjectInputStream class contains readObject() method for deserializing an object.

public final Object readObject()
throws IOException,
ClassNotFoundException

Advantages of Serialization
1. To save/persist state of an object.

2. To travel an object across a network.

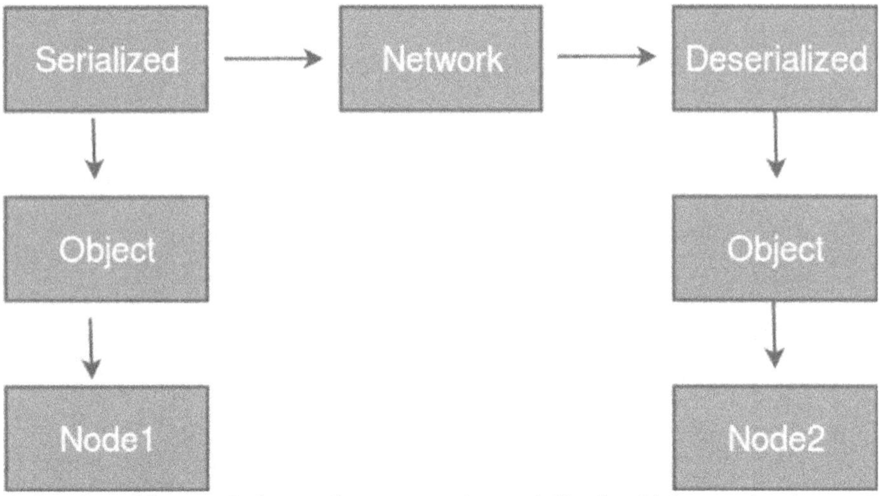

Only the objects of those classes can be serialized which are implementing java.io.Serializable interface. Serializable is a marker interface (has no data member and method). It is used to "mark" java classes so that objects of these classes may get certain capability. Other examples of marker interfaces are:- Cloneable and Remote.

Points to remember

1. If a parent class has implemented Serializable interface then child class doesn't need to implement it but vice-versa is not true.
2. Only non-static data members are saved via Serialization process.
3. Static data members and transient data members are not saved via Serialization process. So, if you don't want to save value of a non-static data member then make it transient.
4. Constructor of object is never called when an object is deserialized.
5. Associated objects must be implementing Serializable interface. Example :

```
class A implements Serializable{

// B also implements Serializable
// interface.
B ob=new B();
}
```

SerialVersionUID The Serialization runtime associates a version number with each Serializable class called a SerialVersionUID, which is used during Deserialization to verify that sender and receiver of a serialized object have loaded classes for that object which are compatible with respect to serialization. If the receiver has loaded a class for the object that has different UID than that of corresponding sender's class, the Deserialization will result in an InvalidClassException.

A Serializable class can declare its own UID explicitly by declaring a field name. It must be static, final and of type long. i.e- ANY-ACCESS-MODIFIER static final long serialVersionUID=42L; If a serializable class doesn't explicitly declare a serialVersionUID, then the serialization runtime will calculate a default one for that class based on various aspects of class, as described in Java Object Serialization Specification. However it is strongly recommended that all serializable classes explicitly declare serialVersionUID value, since its computation is highly sensitive to class details that may vary depending on compiler implementations, any change in class or using different id may affect the serialized data. It is also recommended to use private modifier for UID since it is not useful as inherited member. serialver The serialver is a tool that comes with JDK. It is used to get serialVersionUID number for Java classes.

You can run the following command to get serialVersionUID serialver [-classpath classpath] [-show] [classname…] Example 1:

```
// Java code for serialization and deserialization
// of a Java object
import java.io.*;

class Demo implements java.io.Serializable
{
public int a;
```

```
public String b;

// Default constructor
public Demo(int a, String b)
{
this.a = a;
this.b = b;
}

}

class Test
{
public static void main(String[] args)
{
Demo object = new Demo(1, "geeksforgeeks");
String filename = "file.ser";

// Serialization
try
{
//Saving of object in a file
FileOutputStream file = new FileOutputStream(filename);
ObjectOutputStream out = new ObjectOutputStream(file);

// Method for serialization of object
out.writeObject(object);

out.close();
file.close();

System.out.println("Object has been serialized");

}

catch(IOException ex)
{
System.out.println("IOException is caught");
}


Demo object1 = null;

// Deserialization
try
{
// Reading the object from a file
FileInputStream file = new FileInputStream(filename);
ObjectInputStream in = new ObjectInputStream(file);

// Method for deserialization of object
object1 = (Demo)in.readObject();

in.close();
file.close();
```

```
System.out.println("Object has been deserialized ");
System.out.println("a = " + object1.a);
System.out.println("b = " + object1.b);
}

catch(IOException ex)
{
System.out.println("IOException is caught");
}

catch(ClassNotFoundException ex)
{
System.out.println("ClassNotFoundException is caught");
}

}
}
```

Output :

```
Object has been serialized
Object has been deserialized
a = 1
b = geeksforgeeks
```

Example 2:

```
// Java code for serialization and deserialization
// of a Java object
import java.io.*;

class Emp implements Serializable {
private static final long serialversionUID =
129348938L;
transient int a;
static int b;
String name;
int age;

// Default constructor
public Emp(String name, int age, int a, int b)
{
this.name = name;
this.age = age;
this.a = a;
this.b = b;
}

}

public class SerialExample {
public static void printdata(Emp object1)
{

System.out.println("name = " + object1.name);
System.out.println("age = " + object1.age);
System.out.println("a = " + object1.a);
```

```
System.out.println("b = " + object1.b);
}

public static void main(String[] args)
{
Emp object = new Emp("ab", 20, 2, 1000);
String filename = "shubham.txt";

// Serialization
try {

// Saving of object in a file
FileOutputStream file = new FileOutputStream
(filename);
ObjectOutputStream out = new ObjectOutputStream
(file);

// Method for serialization of object
out.writeObject(object);

out.close();
file.close();

System.out.println("Object has been serialized\n"
+ "Data before Deserialization.");
printdata(object);

// value of static variable changed
object.b = 2000;
}

catch (IOException ex) {
System.out.println("IOException is caught");
}

object = null;

// Deserialization
try {

// Reading the object from a file
FileInputStream file = new FileInputStream
(filename);
ObjectInputStream in = new ObjectInputStream
(file);

// Method for deserialization of object
object = (Emp)in.readObject();

in.close();
file.close();
System.out.println("Object has been deserialized\n"
+ "Data after Deserialization.");
printdata(object);

// System.out.println("z = " + object1.z);
```

```
}

catch (IOException ex) {
System.out.println("IOException is caught");
}

catch (ClassNotFoundException ex) {
System.out.println("ClassNotFoundException" +
" is caught");
}
}
}
```

Output:

```
Object has been serialized
Data before Deserialization.
name = ab
age = 20
a = 2
b = 1000
Object has been deserialized
Data after Deserialization.
name = ab
age = 20
a = 0
b = 2000
```

Description for Output: You have seen while deserializing the object the values of a and b has changed. The reason being a was marked as transient and b was static.

In case of transient variables:- A variable defined with transient keyword is not serialized during serialization process.This variable will be initialized with default value during deserialization. (e.g: for objects it is null, for int it is 0).

In case of static Variables:- A variable defined with static keyword is not serialized during serialization process.This variable will be loaded with current value defined in the class during deserialization.

Transient Vs Final:
final variables will be participated into serialization directly by their values.
Hence declaring a final variable as transient there is no use.
//the compiler assign the value to final variable

example:

```
final int x= 10;
int y = 20;
System.out.println(x);// compiler will replace this as System.out.println(10)->10
because x is final.
System.out.println(y);//20
```

Example 3:

```
//java code for final with transient

import java.io.*;
```

```
class Dog implements Serializable{
int i=10;
transient final int j=20;
}
class GFG {
public static void main (String[] args)throws IOException,ClassNotFoundException
{
Dog d1=new Dog();
//Serialization started
System.out.println("serialization started");
FileOutputStream fos= new FileOutputStream("abc.ser");
ObjectOutputStream oos=new ObjectOutputStream(fos);
oos.writeObject(d1);
System.out.println("Serialization ended");

//Deserialization started
System.out.println("Deserialization started");
FileInputStream fis=new FileInputStream("abc.ser");
ObjectInputStream ois=new ObjectInputStream(fis);
Dog d2=(Dog) ois.readObject();
System.out.println("Deserialization ended");
System.out.println("Dog object data");
//final result
System.out.println(d2.i+"\t" +d2.j);
}
}
```

Output

```
serialization started
Serialization ended
Deserialization started
Deserialization ended
Dog object data
10   20
```

12.2 Containerization (Docker)

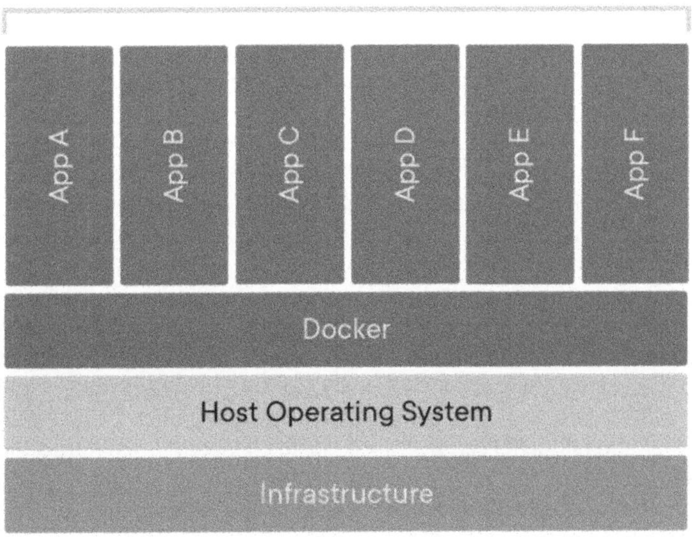

Serialization is a mechanism of converting the state of an object into a byte stream. Deserialization is the reverse process where the byte stream is used to recreate the actual Java object in memory. This mechanism is used to persist the object. serialize-deserialize-java
The byte stream created is platform independent. So, the object serialized on one platform can be deserialized on a different platform. To make a Java object serializable we implement the java.io.Serializable interface. The ObjectOutputStream class contains writeObject() method for serializing an Object.

```
public final void writeObject(Object obj)
throws IOException
```

The ObjectInputStream class contains readObject() method for deserializing an object.

```
public final Object readObject()
throws IOException,
ClassNotFoundException
```

Advantages of Serialization
To save/persist state of an object.
To travel an object across a network.
Only the objects of those classes can be serialized which are implementing java.io.Serializable interface. Serializable is a marker interface (has no data member and method). It is used to "mark" java classes so that objects of these classes may get certain capability. Other examples of marker interfaces are:- Cloneable and Remote.

Points to remember
1. If a parent class has implemented Serializable interface then child class doesn't need to implement it but vice-versa is not true. 2. Only non-static data members are saved via Serialization process.
3. Static data members and transient data members are not saved via Serialization process. So, if you don't want to save value of a non-static data member then make it transient.
4. Constructor of object is never called when an object is deserialized.
5. Associated objects must be implementing Serializable interface. Example :

```
class A implements Serializable{
// B also implements Serializable
// interface.
B ob=new B();
}
```

SerialVersionUID The Serialization runtime associates a version number with each Serializable class called a SerialVersionUID, which is used during Deserialization to verify that sender and receiver of a serialized object have loaded classes for that object which are compatible with respect to serialization. If the receiver has loaded a class for the object that has different UID than that of corresponding sender's class, the Deserialization will result in an InvalidClassException.
A Serializable class can declare its own UID explicitly by declaring a field name. It must be static, final and of type long. i.e- ANY-ACCESS-MODIFIER static final long serialVersionUID=42L; If a serializable class doesn't explicitly declare a serialVersionUID, then the serialization runtime will calculate a default one for that class based on various aspects of class, as described in Java Object Serialization Specification. However it is strongly recommended that all serializable classes explicitly declare serialVersionUID value, since its computation is highly sensitive to class details that may vary depending on compiler implementations, any change in class or using different id may affect the serialized data. It is also recommended to use private modifier for UID since it is not useful as inherited member. serialver The serialver is a tool that comes with JDK. It is used to get serialVersionUID number for Java classes.
You can run the following command to get serialVersionUID serialver [-classpath classpath] [-show] [classname…]
Package Software into Standardized Units for Development, Shipment and Deployment
A container is a standard unit of software that packages up code and all its dependencies so the application runs quickly and reliably from one computing environment to another. A Docker container image is a lightweight, standalone, executable package of software that includes everything needed to run an application: code, runtime, system tools, system libraries and settings.

Container images become containers at runtime and in the case of Docker containers – images become containers when they run on Docker Engine. Available for both Linux and Windows-based applications, containerized software will always run the same, regardless of the infrastructure. Containers isolate software from its environment and ensure that it works uniformly despite differences for instance between development and staging.
Docker containers that run on Docker Engine:
Standard: Docker created the industry standard for containers, so they could be portable anywhere
Lightweight: Containers share the machine's OS system kernel and therefore do not require an OS per application, driving higher server efficiencies and reducing server and licensing costs
Secure: Applications are safer in containers and Docker provides the strongest default isolation capabilities in the industry. Docker Containers Are Everywhere: Linux, Windows, Data center, Cloud, Serverless, etc.
Docker container technology was launched in 2013 as an open source Docker Engine.
It leveraged existing computing concepts around containers and specifically in the Linux world, primitives known as cgroups and namespaces. Docker's technology is unique because it focuses on the requirements of developers and systems operators to separate application dependencies from infrastructure.
Success in the Linux world drove a partnership with Microsoft that brought Docker containers and its functionality to Windows Server.
Technology available from Docker and its open source project, Moby has been leveraged by all major data center vendors and cloud providers. Many of these providers are leveraging Docker for their container-native IaaS offerings. Additionally, the leading open source serverless frameworks utilize Docker container technology.

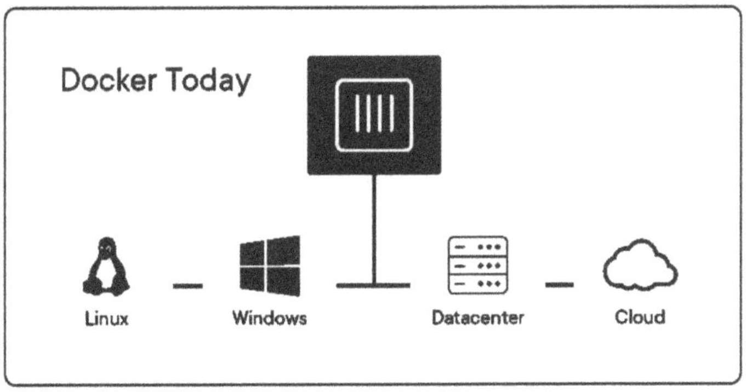

Comparing Containers and Virtual Machines
Containers and virtual machines have similar resource isolation and allocation benefits, but function differently because containers virtualize the operating system instead of hardware. Containers are more portable and efficient.

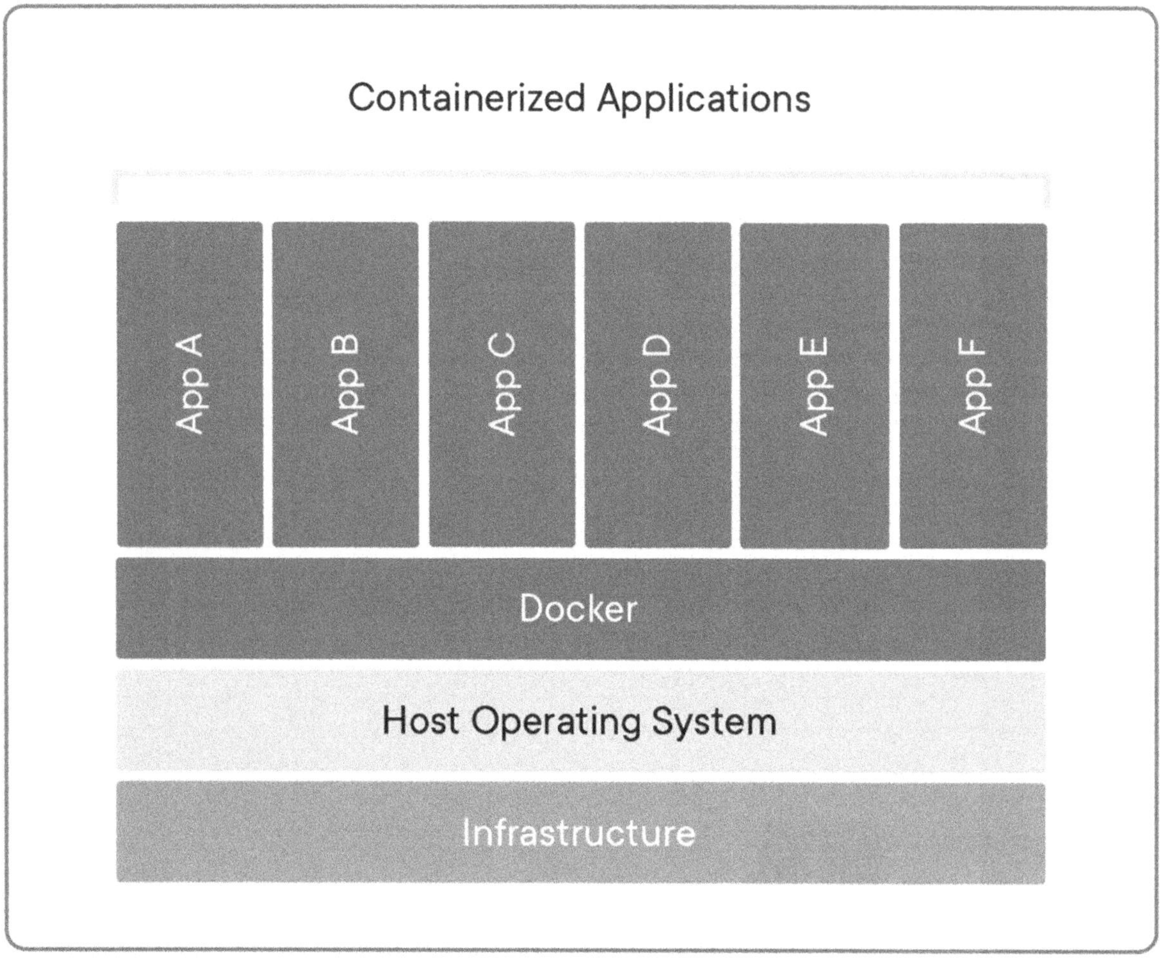

CONTAINERS

Containers are an abstraction at the app layer that packages code and dependencies together. Multiple containers can run on the same machine and share the OS kernel with other containers, each running as isolated processes in user space. Containers take up less space than VMs (container images are typically tens of MBs in size), can handle more applications and require fewer VMs and Operating systems.

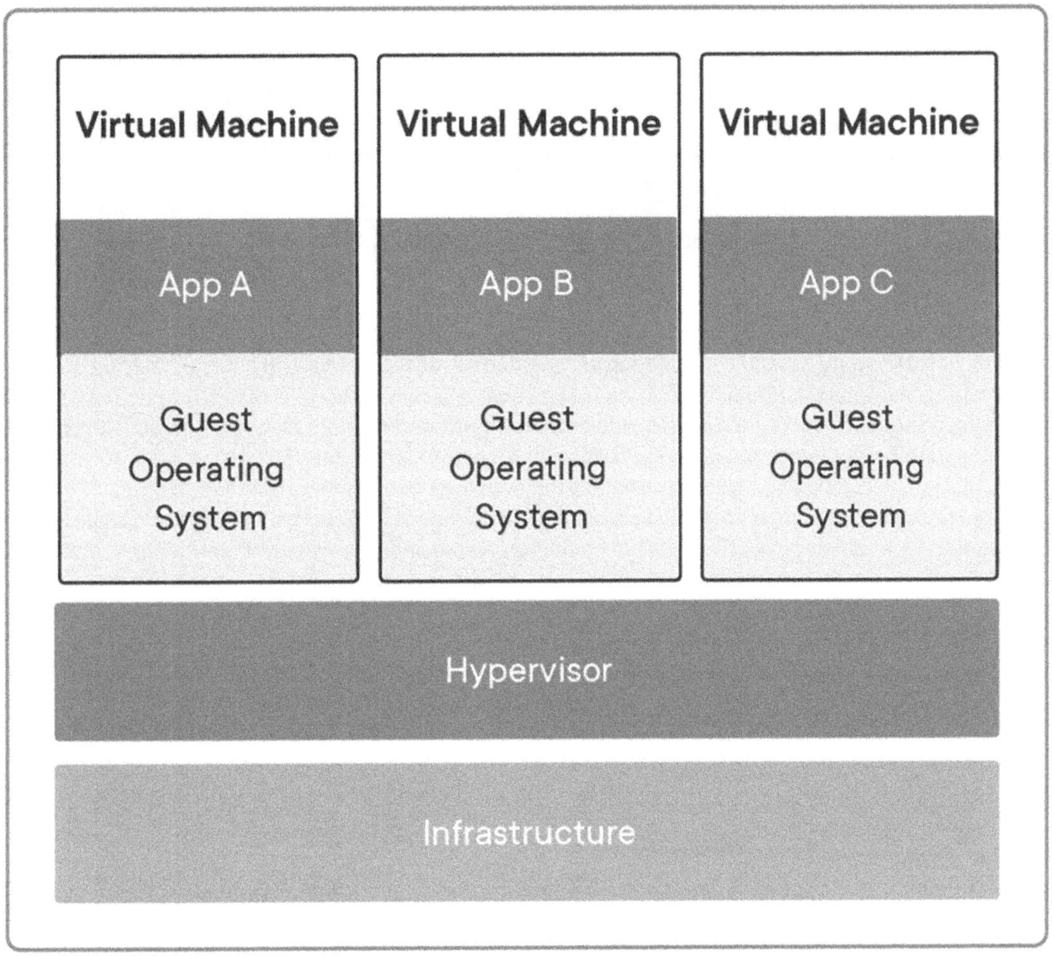

VIRTUAL MACHINES

Virtual machines (VMs) are an abstraction of physical hardware turning one server into many servers. The hypervisor allows multiple VMs to run on a single machine. Each VM includes a full copy of an operating system, the application, necessary binaries and libraries – taking up tens of GBs. VMs can also be slow to boot.

Containers and Virtual Machines Together

Containers and VMs used together provide a great deal of flexibility in deploying and managing app

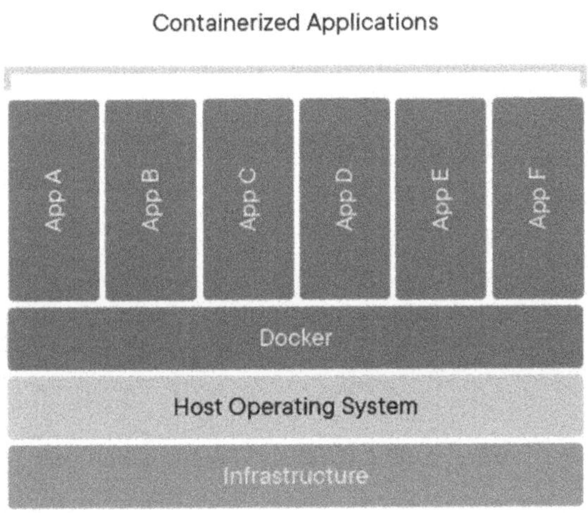

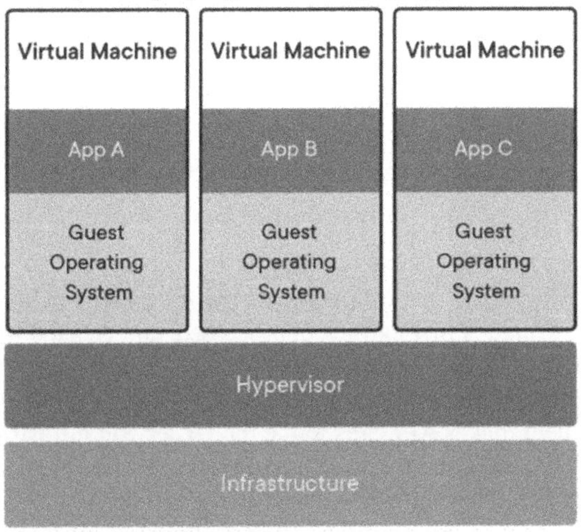

Container Standards and Industry Leadership

The launch of Docker in 2013 jump started a revolution in application development – by democratizing software containers. Docker developed a Linux container technology – one that is portable, flexible and easy to deploy. Docker open sourced libcontainer and partnered with a worldwide community of contributors to further its development. In June 2015, Docker donated the container image specification and runtime code now known as runc, to the Open Container Initiative (OCI) to help establish standardization as the container ecosystem grows and matures.
Following this evolution, Docker continues to give back with the containerd project, which Docker donated to the Cloud Native Computing Foundation (CNCF) in 2017. containerd is an industry-standard container runtime that leverages runc and was created with an emphasis on simplicity, robustness and portability. containerd is the core container runtime of the Docker Engine

12.3 Model Serving with RESTful APIs

TensorFlow Serving Architecture

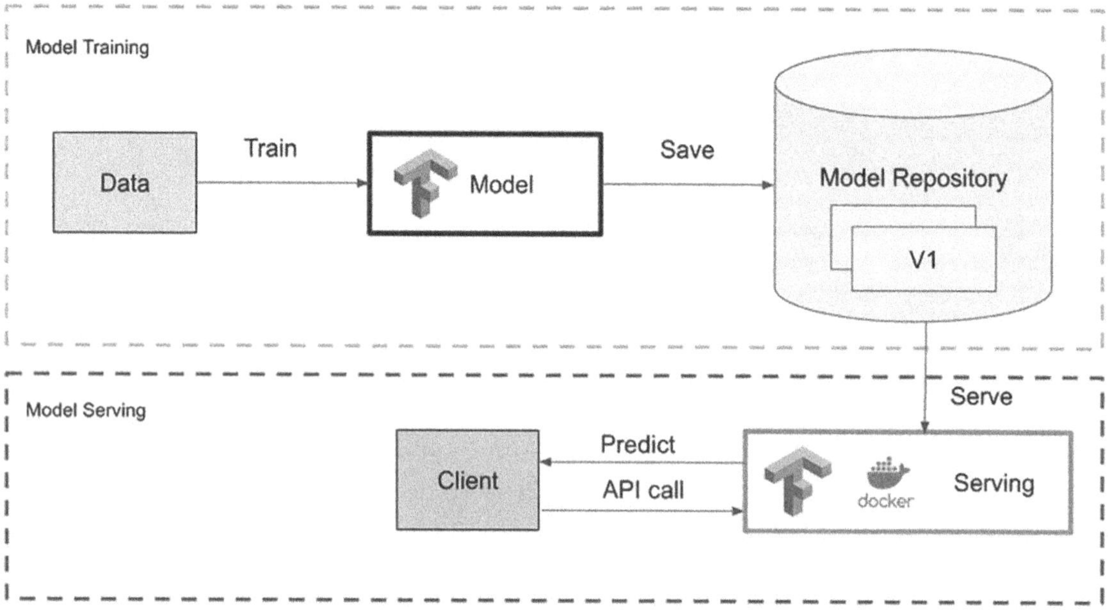

REST Architecture

REST Architecture comprises of the following stages:

The raw data is first extracted, processed, and cleaned to be able to be trained to build TensorFlow models.
These models are now saved as different versions in a model repository.
A specified version of the model is now served through Docker and TensorFlow serving.
The client makes API calls to the model serving infrastructure and receives the model prediction as output.
However, since the focus of the tutorial is on serving a model, hence we are skipping the first step of model training and directly starting with model saving and serving.
Here, we will use a pre-trained TensorFlow Imagenet (ILSVRC-2012-CLS) classification with EfficientNet V2 model from the TensorFlow hub for our image classification.
Step: 0. Prerequisites

Make sure you're using Python 3.x
Make sure you have docker installed. If not you can do it from here.
Follow a similar project structure as shown in the code repository.
Create a virtual environment and activate it
virtualenv venv
source venv/bin/activate
Install dependencies
— Create the requirements.txt file as following
— Now install the requirements as pip3 install -r requirements.txt
Pillow==9.1.1
tensorflow
tensorflow_hub
requests
numpy
6. Install TensorFlow Serving using docker
The first step to getting started with TensorFlow Serving is to pull the latest docker image from the command line as follows:
docker pull tensorflow/serving
To see if you have the right image, you can check from the terminal as docker images and it should generate the following:
List of docker images
Step 1: (Load and) Save (pre-trained) Model
In the load_model() we load the pre-trained TensorFlow ImageNet model from the TensorFlow hub.
In the save_model(), we save the model under the /models/ folder so that later our API can access it.
Step 2: Serve Model using TF Serving
Step 3: Run TF Serving through REST API
The next step is to run the container from the pulled image.
docker run --name myTFServing
-it
-v path/to/repository/img-classifier-tfx:/img-classifier-tfx
-p 9001:9001 --entrypoint /bin/bash tensorflow/serving
Explanations:
docker run --name <myContainerName> : creates a container named myTFServing (you can use any name here). The name of the container is later used for identification purposes.
-it : runs the container in interactive mode
-v path/to/repository/img-classifier-tfx:/img-classifier-tfx binds a volume from the host to a directory inside the container.
-p <host_port>:<container_port> maps the port of the host to a port of the container.
--entrypoint /bin/bash : specifies that /bin/bash executable should run when the container is started.
tensorflow/serving is the name of the image from which the container is derived.
Step 4: Serve the model (using REST end-points)
Once we have the container up and running, our next goal is to serve the model as REST endpoints.
From inside the running docker container, we start the TensorFlow Serving as follows:
cd img-classifier-tfx/

--rest_api_port=9001
--model_name=<model_name>
--model_base_path=/img-classifier-tfx/src/pred/path/to/models/
Note that we are using the same port 9001 that we had mapped earlier.
The parameters --model_name and --model_base_path denote the name under which the model has been saved and the model location respectively.
Step 5: Check if the model is working
You can check whether your model end-points are working using the following curl statements:
GET Request
curl -X GET http:/localhost:9001/v1/models/<model_name>

Your browser athttp:/localhost:9001/v1/models/<model_name> should also return the following if your model could be successfully accessed through the API.

{"model_version_status": [
{
"version": "1657646009",
"state": "AVAILABLE",
"status": {
"error_code": "OK",
"error_message": ""
}}]}

POST Request

curl -X POST http:/localhost:9001/v1/models/<model_name>:predict
-H “Content-Type: application/json”
-d @data.json

To check whether the model prediction works as expected we can send a POST request to our API. Here, we dump the data that needed to be sent as input to our end-point in a JSON file called data.json and pass it with our curl statement.

As a result, we should get a list of the predictions which need to be decoded to get the predicted class name and the prediction confidence.

Voila! If you’ve successfully reached here, you can already celebrate your first ML model serving using TF Serving! You can also define a main function, where you call the serve_rest() with an image URL as its parameter and get your predicted results !!

Our input/output

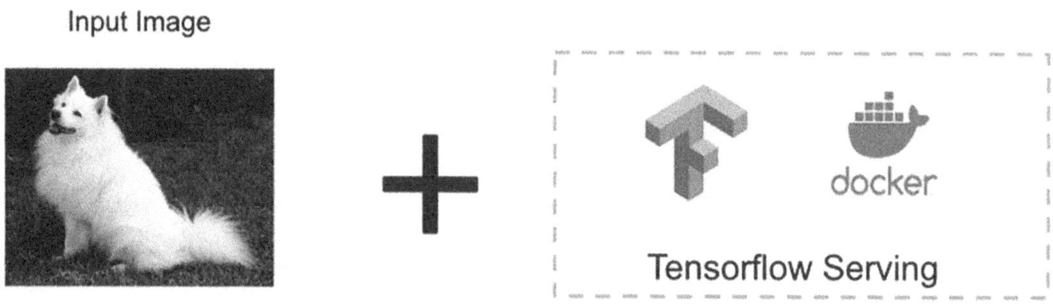


```
{'predicted_label': 'Great Pyrenees', 'probability': 0.771522045135498}
```

Handy Debugging Tips while using TF Serving with REST APIs

It is highly recommended to use TF Serving via Docker containers, owing to their easy integration abilities.

Even though TF Serving provides out-of-the-box integration with TensorFlow models, it is often not too straightforward to extend it to non-TensorFlow models.

If you’re working with larger datasets during inference, using a gRPC as your end-point could possibly be more efficient than its REST counterpart.

In case you run into path errors while loading models during the docker run stage, try replacing the paths with absolute path instead of a relative one.

In case the specified port (9001 in this case) may be unavailable or in use by other system processes, it can be easily changed to another port when running the Docker image.

Sometimes, if you try re-running the docker container, you could get container already in use error. In that case, terminate the container, remove it by docker rm <containerName> and re-run your container.

RESTful API

In addition to gRPC APIs TensorFlow ModelServer also supports RESTful APIs. This page describes these API endpoints and an end-to-end example on usage.

The request and response is a JSON object. The composition of this object depends on the request type or verb. See the API specific sections below for details.

In case of error, all APIs will return a JSON object in the response body with error as key and the error message as the value:

```
{
"error": <error message string>
}
```

Model status API

This API closely follows the ModelService.GetModelStatus gRPC API. It returns the status of a model in the ModelServer.

URL

GET http://host:port/v1/models/${MODEL_NAME}[/versions/${VERSION}|/labels/${LABEL}]

Including /versions/${VERSION} or /labels/${LABEL} is optional. If omitted status for all versions is returned in the response.

Response format

If successful, returns a JSON representation of GetModelStatusResponse protobuf.

Model Metadata API

This API closely follows the PredictionService.GetModelMetadata gRPC API. It returns the metadata of a model in the ModelServer.

URL

GET http://host:port/v1/models/${MODEL_NAME}[/versions/${VERSION}|/labels/${LABEL}]/metadata

Including /versions/${VERSION} or /labels/${LABEL} is optional. If omitted the model metadata for the latest version is returned in the response.

Response format

If successful, returns a JSON representation of GetModelMetadataResponse protobuf.

Classify and Regress API

This API closely follows the Classify and Regress methods of PredictionService gRPC API.

URL

POST

http://host:port/v1/models/${MODEL_NAME}[/versions/${VERSION}|/labels/${LABEL}]:(classify|regress)

Including /versions/${VERSION} or /labels/${LABEL} is optional. If omitted the latest version is used.

Request format

The request body for the classify and regress APIs must be a JSON object formatted as follows:

```
{
// Optional: serving signature to use.
// If unspecifed default serving signature is used.
"signature_name": <string>,
// Optional: Common context shared by all examples.
// Features that appear here MUST NOT appear in examples (below).
"context": {
"<feature_name3>": <value>|<list>
"<feature_name4>": <value>|<list>
},
// List of Example objects
"examples": [
{
// Example 1
"<feature_name1>": <value>|<list>,
"<feature_name2>": <value>|<list>,
...
},
{
// Example 2
"<feature_name1>": <value>|<list>,
"<feature_name2>": <value>|<list>,
...
}
```

```
...
]
}
```

<value> is a JSON number (whole or decimal), JSON string, or a JSON object that represents binary data (see the Encoding binary values section below for details). <list> is a list of such values. This format is similar to gRPC's ClassificationRequest and RegressionRequest protos. Both versions accept list of Example objects.

Response format

A classify request returns a JSON object in the response body, formatted as follows:

```
{
"result": [
// List of class label/score pairs for first Example (in request)
[ [<label1>, <score1>], [<label2>, <score2>], ... ],

// List of class label/score pairs for next Example (in request)
[ [<label1>, <score1>], [<label2>, <score2>], ... ],
...
]
}
```

<label> is a string (which can be an empty string "" if the model does not have a label associated with the score). <score> is a decimal (floating point) number.

The regress request returns a JSON object in the response body, formatted as follows:

```
{
// One regression value for each example in the request in the same order.
"result": [ <value1>, <value2>, <value3>, ...]
}
```

<value> is a decimal number.

Users of gRPC API will notice the similarity of this format with ClassificationResponse and RegressionResponse protos.

Predict API

This API closely follows the PredictionService.Predict gRPC API.

URL

POST http://host:port/v1/models/${MODEL_NAME}[/versions/${VERSION}|/labels/${LABEL}]:predict

Including /versions/${VERSION} or /labels/${LABEL} is optional. If omitted the latest version is used.

Request format

The request body for predict API must be JSON object formatted as follows:

```
{
// (Optional) Serving signature to use.
// If unspecifed default serving signature is used.
"signature_name": <string>,

// Input Tensors in row ("instances") or columnar ("inputs") format.
// A request can have either of them but NOT both.
"instances": <value>|<(nested)list>|<list-of-objects>
"inputs": <value>|<(nested)list>|<object>
}
```

Specifying input tensors in row format.

This format is similar to PredictRequest proto of gRPC API and the CMLE predict API. Use this format if all named input tensors have the same 0-th dimension. If they don't, use the columnar format described later below.

In the row format, inputs are keyed to instances key in the JSON request.

When there is only one named input, specify the value of instances key to be the value of the input:

```
{
```

// List of 3 scalar tensors.
"instances": ["foo", "bar", "baz"]
}

{
// List of 2 tensors each of [1, 2] shape
"instances": [[[1, 2]], [[3, 4]]]
}
Tensors are expressed naturally in nested notation since there is no need to manually flatten the list.

For multiple named inputs, each item is expected to be an object containing input name/tensor value pair, one for each named input. As an example, the following is a request with two instances, each with a set of three named input tensors:
{
"instances": [
{
"tag": "foo",
"signal": [1, 2, 3, 4, 5],
"sensor": [[1, 2], [3, 4]]
},
{
"tag": "bar",
"signal": [3, 4, 1, 2, 5]],
"sensor": [[4, 5], [6, 8]]
}
]
}
Note, each named input ("tag", "signal", "sensor") is implicitly assumed have same 0-th dimension (two in above example, as there are two objects in the instances list). If you have named inputs that have different 0-th dimension, use the columnar format described below.
Specifying input tensors in column format.
Use this format to specify your input tensors, if individual named inputs do not have the same 0-th dimension or you want a more compact representation. This format is similar to the inputs field of the gRPC Predict request.
In the columnar format, inputs are keyed to inputs key in the JSON request.
The value for inputs key can either a single input tensor or a map of input name to tensors (listed in their natural nested form). Each input can have arbitrary shape and need not share the/ same 0-th dimension (aka batch size) as required by the row format described above.
Columnar representation of the previous example is as follows:

{
"inputs": {
"tag": ["foo", "bar"],
"signal": [[1, 2, 3, 4, 5], [3, 4, 1, 2, 5]],
"sensor": [[[1, 2], [3, 4]], [[4, 5], [6, 8]]]
}
}
Note, inputs is a JSON object and not a list like instances (used in the row representation). Also, all the named inputs are specified together, as opposed to unrolling them into individual rows done in the row format described previously. This makes the representation compact (but maybe less readable).

Response format
The predict request returns a JSON object in response body.

A request in row format has response formatted as follows:

```
{
"predictions": <value>|<(nested)list>|<list-of-objects>
}
```

If the output of the model contains only one named tensor, we omit the name and predictions key maps to a list of scalar or list values. If the model outputs multiple named tensors, we output a list of objects instead, similar to the request in row-format mentioned above.

A request in columnar format has response formatted as follows:

```
{
"outputs": <value>|<(nested)list>|<object>
}
```

If the output of the model contains only one named tensor, we omit the name and outputs key maps to a list of scalar or list values. If the model outputs multiple named tensors, we output an object instead. Each key of this object corresponds to a named output tensor. The format is similar to the request in column format mentioned above.

Output of binary values

TensorFlow does not distinguish between non-binary and binary strings. All are DT_STRING type. Named tensors that have _bytes as a suffix in their name are considered to have binary values. Such values are encoded differently as described in the encoding binary values section below.

JSON mapping

The RESTful APIs support a canonical encoding in JSON, making it easier to share data between systems. For supported types, the encodings are described on a type-by-type basis in the table below. Types not listed below are implied to be unsupported.

TF Data Type	JSON Value	JSON example	Notes
DT_BOOL	true, false	true, false	
DT_STRING	string	"Hello World!"	If DT_STRING represents binary bytes (e.g. serialized image bytes or protobuf), encode these in Base64. See Encoding binary values for more info.
DT_INT8, DT_UINT8, DT_INT16, DT_INT32, DT_UINT32, DT_INT64, DT_UINT64	number	1, -10, 0	JSON value will be a decimal number.
DT_FLOAT, DT_DOUBLE	number	1.1, -10.0, 0, NaN, Infinity	JSON value will be a number or one of the special token values - NaN, Infinity, and -Infinity. See JSON conformance for more info. Exponent notation is also accepted.

Floating Point Precision

JSON has a single number data type. Thus it is possible to provide a value for an input that results in a loss of precision. For instance, if the input x is a float data type, and the input {"x": 1435774380} is sent to the model running on hardware based on the IEEE 754 floating point standard (e.g. Intel or AMD), then the value will be silently converted by the underyling hardware to 1435774336 since 1435774380 cannot be exactly represented in a 32-bit floating point number. Typically, the inputs to serving should be the same distribution as training, so this generally won't be problematic because the same conversions happened at training time. However, in case full precision is needed, be sure to use an underlying data type in your model that can handle the desired precision and/or consider client-side checking.

Encoding binary values

JSON uses UTF-8 encoding. If you have input feature or tensor values that need to be binary (like image bytes), you must Base64 encode the data and encapsulate it in a JSON object having b64 as the key as follows:

```
{ "b64": <base64 encoded string> }
```

You can specify this object as a value for an input feature or tensor. The same format is used to encode output response as well.

A classification request with image (binary data) and caption features is shown below:

```
{
"signature_name": "classify_objects",
"examples": [
{
"image": { "b64": "aW1hZ2UgYnl0ZXM=" },
"caption": "seaside"
},
{
"image": { "b64": "YXdlc29tZSBpbWFnZSBieXRlcw==" },
"caption": "mountains"
}
]
}
```

JSON conformance

Many feature or tensor values are floating point numbers. Apart from finite values (e.g. 3.14, 1.0 etc.) these can have NaN and non-finite (Infinity and -Infinity) values. Unfortunately the JSON specification (RFC 7159) does NOT recognize these values (though the JavaScript specification does).

The REST API described on this page allows request/response JSON objects to have such values. This implies that requests like the following one are valid:

```
{
"example": [
{
"sensor_readings": [ 1.0, -3.14, Nan, Infinity ]
}
]
}
```

A (strict) standards compliant JSON parser will reject this with a parse error (due to NaN and Infinity tokens mixed with actual numbers). To correctly handle requests/responses in your code, use a JSON parser that supports these tokens.

NaN, Infinity, -Infinity tokens are recognized by proto3, Python JSON module and JavaScript language.

Example

We can use the toy half_plus_three model to see REST APIs in action.

Start ModelServer with the REST API endpoint

Download the half_plus_three model from git repository:

```
$ mkdir -p /tmp/tfserving
$ cd /tmp/tfserving
$ git clone --depth=1 https://github.com/tensorflow/serving
```

We will use Docker to run the ModelServer. If you want to install ModelServer natively on your system, follow setup instructions to install instead, and start the ModelServer with --rest_api_port option to export REST API endpoint (this is not needed when using Docker).

```
$ cd /tmp/tfserving
$ docker pull tensorflow/serving:latest
$ docker run --rm -p 8501:8501 \
--mount type=bind,source=$(pwd),target=$(pwd) \
-e MODEL_BASE_PATH=$(pwd)/serving/tensorflow_serving/servables/tensorflow/testdata \
```

```
-e MODEL_NAME=saved_model_half_plus_three -t tensorflow/serving:latest
...
.... Exporting HTTP/REST API at:localhost:8501 ...
```

Make REST API calls to ModelServer
In a different terminal, use the curl tool to make REST API calls.

Get status of the model as follows:

```
$ curl http://localhost:8501/v1/models/saved_model_half_plus_three
{
"model_version_status": [
{
"version": "123",
"state": "AVAILABLE",
"status": {
"error_code": "OK",
"error_message": ""
}
}
]
}
```

A predict call would look as follows:

```
$ curl -d '{"instances": [1.0,2.0,5.0]}' -X POST http://localhost:8501/v1/models/saved_model_half_plus_three:predict
{
"predictions": [3.5, 4.0, 5.5]
}
```

And a regress call looks as follows:

```
$ curl -d '{"signature_name": "tensorflow/serving/regress", "examples": [{"x": 1.0}, {"x": 2.0}]}' \
-X POST http://localhost:8501/v1/models/saved_model_half_plus_three:regress
{
"results": [3.5, 4.0]
}
```

Note, regress is available on a non-default signature name and must be specified explicitly. An incorrect request URL or body returns an HTTP error status.

```
$ curl -i -d '{"instances": [1.0,5.0]}' -X POST http://localhost:8501/v1/models/half:predict
HTTP/1.1 404 Not Found
Content-Type: application/json
Date: Wed, 06 Jun 2018 23:20:12 GMT
Content-Length: 65

{ "error": "Servable not found for request: Latest(half)" }
$
```

12.4 Continuous Integration and Continuous Deployment (CI/CD)

Continuous integration (CI) and continuous delivery (CD), also known as CI/CD, embodies a culture, operating principles, and a set of practices that application development teams use to deliver code changes more frequently and reliably.

CI/CD is a best practice for devops teams. It is also a best practice in agile methodology. By automating integration and delivery, CI/CD lets software development teams focus on meeting business requirements while ensuring code quality and software security.

Continuous integration is a coding philosophy and set of practices that drive development teams to frequently implement small code changes and check them in to a version control repository. Most modern applications require developing code using a variety of platforms and tools, so teams need a consistent mechanism to integrate and validate changes. Continuous integration establishes an automated way to build, package, and test their applications. Having a consistent integration process encourages developers to commit code changes more frequently, which leads to better collaboration and code quality.

Continuous delivery picks up where continuous integration ends, and automates application delivery to selected environments, including production, development, and testing environments. Continuous delivery is an automated way to push code changes to these environments.

Automating the CI/CD pipeline

CI/CD tools help store the environment-specific parameters that must be packaged with each delivery. CI/CD automation then makes any necessary service calls to web servers, databases, and other services that need restarting. It can also execute other procedures following deployment.

Because the objective is to deliver quality code and applications, CI/CD also requires continuous testing. In continuous testing, a set of automated regression, performance, and other tests are executed in the CI/CD pipeline.

A mature devops team with a robust CI/CD pipeline can also implement continuous deployment, where application changes run through the CI/CD pipeline and passing builds are deployed directly to the production environment. Some teams practicing continuous deployment elect to deploy daily or even hourly to production, though continuous deployment isn't optimal for every business application.

Nominations are open for the 2024 Best Places to Work in IT

Organizations that implement a CI/CD pipeline often have several devops best practices in place, including microservices development, serverless architecture, continuous testing, infrastructure as code, and deployment containers. Each of these practices improves process automation and increases the robustness of cloud computing environments. Together, these practices provide a strong foundation to support continuous deployment.

How continuous integration improves collaboration and code quality

Continuous integration is a development philosophy backed by process mechanics and automation. When practicing continuous integration, developers commit their code into the version control repository frequently; most teams have a standard of committing code at least daily. The rationale is that it's easier to identify defects and other software quality issues on smaller code differentials than on larger ones developed over an extensive period. In addition, when developers work on shorter commit cycles, it is less likely that multiple developers will edit the same code and require a merge when committing.

Teams implementing continuous integration often start with the version control configuration and practice definitions. Although checking in code is done frequently, agile teams develop features and fixes on shorter and longer timeframes. Development teams practicing continuous integration use different techniques to control what features and code are ready for production.

Many teams use feature flags, a configuration mechanism to turn features and code on or off at runtime. Features that are still under development are wrapped with feature flags in the code, deployed with the main branch to production, and turned off until they are ready to be used. In recent research, devops teams using feature flags had a ninefold increase in development frequency. Feature flagging tools such as CloudBees, Optimizely Rollouts, and LaunchDarkly integrate with CI/CD tools to support feature-level configurations.

Automated builds

In an automated build process, all the software, database, and other components are packaged together. For example, if you were developing a Java application, continuous integration would package all the static web server files such as HTML, CSS, and JavaScript along with the Java application and any database scripts.

Continuous integration not only packages all the software and database components, but the automation will also execute unit tests and other types of tests. Testing provides vital feedback to developers that their code changes didn't break anything.

Most CI/CD tools let developers kick off builds on demand, triggered by code commits in the version control repository, or on a defined schedule. Teams need to determine the build schedule that works best for the size of the team, the number of daily commits expected, and other application considerations. A best practice is to ensure that commits and builds are fast; otherwise, these processes may impede teams trying to code quickly and commit frequently.

Continuous testing and security automation

Automated testing frameworks help quality assurance engineers define, execute, and automate various types of tests that can help development teams know whether a software build passes or fails. They include functionality tests developed at the end of every sprint and aggregated into a regression test for the entire application. The regression test informs the team whether a code change failed one or more of the tests developed across the functional areas of the application where there is test coverage.

A best practice is to enable and require developers to run all or a subset of regression tests in their local environments. This step ensures developers only commit code to version control after code changes have passed regression tests.

Regression tests are just the beginning, however. Devops teams also automate performance, API, browser, and device testing. Today, teams can also embed static code analysis and security testing in the CI/CD pipeline for shift-left testing. Agile teams can also test interactions with third-party APIs, SaaS, and other systems outside of their control using service virtualization. The key is being able to trigger these tests through the command line, a webhook, or a web service, and get a success or failure response.

Continuous testing implies that the CI/CD pipeline integrates test automation. Some unit and functionality tests will flag issues before or during the continuous integration process. Tests that require a full delivery environment, such as performance and security testing, are often integrated into continuous delivery and done after a build is delivered to its target environments.

Stages in the continuous delivery pipeline

Continuous delivery is the automation that pushes applications to one or more delivery environments. Development teams typically have several environments to stage application changes for testing and review. A devops engineer uses a CI/CD tool such as Jenkins, CircleCI, AWS CodeBuild, Azure DevOps, Atlassian Bamboo, Argo CD, Buddy, Drone, or Travis CI to automate the steps and provide reporting.

For example, Jenkins users define their pipelines in a Jenkinsfile that describes different stages such as build, test, and deploy. Environment variables, options, secret keys, certifications, and other parameters are declared in the file and then referenced in stages. The post section handles error conditions and notifications.

A typical continuous delivery pipeline has build, test, and deploy stages. The following activities could be included at different stages:

Pulling code from version control and executing a build.

Enabling stage gates for automated security, quality, and compliance checks and supporting approvals when required.

Executing any required infrastructure steps automated as code to stand up or tear down cloud infrastructure.

Moving code to the target computing environment.

Managing environment variables and configuring them for the target environment.

Pushing application components to their appropriate services, such as web servers, APIs, and database services.

Executing any steps required to restart services or call service endpoints needed for new code pushes.

Executing continuous tests and rollback environments if tests fail.

Providing log data and alerts on the state of the delivery.

Updating configuration management databases and sending alerts to IT service management workflows on completed deployments.

A more sophisticated continuous delivery pipeline might have additional steps such as synchronizing data, archiving information resources, or patching applications and libraries.

Teams using continuous deployment to deliver to production may use different cutover practices to minimize downtime and manage deployment risks. One option is configuring canary deployments with an orchestrated shift of traffic usage from the older software version to the newer one.

CI/CD tools and plugins

CI/CD tools typically support a marketplace of plugins. For example, Jenkins lists more than 1,800 plugins that support integration with third-party platforms, user interface, administration, source code management, and build management.

Once the development team has selected a CI/CD tool, it must ensure that all environment variables are configured outside the application. CI/CD tools allow development teams to set these variables, mask variables such as passwords and account keys, and configure them at the time of deployment for the target environment.

Continuous delivery tools also provide dashboard and reporting functions, which are enhanced when devops teams implement observable CI/CD pipelines. Developers are alerted if a build or delivery fails. The dashboard and reporting functions integrate with version control and agile tools to help developers determine what code changes and user stories made up the build.

Measuring CI/CD success with devops KPIs

The impact of implementing CI/CD pipelines can be measured as a devops key performance indicator (KPI). Indicators such as deployment frequency, change lead time, and incident meantime to recovery (MTTR) are often improved by

implementing CI/CD with continuous testing. However, CI/CD is just one process that can drive these improvements, and there are other prerequisites to improving deployment frequencies.
CI/CD with Kubernetes and serverless architectures
Many teams operating CI/CD pipelines in cloud environments also use containers such as Docker and orchestration systems such as Kubernetes. Containers allow for packaging and shipping applications in a standard, portable way. Containers make it easy to scale up or tear down environments with variable workloads.
There are many approaches to using containers, infrastructure as code (IaC), and CI/CD pipelines together. Free tutorials such as Kubernetes with Jenkins or Kubernetes with Azure DevOps can help you explore your options.
Another option is to use a serverless architecture to deploy and scale your applications. In a serverless environment, the cloud service provider manages the infrastructure, and the application consumes resources as needed based on its configuration. On AWS, for example, serverless applications run as Lambda functions and deployments can be integrated into a Jenkins CI/CD pipeline with a plugin. Azure serverless and GPS serverless computing are similar services.
Next generation CI/CD applications
You may be wondering about some of the more advanced areas for CI/CD pipeline development and management. Here are a few notable ones:
MLOps is the IaC and CI/CD of Machine Learning models and supports infrastructure, integration, and deployment to training and production environments.
Synthetic data generation techniques use Machine Learning to create data sets used by test automation engineers to test APIs and by data scientists to train models.
AIOps platforms, or Machine Learning and automation in IT Ops, aggregate observability data and correlates alerts from multiple sources into incidents. Automations can trigger CI/CD deployments and rollbacks as required.
Teams working on microservices create reusable pipelines to support and scale development and review options on Azure and AWS.
Engineers use CI/CD in other areas, including network configuration, embedded systems, database changes, IoT, and AR/VR.

Exercise

True Or False

1.Model serialization is the process of converting a trained model into a format that can be easily saved and loaded.
2.Deserialization is the process of deploying a model into a production environment.
3.Docker is a platform that allows you to create, deploy, and run applications in isolated containers.
4.Containerization helps to ensure consistent and reliable deployment of applications across different environments.
5.Docker images include both the application code and the entire operating system.
6.RESTful APIs provide a standardized way for different software components to communicate over the internet.
7.Model serving with RESTful APIs enables real-time predictions by exposing the model through HTTP endpoints.
8.CI/CD stands for Computer Integration and Continuous Deployment.
9.Continuous Integration (CI) is the practice of frequently merging code changes into a shared repository.
10.Continuous Deployment (CD) is the process of automatically deploying code changes to production.
11.CI/CD pipelines help streamline the development, testing, and deployment process.
12.Kubernetes is a container orchestration platform that automates the deployment, scaling, and management of containerized applications.
13.In model serialization, the model's architecture, weights, and training configuration are typically saved.
14.Model deserialization involves loading a saved model and making predictions without any additional steps.
15.Docker containers provide full virtualization, allowing applications to run with minimal performance overhead.
16.RESTful APIs are only used for data retrieval and cannot be used for sending data to the server.
17.Swagger is a tool used for containerization of Machine Learning models.
18.Docker images can be easily moved and executed across different environments without modification.
19.Model serving with RESTful APIs is suitable only for batch processing, not real-time applications.
20.Jenkins is a popular tool used for implementing CI/CD pipelines.
21.Kubernetes can automatically scale the number of container instances based on demand.
22.Model serialization is not necessary when deploying Machine Learning models in production.
23.Docker containers can run on Windows and macOS, but not on Linux.

24.Model deserialization is the process of converting a model's predictions into a readable format.
25.CI/CD pipelines help to reduce manual errors and improve software quality.
26.Kubernetes provides built-in monitoring and logging for deployed applications.
27.Model serving APIs allow you to perform only one type of operation on the model, such as prediction.
28.Docker containers are typically larger in size compared to virtual machines.

ANSWERS- True, False, True, True, False, True, True, False, True, True, True, True, True, True, False, False, False, True, False, True, True, False, False, False, True, True, False, False

MCQ

1.What is the purpose of model serialization in the context of deployment?
a) Capturing real-time data for training
b) Storing the model's architecture in a file
c) Converting the model into a binary format for storage
d) Enhancing the interpretability of the model
Answer: c

2.Which format is commonly used for serializing Machine Learning models?
a) JSON
b) XML
c) CSV
d) Pickle
Answer: d

3.What is the main advantage of containerization, such as Docker, in model deployment?
a) It allows direct execution of Python code.
b) It simplifies the model training process.
c) It ensures compatibility across different environments.
d) It automatically generates APIs for model serving.
Answer: c

4.Which component allows Docker containers to share resources while remaining isolated?
a) Hypervisor
b) Virtual Private Network (VPN)
c) Bridge network
d) Container runtime
Answer: a

5.What does RESTful stand for in the context of model serving?
a) Responsive State Transfer for Effective Loading
b) Representational State Transfer with Exceptional Transfer
c) Remote Execution of Stateful Transactions
d) Representational State Transfer
Answer: d

6.What HTTP methods are typically used in RESTful APIs for model serving?
a) GET and POST
b) PUT and DELETE
c) PATCH and HEAD
d) CONNECT and OPTIONS
Answer: a

7.What is the main goal of Continuous Integration (CI) in model deployment?
a) Ensuring the model always performs at 100% accuracy
b) Automatically integrating new code changes into the main codebase
c) Deploying the model to production servers without manual intervention
d) Generating comprehensive documentation for the model
Answer: b

Short Question And Answers

Q1.What is model serialization?
Q2.Why is model deserialization important?
Q3.What are some common serialization formats for Machine Learning models?
Q4.What is Docker?
Q5.Why is Docker useful for model deployment?
Q6.What is a Docker image?
Q7.What is a RESTful API?
Q8.How can Machine Learning models be served using RESTful APIs?
Q9.What are the advantages of using RESTful APIs for model deployment?
Q10.What is Continuous Integration (CI)?
Q11.What is Continuous Deployment (CD)?
Q12.How does CI/CD benefit model deployment?
Q13.What are some popular CI/CD tools?
Jenkins, Travis CI, CircleCI, and GitLab CI/CD are some popular tools for implementing CI/CD pipelines.
Q14.How can Docker be integrated into a CI/CD pipeline for model deployment?
Q15.Explain the process of deploying a serialized Machine Learning model using Docker and RESTful API.
Q16.Why is it important to ensure consistency between the training environment and the production environment in model deployment?
Q17.How can you monitor and manage a Machine Learning model deployed through a RESTful API?
Q18.What role does version control play in model deployment and production?
Q19.Describe an example scenario where CI/CD is beneficial for deploying and updating a Machine Learning model.
Q20.What security considerations should be taken into account when deploying Machine Learning models using Docker and RESTful APIs?

Online Resources
Online Exam Papers
True/False Exam

Link https://forms.gle/ag2vmeDxGqkthiVS6

QR Code

YouTube Video Playlist Link
Chapter 12
Link
https://www.youtube.com/playlist?list=PLzlh_31VWEFqlWc2eJSJRwMCa-T4LBidQ
QR Code

Chapter 13: Ethical and Fair Machine Learning

Ethical and fair Machine Learning refers to the development and deployment of Machine Learning models and algorithms that consider and mitigate potential biases, respect privacy, promote transparency, and prioritize the well-being of individuals and communities impacted by these technologies. Ensuring ethics and fairness in Machine Learning is crucial to prevent harmful consequences, discrimination, and inequitable outcomes.

Here are some key principles and practices for ethical and fair Machine Learning:

1. Data Bias Mitigation: Machine Learning models often learn from historical data, which can contain biases that perpetuate societal inequalities. To address this, it's essential to identify and mitigate biases in the training data to prevent biased decision-making.

2. Transparency and Explainability: Machine Learning models should be interpretable and provide explanations for their predictions. This helps build trust in the technology and enables humans to understand and challenge the outcomes when necessary.

3. Privacy Protection: Machine Learning systems must respect the privacy of individuals and adhere to data protection laws and regulations. Techniques like differential privacy can be used to ensure data anonymity.

4. Inclusive Design: Developing Machine Learning systems with diverse teams that include individuals from different backgrounds and experiences can help in identifying and addressing potential biases and ensuring the technology meets the needs of a broader population.

5. Fairness-aware Algorithms: Researchers and developers should focus on designing algorithms that explicitly consider fairness criteria and avoid reinforcing existing biases.

6. Ongoing Monitoring and Evaluation: Machine Learning models should be continuously monitored in real-world settings to identify and rectify any emerging biases or ethical concerns.

7. Consent and Autonomy: Users should have control over their data and the ability to give informed consent for the use of their information in Machine Learning systems.

8. Responsible AI Use: Developers and organizations should be mindful of the contexts in which Machine Learning models are deployed and consider the potential impact on various stakeholders.

9. Accountability and Regulation: There should be clear accountability for the design, development, and deployment of Machine Learning systems. Policymakers and regulatory bodies play a critical role in setting guidelines and enforcing ethical practices.

10. Social and Ethical Impact Assessments: Organizations should conduct impact assessments to identify and address potential ethical challenges before deploying Machine Learning systems.

By adhering to these principles and practices, developers can build more ethical and fair Machine Learning systems that benefit society as a whole and mitigate potential risks and harms. Additionally, it's essential to involve ethicists, sociologists, and other domain experts in the development process to gain diverse perspectives and insights.

13.1 Bias and Fairness in ML

Bias and fairness in Machine Learning are critical issues that arise due to various factors, including biased training data, algorithmic design, and societal influences. Let's explore these concepts further:

1. Bias in Machine Learning:

- **Data Bias:** Bias in Machine Learning often originates from biased training data, which may reflect historical discrimination or social inequalities. If the training data is not representative or contains unfair patterns, the model may perpetuate these biases in its predictions.

- Algorithmic Bias: Bias can also be introduced by the design of Machine Learning algorithms. Certain algorithms may inherently favor or penalize certain groups, leading to unfair outcomes.

- Societal Bias: Bias can be a reflection of societal stereotypes and prejudices. Machine Learning algorithms may learn and amplify these biases if not properly addressed.

2. Fairness in Machine Learning:
- Fairness: In the context of Machine Learning, fairness refers to the absence of discrimination or unjust treatment in the decisions made by the model.

- Fairness Criteria: There are different definitions of fairness, such as statistical parity, equal opportunity, and individual fairness, which can be used to measure and enforce fairness in Machine Learning models.

- Fairness-aware Algorithms: Researchers and developers work on designing algorithms that explicitly consider fairness criteria to avoid biased decision-making.

3. Types of Fairness:
- Group Fairness: Group fairness aims to ensure fairness for specific groups, such as gender, race, or age. It ensures that predictions do not disproportionately benefit or harm any particular group.

- Individual Fairness: Individual fairness focuses on treating similar individuals similarly. It means that similar individuals should receive similar predictions from the model.

- Intersectional Fairness: Intersectional fairness considers the overlapping effects of multiple protected characteristics (e.g., race and gender) to avoid compounding biases.

4. Challenges:
- Trade-offs: Ensuring fairness often involves trade-offs with other desirable properties, such as accuracy. Striking the right balance is challenging.

- Data Collection: Obtaining representative and unbiased data can be difficult, especially for underrepresented groups.

- Interpretablility: Fairness can become more complex when using complex and black-box models, as it may be challenging to explain how the model arrived at its decisions.

5. Mitigation Techniques:
- Pre-processing: Techniques like data augmentation, re-weighting, and sampling can be used to reduce bias in the training data.

- In-processing: Modifying the learning process to include fairness constraints or adjusting the model's outputs to satisfy fairness criteria.

- Post-processing: Adjusting the model's outputs after training to ensure fairness while maintaining accuracy to some extent.

- Ensuring fairness in Machine Learning is an ongoing area of research, and it requires collaboration between technologists, ethicists, policymakers, and affected communities to address the complex challenges and create more equitable AI systems.

13.2 Privacy and Data Protection

Privacy and data protection are crucial aspects when dealing with personal information in the digital age. They involve safeguarding individuals' data, ensuring its confidentiality, integrity, and accessibility only to authorized parties. Here's a breakdown of these concepts:
1. Privacy: Privacy refers to the right of individuals to control their personal information and to decide how, when, and to what extent that information is shared with others. Privacy is essential in maintaining personal autonomy, protecting against identity theft, ensuring confidentiality, and fostering trust in digital systems.

2. Data Protection: Data protection refers to the practices, policies, and legal frameworks designed to safeguard personal data from unauthorized access, use, disclosure, alteration, or destruction. It involves a comprehensive approach to handling personal data responsibly and ethically.

Key Principles of Data Protection:
Consent: Individuals should give informed and unambiguous consent for their data to be collected, processed, and used for specific purposes.

1. Purpose Limitation: Data should be collected for specified, explicit, and legitimate purposes and not used for unrelated or incompatible reasons.

2. Data Minimization: Only the minimum amount of personal data necessary for the intended purpose should be collected and processed.

3. Accuracy: Organizations should ensure that the data they hold is accurate, up-to-date, and relevant.

Storage Limitation: Personal data should be retained only for as long as necessary for the specified purposes.

1. Integrity and Confidentiality: Organizations should take appropriate security measures to protect personal data from unauthorized access, alteration, or destruction.

2. Transparency: Individuals have the right to know how their data is being processed and used.

3. Accountability: Organizations are responsible for complying with data protection laws and demonstrating their adherence to privacy principles.

4. Data Protection Laws and Regulations:

Many countries and regions have established data protection laws and regulations to ensure the responsible handling of personal data. Some prominent examples include:

1. General Data Protection Regulation (GDPR): Enforced in the European Union, GDPR sets stringent rules for data protection, privacy, and consent.

California Consumer Privacy Act (CCPA): Enacted in California, USA, CCPA gives California residents control over their personal information.

Personal Information Protection and Electronic Documents Act (PIPEDA): In Canada, PIPEDA governs the collection, use, and disclosure of personal information in the private sector.

Health Insurance Portability and Accountability Act (HIPAA): In the United States, HIPAA safeguards health-related data.

Responsible Data Handling:

Organizations and individuals should adopt responsible data handling practices, including:

Implementing strong security measures to protect data from breaches and unauthorized access.

Regularly updating privacy policies to align with current practices and regulations.

Providing clear and accessible information to users about data collection, processing, and usage.

Seeking explicit consent when collecting and using personal data.

Using anonymization and aggregation techniques to minimize privacy risks when possible.

By respecting privacy and adhering to data protection principles, we can build trust, foster responsible data-driven innovation, and protect individuals' rights in the digital ecosystem.

13.3 Explainable AI (XAI)

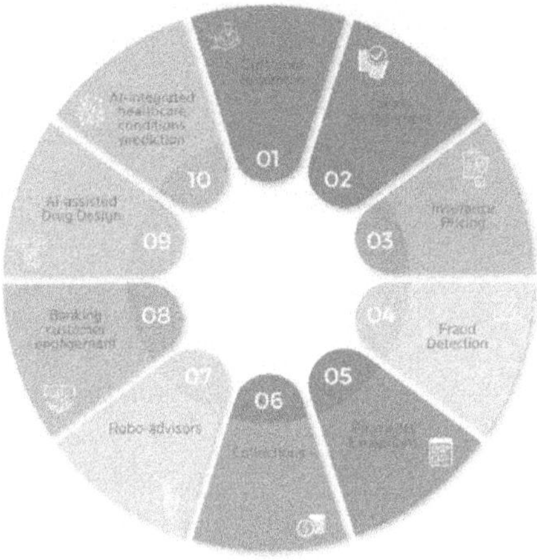

Explainable Artificial Intelligence (XAI) refers to the ability of AI systems to provide understandable and transparent explanations for their decisions and actions. The lack of interpretability in AI models has been a significant concern, especially in critical applications like healthcare, finance, and autonomous systems, where the consequences of AI decisions can have significant real-world impacts.

Traditional Machine Learning models, especially deep learning algorithms, are often considered black-box models, meaning they can produce accurate predictions, but it is challenging to understand how they arrive at those decisions. This lack of transparency can raise ethical, legal, and trust issues, as users and stakeholders may be reluctant to rely on AI systems without understanding the reasoning behind their decisions.

Explainable AI aims to address these challenges by providing human-understandable explanations for AI model outputs.

Some key aspects of XAI include:

1. Interpretability: XAI techniques aim to make AI models more interpretable by revealing the underlying reasoning, features, or patterns that led to a particular prediction. This could involve highlighting relevant data points, features, or connections in the model.

2. Model-specific and Post-hoc Techniques: XAI methods can be model-specific, designed to make inherently interpretable models, or post-hoc, applied to black-box models to provide explanations afterward.

3. Local vs. Global Explanations: Local explanations focus on explaining individual predictions, while global explanations aim to provide insights into the model's behavior as a whole.

4. Trade-offs: There's often a trade-off between model complexity and accuracy and the level of interpretability. Simplifying models for better explanations may result in a slight reduction in performance.

5. User Trust: Explainable AI can enhance user trust by increasing transparency and enabling users to validate the model's decisions, especially in high-stakes applications.

6. Fairness and Bias: XAI can help identify and address biases in AI models, making it easier to understand if the model is discriminating against certain groups.

Legal and Regulatory Compliance: In certain domains, such as healthcare and finance, regulations may require AI systems to be explainable to ensure accountability and compliance.

Some common techniques used in Explainable AI include:

1. Feature Visualization: Showing how different input features influence the model's output, often through visualizations.

2. LIME (Local Interpretable Model-agnostic Explanations): Creating interpretable local approximations of complex models to explain specific predictions.

3. SHAP (SHapley Additive exPlanations): A game-theoretic approach that assigns contributions to each feature in a prediction, considering all possible combinations.

4. Attention Mechanisms: Highlighting specific parts of input data that the model attended to during the decision-making process.

5. Rule-based Models: Using interpretable rule sets or decision trees to replace black-box models.

As the field of Explainable AI continues to advance, it is becoming increasingly important to strike a balance between accuracy and interpretability while ensuring that explanations provided are both meaningful and trustworthy to users and stakeholders. XAI is a crucial step towards responsible AI deployment and the integration of AI technologies into critical systems with human oversight and understanding.

Excercise

True Or False

1.Bias and fairness in Machine Learning refer to addressing potential discriminatory effects of algorithms.
2.Fairness in Machine Learning aims to treat all data points equally during training.
3.Privacy and data protection are not significant concerns in Machine Learning.
4.Data anonymization involves disguising individual identities in the data to protect privacy.
5.Explainable AI (XAI) aims to make AI models more complex and difficult to interpret.
6.XAI methods provide transparency and insights into AI model decisions.
7.Bias in Machine Learning can arise from human prejudices reflected in the data.
8.Group fairness in Machine Learning focuses on treating similar individuals or cases similarly.
9.Disparate impact refers to the fair distribution of resources in Machine Learning.
10.Data utility refers to the total amount of data collected by an organization.
11.Regular monitoring and auditing of model performance can help mitigate bias in Machine Learning.
12.Model interpretability refers to the ability to explain how the model arrives at its decisions.
13.Ignoring bias in Machine Learning is an effective strategy to achieve accurate predictions.
14.Ensuring algorithmic fairness means treating all individuals exactly the same.
15.Explainable AI (XAI) techniques always provide comprehensive insights into model behavior.
16.Data minimization is a privacy principle that encourages collecting as much data as possible.
17.Fairness in Machine Learning can be achieved by eliminating all sources of bias in the data.
ANSWERS-True, True, False, True, False, True, True, True, False, False, True, True, False, False, False, False, True

MCQ
1.What is the main concern addressed in Chapter?
a) Model deployment techniques c) Ethical and fair Machine Learning
b) Data preprocessing methods d) Advanced feature engineering
Answer: c) Ethical and fair Machine Learning

2.Bias and fairness in Machine Learning refer to:
a) Ensuring that models are always accurate c) Addressing the potential discriminatory effects of ML algorithms
b) Minimizing the impact of human errors in data labeling d) Maximizing model complexity for better performance
Answer: c) Addressing the potential discriminatory effects of ML algorithms

3.What is one major reason for the presence of bias in Machine Learning models?
a) Models are too simple to capture complex patterns c) Human prejudices reflected in the data
b) Lack of labeled training data d) Lack of computational power
Answer: c) Human prejudices reflected in the data

4.Fairness in Machine Learning refers to:

a) Ensuring that models are always correct
b) Treating all data points equally during training
c) Eliminating all sources of variability in model predictions
d) Avoiding discriminatory outcomes across different groups
Answer: d) Avoiding discriminatory outcomes across different groups

5.Which of the following is a potential consequence of biased Machine Learning models?
a) Reduced computational efficiency
b) Improved generalization to diverse populations
c) Discriminatory decisions and actions
d) Increased model complexity
Answer: c) Discriminatory decisions and actions

6.Privacy and data protection in Machine Learning involve:
a) Disclosing all collected data publicly
b) Minimizing the impact of data breaches
c) Sharing sensitive user information without consent
d) Ignoring data privacy regulations
Answer: b) Minimizing the impact of data breaches

7.Which of the following is NOT a common privacy concern in Machine Learning?
a) Unauthorized access to personal data
b) Unintended information leakage
c) Overfitting of Machine Learning models
d) Re-identification of anonymized data
Answer: c) Overfitting of Machine Learning models

8.Explainable AI (XAI) aims to:
a) Make AI models more complex and harder to interpret
b) Provide transparency and insights into AI model decisions
c) Automate data labeling processes
d) Maximize predictive accuracy at the cost of interpretability
Answer: b) Provide transparency and insights into AI model decisions

9.Which of the following is a benefit of using Explainable AI (XAI)?
a) Increasing the complexity of Machine Learning models
b) Hiding the decision-making process from users
c) Enhancing user trust and understanding of AI decisions
d) Reducing the need for data preprocessing
Answer: c) Enhancing user trust and understanding of AI decisions

10.What is one common method used for addressing bias and fairness in Machine Learning?
a) Ignoring the presence of bias in the data
b) Avoiding the use of large datasets
c) Tweaking model parameters without analyzing bias
d) Fair data sampling and algorithmic adjustments
Answer: d) Fair data sampling and algorithmic adjustments

11.What does the term "algorithmic fairness" refer to?
a) Ensuring algorithms are highly complex for accuracy
b) Eliminating all sources of bias in data
c) Balancing predictive accuracy and fairness in model outcomes
d) Automating data collection and preprocessing
Answer: c) Balancing predictive accuracy and fairness in model outcomes

12.In the context of Machine Learning, what is "group fairness"?
a) Training models on a single homogeneous group
b) Ensuring that every individual receives the same prediction
c) Addressing disparities in model outcomes across different groups
d) Ignoring the concept of fairness to prioritize accuracy
Answer: c) Addressing disparities in model outcomes across different groups

13.Which of the following is an example of a privacy-preserving technique?
a) Sharing raw and unprocessed data openly

b) Anonymizing sensitive data before analysis
c) Collecting more personal data to improve model accuracy
d) Storing user data without encryption
Answer: b) Anonymizing sensitive data before analysis

14.What is the purpose of a "data protection impact assessment"?
a) To optimize Machine Learning model accuracy
b) To evaluate the ethical implications of AI models
c) To assess the potential risks to individuals' data privacy
d) To collect and label training data
Answer: c) To assess the potential risks to individuals' data privacy

15.Which of the following statements is true about Explainable AI (XAI)?
a) XAI aims to hide the decision-making process from users
b) XAI methods are only applicable to simple Machine Learning models
c) XAI helps users understand how AI models arrive at their decisions
d) XAI is primarily concerned with maximizing predictive accuracy
Answer: c) XAI helps users understand how AI models arrive at their decisions

16.Which aspect of fairness focuses on treating similar individuals or cases similarly?
a) Individual fairness
b) Group fairness
c) Model fairness
d) Predictive fairness
Answer: a) Individual fairness

17.Which of the following is an example of a potential bias in Machine Learning?
a) Using large and diverse datasets for training
b) Assigning higher weights to certain data points during training
c) Regularly updating and retraining the model
d) Implementing complex algorithms to increase model accuracy
Answer: b) Assigning higher weights to certain data points during training

18.Which type of bias occurs when certain groups are systematically underrepresented in the training data?
a) Selection bias
b) Sampling bias
c) Algorithmic bias
d) Predictive bias
Answer: a) Selection bias

19.Which privacy principle states that data should only be collected for a specific purpose and not used for other unrelated purposes?
a) Data minimization
b) Data anonymization
c) Data transparency
d) Data sharing
Answer: a) Data minimization

20.How does data anonymization contribute to privacy protection?
a) By encrypting data during storage
b) By removing all data from the system
c) By making data publicly available
d) By disguising individual identities in the data
Answer: d) By disguising individual identities in the data

21.Which term refers to the ability of an AI system to provide reasons for its decisions in a human-understandable manner?
a) Predictive modeling
b) Algorithmic complexity
c) Explainable AI (XAI)
d) Data preprocessing
Answer: c) Explainable AI (XAI)

22.What is the primary objective of addressing bias and fairness in Machine Learning?
a) To ensure 100% accuracy of the model
b) To achieve maximum complexity in model architecture
c) To prevent the model from overfitting
d) To minimize unjust discrimination in model predictions
Answer: d) To minimize unjust discrimination in model predictions

23.In the context of fairness, what does "disparate impact" refer to?
a) Fair distribution of resources
b) Equal treatment of all individuals
c) Unintended discriminatory effects on different groups
d) Predictive accuracy of the model
Answer: c) Unintended discriminatory effects on different groups

24.Which ethical principle emphasizes the responsibility to ensure that AI systems do not reinforce existing biases or create new forms of discrimination?
a) Transparency
b) Accountability
c) Fairness
d) Accuracy
Answer: c) Fairness

25.What is "data utility" in the context of privacy and data protection?
a) The value of raw, unprocessed data
b) The ability to generate insights from data
c) The degree to which data is useful for a specific purpose
d) The total amount of data collected by an organization
Answer: c) The degree to which data is useful for a specific purpose

Short Question And Answers

Q1. What is bias in Machine Learning?
Q2. Why is bias in Machine Learning a concern?
Q3. How can bias be mitigated in Machine Learning?
Q4. What is fairness-aware Machine Learning?
Q5. What is disparate impact and how does it relate to bias?
Q6. What are some fairness metrics used in evaluating ML models?
Q7. Why is privacy important in Machine Learning?.
Q8. What is the difference between data privacy and data security?
Q9. What is the General Data Protection Regulation (GDPR)?
Q10. How can differential privacy enhance data privacy in Machine Learning?
Q11. What is data anonymization?
Q12. Why is explainable AI important?
Q13. What is a black-box model?
Q14. What are some techniques for achieving explainability in AI?
Q15. How does model complexity affect explainability?
Q16. What is a surrogate model in the context of explainable AI?
Q17. How does explainable AI relate to bias and fairness?

Q18. Is there a trade-off between model performance and explainability?
Q19. How does explainability benefit regulatory compliance?
Q20. What are some challenges in implementing XAI in real-world applications?

Online Resources

Online Exam Papers
True/False Exam

Link: https://forms.gle/jdXk5QtcUeaX287a7

QR Code

YouTube Video Playlist Link

Chapter 13
Link: https://www.youtube.com/playlist?list=PLzlh_31VWEFpZF4IVouxkk3DCce879SxT
QR Code

Chapter 14: Viva Voce Questions

Q 1: What is Machine Learning?
Answer: Machine Learning is a subset of artificial intelligence that involves the development of algorithms that enable computers to learn from and make predictions based on data. These algorithms build a mathematical model based on sample data, known as "training data," in order to make predictions or decisions without being explicitly programmed to perform the task.

Q 2: Can you describe the history of Machine Learning?
Answer: The history of Machine Learning dates back to the mid-20th century. Early milestones include Alan Turing's proposal of the Turing Test, Arthur Samuel's work on self-learning checkers in the 1950s, and the development of neural networks in the 1980s. Significant advancements have been made in the 21st century, particularly with the advent of deep learning and the availability of large datasets and powerful computing resources.

Q 3: Why should we learn Machine Learning?
Answer: Learning Machine Learning is crucial as it equips individuals with the skills to develop intelligent systems that can automate decision-making, improve efficiency, and uncover patterns in data. It is widely applicable across various industries, including healthcare, finance, transportation, and more, making it a valuable skill for career growth.

Q 4: What are the types of Machine Learning?
Answer: The main types of Machine Learning are supervised learning, unsupervised learning, semi-supervised learning, and reinforcement learning. Supervised learning involves learning from labeled data, unsupervised learning deals with unlabeled data, semi-supervised learning uses a mix of labeled and unlabeled data, and reinforcement learning focuses on learning through interactions with an environment to maximize rewards.

Q 5: What are some real-world applications of Machine Learning?
Answer: Machine Learning is used in various applications such as spam detection in emails, recommendation systems on streaming platforms, fraud detection in banking, self-driving cars, medical diagnosis, and natural language processing tasks like translation and sentiment analysis.

Q 6: What is supervised learning?
Answer: Supervised learning is a type of Machine Learning where the model is trained on labeled data, meaning each training example is paired with an output label. The goal is to learn a mapping from inputs to outputs that can generalize well to unseen data.

Q 7: What are Linear Models of classification?
Answer: Linear Models of classification are algorithms that classify data points by finding a linear decision boundary. Examples include Logistic Regression and Support Vector Machines (SVM), which attempt to separate different classes with a hyperplane.

Q 8: Explain Forward Network Functions in the context of Supervised Learning.
Answer: Forward Network Functions refer to the process in which input data is passed through the layers of a neural network to produce an output. This process involves computing the weighted sum of inputs, passing it through an activation function, and propagating it through subsequent layers until the final output is obtained.

Q 9: What is clustering in Machine Learning?
Answer: Clustering is an unsupervised learning technique used to group similar data points together based on their features. Common algorithms include K-means clustering, hierarchical clustering, and DBSCAN.

Q 10: What are Mixtures of Gaussians?
Answer: Mixtures of Gaussians is a probabilistic model that represents a distribution as a combination of several Gaussian distributions. It is used for clustering and density estimation, assuming that the data points are generated from a mixture of several normal distributions.
Q 11: Explain Dimensionality Reduction and its importance.

Answer: Dimensionality Reduction involves reducing the number of random variables under consideration by obtaining a set of principal variables. Techniques like Principal Component Analysis (PCA) and t-SNE are used to simplify models, reduce computational cost, and mitigate the curse of dimensionality.

Q 12: What are Directed Graphical Models?
Answer: Directed Graphical Models, also known as Bayesian Networks, represent the conditional dependencies between random variables using directed edges in a graph. They are used for probabilistic inference and decision making.

Q 13: Explain Naive Bayes Classifiers.
Answer: Naive Bayes Classifiers are probabilistic models based on Bayes' theorem with the assumption of independence between features. Despite their simplicity, they perform well in text classification and other applications.

Q 14: What is a Hidden Markov Model (HMM)?
Answer: An HMM is a statistical model that represents systems with hidden states. It is used for time series analysis and sequence modeling, such as speech recognition and bioinformatics.

Q 15: What is Reinforcement Learning?
Answer: Reinforcement Learning is a type of Machine Learning where an agent learns to make decisions by performing actions in an environment to maximize cumulative rewards. It involves key elements like states, actions, rewards, and policies.

Q 16: How is Computer Vision applied in Machine Learning?
Answer: Computer Vision involves using Machine Learning techniques to interpret and process visual data from the world. Applications include image recognition, object detection, and autonomous driving.

Q 17: Explain the importance of Natural Language Processing (NLP).
Answer: NLP focuses on the interaction between computers and human languages. It enables machines to understand, interpret, and generate human language, with applications in translation, sentiment analysis, and chatbots.

Q 18: Why is Python popular for Machine Learning?
Answer: Python is popular due to its simplicity, readability, extensive libraries (like TensorFlow, Keras, and Scikit-Learn), strong community support, and ease of integration with other technologies.

Q 19: Describe the k-Nearest Neighbor (k-NN) Classifier.
Answer: The k-NN classifier is a simple, instance-based learning algorithm that classifies new data points based on the majority class among its k-nearest neighbors in the feature space. It is used for classification and regression tasks.

Q 20: How do you split data into training and test sets?
Answer: Splitting data into training and test sets involves dividing the dataset into two subsets: one for training the model and one for evaluating its performance. This helps to assess how well the model generalizes to unseen data.

Q 21: What is Cross-Validation?
Answer: Cross-Validation is a technique for assessing the performance of a model by partitioning the data into multiple subsets, training the model on some subsets, and validating it on the remaining ones. It helps to reduce overfitting and provides a better estimate of model performance.

Q 22: Explain the F1 Score.
Answer: The F1 Score is the harmonic mean of precision and recall, providing a balance between the two metrics. It is particularly useful when dealing with imbalanced datasets, where one class is more prevalent than the others.

YouTube Link for Viva Voce Questions:
https://www.youtube.com/playlist?list=PLzlh_31VWEFpZB1SUKpkxYHQKHLlw_iME

QR Code:

Additional Resources

Machine learning Videos Playlist-

Link: https://www.youtube.com/playlist?list=PLzlh_31VWEFo1bkONeV8eBmfAz5WgIBn0

QR Code:

YouTube Videos Playlists for all Chapters

CHAPTER 1
Link: https://www.youtube.com/playlist?list=PLzlh_31VWEFrIZhYhxIF-Ytm1kF0CkByv
QR Code

CHAPTER 2
Link: https://www.youtube.com/playlist?list=PLzlh_31VWEFqa2Hew9xX5KsNH3nknyRhf
QR Code

CHAPTER 3
Link: https://www.youtube.com/playlist?list=PLzlh_31VWEFpVQDTpixKob7GPKELIrzzo
QR Code

CHAPTER 4
Link: https://www.youtube.com/playlist?list=PLzlh_31VWEFo4U-NXdbbGRiyW0sO7JXGh
QR Code

CHAPTER 5
Link: https://www.youtube.com/playlist?list=PLzlh_31VWEFoBaaSxMx4782wb82nztpGE
QR Code

CHAPTER 6
Link: https://www.youtube.com/playlist?list=PLzlh_31VWEFq5-MUdQUQDfxkff0IOMLSH
QR Code

CHAPTER 7
Link : https://www.youtube.com/playlist?list=PLzlh_31VWEFoRPdSlkRBu9A2BUOWx2lkM
QR Code

Chapter 8
Link: https://www.youtube.com/playlist?list=PLzlh_31VWEFoRPdSlkRBu9A2BUOWx2lkM
QR Code

CHAPTER 9
Link
https://www.youtube.com/playlist?list=PLzlh_31VWEFqTsAnVKeNEV90e6sorM9xw
QR Code

CHAPTER 10
Link: https://www.youtube.com/playlist?list=PLzlh_31VWEFqTgiDaY80qF20LmqP_OowB
QR Code

CHAPTER 11
Link: https://www.youtube.com/playlist?list=PLzlh_31VWEFoPlkcjztJMUiCV5-u15r3A
QR Code

CHAPTER 12
Link: https://www.youtube.com/playlist?list=PLzlh_31VWEFqlWc2eJSJRwMCa-T4LBidQ
QR Code

CHAPTER 13
Link: **https://www.youtube.com/playlist?list=PLzlh_31VWEFpZF4IVouxkk3DCce879SxT**
QR Code

9 789369 914180

Printed at Repro India Ltd.